GREAT
MOMENTS

IN COOKING

GREAT MOMENTS IN COOKING

Readon Publications

CONCEPT:
Communiplex Marketing Inc.

LAYOUT AND GRAPHICS:
Publicola

PHOTOGRAPHY AND STYLING:
Bodson Gauthier et Associés

RECIPE SELECTION:
Lorraine Fortin
Claire Hébert

PREPARATION AND STANDARDIZATION OF RECIPES:
Chef Michel Simonnet

ENGLISH ADAPTATION:
Robyn Bryant
Sabine Davies
Ann Rajan

This 1991 edition published by Readon Publications Inc. by arrangement with
Communiplex Marketing Inc.

Readon Publications Inc.
345 Nugget Ave.
Unit 15
Scarborough, Ont., Canada   M1S 4J4
Tel.: (416) 754-0162
Fax: (416) 754-4984

ISBN: 2-9801481-2-1

Printed and bound in U.S.A.

INTRODUCTION

The eating habits and lifestyles of today's households have changed considerably in recent years. Work, social and business obligations, and the faster pace of day-to-day living leave little time for cooking or entertaining. Celebrating with family and friends, whether it be a truly grand occasion or an informal get-together, is therefore more challenging than ever.

We all know that sharing good food with loved ones nourishes not only the body but also the soul. The menus and recipes in this book have been carefully selected to encourage you to experience the pleasures of festive dining more often. You will find a variety of exciting menus to fit every occasion, ranging from the traditional Christmas dinner to the casually elegant pool-side party, from birthday parties for children to ethnic meals.

We hope that *Great Moments in Cooking* will serve as a source of inspiration for expanding your cooking skills and extending your spirit of hospitality.

NOTE

The equivalencies for metric and standard weights and measures used in the recipes in this book are derived in part from a table in "La Cuisine Five Roses" published by Lake of the Woods Mills Inc.

The microwave recipes and microwave information were designed and tested for 650/700 watt ovens.
- If you use a 600 watt microwave oven, add 20 seconds to each minute of suggested cooking time.
- If you use a 500 watt oven, add up to 40 seconds to every minute of suggested cooking time for all recipes containing fresh ingredients which are to be cooked at HIGH or MAXIMUM power. In other cases, the additional necessary cooking time will not be as long. We suggest that you check the results after the recommended standing time has elapsed.

The contributors, editors and publisher have made every effort to ensure the accuracy of the information contained herein, but the publisher cannot guarantee the specific results which may be obtained by following the instructions.

Contents

TRADITIONAL HOLIDAYS

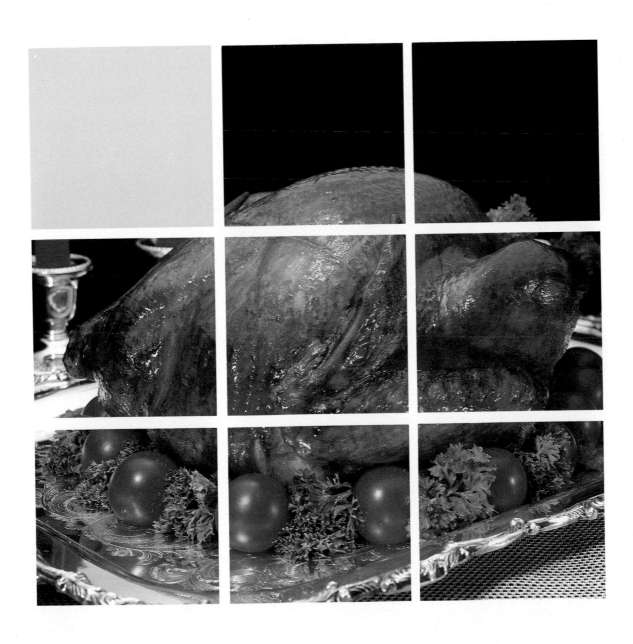

CHRISTMAS EVE REVEILLON

This Christmas Eve midnight feast features traditional Quebec dishes.

Serve with white medium-dry wine, sparkling wine or champagne.

MENU

Serves 8 to 10

Vegetable Aspic
Cipâte
Lac Saint-Jean Tourtière
Galantine of Chicken
Carrot and Cabbage Salad with Coriander
Mocha Cake with Chocolate Butter Crème
Fruit Cake

VEGETABLE ASPIC

Standard	Metric
3/4 cup lemon jelly powder	150 ml lemon jelly powder
2-3/4 cups boiling water	650 ml boiling water
3 tbsp lemon juice	45 ml lemon juice
3/4 cup diced celery	150 ml diced celery
1/2 cup grated carrot	125 ml grated carrot
1/2 cup diced green pepper	125 ml diced green pepper
1/2 cup diced sweet red pepper	125 ml diced sweet red pepper
1 cup shredded lettuce	250 ml shredded lettuce
1/2 cup chopped cabbage	125 ml chopped cabbage
1/2 cup stuffed olives	125 ml stuffed olives
Carrot curls	Carrot curls
Salt and pepper	Salt and pepper

Dissolve jelly powder in boiling water. Pour into an aspic mold. Stir in the lemon juice, salt and pepper. Add the vegetables. Decorate with carrot curls. Chill in refrigerator until set.

CIPÂTE

Standard	Metric
1 boned chicken	1 boned chicken
2 lb pork, shoulder or butt cut	1 kg pork, shoulder or butt cut
2 lb cubed beef	1 kg cubed beef
1 lb veal or rabbit	500 g veal or rabbit
1 piece salt pork	1 piece salt pork
1 onion	1 onion
3 lb potatoes, in chunks	1.5 kg potatoes, in chunks
Salt, pepper and mixed spices	Salt, pepper and mixed spices
Pie crust	Pie crust

Cipâte

Preheat the oven to 350°F (180°C). Cut all the meats into cubes. Add the onion and spices.

Line a baking pan with sliced salt pork. Cover with a layer of potatoes, then a layer of meat. Arrange small squares of pastry on top (see pastry recipe for Christmas Tart on page 26).

Continue making layers of potatoes and meat, ending with a layer of pastry squares. Add water to the top of the layers if the pan is shallow. If you are using a deep pan, reduce the amount of water. Top with a pastry crust. Cover.

Bake until the bottom pastry layer has absorbed some of the fat; leave the pan uncovered for about an hour to brown the top crust.

Then reduce the heat to 300°F (150°C) and continue baking, covered, for 6 to 8 hours.

Lac Saint-Jean Tourtière

Standard	Metric
1-1/2 lb pork	750 g pork
1 lb beef	500 g beef
1 lb veal	500 g veal
1/2 chicken	1/2 chicken
3 sliced onions	3 sliced onions
1 rabbit or	1 rabbit or
1 hare	1 hare
1 lb venison or	500 g venison or
1 lb caribou	500 g caribou
1/4 lb salt pork	125 g salt pork
Salt and pepper	Salt and pepper
Potatoes	Potatoes
2 pastry crusts 1/4 inch thick	2 pastry crusts 5 mm thick

This meat pie is traditionally made with whatever game is available. You can substitute game or meat available locally, as long as you have a combined total of about 5 lb (2.5 kg).

Remove the bones from the chicken and meat and cut all into pieces about 3/4 inch (2 cm) square. Combine the meats and let sit for about 12 hours. Peel a quantity of potatoes equal to the amount of meat and dice the same size as the meat. Add the salt pork.

Line a deep heavy casserole with a layer of pastry (see recipe for pastry crust, Christmas Tart, page 26). Mix the meat, potatoes and salt pork well and turn into pastry-lined pan. Pour on water to cover and seal with second layer of pastry. Cover with casserole lid. Bake in 350°F (180°C) oven for about 2

Lac Saint-Jean Tourtière

Galantine of Chicken

hours. Continue cooking another 10 hours at 200°F (100°C).

Serve directly from the casserole.

Galantine of Chicken

Standard	Metric
3/4 cup cooked chicken	150 ml cooked chicken
1 cup homemade chicken stock	250 ml homemade chicken stock
1/2 tsp salt	2 ml salt
1/8 tsp pepper	0.5 ml pepper
8 cherry tomatoes	8 cherry tomatoes
1 tbsp grated carrot	15 ml grated carrot
1 tbsp grated parsnip	15 ml grated parsnip
1 tbsp grated onion	15 ml grated onion
1 tbsp grated celery	15 ml grated celery
1/8 tsp savory or thyme	0.5 ml savory or thyme
1 tbsp gelatin	15 ml gelatin

Bring the chicken stock to a boil and add all ingredients except chicken and tomatoes. Cover and simmer gently until vegetables are cooked.

Arrange the tomatoes in an oiled mold. Arrange pieces of chicken over tomatoes. Pour the chicken stock and vegetables on top. Cover and refrigerate about 12 hours.

Carrot and Cabbage Salad with Coriander

Standard	Metric
1 grated cabbage	1 grated cabbage
3 grated carrots	3 grated carrots
1 tbsp crushed coriander seed	15 ml crushed coriander seed
1 tbsp Dijon mustard	15 ml Dijon mustard
4 tbsp wine vinegar	60 ml wine vinegar
1/2 cup vegetable oil	125 ml vegetable oil
1 tbsp salt	15 ml salt
1 tbsp sugar	15 ml sugar

Combine all ingredients except carrots and cabbage to make a vinaigrette. Stir into the vegetables. Serve arranged on lettuce leaves.

FRUIT CAKE

Standard	Metric
1/2 cup white sugar	125 ml white sugar
1/2 cup molasses	125 ml molasses
1/2 cup vegetable shortening	125 ml vegetable shortening
1 cup sour milk	250 ml sour milk
1 tsp baking soda (if milk is very sour)	5 ml baking soda (if milk is very sour)
1 tsp baking powder	5 ml baking powder
2 cups pastry flour	500 ml pastry flour
1 cup raisins	250 ml raisins
1/2 cup dried currants	125 ml dried currants
1/2 cup chopped dates	125 ml chopped dates
1/2 cup almonds	125 ml almonds
1/2 cup candied fruit	125 ml candied fruit
Lemon to taste	Lemon to taste
1/2 tsp cinnamon	2 ml cinnamon
1/2 tsp allspice	2 ml allspice
1/2 tsp salt	2 ml salt
1/2 tsp nutmeg	2 ml nutmeg

Cream together shortening, sugar and molasses. Sift together dry ingredients. Stir in dry ingredients, milk, fruit and nuts. Turn mixture into greased cake pan. Bake at 350°F (180°C) about 1 hour.

Mocha Cake with Chocolate Butter Crème

MOCHA CAKE WITH CHOCOLATE BUTTER CRÈME

Standard	Metric
1 cup pastry flour	250 ml pastry flour
1 tsp baking powder	5 ml baking powder
1/4 tsp salt	1 ml salt
2 egg yolks, beaten	2 egg yolks, beaten
1/2 cup cold water	125 ml cold water
1 tsp orange zest	5 ml orange zest
3/4 cup sugar	150 ml sugar
2 egg whites, beaten stiff	2 egg whites, beaten stiff
3 tbsp orange juice	45 ml orange juice
2 tbsp icing sugar	30 ml icing sugar
2 tbsp sugar	30 ml sugar

Sift together the flour, salt and baking powder 3 times. Set aside. With an electric mixer, beat the egg yolks and 3/4 cup (150 ml) sugar for 5 minutes. Gradually beat in the flour and cold water.

Beat the egg whites stiff. As they begin to form peaks, beat in the 2 tbsp (30 ml) icing sugar. Fold gently into flour mixture.

Turn the batter into 2 well-greased 8 inch (20 cm) aluminum cake pans. Bake at 350°F (180°C) 25 minutes. In a small pot, bring the orange juice and 2 tbsp (30 ml) sugar to a boil. Saturate the cakes with juice mixture.

Let cool and unmold. Use Chocolate Butter Crème recipe to fill between the layers and frost.

Chocolate Butter Crème

Standard	Metric
3 egg yolks	3 egg yolks
1 cup sugar	250 ml sugar
1/2 tsp cream of tartar	2 ml cream of tartar
1/2 cup water	125 ml water
1/2 lb unsalted butter	250 g unsalted butter
1/2 lb vegetable shortening	250 g vegetable shortening
1/2 lb sweet chocolate	250 g sweet chocolate
2 tbsp instant coffee	30 ml instant coffee
2 tbsp dark rum	30 ml dark rum
Pinch of salt	Pinch of salt

Beat egg yolks until pale and foamy. Put the water, sugar and cream of tartar in a saucepan; cook to a thick syrupy consistency. Remove from heat and stir in the instant coffee.

Slowly pour the hot (not boiling) syrup over the egg yolks, beating constantly; continue beating until thick and lukewarm.

Gradually beat in the butter and shortening and beat until mixture is completely smooth.

Fold in the melted chocolate. Beat again.

CHRISTMAS BREAKFAST

Ring in the morning with a substantial and unusual menu.

Serve with rosé or sparkling wine.

MENU

Serves 6 to 8

Surprise Fruit Baskets
Baked French Toast
Dreamy Omelet
Apricot Loaf
Grapes with Yogurt
Seven Layer Strawberry Meringue Crêpes
Sparkling Wine Mimosa
Café Brûlot

SURPRISE FRUIT BASKETS

Cut grapefruit in half and remove the flesh, being careful not to cut through the skin. Cut the flesh into chunks, and add green grapes and orange slices.

Stuff the grapefruit halves with the fruit mixture, sprinkle with fine sugar, and refrigerate.

Before serving, sprinkle the fruit with icing sugar and arrange the grapefruit halves on lettuce leaves.

Surprise Fruit Baskets

BAKED FRENCH TOAST

Standard	Metric
Butter	Butter
4 eggs	4 eggs
1 cup milk	250 ml milk
1 tbsp sugar	15 ml sugar
1 tsp vanilla	5 ml vanilla
1/4 tsp nutmeg	1 ml nutmeg
Maple syrup	Maple syrup
Sliced stale bread	Sliced stale bread

Combine all ingredients except bread and syrup. Carefully dip bread slices in the egg mixture, and arrange on a rimmed tray or plate.

After a few minutes, turn the slices over, so that the egg mixture completely permeates the bread.

Arrange the bread on a baking sheet, baste with melted butter and brown in a 375°F (190°C) oven. Turn over, baste with butter, and brown for about 10 minutes. Warm the syrup and butter in a saucepan. Serve with the French toast.

DREAMY OMELET

Standard	Metric
12 slices bacon	12 slices bacon
12 eggs	12 eggs
2 cups milk	500 ml milk
Salt and pepper	Salt and pepper

Brown the bacon in an ovenproof skillet. Drain off the excess fat. Beat the egg whites until stiff. In a separate bowl, beat the yolks together with the milk, salt and pepper. Fold in the egg whites. Spread the mixture over the bacon and bake in a 350°F (180°C) oven until golden.

APRICOT LOAF

Standard	Metric
1/2 cup dried apricots, chopped	125 ml dried apricots, chopped
3 cups all-purpose flour (or partly whole wheat flour)	750 ml all-purpose flour (or partly whole wheat flour)
1 tbsp baking powder	15 ml baking powder
1/4 tsp baking soda	1 ml baking soda
1 tsp salt	5 ml salt
1 cup brown sugar	250 ml brown sugar
1/2 cup chopped dates	125 ml chopped dates
1 cup chopped nuts	250 ml chopped nuts
1 well-beaten egg	1 well-beaten egg
1 cup milk	250 ml milk
1/2 cup maple syrup	125 ml maple syrup

Baked French Toast, Dreamy Omelet, Apricot Loaf, and Sparkling Wine Mimosa

Cover the dried, chopped apricots with boiling water and leave to steep for about 15 minutes. Drain.

Sift together the flour, baking powder, baking soda and salt. Stir in the brown sugar, dates, apricots, and nuts. Beat together the egg, milk and maple syrup and stir into the flour mixture. Pour into a greased loaf pan and let rest for 20 minutes. Bake at 350°F (180°C) for about 1 hour 15 minutes or until a toothpick inserted in the center comes out clean.

Let cool. Ice with cream cheese and garnish with chopped nuts.

GRAPES WITH YOGURT

Standard	Metric
4 cups seedless grapes, sliced in half	1 liter seedless grapes, sliced in half
1 cup plain yogurt	250 ml plain yogurt
1 tbsp chopped candied ginger	15 ml chopped candied ginger

Mix all ingredients. Chill before serving.

SPARKLING WINE MIMOSA

Standard	Metric
2 bottles sparkling wine	2 bottles sparkling wine
3 cups orange juice	750 ml orange juice

Chill the wine in the refrigerator for 3 to 4 hours before adding the orange juice.

Before serving, place a sprig of spruce or fir in the bottom of each glass.

Pour in a little orange juice and fill with sparkling wine.

Note: You can turn this into Sparkling Wine Cardinale by replacing the orange juice with a raspberry coulis (boil a package of frozen raspberries with a little sugar for 1 minute. Puree in the food processor, then force the coulis through a strainer). Pour the wine over the coulis very carefully so that it doesn't foam over.

CAFÉ BRÛLOT

Standard	Metric
1-1/2 cinnamon sticks, broken in pieces	1-1/2 cinnamon sticks, broken in pieces
Rind of 1/2 lemon	Rind of 1/2 lemon
1/2 tsp allspice	2 ml allspice
Rind of 2 oranges	Rind of 2 oranges
4 tsp sugar	20 ml sugar
1/2 cup cognac	125 ml cognac
3 cups very strong black coffee	750 ml very strong black coffee

Place a piece of cinnamon in each cup. In a saucepan, mix the allspice, lemon and orange rinds and sugar. Add the cognac and heat. Flame and allow to burn for 1 minute. Carefully blow out the flames and stir in the hot coffee.

Strain the coffee into small cups. Serve very hot.

Variations:

Mexican Coffee: Flavor with Tia Maria or other coffee-flavored liqueur.

Caribbean Coffee: Flavor with dark rum.

Spiced Orange Coffee: Flavor with orange liqueur; add a pinch of ground cinnamon and cloves.

Seven Layer Strawberry Meringue Crêpes

SEVEN LAYER STRAWBERRY MERINGUE CRÊPES

Standard	Metric
7 large crêpes, about 8 inch diameter	7 large crêpes, about 20 cm diameter
Strawberry jam	Strawberry jam
Egg whites	Egg whites
Icing sugar	Icing sugar

Crêpe Batter

Standard	Metric
1 cup all-purpose flour	250 ml all-purpose flour
1/4 tsp salt	1 ml salt
1 tbsp sugar	15 ml sugar
2 large eggs	2 large eggs
1-1/2 cups milk	375 ml milk
1 tsp rum	5 ml rum
1 tsp vanilla	5 ml vanilla
1 tbsp melted butter	15 ml melted butter

Sift together the flour, salt and sugar into a bowl. Make a well in the center of the flour and break the eggs into it; beat with a whisk, gradually incorporating all the flour. Add the milk and beat to a smooth texture. Stir in the rum, vanilla and melted butter. Let rest for 1 hour at room temperature. If the batter contains any lumps, pass it through a sieve.

Cooking the Crêpes

Heat a skillet and wipe it with a paper towel dipped in oil. Pour in enough crêpe batter just to cover the bottom of the pan. Cook and brown well on both sides. Slide the crêpe onto a plate and repeat the procedure.

Meringue

Standard	Metric
7 tbsp egg whites	105 ml egg whites
1 cup icing sugar	250 ml icing sugar

Beat together the egg whites and sugar with a beater or whisk until the eggs are very firm.

Building the Seven Layer Crêpe

Spread a thin layer of strawberry jam on the first crêpe. Cover with a second crêpe. Continue building layers with all 7 crêpes. Put the meringue mixture in a large pastry bag with a large nozzle. Decorate the crêpes with meringue rosettes. Brown the meringue under the grill or broiler, watching carefully to avoid burning. Garnish with fresh strawberries. Cut in wedges to serve.

Technique: Seven Layer Strawberry Meringue Crêpe

1 Sift together the flour, salt and sugar.

2 Make a well in the flour and break the eggs into it.

3 With a whisk, gradually beat in the flour.

4 Add the milk, rum, vanilla and melted butter. Pass the batter through a sieve.

5 Heat a pan and oil it with a paper towel.

6 Pour in enough batter to cover the bottom of the pan.

7 Turn the crêpe and cook until golden.

8 Beat the egg whites and sugar with a mixer

9 ... until stiff.

10 Spread a thin layer of strawberry jam over the first crêpe.

11 Cover with a second crêpe and repeat procedure.

12 Put the meringue in a large-tipped pastry bag and decorate the crêpes.

13 Pass under the broiler until golden.

Caution :

Leave the oven door open when browning the meringue. Watch carefully because the meringue can burn quickly.

Decoration:

Garnish with fresh strawberries if available. Cut into wedges to serve.

Christmas Day Brunch

An easy and elegant meal with some make-ahead recipes.

Serve with rosé, medium-dry white wine or sparkling wine.

Menu

Serves 8 to 10

Wake-Up Grapefruit with Cognac
Poached Eggs Benedict
Hollandaise Sauce
Kiwi and Orange Glazed Ham
Parmesan Muffins
Light Spinach Salad
Maple Walnut Brioche
Old-Fashioned Doughnuts

Wake-up Grapefruit with Cognac

Standard	Metric
1/2 grapefruit per person	1/2 grapefruit per person
A little brown sugar	A little brown sugar
1 tbsp of cognac per grapefruit	15 ml of cognac per grapefruit
Cherries	Cherries

Slice the grapefruit in half. Sprinkle a little brown sugar on each half. Garnish with a maraschino cherry. Sprinkle cognac on top.

Place under the grill or broiler for a few minutes.

Poached Eggs Benedict

10 poached eggs
10 thin slices cooked ham
5 English muffins cut in half

In a large shallow saucepan, put 3/4 tsp (3 ml) of vinegar for each 4 cups (1 liter) of water. Do not add salt. Bring the water just to a simmer, (boiling water will cause the eggs to break). Break the eggs individually into a saucer and slide gently into the water.

Use a spoon to gently shape the egg whites close to the yolks. Let cook for 2 to 3 minutes. Arrest the cooking process by setting the eggs in chilled water. (The egg yolks should not be too cooked.) Drain on a towel and use scissors to trim ragged edges from the whites.

Lightly toast the muffin halves and butter them. Cover each muffin half with a slice of ham sautéed in butter. Reheat the eggs in simmering water for about 30 seconds and lay

them on top of the ham slices. Top with hollandaise sauce before serving.

Hollandaise Sauce

Standard	Metric
1/2 cup well-chilled butter in pieces	125 ml well-chilled butter in pieces
4 egg yolks	4 egg yolks
2 tbsp lemon juice	30 ml lemon juice
Pinch of salt	Pinch of salt
Pinch of cayenne and white pepper	Pinch of cayenne and white pepper

Put all ingredients in a small saucepan with an enamel bottom. Heat on a very low flame. Beat constantly with a whisk until the sauce is the consistency of mayonnaise.

If the sauce separates, add 2 ice cubes and beat again until the proper consistency.

If the sauce is too thin, put 1 egg yolk in a clean bowl and add the sauce slowly, almost drop by drop, beating constantly.

Microwave Method

Poached Eggs

Put 2 tbsp (30 ml) of water and 1/4 tsp (1 ml) vinegar in a ramekin or small baking dish.

Cover with plastic wrap. Heat at HIGH for 30 or 40 seconds until the water comes to a boil.

Break an egg and slide it slowly into the water. Prick the yolk twice and cover with plastic wrap.

Microwave on MEDIUM for 45 seconds to 1-1/4 minutes until the egg is barely cooked. (For more than one egg, use the following guide: two eggs - 1-1/4 to 1-1/2 minutes; three eggs - 2-1/2 to 3 minutes; 4 eggs - 3-1/2 to 4 minutes. The eggs should be in individual ramekins arranged in a circle; rotate each container every 45 seconds.)

Let the eggs stand for 2 to 3 minutes. Do not remove the plastic wrap until standing time is complete.

Drain each egg. If you find that the bottom of the egg is not cooked to your taste, transfer the egg to a cup and microwave for another couple of seconds.

LIGHT SPINACH SALAD

Standard	Metric
1 cup fresh spinach, washed and torn	250 ml fresh spinach, washed and torn
3 sliced tomatoes	3 sliced tomatoes
4 hard-boiled eggs	4 hard-boiled eggs
1/4 cup plain yogurt	50 ml plain yogurt
2 tsp lemon juice	10 ml lemon juice
4 chopped shallots (or onion rings)	4 chopped shallots (or onion rings)
Pepper	Pepper
Marjoram	Marjoram

In a salad bowl, combine the yogurt, lemon juice, shallots and spinach. Toss. Sprinkle with chopped eggs and decorate with tomato slices.

PARMESAN MUFFINS

Standard	Metric
1 egg	1 egg
1 cup plain yogurt	250 ml plain yogurt
1/2 cup milk	125 ml milk
4 tbsp melted butter	60 ml melted butter
1/4 tsp rosemary	1 ml rosemary
2 cups flour	500 ml flour
1 tbsp baking powder	15 ml baking powder
1 tbsp sugar	15 ml sugar
1/2 tsp salt	2 ml salt
4 tbsp golden corn meal	60 ml golden corn meal
1/2 cup grated Parmesan cheese	125 ml grated Parmesan cheese

In a bowl, mix together the egg, yogurt, milk and butter. Stir in the rosemary. Set aside.

Combine the flour, baking powder, sugar, salt and corn meal and Parmesan cheese in a second bowl.

Rapidly stir the dry ingredients into the liquid ingredients. Avoid overmixing, or the muffins will be tough.

Pour the batter into 12 well-greased muffin tins, and bake at 400°F (200°C) for 20 to 25 minutes (until the the top of the muffins spring back when pressed lightly with a finger.) Serve warm.

MICROWAVE METHOD

Baking Muffins

Line microwave muffin tins with two layers of paper muffin molds. Fill the molds half full. Microwave on HIGH for 2 to 2-1/2 minutes, turning the pan halfway through.

Let muffins stand for 3 to 4 minutes, then remove from pans and let cool. Repeat with remaining muffin mixture.

Facing page: Poached Eggs Benedict
Above: Kiwi and Orange Glazed Ham

KIWI AND ORANGE GLAZED HAM

Standard	Metric
1 ham, 8 to 12 lb	1 ham, 4 to 6 kg
1-1/2 cups orange marmalade	375 ml orange marmalade
1/2 cup orange juice	125 ml orange juice
1 tsp rum extract or brandy	5 ml rum extract or brandy
2 kiwis, peeled and sliced	2 kiwis, peeled and sliced
2 oranges, peeled and sliced	2 oranges, peeled and sliced

Bake the ham at 350°F (160°C) for 5 to 7 minutes per pound, (10 to 17 minutes per kg), or until it is completely cooked.

Meanwhile, simmer the orange juice and marmalade in a small saucepan for 2 or 3 minutes. Add the rum extract or brandy and let cool.

One half hour before the ham is done, arrange the kiwi and orange slices on top, anchoring with toothpicks. Spoon the orange syrup on top.

Continue baking, basting once or twice with the orange syrup.

Reheat any remaining orange syrup and bits of fruit, and serve in a sauceboat.

21

OLD-FASHIONED DOUGHNUTS

Standard	Metric
2-1/2 cups all-purpose flour, sifted	625 ml all-purpose flour, sifted
1/4 tsp nutmeg	1 ml nutmeg
1 cup sugar	250 ml sugar
1 tsp vanilla	5 ml vanilla
3/4 cup milk	150 ml milk
4 tsp baking powder	20 ml baking powder
1/2 tsp salt	2 ml salt
1/4 cup butter or vegetable shortening	50 ml butter or vegetable shortening
2 egg yolks	2 egg yolks
2 egg whites	2 egg whites

Cream the butter. Beat the egg yolks; gradually work in the sugar, butter, salt, nutmeg, vanilla, and 2 tbsp (30 ml) of the milk. Set aside.

Beat the egg whites; fold into the first mixture.

Sift together the flour and baking powder several times; mix the flour into the first mixture, alternating with the remaining milk, beginning and ending with dry ingredients.

Knead the dough gently, and roll it out to a thickness of about 1/2 inch (1.25 cm). Cut with a doughnut cutter, and deep-fry a few at a time at 360°F (185°C) for about 3 minutes, turning once. (The oil is the correct temperature when a cube of bread browns and comes to the surface after 1 minute.) Let the doughnuts drain on plain unwaxed brown paper, and dust with icing sugar.

Makes 3 dozen doughnuts.

MAPLE WALNUT BRIOCHE

Standard	Metric
2 cups flour	500 ml flour
2 tsp salt	10 ml salt
1 tbsp fresh yeast	15 ml fresh yeast
2 tbsp sugar	30 ml sugar
1/3 cup milk	75 ml milk
7 eggs	7 eggs
1-1/4 cups soft butter	300 ml soft butter

Topping

Standard	Metric
1 cup maple syrup	250 ml maple syrup
1 cup sugar	250 ml sugar
1 cup thick cream (35%)	250 ml thick cream (35%)

Dissolve the sugar and salt in the cold milk and stir for 1 minute. Add the flour and yeast. Add the eggs 2 at a time, mixing well after each addition.

If the batter is still not smooth enough, add 1 or 2 more eggs. Knead the dough until it is supple and elastic. Work in the softened butter in 3 stages.

Put the dough into a bowl, cover it, and refrigerate overnight.

The next day, grease a round cake pan, form the dough into small balls, and arrange them in concentric circles in the pan. (The dough should fill about 1/3 the height of the pan.) Cover, and let stand in a warm place (not in the oven) until the dough has risen to half the height of the pan.

Brush the top gently with a beaten egg, and bake at 375°F (190°C) for about 40 minutes.

Boil together the maple syrup and sugar for 4 to 5 minutes and pour it evenly over the brioche. Once the syrup has set, decorate the top with whipped cream piped in rosettes and chopped nuts.

MICROWAVE METHOD

Raising Dough

Place the dough in a greased bowl. Cover with wax paper or a sheet of plastic wrap, punctured.

Put in the microwave at the lowest power setting and leave for 15 minutes, or until the dough has doubled in volume.

Maple Walnut Brioche

CHRISTMAS LUNCHEON

You can prepare almost everything a day or two in advance, and relax Christmas day.

Serve a light red wine, red Bordeaux or a sparkling rosé.

MENU

Serves 6 to 8

Homemade Terrine
Herbed Bread
Avocado Dip and Vegetables
Zucchini-Stuffed Tomatoes
Christmas Tart
Fruit Salad with Grand Marnier
Chocolate Almond Squares

HOMEMADE TERRINE

You will need enough thin sliced bacon or lard to line the interior of the mold or loaf pan.

Standard	Metric
1/2 lb lean shoulder or filet of pork	250 g lean shoulder or filet of pork
1/2 lb lean veal, shoulder cut	250 g lean veal, shoulder cut
1/2 lb pork, veal or chicken liver	250 g pork, veal or chicken liver
1/2 lb fresh lard	250 g fresh lard
1/4 lb smoked ham, cubed or chopped (not ground)	125 g smoked ham, cubed or chopped (not ground)
1 tsp brandy	5 ml brandy
4 eggs	4 eggs
1 medium onion or 3 shallots, chopped fine and sautéed in butter	1 medium onion or 3 shallots, chopped fine and sautéed in butter
1 tsp allspice	5 ml allspice
1 tsp each salt and pepper	5 ml each salt and pepper
1 bay leaf, pulverized	1 bay leaf, pulverized
1/4 tsp thyme	1 ml thyme
1 garlic clove, minced	1 garlic clove, minced
1 bay leaf for decoration	1 bay leaf for decoration

Line a 4 x 8 inch (10 x 20 cm) loaf pan or 6 cup (1.5 liter) terrine mold with strips of lard or bacon slices (simmered until soft), letting the slices overhang the edges of the mold 1 or 2 inches (2.5 to 5 cm).

Preheat the oven to 350°F (180°C); half fill a roasting pan with water and put in the oven.

Chop the meat fine, by hand or with the aid of a meat grinder.

In a large bowl, mix the meat, spices, herbs, brandy, eggs,

Homemade Terrine

onion and garlic. Put the meat into the pan, molding it into a loaf shape. Fold the bacon ends over top.

Place the bay leaf on top, and seal the pan tightly in two layers of aluminum foil.

Put the pan or mold into the roasting pan of hot water, and bake for about 2 hours, or until a skewer inserted in the center comes out clean and the juice runs a clear amber color.

Let the terrine cool, then put it in the refrigerator for a day or two, weighted down under a weight (a brick for example) to make the texture firm.

Unmold, or slice directly in the pan.

Facing page: Christmas Tart and Zucchini-Stuffed Tomatoes
Above: Avocado Dip and Vegetables

AVOCADO DIP AND VEGETABLES

2 carrots, cut on the bias or into sticks
4 celery stalks, cut on the bias
15 whole radishes
1 cauliflower, broken into flowerets
15 cherry tomatoes
2 green peppers, cut into sticks

Avocado Dip

Standard	Metric
1/2 cup cream cheese	125 ml cream cheese
1/2 cup milk or heavy cream (35%)	125 ml milk or heavy cream (35%)
Salt and pepper	Salt and pepper
2 tbsp chopped green onions	30 ml chopped green onions
2 ripe avocados	2 ripe avocados
Juice of 1 lemon	Juice of 1 lemon
2 tbsp chopped parsley	30 ml chopped parsley
2 tbsp minced chives	30 ml minced chives
Pinch cayenne pepper	Pinch cayenne pepper

Leave the cream cheese at room temperature for several hours before using. Peel and cube the avocado. In a food processor, combine all ingredients and season to taste.

ZUCCHINI-STUFFED TOMATOES

Standard	Metric
6 medium-sized tomatoes	6 medium-sized tomatoes
2 tbsp butter	30 ml butter
1 zucchini, chopped fine	1 zucchini, chopped fine
4 tsp minced onion	20 ml minced onion
1 garlic clove, minced	1 garlic clove, minced
1/2 tsp dried basil	2 ml dried basil
1 cup small toasted croutons	250 ml small toasted croutons
Salt and pepper	Salt and pepper

Cut a thin slice off the top of each tomato and remove the pulp, leaving a shell about 1/4 inch (5 mm) thick. Chop the tomato pulp, drain off the juice, and set aside. Combine the butter, chopped zucchini, onion, garlic, basil, tomato pulp and croutons in a deep 8 cup (2 liter) saucepan. Add salt and pepper.

Cook the vegetable mixture for 7 to 8 minutes, then fill the tomato shells. Arrange in a baking dish and bake at 400°F (200°C) for 10 minutes.

HERBED BREAD

Standard	Metric
1 large loaf country-style bread (or other crusty bread)	1 large loaf country-style bread (or other crusty bread)
8 chopped shallots	8 chopped shallots
1 large bunch parsley, chopped	1 large bunch parsley, chopped
2 tbsp chopped fresh or dried tarragon	30 ml chopped fresh or dried tarragon
1 tsp thyme	5 ml thyme
1 tsp monosodium glutamate	5 ml monosodium glutamate
2 tsp chervil	10 ml chervil
Salt and pepper	Salt and pepper
Butter	Butter

Cut the bread into large slices and butter them. Mix together all the other ingredients and sprinkle over the bread slices. Arrange in a bread basket or serving plate. This recipe is particularly delicious served with patés, terrines or steamed mussels. Feel free to substitute herbs of your choice.

MICROWAVE METHOD

Zucchini-Stuffed Tomatoes

Cover the vegetable mixture and microwave on HIGH for 3 to 4 minutes, or until the zucchini is tender. Stuff the tomatoes. Arrange them on a plate and microwave on HIGH for 2 to 3 minutes before serving.

CHRISTMAS TART

Standard
1 chopped onion
1 tbsp butter
2 bags spinach
1/2 lb sliced ham
1 lb sliced mozzarella
1 sweet red pepper, sliced thin
6 eggs, well-beaten

Metric
1 chopped onion
15 ml butter
2 bags spinach
250 g sliced ham
500 g sliced mozzarella
1 sweet red pepper, sliced thin
6 eggs, well-beaten

Sauté the onion in butter. Add the spinach, and cook just until it wilts. Drain well.

Cover the bottom of a pie mold with a layer of pastry about 1/4 inch (5 mm) thick.

Cover the pastry with a layer of half the ham, half the cheese, half the spinach mixture and half the red pepper. Pour half the beaten eggs over top.

Now continue building a second layer of the ingredients in the same order. Pour the second half of the beaten eggs on top.

Seal the ingredients under a second pastry layer about 1/4 inch (5 mm) thick.

Baste the top crust lightly with a little light cream. Bake at 400°F (200°C) for 40 to 45 minutes. Let cool before serving.

Pastry Crust

Standard
2 cups bread flour
3/4 cup lard
2 eggs
1/2 tsp salt
1 cup tepid water

Metric
500 ml bread flour
150 ml lard
2 eggs
2 ml salt
250 ml tepid water

In a bowl, beat the eggs, salt and tepid water. Set aside.

Work the flour and lard together between your fingers until it reaches the consistency of breadcrumbs.

Make a well in the center of the flour mixture and pour in the egg mixture. Work into the flour with a knife. (Avoid working the dough too much; it should not become elastic.) If the dough is too sticky, add flour in small quantities. Stop handling the dough as soon as it forms a ball. Cover and refrigerate for 1 hour before using.

Note: The lard can be replaced with butter or margarine. Recipe makes 1 pie.

Technique: Pie Crust

1 Beat the eggs, warm water and salt with a whisk.

2 Work together the flour and lard with your fingers

3 ...to the consistency of breadcrumbs.

4 Make a well in the flour mixture.

5 Pour in the egg mixture.

6 Cut the egg mixture into the flour with a knife.

7 Stop working the dough as soon as it forms a ball easily.

8 Cover and refrigerate for 1 hour. (Can also be frozen.)

Fruit Salad with Grand Marnier and Chocolate Almond Squares

FRUIT SALAD WITH GRAND MARNIER

Standard
1 fresh pineapple, crushed
1/2 cantaloupe, cubed
2 pears, cubed
15 seedless red grapes, halved
2 oranges, peeled and cut up
1 large apple, cubed
1 banana, sliced thin
1/3 cup sugar
1/2 cup orange juice or Seven-Up
2 tbsp Grand Marnier or cognac
A few maraschino cherries for color

Metric
1 fresh pineapple, crushed
1/2 cantaloupe, cubed
2 pears, cubed
15 seedless red grapes, halved
2 oranges, peeled and cut up
1 large apple, cubed
1 banana, sliced thin
75 ml sugar
125 ml orange juice or Seven-Up
30 ml Grand Marnier or cognac
A few maraschino cherries for color

Make a syrup with the sugar, the orange juice and a bit of maraschino cherry juice. Add the Grand Marnier or cognac. Stir well, and add the prepared fruits. Make this recipe one day in advance to allow the flavors to blend completely.

CHOCOLATE ALMOND SQUARES

Standard
1/3 cup vegetable oil
2 squares unsweetened chocolate
3/4 cup water
1 cup sugar
1-1/4 cups flour
1 egg
1/2 tsp salt
1/2 tsp baking soda
1 tsp almond extract
1 package semi-sweet chocolate bits
1/3 cup slivered almonds

Metric
75 ml vegetable oil
2 squares unsweetened chocolate
150 ml water
250 ml sugar
300 ml flour
1 egg
2 ml salt
2 ml baking soda
5 ml almond extract
1 package semi-sweet chocolate bits
75 ml slivered almonds

Heat the oven to 350°F (180°C) and heat the vegetable oil and chocolate squares for about 4 minutes. Remove from oven and add the rest of ingredients (except chocolate bits and almonds). Beat with a fork about 2 minutes until mixture is smooth.

Spread the batter evenly in a greased and floured cake pan. Sprinkle chocolate bits and almonds on top.

Bake about 40 minutes or until a skewer inserted in the center of the squares comes out clean.

CHRISTMAS DINNER

A veritable feast featuring the traditional turkey with a twist.

Serve with white Bordeaux, red Bordeaux, and cognac to finish.

MENU

Serves 8 to 10

Tomato Soup with Gin

Pâté de Campagne with Pink Peppercorns

Roast Turkey with Two Stuffings

Veal and Pork Pie

Duchess Potatoes

Puréed Turnips Amandine

Beet and Onion Salad

Rum or Cognac Cake

Tomato Soup with Gin

TOMATO SOUP WITH GIN

Standard	Metric
5 fresh tomatoes, peeled	5 fresh tomatoes, peeled
2 garlic cloves, minced	2 garlic cloves, minced
2 cups beef broth or bouillon	500 ml beef broth or bouillon
1 tsp thyme	5 ml thyme
Salt and freshly ground pepper	Salt and freshly ground pepper
4 slices bacon	4 slices bacon
1/4 cup butter	50 ml butter
1/2 lb mushrooms	250 g mushrooms
1/3 cup dry gin	75 ml dry gin
1 cup heavy cream (35%)	250 ml heavy cream (35%)

Melt the butter in a small saucepan and add the bacon, mushrooms, one garlic clove and the freshly ground pepper. Sauté and drain.

Put the tomatoes, the second garlic clove, the beef broth, thyme, salt along with the cooked mushroom mixture in a food processor; process at medium speed.

Pour the tomato mixture into a soup pot and add the gin. Cook for about 8 minutes. Stir in the cream just before serving.

PÂTÉ DE CAMPAGNE WITH PINK PEPPERCORNS

Standard	Metric
1 lb ground pork liver	450 g ground pork liver
3 lb ground fresh pork	1.5 kg ground fresh pork
6 shallots, minced fine	6 shallots, minced fine
1 cup heavy cream (35%)	250 ml heavy cream (35%)
4 eggs	4 eggs
1 tsp salt	5 ml salt
1 tsp brown sugar	5 ml brown sugar
1 tbsp pink peppercorns, crushed	15 ml pink peppercorns, crushed
1/2 tsp marjoram	2 ml marjoram
1/4 tsp mace	1 ml mace
1/4 tsp ginger	1 ml ginger
1/4 tsp ground cardamom	1 ml ground cardamom
1/2 lb thin strips of lard	250 g thin strips of lard
2 slices bacon	2 slices bacon

Combine the pork, pork liver and shallots. Add all the other ingredients except lard and bacon strips, and mix in the food processor (using the plastic blades) or with an electric mixer.

Line the bottom and sides of a loaf pan or terrine mold with the lard. Shape the meat mixture into the pan. Arrange the bacon slices on top. Cover the pâté with aluminum foil and insert a meat thermometer in the center.

Fill a roasting pan with 3 inches (7.5 cm) of water. Set the mold in the roasting pan, and bake at 325°F (160°C) for 1 hour, or until the thermometer registers 130° to 140°F (50° to 60°C). Drain off the excess fat and set the pâté under a heavy weight (a brick for example) overnight.

This recipe makes about 4 pounds (2 kg) of pâté. It will keep in the refrigerator for 3 to 4 weeks. The meat mixture can also be frozen before baking.

ROAST TURKEY WITH TWO STUFFINGS

To serve 8 to 12 people, you will need a 13-1/2 to 18 lb (6.75 to 9 kg) bird. Wipe the turkey inside and out with paper towels. Sprinkle a little salt inside the cavities.

Stuff the neck cavity with the wild rice stuffing, and the other end with the sausage mushroom mixture. Sew the openings shut or close with skewers. Tie the wings against the body of the bird. Baste the bird all over with butter and place it in a roasting pan. We suggest that you cover the turkey with heavy brown paper. You won't have to baste as often, as the brown paper soaks up the grease and bastes the bird continuously, without giving the "stewed" flavor produced if you cover it with aluminum foil or the lid of the roasting pan.

Roast the bird in a preheated oven at 275° to 300°F (130° to 150°C) for 20 to 25 minutes per pound (500 g).

To give the turkey a festive air, present it on a platter surrounded with cherry tomatoes interspersed with parsley sprigs.

Sausage Mushroom Stuffing

Standard	Metric
1/4 cup butter or margarine	50 ml butter or margarine
1 large onion, minced	1 large onion, minced
1/2 cup chopped mushrooms	125 ml chopped mushrooms
3/4 lb pork sausage meat	375 g pork sausage meat
1 cup chopped ham	250 ml chopped ham
3/4 lb chicken liver, chopped	375 g chicken liver, chopped
3 eggs, lightly beaten	3 eggs, lightly beaten
1 cup breadcrumbs	250 ml breadcrumbs
3/4 cup chicken stock or dry white wine	150 ml chicken stock or dry white wine
1/4 cup chopped parsley	50 ml chopped parsley
1 tsp sage	5 ml sage
1 tsp salt	5 ml salt
Freshly ground black pepper	Freshly ground black pepper

Sauté the onions and mushrooms in the butter. Add the pork and cook until the meat is almost done. Add the meat and

Roast Turkey with Two Stuffings

29

chicken livers and cook a few more minutes. Let cool. Add the rest of the ingredients and mix well.

Makes about 5 cups.

Wild Rice Stuffing

Standard	Metric
1/2 cup wild rice	125 ml wild rice
2 chicken bouillon cubes	2 chicken bouillon cubes
The turkey giblets	The turkey giblets
1/4 cup butter	50 ml butter
1 small chopped onion	1 small chopped onion
1/2 lb mushrooms, chopped fine	250 g mushrooms, chopped fine
1/2 tsp thyme	2 ml thyme
1/4 tsp rosemary	1 ml rosemary
Pinch of nutmeg	Pinch of nutmeg
Salt and pepper	Salt and pepper
1/4 cup brandy	50 ml brandy

Rinse the rice several times. Drain and place in a saucepan with 4 cups (1 liter) water and the bouillon cubes. Bring to a boil and let simmer, partially covered, for about 1 hour or until the rice is tender and the water has evaporated.

Meanwhile, melt the butter in a heavy skillet and sauté the onion, mushrooms, and turkey liver and gizzard, stirring frequently.

Pour on the brandy and flame. Once the flame has died, remove the giblets, and stir in the rice and seasonings.

MICROWAVE METHOD

Cooking a 15 lb (6.75 kg) Turkey

Baste the turkey with a browning mix. Cook at HIGH for 26 minutes. Turn the bird on its side, baste with browning mix and the cooking juices, and cook for another 26 minutes. Turn the bird on its other side, baste again, and cook 26 minutes. Place the turkey breast side up, baste and microwave for a final 27 minutes. Let stand for 25 minutes before serving.

DUCHESS POTATOES

Standard	Metric
2 lb potatoes, peeled and diced large	1 kg potatoes, peeled and diced large
4 egg yolks	4 egg yolks
3 tbsp butter	45 ml butter
Salt and pepper	Salt and pepper
Pinch nutmeg	Pinch nutmeg
Pinch paprika	Pinch paprika

Cook the potatoes in boiling salted water just until done; do not overcook or they will be soggy. Drain the potatoes and let them dry on a platter in the oven, stirring from time to time.

Put the potatoes through a food mill into a casserole dish over low heat. Beat in the egg yolks, nutmeg and butter briskly with a wooden spoon. Stuff the potatoes into a pastry bag fitted with a large fluted tip and pipe the potatoes into mounds on a buttered baking sheet. Pour a little melted butter over each mound and sprinkle with paprika. Bake at 325°F (160°C) for about 15 minutes.

PURÉED TURNIPS AMANDINE

Standard	Metric
1-1/2 cups mashed potatoes	375 ml mashed potatoes
2 cups puréed turnips	500 ml puréed turnips
6 tbsp heavy cream (35%)	90 ml heavy cream (35%)
3 tbsp butter	45 ml butter
4 tsp powdered almonds	20 ml powdered almonds
2 tbsp finely chopped fresh parsley	30 ml finely chopped fresh parsley
1/4 tsp nutmeg	1 ml nutmeg
Salt and pepper to taste	Salt and pepper to taste

In separate pots of boiling salted water, cook enough potatoes and turnips to give at least 3-1/2 cups (875 ml) of puréed vegetables. Combine with the rest of the ingredients and mix well.

VEAL AND PORK PIE

Standard	Metric
1 recipe for 2-crust pie pastry	1 recipe for 2-crust pie pastry
1/2 lb ground veal	250 g ground veal
1/2 lb ground pork	250 g ground pork
1 medium onion	1 medium onion
1/4 cup water	50 ml water
3/4 tsp salt	4 ml salt
1/4 tsp pepper	1 ml pepper
Pinch ground cloves	Pinch ground cloves
Pinch of cinnamon	Pinch of cinnamon
Pinch of savory	Pinch of savory

Preheat the oven to 450°F (230°C). Prepare the pastry. Line a pie plate with a layer of pastry. Mix together the remaining ingredients in a large pan. Cook on the stove top until the meat is cooked but not dry. Correct seasonings. Let cool a little and turn into the unbaked pastry shell. Cover with the second pastry layer, seal and crimp the edges, and slash the top crust for steam to escape.

Baste the crust with a mixture of egg yolk and milk. Bake for about 20 to 25 minutes or until the crust is browned.

Rum or Cognac Cake

Beet and Onion Salad

BEET AND ONION SALAD

Standard	Metric
1 lb beets, cooked	500 g beets, cooked
1 tsp mustard	5 ml mustard
1 tbsp wine vinegar	15 ml wine vinegar
1 or 2 drops Tabasco sauce	1 or 2 drops Tabasco sauce
Salt and pepper	Salt and pepper
3 tbsp olive oil	45 ml olive oil
3 small onions	3 small onions
1 head lettuce	1 head lettuce
2 tbsp fresh parsley	30 ml fresh parsley

Peel and slice the beets into rounds. Arrange them in deep plate. In a bowl, combine the mustard, vinegar and Tabasco. Add salt and pepper and the olive oil. Mix well, pour the sauce over the beets and let stand for 2 hours.

Meanwhile, peel the onions and slice into thin rounds. Separate into rings and add them to the beets. Gently combine the ingredients and arrange on a bed of lettuce. Sprinkle with chopped fresh parsley.

RUM OR COGNAC CAKE

Standard	Metric
6 eggs	6 eggs
1 cup icing sugar	250 ml icing sugar
1 cup flour	250 ml flour
1 tsp instant coffee	5 ml instant coffee
1/2 tsp baking powder	2 ml baking powder
1/2 cup chopped nuts	125 ml chopped nuts

Break the eggs into a bowl, add the icing sugar and beat with an electric mixer for 6 to 7 minutes. Blend in the rest of the ingredients with a spatula.

Turn the mixture into 2 greased 9 inch (22 cm) cake pans, which have been lined with wax paper cut to size. Bake at 325°F (160°C) for 20 minutes. Unmold. With a pastry brush, spread the rum or cognac icing over the cake. Decorate with empty walnut shell halves filled with maple syrup.

Icing

Standard	Metric
1 cup heavy cream (35%)	250 ml heavy cream (35%)
3/4 cup icing sugar	50 ml icing sugar
1 tsp instant coffee diluted in	5 ml instant coffee diluted in
1 tbsp cognac or dark rum	15 ml cognac or dark rum

Beat the cream just until thick; and gradually beat in the icing sugar. Stir in the coffee cognac (or rum) mixture. The icing should have the consistency of very thick cream.

MICROWAVE METHOD

Rum or Cognac Cake

Modify the ingredients as follows:

Standard	Metric
3/4 cup butter	150 ml butter
1 cup icing sugar	250 ml icing sugar
1 cup flour	250 ml flour
1 tsp instant coffee	5 ml instant coffee
5 eggs	5 eggs
2 tbsp milk	30 ml milk
1/2 cup chopped nuts	125 ml chopped nuts

Cream the butter and sugar together, then beat in the rest of the ingredients.

Turn the batter into a microwave cake mold. Microwave on HIGH for 6 to 8 minutes, rotating the pan a quarter turn 4 times during the cooking process. Let stand for 15 minutes. Unmold.

CHRISTMAS DINNER II

An elegant meal featuring a novel and delicious recipe for quail.

Serve with a rosé, white Bordeaux, or champagne.

MENU

Serves 6 to 8

Oyster Chowder
Chicken Liver Mousse with Port
Stuffed Quail Francillon
Broccoli with Pears
Brussels Sprouts Amandine
Tomato Fan Salad
Strawberry Almond Roll
Mocha Christmas Log

OYSTER CHOWDER

Standard	Metric
8 slices bacon, diced small	8 slices bacon, diced small
4 onions, chopped fine	4 onions, chopped fine
5 medium potatoes, diced	5 medium potatoes, diced
1/4 cup green pepper, diced	50 ml green pepper, diced
1 celery stalk, diced	1 celery stalk, diced
1 garlic clove, minced fine	1 garlic clove, minced fine
2 pints shucked oysters, drained (reserve the juice and add enough milk to make 3 cups)	1 liter shucked oysters, drained (reserve the juice and add enough milk to make 750 ml)
2 tsp salt	10 ml salt
1 carrot, diced	1 carrot, diced
1 tsp pepper	5 ml pepper
1 tsp Worcestershire sauce	5 ml Worcestershire sauce
4 drops Tabasco sauce	4 drops Tabasco sauce

Sauté the bacon until crisp. Add all the other ingredients except the drained oysters. Simmer until the vegetables are tender, then purée the mixture. Add the oysters and simmer for 2 minutes at low heat. Return the mixture to the food processor and process rapidly; you want to leave small chunks of oyster. If the chowder is too thick, add a little milk or cream.

CHICKEN LIVER MOUSSE WITH PORT

Standard	Metric
1 lb chicken livers	500 g chicken livers
4 tbsp grated onion	60 ml grated onion
2 garlic cloves, minced	2 garlic cloves, minced
2 tbsp fresh parsley, chopped	30 ml fresh parsley, chopped
1 tsp sugar	5 ml sugar
1/4 cup port	50 ml port
Salt and pepper	Salt and pepper
1/2 lb butter or lard	250 g butter or lard

Remove the membranes and filaments from the livers, rinse, then sauté them in a saucepan with a little butter until cooked but still pink. Set aside the livers, and add to the saucepan the onion, garlic, parsley, sugar, salt and pepper; cook for 5 minutes. Drain. Put the livers and onion mixture in a food processor and process to a mousse-like consistency. When the liver mixture has cooled, blend in the port and the softened butter. Put the mousse into a bowl, cover and refrigerate for at least 2 hours. Serve with thin slices of toasted herbed bread. This mousse freezes well.

Oyster Chowder

BRUSSELS SPROUTS AMANDINE

Standard	Metric
1-1/2 lb Brussels sprouts	750 g Brussels sprouts
1/3 cup butter	75 ml butter
2-1/2 cups chicken stock	625 ml chicken stock
1/2 cup almonds, sliced and toasted	125 ml almonds, sliced and toasted
Juice of 1 lemon	Juice of 1 lemon
1/4 cup chopped fresh parsley	50 ml chopped fresh parsley

Trim the sprouts and boil them for about 8 minutes in the chicken stock. Melt the butter in a pan and add the almonds; cook until golden. Stir in the drained Brussels sprouts, and season with lemon juice and chopped parsley.

BROCCOLI WITH PEARS

Standard	Metric
2 heads broccoli	2 heads broccoli
3 tbsp butter	45 ml butter
5 pear halves in syrup, drained	5 pear halves in syrup, drained

Trim and cut the broccoli into flowerets and cook for 7 minutes, uncovered, in boiling salted water. Dice the pears and sauté them gently in a saucepan with the butter. Drain the broccoli and add to the pears to heat. Stir gently to avoid crushing the fruit.

TOMATO FAN SALAD

Standard	Metric
1 tomato per serving	1 tomato per serving
1 can baby peas	1 can baby peas
1 green pepper, diced	1 green pepper, diced
1 tsp mayonnaise per tomato	5 ml mayonnaise per tomato
Vinaigrette, homemade or commercial	Vinaigrette, homemade or commercial
Parsley sprigs	Parsley sprigs
1/2 slice white cheese per serving	1/2 slice white cheese per serving

Wash and dry the tomatoes, and slice a piece off the stem end so tomatoes sit flat. Slice the tomatoes into fan shapes. Arrange on a platter surrounding a mound of peas and green peppers dressed with vinaigrette. Garnish with cheese slices.

Technique: Tomato Fan

1 Gather your ingredients.

2 Cut a slice off each tomato so it will sit flat.

3 Make the first incision in a V-shape. Detach but do not remove.

4 Make a second V-shaped cut.

5 Make a third incision

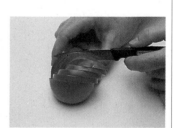

6 ...and a fourth.

7 Shift the cut pieces to make a fan shape.

8 You can use the same technique with potatoes, carrots, and other vegetables.

Stuffed Quail Francillon

Standard	Metric
20 small quails, cleaned	20 small quails, cleaned
1 small white cabbage, grated	1 small white cabbage, grated
1 cup rice, cooked and lightly buttered	250 ml rice, cooked and lightly buttered
Salt, pepper and thyme	Salt, pepper and thyme
7 tbsp butter and oil (half and half)	105 ml butter and oil (half and half)
10 slices bacon	10 slices bacon
1/2 cup dry white wine	125 ml dry white wine
1 red cabbage, chopped	1 red cabbage, chopped
1-1/2 cups vinaigrette	375 ml vinaigrette
1/2 cup heavy cream (35%)	125 ml heavy cream (35%)

Wash the quails, clean out the interiors, and season the cavities lightly with salt, pepper and thyme. Set aside.

Cook the white cabbage in boiling salted water for 5 minutes; drain it and add it to a saucepan containing the bacon, diced small. Cover and cook gently for 15 minutes. Meanwhile, cook the rice. Stir some butter into the rice, and add it to the white cabbage. Mix well.

Stuff the quails tightly with the cabbage mixture. To close the cavities, make an incision in one leg of each quail with a knife and poke the other leg through the incision. Arrange the quails in a roasting pan with the butter and oil. Season and roast in the oven at 375°F (190°C) for about 25 minutes.

Meanwhile, cook the chopped red cabbage in boiling salted water for 10 minutes. Drain, then braise in butter for 10 minutes. Keep warm.

When the quails are cooked, arrange the cooked red cabbage on a large serving platter with the quails arranged on top. Keep warm.

Pour off excess grease from the roasting pan and add the white wine. Set to boil on burner for 3 minutes, then stir in

Stuffed Quail Francillon

1-1/2 cups (375 ml) of vinaigrette and 1/2 cup (125 ml) heavy cream. Pour this sauce over the quails.

Technique: Stuffed Quail

1 Stuff the quail with cabbage rice mixture.

2 Make a small incision in one thigh with a knife.

3 Slip the other leg through the incision.

4 Put the quails in a roasting pan with the butter and oil.

Microwave Method

Stuffed Quail

Prepare the quails as for conventional cooking method. Brush the breasts and legs with butter.

Heat a browning dish at HIGH for 5 minutes, or according to manufacturer's instructions. Brown the quails on all sides.

Cook the quails in batches of 4, arranged breast side down. Cover with paper towels and cook at HIGH for 5 to 6 minutes. Turn the quails breast side up, and make a small incision in the thigh to check doneness; you should see pink juice. If so, microwave the quails another 2 minutes, breast side up, then check degree of doneness again. Cook a minute or two longer if necessary. When cooked, the skin should be slightly dry.

STRAWBERRY ALMOND ROLL

Standard	Metric
6 egg whites	6 egg whites
6 egg yolks	6 egg yolks
1 cup sugar	250 ml sugar
1/2 tsp vanilla	2 ml vanilla
1 cup pastry flour	250 ml pastry flour
1 tsp baking powder	5 ml baking powder
1 tsp cornstarch	5 ml cornstarch
1/4 tsp salt	1 ml salt
1 cup strawberry jam	250 ml strawberry jam
1-1/2 cups whipped cream	375 ml whipped cream
1/2 cup almonds, chopped and toasted	125 ml almonds, chopped and toasted

Beat the egg whites into stiff peaks, gradually beating in half the sugar.

Beat the egg yolks together with the other 1/2 cup (125 ml) sugar until thick. Blend in the vanilla. Fold the yolk mixture into the whites.

Sift together all the dry ingredients, then fold them gently into the egg mixture.

Line a jelly roll pan with greased wax paper, and spread the batter in it. Bake in a preheated oven at 375°F (190°C) for 12 minutes.

Turn the cake out on a clean, dry tea towel. Gently pull off the wax paper and roll the cake inside the towel to draw off the excess moisture.

Unroll the cake, spread it with a layer of strawberry jam, and roll it jelly-roll fashion. Chill. Spread the roll with whipped cream. Decorate the cake with fresh strawberries or with a strawberry coulis (made of frozen berries and sugar, run through the blender). Sprinkle the cake with chopped toasted almonds.

Mocha Christmas Log

MOCHA CHRISTMAS LOG

Rolled Biscuit Dough

Standard	Metric
1/2 cup sugar	125 ml sugar
1/2 cup pastry flour	125 ml pastry flour
2 tbsp melted unsalted butter	30 ml melted unsalted butter
4 egg whites	4 egg whites
5 egg yolks	5 egg yolks

Preheat the oven to 350°F (180°C). Melt the butter in a saucepan. Set aside.

Beat together the egg yolks and sugar for 5 minutes with an electric mixer. Beat in the flour, being careful not to beat too much. Whip the egg whites into stiff peaks. As soon as the whites start to stiffen, beat in 1 tsp (5 ml) sugar. Add the egg whites and melted butter to the egg yolk mixture, and fold in gently with a rubber spatula.

Cover a pastry sheet with greased wax paper, and spread the batter on top to a thickness of about 3/4 inch (2 cm). Spread the batter as smoothly as possible so it cooks evenly. Bake for 7 to 10 minutes.

Turn the pastry onto a tea towel generously sprinkled with icing sugar. Gently pull off the wax paper, trim the edges, and roll the cake up in the towel. Chill before using.

Note: You can roll the pastry in plastic wrap and freeze as is.

Mocha Butter Crème

Standard	Metric
2 cups whole milk	500 ml whole milk
1 tsp vanilla	5 ml vanilla
5 egg yolks	5 egg yolks
3/4 cup sugar	150 ml sugar
1/4 cup pastry flour	50 ml pastry flour
1 tbsp instant coffee	15 ml instant coffee
1-1/4 cups soft butter	300 ml soft butter

In a saucepan, bring the milk, coffee and vanilla just to a boil. Meanwhile, beat together the egg yolks and sugar with an electric mixer at medium speed. Beat in the flour.

When the milk reaches the boiling point, pour half of it over the egg yolk mixture and beat vigorously. Turn this mixture into the rest of the milk and boil for 3 minutes, beating occasionally.

Remove the pan from the heat. When the mixture is nearly cool, work in the softened butter, bit by bit, beating well.

If you are assembling the Christmas log immediately, use the crème as is. Otherwise, refrigerate, and let stand at room temperature 2 hours before using.

Assembling the Christmas Log

Unroll the pastry. Spread a thin layer of mocha crème over the entire surface and roll up again. Cut 2 slices about 1 inch (2.5 cm) thick on the bias and arrange them on the log to give the shape of a cut branch, attaching them with a bit of the mocha crème.

Ice the cake with mocha butter crème using a ribbed pastry nozzle, or use a fork to score the icing. Don't ice the ends.

Sprinkle icing sugar over top and decorate with holly leaves and small red candies.

For an added decorative touch, shape a little snowman out of almond paste. Use honey to glue on arms. Use toothpicks to fasten the hat and head to the body.

Technique: Mocha Christmas Log and Decorative Snowman

1 Spread the batter on a baking pan covered with a layer of greased wax paper.

2 Smooth the batter to a uniform 3/4 inch (2 cm) thickness and bake for 7 to 10 minutes.

3 Turn the cake out on a towel sprinkled with icing sugar. Remove the pan and peel off the wax paper.

4 Trim the edges even and carefully roll the cake into a jelly roll shape, using the towel.

5 Unroll the cake. Spread with a thin layer of mocha crème.

6 Roll the cake up again.

7 Cut two 1 inch (2.5 cm) slices on the bias and arrange on the roll to give the effect of a cut branch.

8 Use a pastry bag or spatula to cover the roll with mocha crème. Make grooves on the icing to look like bark.

9 Make two different size balls of almond paste. Roll two cylinder shapes for arms.

10 To make the hat, shape a ball and use a knife to make an indentation on the bottom.

11 One toothpick will hold the hat, head and body together.

12 Use chocolate to make the mouth and eyes, as shown.

NEW YEAR'S EVE

A hearty midnight feast.

Serve with a white Burgundy, a red Bordeaux or a sparkling wine.

MENU

Serves 8 to 10

Rum Punch
Fancy Pea Soup
Lemony Carrots in Aspic
Chicken Vegetable Pie
Ham Turnovers
Pig Knuckles with Meatballs
Red Cabbage and Cauliflower Vinaigrette
Molasses and Brown Sugar Pie

RUM PUNCH

Standard	Metric
24 cups apple cider	6 litres apple cider
1 cup dark rum	250 ml of dark rum
1 cup brandy	250 ml of brandy
1/2 tsp mace	2 ml mace
1/2 tsp allspice	2 ml allspice
2 or 3 cinnamon sticks	2 or 3 cinnamon sticks

Combine all the ingredients and let simmer for 30 minutes. May be served piping hot or iced.

FANCY PEA SOUP

Standard	Metric
1 lb dried yellow peas	500 g dried yellow peas
1/4 lb salt pork or bacon	125 g salt pork or bacon
or	or
1 ham bone	1 ham bone
14 cups water	3.5 liters water
3 medium onions, chopped	3 medium onions, chopped
2 carrots, diced	2 carrots, diced
2 bay leaves	2 bay leaves
1 handful chopped celery leaves	1 handful chopped celery leaves
1 tbsp savory	15 ml savory
Salted herbs to taste	Salted herbs to taste

Wash and drain the peas thoroughly and let them soak in water for 12 to 24 hours. Pour the contents into a large uncovered pot. Add the remaining ingredients and boil for two minutes.

Remove from heat and let stand for 1 hour.

Return the contents to burner and bring to a boil. Reduce the heat, cover the pot and let simmer for approximately one hour or until the peas are tender. Add salt and pepper to taste.

Serve as is or purée in a food mill or blender.

Note: The peas will cook better if you add 1/2 tsp (2 ml) of baking soda to the water when soaking the peas.

Fancy Pea Soup

LEMONY CARROTS IN ASPIC

Standard
3 medium-sized carrots, grated
1 package lemon gelatin mix
1 cup boiling water
1 cup cold water
1 pinch of salt
1 can of crushed pineapple with juice

Metric
3 medium-sized carrots, grated
1 package lemon gelatin mix
250 ml boiling water
250 ml cold water
1 pinch of salt
1 can of crushed pineapple with juice

Dissolve the gelatin mix in the boiling water. Add the cold water, salt and pineapple, including the juice. Refrigerate until the gelatine just begins to set. Stir in the grated carrots.

Pour the contents into a 1 quart (1 liter) mold, or into six individual molds. Refrigerate until firm.

To decorate: Take approximately ten pineapple leaves about 4 inches (10 cm) long from a fresh pineapple. Wash and dry them, then dip them into egg whites and then into cherry-flavoured gelatin crystals. Arrange the leaves around the mold.

CHICKEN VEGETABLE PIE

Standard
Pastry dough
2 cups cooked chicken
1 cup wax beans
1 cup carrots, diced
1 cup celery, diced
1 cup turnip, diced
1 cup cabbage, chopped
1 cup onion, diced
1 cup mushrooms, chopped
1 can cream of mushroom soup (undiluted)
1 can cream of celery soup (undiluted)

Metric
Pastry dough
500 ml cooked chicken
250 ml wax beans
250 ml carrots, diced
250 ml celery, diced
250 ml turnip, diced
250 ml cabbage, chopped
250 ml onion, diced
250 ml mushrooms, chopped
1 can cream of mushroom soup (undiluted)
1 can cream of celery soup (undiluted)

Prepare enough pastry dough to line and cover a large baking dish.

Place all the other ingredients in a pot with the cream of mushroom and cream of celery soups. Simmer for 15 minutes.

Remove from heat and let cool. Pour the mixture into the pastry-lined baking dish. Cover with a top layer of pastry and seal well. Bake in a 350°F (180°C) oven for approximately 20 minutes.

Lemony Carrots in Aspic

HAM TURNOVERS

Standard
5 cups flour
1 tsp brown sugar
1 tsp salt
1 tsp baking powder
1 lb lard
or
2-1/3 cups shortening
3/4 cup cold water
1 egg
2 tsp vinegar

Metric
1.25 liters flour
5 ml brown sugar
5 ml salt
5 ml baking powder
500 g lard
or
575 g shortening
150 ml cold water
1 egg
10 ml vinegar

Filling

Standard
1-1/2 lb cooked ham, chopped
2 tbsp green pepper, diced
2 tbsp sweet red pepper, diced
1 tbsp onion, chopped
1 can cream of mushroom soup
or
1 can cream of celery soup
1 pinch garlic salt
Sesame or poppy seeds

Metric
750 g cooked ham, chopped
30 ml green pepper, diced
30 ml sweet red pepper, diced
15 ml onion, chopped
1 can cream of mushroom soup
or
1 can cream of celery soup
1 pinch garlic salt
Sesame or poppy seeds

Mix all the dry ingredients together in a bowl. Work in half the lard and then the other half until the mixture forms pea-sized balls. In a separate bowl, mix together the water, egg and vinegar and work into the dough mixture. Refrigerate.

Roll out the pastry dough and cut out approximately 50 pieces, 4 or 6 inches (10 or 15 cm) in diameter.

Cut the ham into small pieces or put through a meat grinder. Add the remaining ingredients to the ham. Fill each piece of pastry, moisten the edges and fold, sealing the edges with a fork. Brush the top of the turnovers with beaten egg.

Sprinkle the turnovers with sesame or poppy seeds. Pierce the pastry shells with a fork to ensure even cooking.

Bake at 400°F (200°C) for 15 to 20 minutes.

Makes approximately fifty turnovers. Can be stored in the freezer.

Pig Knuckles with Meatballs

Standard	Metric
2 pig knuckles	2 pig knuckles
2 lb ground pork	1 kg ground pork
1 onion	1 onion
1 celery stalk, chopped	1 celery stalk, chopped
1 tsp allspice	5 ml allspice
3 cloves	3 cloves
Cold water	Cold water
Toasted flour	Toasted flour
Salt and pepper	Salt and pepper

To the ground pork add:

Standard	Metric
1 finely chopped onion	1 finely chopped onion
1/4 cup finely chopped celery	50 ml finely chopped celery
1 egg lightly beaten with a fork	1 egg beaten lightly with a fork
1/4 tsp ground nutmeg	1 ml ground nutmeg
1/2 tsp ground cloves	2 ml ground cloves
1/2 tsp ground cinnamon	2 ml ground cinnamon
Salt and pepper	Salt and pepper

Put the pig knuckles in a pot of cold water. Add the onion, celery, allspice, salt and pepper. Let simmer for 4 hours until the meat is well- cooked.

Mix the ground pork with the other meatball ingredients and shape into little balls.

Once the pig knuckles are cooked, remove from the pot and leave them to cool on a plate. Pour the stock through a strainer and return it to the pot. Bring the stock to a furious boil and gently drop in the meatballs one at a time.

Reduce the heat and let simmer for 1-1/2 hours. Using a strainer, gently sift 3/4 to 1 cup (150 to 250 ml) toasted flour into the stock, to thicken to desired consistency.

Simmer for 1/2 hour.

Add the pig knuckles and keep at a simmer until you are ready to serve.

Pig Knuckles with Meatballs

Molasses and Brown Sugar Pie

RED CABBAGE AND CAULIFLOWER VINAIGRETTE

Standard	Metric
2 lb red cabbage, shredded	1 kg red cabbage, shredded
1 tsp salt	5 ml salt
3 cups boiling water	750 ml boiling water
1/3 cup lemon juice	75 ml lemon juice
1/2 cup oil	125 ml oil
2 tbsp sugar	30 ml sugar
1/4 tsp pepper	1 ml pepper
1-1/2 cups diced green apples	375 ml diced green apples
1/4 cup onion, chopped	50 ml onion, chopped
1 head of cauliflower	1 head of cauliflower
Several leaves of lettuce	Several leaves of lettuce

Add salt and cabbage to boiling water. Let sit for 10 minutes. Drain.

Mix the lemon juice, oil, sugar and pepper. Pour over the apples. Place the drained cabbage in large bowl and add the apples, onions and vinaigrette. Toss and refrigerate for approximately 30 minutes.

Serve on a bed of lettuce garnished with blanched cauliflower broken up into flowerets.

For a change of flavor, warm the vinaigrette before pouring over the salad.

MOLASSES AND BROWN SUGAR PIE

Standard	Metric
1 cup molasses	250 ml molasses
1 cup brown sugar	250 ml brown sugar
3 eggs, beaten	3 eggs, beaten
2 tbsp butter	30 ml butter
1 cup milk	250 ml milk
2 tbsp cornstarch	30 ml cornstarch
1 tsp lemon	5 ml lemon
1 cup raisins	250 ml raisins

Over medium heat, mix the molasses, brown sugar, eggs, milk and butter. Thicken the mixture with cornstarch.

Add the raisins. Pour this mixture into an unbaked pie shell. Preheat the oven to 350°F (180°C) and bake the pie for 35 to 40 minutes.

(See recipe on page 75 for shortcrust pastry.)

41

New Year's Brunch

A colorful, appetizing and refreshing light meal.

Serve with a sweet white Bordeaux, fruity vin d'Alsace or sparkling wine.

Menu

Serves 6 to 8

Strawberry Eggnog
Oranges and Grapefruit in Hot Syrup
Applenut Crêpes
Brioche with Raspberry Topping
Stewed Fruit with Crème Fraîche
Coffee Cake
Café au Rhum

Strawberry Eggnog

Standard	Metric
4 eggs	4 eggs
3 cups cold milk	750 ml cold milk
30 large strawberries	30 large strawberries
1/3 cup honey	75 ml honey

Blend all the ingredients together in a food processor or blender, and pour into large glasses. Refrigerate and serve cold. Set aside some of the nicer strawberries to decorate the sides of the glasses and sprinkle with icing sugar. Frozen raspberries may be used instead of fresh strawberries.

Oranges and Grapefruit in Hot Syrup

Standard	Metric
6 seedless oranges	6 seedless oranges
3 white grapefruit	3 white grapefruit
3 pink grapefruit	3 pink grapefruit
1 cup corn syrup	250 ml corn syrup
or	or
1 cup maple syrup	250 ml maple syrup
1/2 cup roasted almonds	125 ml roasted almonds
Fresh mint	Fresh mint

Peel the oranges and grapefruit, completely removing the stringy white membrane between segments. Any juice should be set aside. Add this juice to the syrup and bring to a boil.

Arrange segments on small plates, alternating the oranges and grapefruit. Sprinkle with roasted almonds and pour the hot syrup over each portion. Garnish with fresh mint.

Applenut Crêpes

Standard	Metric
2 cups sifted flour	500 ml sifted flour
1 tsp baking soda	5 ml baking soda
1/4 cup sugar	50 ml sugar
3/4 tsp salt	4 ml salt
2 eggs, beaten	2 eggs, beaten
1/4 cup vinegar	50 ml vinegar
1-3/4 cups fresh milk	400 ml fresh milk
1/4 cup melted shortening	50 ml melted shortening

Sift the flour, salt and baking soda; add the sugar and mix well. In another bowl beat in the eggs, vinegar, milk and shortening. Gradually add the dry ingredients to this mixture, stirring constantly, until the batter is smooth.

Heat a skillet. Pour just enough batter to cover the bottom by tilting the skillet. Cook the crêpe over medium heat until little bubbles cover the surface. Flip the crêpe and cook following the same procedure.

Applenut Sauce

Standard	Metric
6 apples, peeled, cored and quartered	6 apples, peeled, cored and quartered
1/2 cup sugar	125 ml sugar
1/2 cup chopped nuts	125 ml chopped nuts
1 tsp ground cinnamon	5 ml ground cinnamon
2 tbsp butter	30 ml butter

Place all the ingredients in a covered saucepan, setting aside a handful of chopped nuts. Cook over low heat for 15 minutes until the fruit is soft. Blend the sauce lightly in a blender. Fill each crêpe with the applenut sauce. Sprinkle with reserved chopped nuts.

Microwave Tip

How to Cook Applesauce

Peel, core and quarter the apples. Place the apples, sugar, cinnamon and butter in a microwave dish and cover with plastic wrap. Cook at HIGH for 5 to 7 minutes until soft. Let stand for 2 minutes.

Strawberry Eggnog

BRIOCHE WITH RASPBERRY TOPPING

Technique: Brioche

Standard

3/4 cup warm water
2 tsp sugar
2 packages of dry yeast
1 cup milk
1/4 cup margarine
1/2 cup sugar
1 tsp salt
1 egg, beaten
3-1/2 to 4-1/2 cups all-purpose flour
or an even mix of whole wheat flour and all-purpose flour

Metric

150 ml warm water
10 ml sugar
2 packages of dry yeast
250 ml milk
50 ml margarine
125 ml sugar
5 ml salt
1 egg, beaten
875 to 1.125 ml all-purpose flour
or an even mix of whole wheat flour and all-purpose flour

Pour the warm water into a large mixing bowl. Stir in 2 tsp (10 ml) sugar. Sprinkle in the yeast and let stand for 10 minutes.

In the meantime pour the milk into a saucepan. Add the margarine and gently heat the contents until the margarine has melted. Stir in 1/2 cup (125 ml) sugar and salt. Pour this mixture into the yeast and water. Stir.

Add the beaten egg and incorporate 1-1/2 cups (375 ml) of flour and beat until smooth. Add approximately 2-1/2 cups (625 ml) of flour until the batter has a dough-like consistency.

Cover and allow to rise for 1 hour until it has doubled in volume. Keep away from drafts (in the oven with only the light on, for instance).

Place the dough on the counter and punch it to let the air out. Knead gently and shape into a loaf.

Place the loaf into a 4 inch-high (10 cm) loaf pan. Allow to rise for 40 to 60 minutes until the dough has once again doubled in volume. Brush the top with a beaten egg.

Bake at 350°F(180°C) for 40 to 45 minutes. Cool and turn out the brioche.

1 Add the beaten egg to the water, yeast and milk mixture. Gradually incorporate the flour.

2 Beat until the batter is smooth.

3 Add the rest of the flour, using a mixer, until the batter has a dough-like consistency.

4 Cover and let rise until the dough doubles in volume (1 hour).

5 Punch the dough to let the air out.

6 Let the dough rise for 40 to 60 minutes.

Brioche with Raspberry Topping

To glaze the brioche, boil water and apricot jam and apply with a brush.

Raspberry Topping

Thaw a package of frozen raspberries and place in a saucepan. Add sugar to taste and boil for 2 minutes. Put this mixture through a blender until smooth. Top each slice of brioche with the topping just before serving.

COFFEE CAKE

Standard	Metric
1/3 cup shortening	75 ml shortening
1/3 cup sugar	75 ml sugar
2 eggs	2 eggs
1/2 tsp vanilla	2 ml vanilla
1-3/4 cups flour	400 ml flour
1 tbsp baking powder	15 ml baking powder
1/2 tsp salt	2 ml salt
2 tbsp instant coffee	30 ml instant coffee
1/3 cup milk	75 ml milk
1/3 cup softened butter	75 ml softened butter
1/2 cup brown sugar	125 ml brown sugar
3/4 cup chopped nuts	150 ml chopped nuts

Heat an oven to 350°F (180°C). Grease a cake pan. In a mixing bowl combine the shortening, eggs, sugar and vanilla. Beat thoroughly.

Sift the flour, baking powder, salt and coffee. Add gradually to the preceding mixture alternating with the milk.

In another bowl, blend the butter, brown sugar and chopped nuts with a fork. Place half of the flour mixture into the pan. Top with the nut mixture. Cover with the rest of the flour mixture.

Bake for 25 to 30 minutes.

CAFÉ AU RHUM

Standard	Metric
8 cups coffee	2 liters coffee
1 cup dark rum	250 ml dark rum
1 cup whipping cream (35%)	250 ml whipping cream (35%)
3 tbsp sugar (white or brown)	45 ml sugar (white or brown)
1 tbsp of cocoa or grated chocolate	15 ml of cocoa or grated chocolate

Pour the coffee into glasses. Whip the cream and place in a pastry bag fitted with a fluted tip. Top each glass with a rosette of cream. Pour 2 tbsp (30 ml) dark rum over each rosette and sprinkle with cocoa or grated chocolate.

STEWED FRUIT WITH CRÈME FRAÎCHE

Standard	Metric
16 medium-sized prunes	16 medium-sized prunes
24 dried apricots	24 dried apricots
1/2 cup sweet white wine	125 ml sweet white wine
5 cooking apples	5 cooking apples
5 fresh pears	5 fresh pears
6 cloves	6 cloves
Pinch nutmeg	Pinch nutmeg
3/4 cup slivered almonds	150 ml slivered almonds
3/4 cup sugar	150 ml sugar
Water	Water

Soak the prunes and apricots in white wine for 8 hours or overnight.

Peel and core apples and pears, and cut into eight pieces. Place them in an enamelled cast iron pot with the cloves, nutmeg, almonds and sugar.

Add just enough water to cover the fruit. Over low heat, gently simmer the fruit until they just begin to soften. Add the prunes, apricots and wine. Heat until hot through.

Cool and serve with crème fraîche.

Crème Fraîche

Standard	Metric
2 cups whipped cream, not too stiff	500 ml whipped cream, not too stiff
2 cups sour cream	500 ml sour cream
1/4 cup brown sugar	50 ml brown sugar
1 tsp vanilla	5 ml vanilla

Mix both the whipped cream and the sour cream together. Gently fold in the brown sugar and vanilla. Pour into a serving bowl. Serve chilled.

Café au Rhum

New Year's Brunch II

A meal to rev up tired holiday appetites.

Serve with a white or red Burgundy, dry white wine or sparkling rosé.

Menu

Serves 6 to 8

Deviled Eggs with Shrimp
Spinach and Cheese Tarts
Poached Salmon Mimosa in a Rich Caper Sauce
Scalloped Potatoes
Holiday Pecan Pie
Pineapple Squares

Deviled Eggs with Shrimp

Standard	Metric
16 hard-boiled eggs	16 hard-boiled eggs
1/2 cup shrimp, peeled and chopped	125 ml shrimp, peeled and chopped
1/2 tsp dry mustard	2 ml dry mustard
1/4 cup celery, chopped	50 ml celery, chopped
1/4 cup mayonnaise	50 ml mayonnaise
Salt and pepper	Salt and pepper
1 tbsp sweet green pepper, chopped	15 ml sweet green pepper, chopped

Cut the eggs in two, lengthwise. Remove the yolks and put through a ricer. Mix together the egg yolks, shrimp, mustard, celery and mayonnaise and fill the egg whites. Garnish each deviled egg with a little cube of pepper and one or two whole shrimp.

Spinach and Cheese Tarts

Standard	Metric
4 eggs	4 eggs
1/2 cup plain yogurt	125 ml plain yogurt
1/2 cup milk	125 ml milk
1/2 tsp dry mustard	2 ml dry mustard
1/2 tsp tarragon	2 ml tarragon
Pinch nutmeg	Pinch nutmeg
1-1/2 cups cooked spinach, drained and chopped	375 ml cooked spinach, drained and chopped
1/2 cup of feta cheese, crumbled	125 ml of feta cheese, crumbled
Salt to taste	Salt to taste

Preheat the oven to 375°F (190°C). Beat the eggs thoroughly. Add the yogurt, milk, salt, mustard, tarragon, nutmeg, spinach and cheese. Using a spoon, fill aluminum tart tins with the mixture. Bake for 25 minutes until firm but not dry.

Scalloped Potatoes

Standard	Metric
4 cups potatoes, thinly sliced	1 liter potatoes, thinly sliced
1 tbsp butter	15 ml butter
1 tbsp flour	15 ml flour
1 tsp salt and pepper	5 ml salt and pepper
1-1/2 cups milk	375 ml milk
1/4 tsp dry mustard	1 ml dry mustard
1 cup grated cheese	250 ml grated cheese

Over low heat, melt the butter and add the flour to form a paste. Add the milk, stirring constantly. Remove from heat. Add the salt, pepper, mustard and half the cheese.

Place alternate layers of potatoes and sauce in a greased ovenproof dish. Sprinkle the remaining cheese over the top.

Bake at 350°F (190°C) for 60 to 90 minutes.

Note: Do not soak the potato slices in water as they will lose their starch.

Microwave Method

How to Cook Scalloped Potatoes

In a 2-cup (500 ml) measuring cup, melt the butter at HIGH for 5 minutes.

Add the flour and mix thoroughly. Blend in the milk and heat at HIGH for 1 minute. Stir. Heat for another minute at HIGH.

Add the seasonings and half the cheese. Stir until the mixture is smooth.

In a greased microwave-safe dish, place alternate layers of potatoes and sauce. Sprinkle the remaining cheese over the top. Cook uncovered at HIGH for 13 to 15 minutes. Let stand for 10 minutes.

Deviled Eggs with Shrimp

POACHED SALMON MIMOSA IN A RICH CAPER SAUCE

Standard	Metric
6 oz salmon filets	175 g salmon filets
(one filet per person)	(one filet per person)
8 hard-boiled eggs	8 hard-boiled eggs
1 bunch parsley, chopped	1 bunch parsley, chopped
3 tbsp French shallots	45 ml French shallots
3 tbsp butter	45 ml butter
1/2 cup white wine	125 ml white wine

Put the eggs through a food mill or food processor. Add the parsley and mix. Dredge each filet in this mixture.

Grease a baking pan, cover with the shallots and place the salmon on top. Pour the wine over the salmon and bake at 350°F (180°C) for 8 to 10 minutes. Place the salmon on a plate and use the strained wine and shallot mixture to make the caper sauce.

Rich Caper Sauce

Standard	Metric
2 tbsp butter	30 ml butter
1/2 cup capers	125 ml capers
1 tbsp flour	15 ml flour
1 cup whipping cream (35%)	250 ml whipping cream (35%)
2 egg yolks	2 egg yolks
Salt and pepper to taste	Salt and pepper to taste

Sauté the capers in butter for 3 minutes. Add the flour and stir 30 seconds. Add the wine and shallot mixture from the salmon.

Cook the above ingredients for 1 or 2 minutes and stir in the cream until the mixture is smooth and creamy. Remove from heat and let cool slightly. Beat in the egg yolks using a whisk.

MICROWAVE METHOD

How to Cook the Salmon

Make sure that the salmon has thawed. Arrange the filets on a microwave-safe plate placing the smaller pieces in the center. Cover and cook at HIGH for 3 minutes or until the salmon becomes opaque and flakes easily.

Technique: Salmon and Caper Sauce

1 Put the eggs through a food mill with the parsley.

2 Coat each filet with the egg mixture.

3 Grease a baking dish. Sprinkle with shallots and arrange the salmon.

4 Pour the white wine over the filets and bake.

5 Sauté the capers in butter over medium heat for 3 minutes.

6 Add the flour and stir for 30 seconds.

7 Add the strained wine and boil over high heat.

8 Add the cream and beat with a whisk. Remove from heat and beat in egg yolks.

Poached Salmon Mimosa in a Rich Caper Sauce

HOLIDAY PECAN PIE

Standard	Metric
1-1/2 cups sugar	375 ml sugar
1/2 tsp salt	2 ml salt
1/2 tsp cinnamon	2 ml cinnamon
1/2 tsp nutmeg	2 ml nutmeg
1/4 tsp allspice	1 ml allspice
1 large apple, peeled, cored and diced	1 large apple, peeled, cored and diced
3 clementines	3 clementines
1 cup seedless raisins	250 ml seedless raisins
1/2 cup chopped pecans	125 ml chopped pecans
1 cup cranberries	250 ml cranberries
Double-crust pastry	Double-crust pastry

Prepare the pastry dough and refrigerate. In a heavy saucepan mix the sugar, salt, spices and chopped apple.

Wash clementines, remove stem and cut in half. Chop the unpeeled clementines in a blender or food processor (use metal blades). Add clementines, cranberries and pecans to saucepan.

Cook over medium heat until the cranberries burst. Cool.

Cover the bottom of a 9 inch (22 cm) pie mold with pastry. Pour in the cooled filling. Cut 1/2 inch (1.2 cm) strips of pastry and weave into a lattice to cover pie.

Bake at 400°F (200°C) for 30 to 35 minutes. May be served with vanilla ice cream.

PINEAPPLE SQUARES

Standard	Metric
1 can crushed pineapple	1 can crushed pineapple
1/4 cup sugar	50 ml sugar
2 tbsp cornstarch	30 ml cornstarch
1 box Graham crackers	1 box Graham crackers
1 cup whipping cream (35%)	250 ml whipping cream (35%)

Line a pan with crushed Graham crackers. In a sauce pan, cook the pineapple, sugar and cornstarch. Pour this mixture into the pan. Cover the top with another layer of Graham crackers. Refrigerate.

May be served with a topping of whipped cream and candied fruit.

NEW YEAR'S DAY BUFFET

Serve with a fruity white wine, white Bordeaux, semi-sweet white wine or a sparkling rosé.

MENU

Serves 6 to 8

Cranberry Punch and Fruit Kebabs
Marinated Artichoke Hearts and Olives
Turkey Vol-au-Vent
Glazed Pork Roast and Sautéed Potatoes with Garlic
Apple Coleslaw
Curried Rice Salad
Mincemeat Tarts
Oka Cheese Fruitcake

CRANBERRY PUNCH AND FRUIT KEBABS

Standard	Metric
7 cups cranberry juice	1.75 liters cranberry juice
1/4 cup lemon juice	50 ml lemon juice
1/4 cup grenadine	50 ml grenadine
1 cup vodka, rosé wine or sparkling cider	250 ml vodka, rosé wine or sparkling cider

Mix all the ingredients together, cover and refrigerate. When ready to serve, add ice cubes. Prepare fruit kebabs made with strawberries, melon balls and orange wedges. Arrange the kebabs inside a scooped-out melon or pineapple. Cut the base of the melon or pineapple to prevent it from falling over.

MARINATED ARTICHOKE HEARTS AND OLIVES

Standard	Metric
1-3/4 cups artichoke hearts	400 ml artichoke hearts
3/4 cup pitted black olives	150 ml pitted black olives
1 small red onion	1 small red onion
3 tbsp lemon juice	45 ml lemon juice
3 tbsp chopped parsley	45 ml chopped parsley
2 cloves garlic, chopped	2 cloves garlic, chopped
1/4 tsp cayenne pepper	1 ml cayenne pepper
3/4 cup olive oil	150 ml olive oil
1 tbsp curry powder	15 ml curry powder
1 tbsp paprika	15 ml paprika
Salt and pepper	Salt and pepper
1 tsp thyme	5 ml thyme

Drain the artichoke hearts and olives and place in a bowl. Purée the remaining ingredients in a food processor. Add the mixture to the olives and artichokes. Cover and marinate for 24 to 48 hours.

APPLE COLESLAW

Standard	Metric
1/2 cup mayonnaise	125 ml mayonnaise
1/2 tsp celery seed	2 ml celery seed
1/8 tsp dry mustard	0.5 ml dry mustard
2 medium apples, cored and diced	2 medium apples, cored and diced
2 tbsp lemon juice	30 ml lemon juice
1/2 cup grated carrots	125 ml grated carrots
4 cups grated cabbage	1 liter grated cabbage

Mix the mayonnaise and seasonings in a small bowl and refrigerate.

Sprinkle the diced apples with lemon juice then add the carrots and cabbage. Toss. When ready to serve add the mayonnaise vinaigrette and toss thoroughly.

Cranberry Punch and Fruit Kebabs

GLAZED PORK ROAST AND SAUTÉED POTATOES WITH GARLIC

Standard	Metric
4 lb pork loin, boned	2 kg pork loin, boned
4 tbsp fresh rosemary	60 ml fresh rosemary
1 cup dry cider	250 ml dry cider
Freshly ground pepper	Freshly ground pepper
4 tbsp icing sugar	60 ml icing sugar
1/3 cup lemon juice	75 ml lemon juice
3 to 4 tbsp calvados	45 to 60 ml calvados

With a sharp knife, make several short, deep cuts in the pork loin along the grain. Finely chop the rosemary and insert 3 tbsp (45 ml) into the cuts. Place the meat on a plate and douse with cider and remaining rosemary. Add a generous amount of pepper and marinate for at least 2 hours, turning several times.

Heat the oven to 425°F (220°C).

Remove the meat from the marinade, sponge dry, roll and tie with string.

Place the roast on a cookie sheet and cook for 15 minutes in a preheated oven. After 15 minutes, reduce the temperature to 350°F (180°C) and continue cooking. After 30 minutes, begin basting the roast.

Mix the remaining ingredients (icing sugar, lemon, calvados), making sure that the sugar dissolves.

After the roast has been cooking for 1 hour, remove it from the oven and degrease the pan. Brush the roast with the lemon-calvados mixture. Put the roast back in the oven for another 30 minutes. Baste every 10 minutes with the mixture. The roast will be glazed and golden. Let the roast sit 10 minutes before carving.

Sautéed Potatoes with Garlic

Standard	Metric
6 potatoes	6 potatoes
4 cloves garlic, slivered	4 cloves garlic, slivered
2 tbsp butter	30 ml butter
2 tbsp oil	30 ml oil

Peel the potatoes and cut them into rectangular shapes measuring 1 by 2 inches (2.5 by 5 cm). Cook for 7 minutes in boiling water (with salt). Cool and drain the potatoes. Make a cut at each end of the potatoes and insert a sliver of garlic.

Fry the potatoes in a large skillet with butter and garlic. Cook until the potatoes are golden brown on all sides, about 20 minutes.

Glazed Pork Roast and Sautéed Potatoes with Garlic

NEW YEAR'S DINNER

Serve with a semi-dry white wine, champagne or sparkling wine.

MENU

Serves 6 to 8

Hot Consommé with Port
Red Tomatoes with Hazelnut Stuffing
Pot Roast Royale
Béarnaise Sauce
Steamed Green Beans
Watercress and Endive Salad

Orange and Pineapple Tulips with Sherry

HOT CONSOMMÉ WITH PORT

Standard	Metric
20 cups cold water	5 liters cold water
4 lb meaty soup bones	2 kg meaty soup bones
1 unpeeled onion	1 unpeeled onion
1 clove	1 clove
4 unpeeled garlic cloves	4 unpeeled garlic cloves
10 sprigs parsley	10 sprigs parsley
2 carrots	2 carrots
1 celery stalk with leaves	1 celery stalk with leaves
1 bay leaf	1 bay leaf
Pinch thyme	Pinch thyme
5 peppercorns	5 peppercorns
1 tsp salt	5 ml salt
1 leek	1 leek
1/2 cup port	125 ml port

Brown the bones on an ungreased cookie sheet in a hot oven. Remove from the oven and place the bones in a pot. Add the cold water and bring to a boil as slowly as possible. Skim off the foam as it rises to the surface. Once all the foam has been removed, add all remaining ingredients and simmer uncovered for 3 hours. Strain the contents through a cheesecloth and refrigerate.

To make clear consommé, degrease the broth while still cold and add 1 egg white for every 6 cups (1.5 liters) of liquid. Bring to a boil stirring constantly and reduce to a slow boil for 20 minutes.

Strain through a double layer of cheesecloth.

For a zestier consommé, add the port just before serving, without letting it boil.

RED TOMATOES WITH HAZELNUT STUFFING

Standard	Metric
2 firm tomatoes	2 firm tomatoes
1 tbsp butter	15 ml butter
1 tbsp finely chopped onion	15 ml finely chopped onion
1/3 cup breadcrumbs	75 ml breadcrumbs
1/3 cup chopped hazelnuts	75 ml chopped hazelnuts
Salt and pepper	Salt and pepper
1 tsp lemon juice	5 ml lemon juice

Heat the oven to 350°F (180°C). Cut off the base of the tomatoes to make a flat surface. Set the pieces aside to use as tops. Scoop out the tomatoes.

In a skillet, heat the butter, add the onion and cook for 5 minutes. Add the remaining ingredients and mix thoroughly.

Stuff the tomatoes with this mixture and sprinkle the top with chopped hazelnuts. Place on a cookie sheet and bake for 10-15 minutes until the tops are golden brown. Place tops on tomatoes.

Makes 2 servings. Increase recipe as required.

Red Tomatoes with Hazelnut Stuffing

Pot Roast Royale

Standard	Metric
1 rolled outside round of beef, about 3 lb	1 rolled outside round of beef, about 1.5 kg
1 tbsp vegetable shortening	15 ml vegetable shortening
1 tsp dry mustard	5 ml dry mustard
1 tsp freshly ground pepper	5 ml freshly ground pepper
1 clove garlic, chopped	1 clove garlic, chopped
1/2 cup carrots, diced	125 ml carrots, diced
1/2 cup onions, chopped	125 ml onions, chopped
3 cups brown sauce	750 ml brown sauce

Heat the vegetable shortening in the bottom of a roasting pan. Season the meat with the mustard, garlic and pepper. Brown the meat on all sides on the stovetop.

Add the remaining ingredients, cover and place in the oven at 325°F (160°C), calculating 25 minutes per pound or until roasting thermometer reads:

    140°F (60°C) - rare
    160°F (70°C) - medium
    170°F (75°C) - well-done

Béarnaise Sauce

Standard	Metric
1 cup wine vinegar	250 ml wine vinegar
4 tbsp fresh or dried tarragon	60 ml fresh or dried tarragon
2 tbsp French shallots, chopped	30 ml French shallots, chopped
1 tbsp crushed black pepper	15 ml crushed black pepper
2 tbsp fresh parsley, chopped	30 ml fresh parsley, chopped
6 egg yolks	6 egg yolks
1 cup sweet butter	250 ml sweet butter
Salt and pepper	Salt and pepper
Pinch cayenne	Pinch cayenne
Juice of 1 lemon	Juice of 1 lemon

Bring the vinegar, tarragon, shallots and pepper to a boil and reduce until only 1/3 cup (75 ml) of liquid is left. Remove from heat. Place in a food processor or blender, add the egg yolks and blend for 5 seconds.

Melt butter in a saucepan. Gently pour into the blender and stop blending once the butter has been incorporated into the mixture. Add salt, pepper, parsley, cayenne and lemon juice. Blend for 5 seconds.

Serve at room temperature.

Steamed Green Beans

Standard	Metric
2 lb green beans	1 kg green beans
3 tbsp butter	45 ml butter
3 tbsp parsley	45 ml parsley
2 tbsp shallots, chopped	30 ml shallots, chopped
1 tsp garlic, chopped	5 ml garlic, chopped

Select beans that have no rust spots and are the same size. Leave them whole or slice them after having removed the threads.

Cook the beans in a steamer until tender.

In a separate saucepan, melt the butter and cook shallots, parsley and garlic for 1 minute. Add the beans, stir and serve.

Any leftovers can be served as a salad by adding a little vinaigrette.

Pot Roast Royale

WATERCRESS AND ENDIVE SALAD

Standard	Metric
4 bunches of watercress	4 bunches of watercress
4 endives	4 endives
2 hard-boiled eggs, chopped	2 hard-boiled eggs, chopped
1 cup croutons	250 ml croutons

Slice the endives and cut up the watercress. Stems may be saved to be used in a soup (they may be frozen).

Place the endives and watercress in a salad bowl and add the chopped eggs. Season with the following vinaigrette.

Vinaigrette

Standard	Metric
1 tsp Dijon mustard	5 ml Dijon mustard
1 tbsp salt	15 ml salt
1/2 tsp pepper	2 ml pepper
4 tbsp vinegar	60 ml vinegar
1/2 cup vegetable oil	125 ml vegetable oil

Mix all the ingredients together in a food processor.

Pre-packaged croutons may be used or croutons may be cut from a loaf of bread. The croutons are then sautéed in oil and butter until golden. Place on a paper towel and sprinkle over the salad.

Orange and Pineapple Tulips with Sherry

ORANGE AND PINEAPPLE TULIPS WITH SHERRY

Standard	Metric
10 seedless oranges	10 seedless oranges
2 cups water	500 ml water
2 cups sugar	500 ml sugar
1 pineapple	1 pineapple
1-1/2 cups sherry	375 ml sherry

Peel the oranges, removing any white pith. Separate the individual pieces removing the membrane. Prepare the pineapple and cut into bite-size pieces. Place the oranges and pineapple in a bowl and pour in the sherry.

Refrigerate for 24 hours.

Tulip Preparation

Standard	Metric
1/4 cup slivered almonds	50 ml slivered almonds
1/4 cup egg whites	50 ml egg whites
1/4 cup sugar	50 ml sugar
3/4 cup flour	150 ml flour
1-1/2 oz melted butter	40 g melted butter
1 tsp vanilla extract	5 ml vanilla extract
2 tsp dark rum	10 ml dark rum

Preheat the oven to 350°F (180°C)

Put all the ingredients through the blender.

Place 2 tbsp (30 ml) of the mixture at a time on a well-greased cookie sheet. Flatten the mixture using a fork dipped in milk to spread as thinly as possible in a circle measuring 7 inches (17 cm) in diameter. Bake until golden.

Take 2 small molds 3 inches (7.5 cm) in diameter, placing one upside down on the counter. While still warm, place the baked tulip over the mold and cover with the second one. This will shape the tulip. Avoid applying too much pressure as the bottom of the tulip will tear.

Cool and remove the molds. Place a tulip on each plate and fill with the oranges and pineapple.

Technique: Tulips

1 Shape the batter into flat circles about 7 inches (17 cm) in diameter.

2 Place the warm tulip over the inverted mold and cover with the second.

New Year's Dinner II

Be a little adventurous with a menu that has an exotic touch.

Serve with a zestful Zinfandel or Syrah red, or a sparkling rosé.

Menu

Serves 6 to 8

Chicken Consommé
Fruit Aspic
Curried Lamb
Date Chutney
Rice Pilaf
Green Salad
Rum Baba

Curried Lamb

Chicken Consommé

Standard	Metric
8 cups chicken stock	2 liters chicken stock
1 cup carrots, diced	250 ml carrots, diced
2 or 3 celery leaves	2 or 3 celery leaves
1/2 cup cooked chicken, cubed	125 ml cooked chicken, cubed
Pepper	Pepper

Cook the carrots and celery leaves in the chicken stock. Add the chicken and pepper. Gently simmer over low heat for 30 minutes. Serve immediately.

Fruit Aspic

Standard	Metric
1 envelope lemon-flavored gelatin	1 envelope lemon-flavored gelatin
3/4 cup boiling water	150 ml boiling water
1 cup pineapple juice	250 ml pineapple juice
1 cup pineapple chunks	250 ml pineapple chunks
1 cup grated carrots	250 ml grated carrots
1/3 cup chopped nuts	75 ml chopped nuts
1/4 tsp salt	1 ml salt
2 tbsp vinegar	30 ml vinegar

Dissolve the gelatin in the boiling water. Add the pineapple juice, salt and vinegar. Cool. When the mixture has almost set, add the pineapple, chopped nuts and carrots. Pour the mixture into individual molds that have been run under cold water. Refrigerate.

Remove from molds and serve on a lettuce leaf. Garnish with cream cheese and mayonnaise balls.

Curried Lamb

Standard	Metric
5 lb lean lamb, cubed	2.25 kg lean lamb, cubed
1 cup butter	250 ml butter
6 medium onions, chopped	6 medium onions, chopped
12 garlic cloves, chopped	12 garlic cloves, chopped
1 tsp freshly ground pepper	5 ml freshly ground pepper
1 tsp paprika	5 ml paprika
1/2 tsp cinnamon	2 ml cinnamon
1/2 tsp ground cloves	2 ml ground cloves
1 tsp fresh ginger, chopped or	5 ml fresh ginger, chopped or
1/2 tsp powdered ginger	2 ml powdered ginger
1/2 tsp thyme	2 ml thyme
1/2 tsp turmeric	2 ml turmeric
1 tsp salt	5 ml salt
8 tomatoes, peeled and chopped	8 tomatoes, peeled and chopped
2-1/2 cups water	625 ml water
1 tbsp curry powder	15 ml curry powder

Heat the butter in a heavy pot with a tight-fitting cover. Add the onions and garlic and cook slowly for several minutes. Add the spices and the cubed lamb and cook over low heat for 10 minutes, stirring occasionally. Add the tomatoes and continue cooking for another 10 minutes.

Add 1 cup (250 ml) water. Cover and cook for 1-1/2 hours until the lamb is tender. If the curry is not thick enough, simmer uncovered during the final minutes of cooking time.

DATE CHUTNEY

Standard	Metric
2 lb pitted dates	1 kg pitted dates
1 lb onions, quartered	500 g onions, quartered
1 tsp powdered ginger	5 ml powdered ginger
1/2 tsp cayenne	2 ml cayenne
2 tbsp coarse salt	30 ml coarse salt
1 tbsp allspice	15 ml allspice
1 tsp peppercorns	5 ml peppercorns
2 cups sugar	500 ml sugar
2 tbsp mustard seed	30 ml mustard seed
1 cup wine vinegar or cider vinegar	250 ml wine vinegar or cider vinegar

Place the allspice, pepper and mustard seed into a piece of cheesecloth tied with string. Chop the dates and onions and place in a heavy cooking pot.

Add the spices and vinegar. Simmer until the mixture thickens.

Add the sugar, coarse salt, ginger and cayenne. Continue cooking until the mixture thickens once more. Stir often to prevent the chutney from sticking.

Store in a closed jar.

RICE PILAF

Standard	Metric
2 cups rice	500 ml rice
1 large onion, chopped	1 large onion, chopped
4 tbsp butter	60 ml butter
6 cups consommé or water	1.5 liters consommé or water
Salt and pepper	Salt and pepper

In a skillet, melt the butter and add the onion. Cook the onion until translucent, about 4 minutes.

Add the rice and fry for 2 minutes, stirring occasionally. Add the liquid, salt and pepper. Bring to a boil. Pour contents into a covered baking dish and bake at 400°F (200°C) for 20 to 30 minutes.

GREEN SALAD

3 heads Boston or Bib lettuce
3 tomatoes
Vinaigrette

Wash and dry the lettuce. Tear up the lettuce and place in a salad bowl. Follow vinaigrette recipe on page 56, Watercress and Endive Salad. Pour this vinaigrette over the lettuce. Arrange quartered tomatoes over the top and serve.

RUM BABA

Standard	Metric
4 egg yolks	4 egg yolks
1 cup sugar	250 ml sugar
1/2 cup boiling water	125 ml boiling water
1-1/2 cups all-purpose flour	375 all-purpose flour
1 tsp baking powder	5 ml baking powder
4 egg whites, beaten	4 egg whites, beaten

Rum Syrup

Standard	Metric
1-1/2 cups sugar	375 ml sugar
3/4 cup water	150 ml water
3/4 cup dark rum	150 ml dark rum
1/2 cup orange juice	125 ml orange juice
1/4 cup lemon juice	50 ml lemon juice

Topping

Standard	Metric
2 cans apricots	2 cans apricots
Maraschino cherries	Maraschino cherries
1/2 cup apricot jam	125 ml apricot jam
1/2 cup whipped cream	125 ml whipped cream

Beat the egg yolks and incorporate 1/2 cup (125 ml) sugar. Add the boiling water, the rest of the sugar, flour and baking powder. Beat the egg whites separately until they form stiff peaks and gently fold into the batter.

Grease and flour a Bundt mold and pour in the batter. Bake at 325°F (160°C) for 1 hour. Cool 5 minutes and remove from mold.

In a wide saucepan, boil the sugar and water for 5 minutes. Add the rum, orange and lemon juices and boil another 5 minutes. Pierce the Baba and soak with the syrup.

Drain the apricots and arrange them on the top of the Baba. To glaze the cake, heat the apricot jelly, cool slightly and pour over the Baba. Decorate the top and base of the Rum Baba with whipped cream. Garnish with the maraschino cherries.

Rum Baba

EASTER BRUNCH

This hearty brunch takes its inspiration from the spring maple syrup crop.

Serve with a dry white wine, or sparkling wine.

MENU

Serves 6 to 8

Fluffy Omelet with Maple Syrup
Baked Beans in Maple Syrup
Glazed Ham with Pears and Maple Syrup
White Asparagus au Gratin
Fancy Fruit Salad
Fruit Biscuits

FLUFFY OMELET WITH MAPLE SYRUP

Standard	Metric
12 eggs	12 eggs
3/4 cup maple syrup	150 ml maple syrup
1/2 tsp vanilla extract	2 ml vanilla extract
Pinch salt	Pinch salt
7 tbsp butter	105 ml butter
1/2 cup slivered almonds	125 ml slivered almonds
7 tbsp sugar	105 ml sugar

Beat the egg yolks, maple syrup, vanilla extract and salt into a thick foam.

Beat egg whites to form stiff peaks. As the egg whites begin to thicken, slowly incorporate 1 tbsp (15 ml) sugar and add this mixture to the egg yolks. In a 8-9 inch (20-22.5 cm) cast-iron skillet, melt the butter over medium heat. Sprinkle the almonds into the skillet, pour in the egg mixture and reduce heat. Cook gently for 8 to 10 minutes. When the bottom of the omelet begins to brown, place the skillet in a 350°F (180°C) oven for 8 minutes. Carefully fold the omelet and slide onto a warm serving dish. Pour hot maple syrup over the omelet and serve immediately.

WHITE ASPARAGUS AU GRATIN

Standard	Metric
2 lb white asparagus spears	1 kg white asparagus spears
2 cups white cheese sauce	500 ml white cheese sauce
1 cup grated cheese	250 ml grated cheese
2 tbsp melted butter	30 ml melted butter

Arrange cooked asparagus in a baking dish. Cover the asparagus with a white cheese sauce. Place a piece of greased paper over the stems. Sprinkle the heads of the asparagus with the grated cheese. Cook the asparagus in a 400°F (200°C) oven until golden. Remove greased paper and serve.

BAKED BEANS IN MAPLE SYRUP

Standard	Metric
4 cups dried navy beans	1 liter dried navy beans
1 small onion	1 small onion
5 strips of bacon cut into 1 inch pieces	5 strips of bacon cut into 1 inch pieces
or	or
Several 1 inch cubes of salt pork	Several 2.5 cm cubes of salt pork
1/2 cup chili sauce	125 ml chili sauce
1 cup maple syrup	250 ml maple syrup
1 tsp dry mustard	5 ml dry mustard
2 tsp salt	10 ml salt

Soak the beans overnight in cold water. Boil the beans for 1 minute. Skim off the foam and simmer for 30 minutes. Drain.

Pour the beans into a crock or in a deep and heavy cooking pot. Bury the onion and the bacon (or salt pork) under the beans. Combine the maple syrup, chili sauce, mustard and salt. Pour this mixture over the beans. Add enough boiling water so that the level of liquid is 1 inch (2.5 cm) higher that that of the beans. Tightly seal the crock (or pot). If need be, cover with aluminum foil before putting on the cover.

Bake in a 275°F (130°C) oven for 5 hours or more, as desired. Check the beans every now and then, adding water when necessary. Remove the onion and serve.

White Asparagus au Gratin

GLAZED HAM WITH PEARS AND MAPLE SYRUP

Standard	Metric
1 cooked ham with bone, about 6 lb	1 cooked ham with bone, about 3 kg
1 can of halved pears with juice	1 can of halved pears with juice
1 cup maple syrup	250 ml maple syrup
40 maraschino cherries	40 maraschino cherries
Cloves	Cloves
Juice of 1 orange	Juice of 1 orange
Juice of 1 lemon or vinegar	Juice of 1 lemon or vinegar
1 cup brown sugar or golden honey	250 ml brown sugar or golden honey
1/4 tsp cinnamon	1 ml cinnamon
1/4 tsp powdered ginger	1 ml powdered ginger
Vegetable oil	Vegetable oil

Place the ham on a baking dish, fat side up, and brush with vegetable oil. Bake for 45 minutes at 325°F (160°C). Remove the ham and degrease the dish. Score the ham in a diamond pattern about 1 inch (2.5 cm) wide and 1/4 inch (5 mm) deep. Insert a clove into each diamond.

Prepare the pear glaze before putting the ham back into the oven.

Pear Glaze

Mix together the pear juice, lemon and orange juice, brown sugar, cinnamon, ginger and maple syrup. Glaze the ham with this mixture and bake at 325°F (160°C) for 45 minutes. Baste frequently to thoroughly glaze the ham. Add pear halves and bake for an additional 10 minutes.

To decorate

String the maraschino cherries together to make several strands. Secure the strands to each end of the ham with a toothpick. Arrange pear halves around the ham, decorating each pear with half a cherry and 3 cloves. Pour the remaining glaze over the ham and pears. Serve.

FANCY FRUIT SALAD

Standard	Metric
3 bananas	3 bananas
5 oranges	5 oranges
1-1/3 cups figs	200 ml figs
1-3/4 cups raisins	400 ml raisins
1/2 cup nuts	125 ml nuts
1/2 cup almonds	125 ml almonds
3/4 cup fruit sugar	150 ml fruit sugar
5 tbsp rum	75 ml rum
5 tbsp water	75 ml water
1/2 cup sugar	125 ml sugar
Juice of 2 lemons	Juice of 2 lemons

Soak the raisins, figs, nuts and almonds in the rum and sugar for 12 hours in the refrigerator. Peel and slice the bananas. Peel and cut 3 oranges into thin slices. Squeeze the other 2 oranges and the lemons. Place all the ingredients into a fruit bowl. Mix gently and serve cold.

FRUIT BISCUITS

Standard	Metric
3/4 cup vegetable shortening	150 ml vegetable shortening
1 cup brown sugar	250 ml brown sugar
2 eggs	2 eggs
2 tbsp milk	30 ml milk
2 cups flour	500 ml flour
1 tsp baking powder	5 ml baking powder
1/4 tsp baking soda	1 ml baking soda
1/4 tsp salt	1 ml salt
1 tsp vanilla extract	5 ml vanilla extract
1/2 cup dates, chopped	125 ml dates, chopped
1/2 cup raisins	125 ml raisins
1/2 cup nuts, chopped	125 ml nuts, chopped
6 cherries, pitted and sliced	6 cherries, pitted and sliced

Mix the fruit and nuts together. Set aside. Cream the shortening and add brown sugar and beaten eggs. Sift the flour, baking powder, baking soda and salt. Add this to the egg mixture. Add the milk, fruit and nuts. Mix thoroughly. Place batter by spoonfuls onto a greased cookie sheet. Bake at 350°F (180°C) for 10 to 12 minutes.

Glazed Ham with Pears and Maple Syrup

Easter Brunch II

You'll find these impressive brunch dishes a snap to prepare.

Serve with a white Bordeaux, and Grand Marnier on the rocks.

Menu

Serves 6 to 8

Egg Cup Muffins
Sunrise Gingerbread
Cheese Soufflé
Ham and Spinach Terrine
Cranberry and Chicken Tarts
Crêpes Suzette

Egg Cup Muffins

Standard	Metric
2 cups whole wheat flour	500 ml whole wheat flour
2 cups oatmeal or bran flour	500 ml oatmeal or bran flour
1/2 cup sugar	125 ml sugar
5 tsp baking powder	25 ml baking powder
1-1/2 tsp salt	7 ml salt
2 eggs	2 eggs
1-1/2 cups milk	375 ml milk
3/4 cup vegetable oil	150 ml vegetable oil
1 cup raisins	250 ml raisins
1/2 cup chopped nuts	125 ml chopped nuts
18 eggs	18 eggs

Place all the dry ingredients in a large bowl. In another bowl, beat 2 eggs and add the milk, oil, nuts and raisins. Mix. Add this mixture to the dry ingredients. Stir until all ingredients are blended together. Spoon the batter into muffin tins lined with cupcake paper. Place an uncooked egg (large end down) on top of the batter. Bake at 400°F (200°C) for 20 minutes, or until the muffins are golden brown.

Sunrise Gingerbread

Standard	Metric
1/2 cup melted butter	125 ml melted butter
1 egg, beaten	1 egg, beaten
1/2 cup sugar	125 ml sugar
2-1/2 cups sifted flour	625 ml sifted flour
1-1/2 tsp baking soda	7 ml baking soda
1 tsp cinnamon	5 ml cinnamon
1 tsp ginger	5 ml ginger
1/2 tsp salt	2 ml salt
1 tbsp orange zest	15 ml orange zest
1/2 cup molasses	125 ml molasses
1/2 cup honey	125 ml honey
1 cup hot water	250 ml hot water

Melt the butter and cool. Mix the eggs and sugar. Set aside. Sift the flour, baking soda, cinnamon, ginger and salt. Add the orange zest. In another bowl, mix the molasses, honey and hot water. Alternately add the flour and the liquid to the butter. Mix thoroughly. Pour the batter into a 9 x 9 x 2 inch (23 x 23 x 5 cm) greased baking pan. Bake at 350°F (180°C) for about 1 hour.

Egg Cup Muffins

HAM AND SPINACH TERRINE

Standard	Metric
1 tsp Dijon mustard	5 ml Dijon mustard
1 lb ground cooked ham	500 g ground cooked ham
1 small onion, chopped	1 small onion, chopped
2 eggs	2 eggs
Salt and pepper	Salt and pepper
1 cup heavy cream (35%)	250 ml heavy cream (35%)
1-1/2 cups frozen mixed vegetables	375 ml frozen mixed vegetables

Breading

Standard	Metric
4-1/2 cups breadcrumbs	1.125 liters breadcrumbs
3/4 cup chicken stock	150 ml chicken stock

Spinach

Standard	Metric
2 packages spinach	2 packages spinach
1 tsp sugar	5 ml sugar

Garnish

Standard	Metric
5 hard-boiled eggs, cut in two	5 hard-boiled eggs, cut in two
1/2 lb asparagus (fresh, cooked or canned)	250 g asparagus (fresh, cooked or canned)

Put the ham, onion, mustard and 2 eggs through the food processor until it forms a paste. Add the cream little by little, without stopping the food processor. Put this mixture into a bowl and stir in the mixed vegetables. Refrigerate. Bring the chicken stock to a boil. Add the bread crumbs, stirring constantly. Incorporate the breading into the ham mixture.

Rinse the spinach and place in a pot with the sugar. Cook the spinach over medium heat and drain if necessary. Set aside.

Grease a 10 x 5 inch (25 x 12.5 cm) loaf pan. Pour half the ham mixture and half the lightly chopped spinach into the pan. Arrange the eggs on top of the spinach. Hide the eggs with a layer of ham mixture. Cover with a layer of asparagus and top with a layer of ham. Cover with a final layer of spinach.

Place the loaf pan in a deep baking pan. Fill the baking pan with water, 1 inch (2.5 cm) from the top edge. Cover well with a sheet of aluminum foil. Bake at 375°F (190°C) for 45 minutes until the terrine has set and slips easily from the pan. Refrigerate overnight.

To serve, remove the terrine from the pan, place on a serving plate.

Garnish with mayonnaise and fresh dill.

CHEESE SOUFFLÉ

Standard	Metric
8 eggs (separate whites and yolks)	8 eggs (separate whites and yolks)
6 tbsp all-purpose flour	90 ml all-purpose flour
2 cups cold milk	500 ml cold milk
1 cup grated cheese	250 ml grated cheese
6 tbsp butter	90 ml butter
Salt and nutmeg	Salt and nutmeg

Heat the butter in a saucepan and add the flour. Stir with a wooden spoon. Slowly add the milk, continue stirring until mixture thickens.

Lightly beat 4 egg yolks and add to the white sauce. Incorporate the grated cheese and mix well. Add salt and nutmeg to taste.

Cool. Whip the 8 egg whites into firm peaks and fold into previous mixture.

Fill 4 individual soufflé dishes (or one large one), that have been buttered and lightly floured. Place the dishes in a pan filled with 1 inch (2.5 cm) of water. Bake at 375°F (190°C) for 10 minutes.

Remove from the oven. Empty the water. Place the soufflés back into the dry pan and cook for another 10 to 15 minutes. Serve immediately.

Cheese Soufflé

Technique: Soufflé

1 Gradually add the flour to the melted butter.

2 Stir until smooth.

3 Slowly add the milk and stir until sauce thickens.

4 Gently add the egg yolks.

5 Incorporate the grated cheese and mix well.

6 Fold in the beaten egg whites.

CRANBERRY AND CHICKEN TARTS

Standard	Metric
Shortcrust pastry	Shortcrust pastry
1 can cranberry sauce	1 can cranberry sauce
4 chicken breasts, skinned and deboned	4 chicken breasts, skinned and deboned
Juice of 1 orange	Juice of 1 orange
2 tsp orange zest	10 ml orange zest
1/2 cup chicken or turkey stock	125 ml chicken or turkey stock

Preheat the oven to 300°F (135°C). Prepare the shortcrust pastry (see page 75, Easter Custard Pie). Line individual tart tins with the shortcrust. Cut the rest into strips.

Flatten the chicken and place in a lightly greased baking dish with the stock. Bake for about 15 minutes. Do not add salt. In a saucepan, heat the cranberry sauce, orange juice, orange zest and chicken drippings. Boil for 4 minutes over high heat.

Cut the chicken into small cubes and place them at the bottom of the pie shells. Fill with cranberry sauce mixture. Twist the strips of pastry to form a lattice over the pies. Cook for 20 to 25 minutes at 375°F (190°C).

Serve cold.

CRÊPES SUZETTE

Standard	Metric
8 large eggs	8 large eggs
3-3/4 cups flour	900 ml flour
3 cups warm milk	750 ml warm milk
3/4 cup sugar	150 ml sugar
1 tsp salt	5 ml salt
1 tsp dry yeast	5 ml dry yeast
4 tbsp brandy	60 ml brandy
2 tbsp orange blossom water or	30 ml orange blossom water or
2 tbsp milk with orange zest	30 ml milk with orange zest
Unsalted butter	Unsalted butter

Prepare the batter the night before. Separate the yolks from the whites. Whip the egg whites into firm peaks. In a mixing bowl, make a well in the flour and add the egg yolks. Mix. Heat the milk in a saucepan and dissolve the sugar and yeast. Gradually add the milk to the flour and eggs. Add the brandy and orange blossom water. Mix in the whipped egg whites. The batter should be quite light. Refrigerate overnight. Whip the batter once more before using. Lightly butter and heat a cast iron skillet or pancake pan. Pour a small amount of batter into the pan or skillet. Quickly spread the batter and make the crêpe as thin as possible. Flip the crêpe once one side is golden.

Sauce

Standard	Metric
1 cup and 3 tbsp unsalted butter	250 ml and 45 ml unsalted butter
1/2 cup sugar	125 ml sugar
Zest of 4 oranges	Zest of 4 oranges
1 cup brandy	250 ml brandy
Dash of Curaçao	Dash of Curaçao

Melt the butter in a heavy skillet over high heat. Mix the sugar and orange zest. Add this sugar to the butter and shake the skillet until the sugar dissolves and becomes golden. Add the Curaçao and half the brandy.

Roll or fold the crêpes into four and place in the sauce to reheat. Add the rest of the brandy and cook gently for several minutes. Carefully light the brandy and flambé the crêpes.

Easter Day Luncheon

A traditional lamb roast with novel accompaniments.

Serve with a red Bordeaux, white semi-dry wine, or sparkling wine.

Menu

Serves 6 to 8

Tomato and Celery Soup
Zucchini Casserole
Lamb Provençale
Baked Carrots and Celery
Creamy Garlic Flan
Mushrooms in Sour Cream
Easter Egg Cake

Tomato and Celery Soup

Standard	Metric
3 tbsp onion, chopped	45 ml onion, chopped
2 cups celery, chopped	500 ml celery, chopped
6 cups water	1.5 liters water
1 can stewed tomatoes	1 can stewed tomatoes
1 tbsp butter or margarine	15 ml butter or margarine
Salt and pepper	Salt and pepper
2 tbsp rice	30 ml rice

Chop the onion and celery. Melt the butter in a large saucepan and add the onion. Cook till golden. Add the celery, tomatoes and water. Cook for 45 minutes. Rinse the rice and add to the soup. Cook for another 30 minutes.

Zucchini Casserole

Standard	Metric
3 cups zucchini, sliced, unpeeled	750 ml zucchini, sliced, unpeeled
1 cup "Bisquick"	250 ml "Bisquick"
1/2 cup onion, chopped	125 ml onion, chopped
1/2 cup grated mozzarella	125 ml grated mozzarella
2 tbsp fresh parsley	30 ml fresh parsley
Salt and pepper	Salt and pepper
1/2 tsp oregano	2 ml oregano
1/2 cup vegetable oil	125 ml vegetable oil
4 eggs, beaten	4 eggs, beaten

Prepare the vegetables. Mix all the ingredients together. Place in a greased 13 x 9 x 2 inch (34 x 22 x 4 cm) pan. Bake at 350°F (180°C) for 25 minutes. Serve hot.

Baked Carrots and Celery

Standard	Metric
3 cups carrots, cut on the bias 1/2 inch thick	750 ml carrots, cut on the bias 1.5 cm thick
2 cups celery, cut on the bias 1/4 inch thick	500 ml celery, cut on the bias 5 mm thick
1/4 cup melted butter	50 ml melted butter
1 tsp parsley	5 ml parsley
1/8 tsp pepper	0.5 ml pepper

Preheat the oven to 350°F (180°C). Mix the carrots and celery and place in a 4-cup (2 liter) ovenproof baking dish. Add the rest of the ingredients and 1/4 cup (50 ml) of water.

Cover and cook for 45 minutes until vegetables are tender.

Zucchini Casserole

Lamb Provençale

LAMB PROVENÇALE

Standard	Metric
1 leg of lamb	1 leg of lamb
1-1/2 cups beef stock	375 ml beef stock
3 garlic cloves, crushed	3 garlic cloves, crushed
1/2 cup chopped parsley	125 ml chopped parsley
1 tsp each of dried rosemary, thyme and crushed bay leaf	5 ml each of dried rosemary, thyme and crushed bay leaf
2 small red peppers (or tomatoes) pickled in water or vinegar	2 small red peppers (or tomatoes) pickled in water or vinegar

Trim the leg of lamb of excess fat. Heat the oven to 325°F (160°C). Pour 1/4 cup (50 ml) of beef stock into a roasting pan. Rub the lamb with the garlic, herbs, salt and pepper. Cook at 350°F (180°C), occasionally basting the roast with the beef stock. Calculate cooking time according to weight. Lamb is at its best when slightly pink. Degrease the lamb drippings and serve.

CREAMY GARLIC FLAN

Standard	Metric
1-1/2 cups heavy cream (35%)	375 ml heavy cream (35%)
15 cloves of garlic	15 cloves of garlic
3 eggs	3 eggs
Salt and pepper	Salt and pepper

Pour the cream into a saucepan. Add the garlic and cook gently being careful not to curdle the cream. When the garlic is tender, put the mixture through the food processor. Add salt and pepper to taste. Cool. Beat and add the eggs.

Generously butter 6 to 8 individual aluminum flan tart tins. Fill each one with the mixture. Place the tart tins in a pan containing 1 inch (2.5 cm) water. Bake at 350°F (180°C) for 25 minutes. The flan is cooked when an inserted toothpick comes out clean.

MUSHROOMS IN SOUR CREAM

Standard	Metric
1 lb mushrooms	500 g mushrooms
1-1/2 cups sour cream	375 ml sour cream
2 lemons	2 lemons
Chopped parsley	Chopped parsley
Mild cheddar cheese	Mild cheddar cheese

Wash the mushrooms and put them in boiling salted water for 2 to 3 minutes. Drain and cool. Thinly slice the mushrooms and place in a serving bowl. Sprinkle the juice of half a lemon over the top. Add the cream and mix gently. Garnish with chopped parsley, cheese strips and very thin slices of lemon. Serve chilled.

EASTER EGG CAKE

Standard	Metric
6 tbsp shortening	90 ml shortening
1 cup sugar	250 ml sugar
2 cups sifted pastry flour	500 ml sifted pastry flour
3 eggs	3 eggs
1/2 cup candied fruit	125 ml candied fruit
1/4 tsp salt	1 ml salt
2 tsp baking powder	10 ml baking powder
1/2 cup milk	125 ml milk
1/2 tsp vanilla extract	2 ml vanilla extract
1/4 cantaloupe	1/4 cantaloupe
Corn syrup	Corn syrup
Shredded coconut	Shredded coconut

Cream the shortening and add the sugar and egg yolks. Mix until smooth.

Sift the flour with the baking powder and salt. Add the sifted ingredients to the egg mixture, alternating with the milk. Mix thoroughly.

Beat the egg whites until stiff and fold into batter. Add the vanilla extract. Pour the batter into a greased and floured cake mold. Bake at 350°F (180°C) for 45 minutes. Remove the cake from the mold. Cool.

Brush the cake with hot corn syrup and sprinkle immediately with shredded coconut.

Cut a hole into the edge of the cake. The hole should be big enough to hold 2 or 3 chocolate Easter eggs. Surround the hole with coconut and a ribbon of cantaloupe cut with a potato peeler to achieve desired effect. Decorate with candied fruit and roasted slivered almonds..

MICROWAVE METHOD

Easter Egg Cake

Bake the cake in two layers. Pour half the batter into a microwave-safe cake mold to avoid overflowing. Set at MEDIUM for the first 6 minutes, then at HIGH for the last 3 minutes until cake no longer sticks to sides. Wait 5 minutes before unmolding.

Repeat for second layer.

Easter Egg Cake

Easter Day Luncheon II

A menu celebrating the fresh flavors of spring.

Serve with a red Bordeaux, or rosé.

MENU

Serves 6 to 8

Cream of Carrot Soup
Pineapple Ham
Potato Croquettes
Spring Peas with Fennel
Gourmet Mandarin Salad
Maple Syrup Pie

CREAM OF CARROT SOUP

Standard	Metric
2 cups carrots, diced	500 ml carrots, diced
1 onion	1 onion
1 tbsp butter	15 ml butter
1/2 cup light cream	125 ml light cream
1 tbsp chopped parsley	15 ml chopped parsley
Salt and pepper	Salt and pepper
1 tbsp sugar	15 ml sugar

Peel and dice the carrots and onion. In a saucepan, sauté the onion in the butter for 2 minutes. Add the carrots and cook for another 2 minutes.

Add 4 cups (1 liter) boiling water. Season to taste and cook for 30 minutes. Add the sugar. Pour the contents of the saucepan into a blender. Blend until smooth. Return the contents to the saucepan. Add the cream. Bring to a boil, stirring constantly. Garnish each soup bowl with chopped parsley and a bit of blanched carrot shavings. Serve.

Cream of Carrot Soup

PINEAPPLE HAM

Standard	Metric
1 smoked ham, 4 to 5 lb	1 smoked ham, 1.75 to 2.25 kg
12 cups water	3 liters water
12 cups beer	3 liters beer
1-1/2 cups pineapple juice	375 ml pineapple juice
1 medium onion, chopped	1 medium onion, chopped
6 cloves	6 cloves
1 cup molasses	250 ml molasses
1 tsp pepper	5 ml pepper
1 carrot	1 carrot
1 bay leaf	1 bay leaf
1 celery stalk	1 celery branch
1/2 cup brown sugar	125 ml brown sugar
1/2 cup breadcrumbs	125 ml breadcrumbs
1 tbsp dry mustard	15 ml dry mustard
Pineapple slices	Pineapple slices
Maraschino cherries	Maraschino cherries

Place the ham in a large cooking pot with the water, beer, pineapple juice, celery, bay leaf, onion, molasses, carrot and pepper. Cook over low heat for 20 minutes per pound (45 minutes per kg). Remove from heat and peel off skin without removing the fat. Cut a diamond pattern into the fat, and insert a clove into each. Mix the brown sugar, breadcrumbs and dry mustard. Glaze entire surface of the ham with this mixture. Place the ham in a 400°F (200°C) oven for 20 minutes. Decorate the ham with pineapple slices and maraschino cherries towards the end of the cooking time.

Decorating Tip

Take a dozen or so pineapple leaves about 3 inches (7.5 cm) long. Dip them in egg whites then in cherry-flavored gelatin. Arrange around base of ham.

Potato Croquettes

Standard	Metric
6 peeled potatoes	6 peeled potatoes
6 egg yolks	6 egg yolks
1/4 cup butter	50 ml butter

Cut the potatoes into large pieces. Cook them in water to which salt has been added. Drain and dry them over low heat for about 10 minutes. Mash the potatoes and add the egg yolks, stirring vigorously with a wooden spoon over the burner. Add the butter. Mix. Shape into croquettes.

Breading

Standard	Metric
2 cups milk	500 ml milk
3 eggs	3 eggs
1 tsp salt	5 ml salt
1 tbsp oil	15 ml oil
Breadcrumbs	Breadcrumbs

Combine the milk, beaten eggs and salt. Roll the croquettes in flour, followed by the milk mixture and then dredge in breadcrumbs. Fry them in the oil in a hot skillet.

Spring Peas with Fennel

Standard	Metric
2 lb frozen peas	1 kg frozen peas
1 tbsp sugar	15 ml sugar
1 fennel bulb, grated	1 fennel bulb, grated
3 tbsp butter	45 ml butter
Salt and pepper	Salt and pepper
Fennel leaves to garnish	Fennel leaves to garnish

Combine the peas, sugar and fennel. Cover with water and boil for 10 to 12 minutes. Drain and stir in melted butter. Serve on a hot plate. Garnish the dish with fennel leaves.

Gourmet Mandarin Salad

Standard	Metric
2 endives	2 endives
2 small heads red leaf lettuce	2 small heads red leaf lettuce
2 heads lamb's lettuce (mache)	2 heads lamb's lettuce (mache)
2 bunches watercress	2 bunches watercress
3/4 cup mandarin pieces	150 ml mandarin pieces

Tear up the lettuce and watercress and slice the endives. Place in a salad bowl and add the mandarins. Add salt, pepper, oil and vinegar to taste. Toss. Serve.

Maple Syrup Pie

Old-Fashioned Pie Crust

Standard	Metric
2 cups pastry flour	500 ml pastry flour
1 tsp salt	5 ml salt
1-1/2 cups oatmeal	375 ml oatmeal
3/4 cup vegetable shortening	150 ml vegetable shortening
Cold water	Cold water

Sift the flour and salt. Add the oatmeal. Add the shortening and blend with a fork. Add water and blend gently with the tip of the fork. The dough must not become elastic. Use just enough water so that the dough forms a ball and does not stick to the bowl. Roll out the pastry and line a pie plate. Bake at 375°F (190°C) for 25 to 30 minutes. Cool.

Filling

Standard	Metric
1 cup milk	250 ml milk
1/4 cup flour	50 ml flour
1/8 tsp salt	0.5 ml salt
2 cups maple syrup	500 ml maple syrup
2 egg yolks	2 egg yolks
1 tbsp butter	15 ml butter
2 egg whites	2 egg whites
Pinch salt	Pinch salt
1/4 cup sugar	50 ml sugar

Heat the milk. Combine the flour and salt and gradually stir this into the maple syrup. Pour this mixture into the warm milk. Cook over low heat, stirring constantly until mixture thickens.

Place the 2 egg yolks in a cup. Heat the yolks by spooning some of the syrup mixture into the cup. Mix the egg yolks into the rest of the sauce. Remove from heat. Add the butter and cool.

Pour the filling into the cooked pie crust and top with meringue. Bake at 450°F (230°C) for about 5 minutes until golden. Decorate with bunches of grapes dipped in caramel.

Maple Syrup Pie

EASTER DINNER

Featuring a new twist with fresh salmon.

Serve with a white semi-dry wine, or sparkling wine.

MENU

Serves 6 to 8

Shrimp Mousse
Asparagus Rolls
Marinated Fresh Salmon
Potato Savarin
Green Beans with Lemon Butter
Waldorf Salad
Pineapple Flambé

Marinated Fresh Salmon

SHRIMP MOUSSE

Standard	Metric
1 small can cream of tomato soup	1 small can cream of tomato soup
1 small can cocktail shrimp	1 small can cocktail shrimp
1 cup cream cheese	250 g cream cheese
1 envelope unflavored gelatin	1 envelope unflavored gelatin
1 cup mayonnaise	250 ml mayonnaise
1/2 cup celery, chopped	125 ml celery, chopped
1/2 cup shallots, chopped	125 ml shallots, chopped

Heat the cream of tomato in a double boiler until bubbles appear. Pour into a blender and add the cream cheese. Blend thoroughly. Pour contents back into double boiler. Add the shrimp, celery, shallots and gelatin. Stir.

Remove from heat and cool. Stir in mayonnaise (see page 75, Nutty Apple Salad). Mix thoroughly and pour the mixture into a mold. Refrigerate at least 4 hours.

ASPARAGUS ROLLS

Standard	Metric
1 lb asparagus, cooked or canned	500 g asparagus, cooked or canned
6 to 8 slices cooked ham	6 to 8 slices cooked ham
1 cup grated Emmenthal cheese	250 ml grated Emmenthal cheese

Place 2 or 3 asparagus spears (depending on size) on a slice of ham. Roll. Repeat procedure. Place the rolled asparagus in a baking dish. Sprinkle with the cheese. Bake at 350°F (180°C) until golden brown. Serve immediately.

MARINATED FRESH SALMON

Standard	Metric
2 lb fresh salmon	1 kg fresh salmon
2 large Spanish onions	2 large Spanish onions
1/2 cup sugar	125 ml sugar
3/4 cup white vinegar	150 ml white vinegar
1/2 cup water	125 ml water
1 tbsp salt	15 ml salt
Pepper	Pepper
1 tsp pickling spices	5 ml pickling spices

Yogurt Sauce

Standard	Metric
1 cup plain yogurt	250 ml plain yogurt
1 tbsp Dijon mustard	15 ml Dijon mustard
2 tbsp chives, chopped	30 ml chives, chopped
Juice of one lemon	Juice of one lemon
3 tbsp Port	45 ml Port
1/4 cup marinade	50 ml marinade

Wash the salmon. Cut into slices, across the grain. Slice the onions and put them on a plate. Arrange the salmon on top of the onions. Cover with the rest of the marinade ingredients. Refrigerate for 2 hours.

Remove the salmon and dry it with paper towel. Cook in a frying pan with butter. Serve hot or cold with the Yogurt Sauce.

Potato Savarin

POTATO SAVARIN

Standard	Metric
1 potato per person	1 potato per person
4 tbsp melted butter	60 ml melted butter
1 cup light cream (15%)	250 ml light cream (15%)
Pinch paprika	Pinch paprika
Pinch grated cheese	Pinch grated cheese
Flour	Flour
1 egg	1 egg

Cut the potatoes into thin juliennes and place them in a buttered ovenproof frying pan. Stack the potatoes tightly and cover with the melted butter. Cook at 425°F (215°C) for 20 to 25 minutes. Turn the potatoes out of the pan onto a serving dish. Pour a white cheese sauce over the potatoes (see section on sauces, use half recipe). May be served without sauce.

GREEN BEANS WITH LEMON BUTTER

Standard	Metric
1 lb green beans	500 g green beans
1 tbsp salt	15 ml salt
3 tbsp melted butter	45 ml melted butter
Juice of one lemon	Juice of one lemon
4 tbsp chopped parsley	60 ml chopped parsley
1 clove garlic, chopped	1 clove garlic, chopped

Remove stems and threads from green beans. Cut into pieces, if desired. Cook uncovered in salted boiling water for about 7 minutes. Run them under cold water. Drain and set aside. Pour the butter and the lemon juice into a saucepan. Add the beans and heat.

WALDORF SALAD

Standard	Metric
6 slightly sour apples	6 slightly sour apples
1 tsp lemon juice	5 ml lemon juice
1 cup green seedless grapes, cut in two	250 ml green seedless grapes, cut in two
1 cup pecans, chopped	250 ml pecans, chopped
2 cups celery, diced	500 ml celery, diced
1 can of mandarins	1 can of mandarins
2 sliced bananas	2 sliced bananas
Mayonnaise	Mayonnaise

Gently mix all the ingredients with the mayonnaise (see page 75, Nutty Apple Salad). Decorate with shredded coconut. Serve on a lettuce leaf.

PINEAPPLE FLAMBÉ

Standard	Metric
16 pineapple slices	16 pineapple slices
1/2 cup sugar	125 ml sugar
4 tbsp butter	60 ml butter
Juice of two oranges	Juice of two oranges
Juice of one lemon	Juice of one lemon
1 tbsp rum	15 ml rum
2 tbsp cognac	30 ml cognac
8 small plums or cherries	8 small plums or cherries
8 scoops of vanilla ice cream	8 scoops of vanilla ice cream

Caramelize the sugar in a heavy skillet. Add the butter, orange and lemon juices. Simmer. Arrange the pineapple slices in the skillet. Cook them on both sides. Add the rum and cognac and light. Add the plums or cherries and let simmer for a few minutes. Put one pineapple slice on each plate. Place a scoop of ice cream in the middle of the pineapple. Place another slice of pineapple on the ice cream. Garnish with plums or cherries and cover with sauce.

Waldorf Salad

Easter Dinner II

Every dish a feast for the eyes.

Serve with a white Bordeaux or sparkling rosé.

Menu

Serves 6 to 8

Leek and Potato Soup
Orange Terrine with Grand Marnier
Stuffed Peach Halves
Piglets in Pastry
Chicken Breasts Stuffed with Shrimp
Delicious Baked Potatoes
Glazed Carrots with Rosemary
Nutty Apple Salad
Easter Custard Pie

Leek and Potato Soup

Standard	Metric
4 leeks (white part only)	4 leeks (white part only)
5 potatoes	5 potatoes
1/4 cup butter	50 ml butter
8 cups chicken stock	2 liters chicken stock
Chervil	Chervil
Salt and pepper	Salt and pepper
6 tbsp heavy cream (35%)	90 ml heavy cream (35%)

Wash and chop the leeks, setting aside the green parts. Peel and dice the potatoes. Melt the butter in a large saucepan. Add the vegetables and simmer over low heat for 5 to 10 minutes. Add the chicken stock (or water), salt and pepper. Cook for 20 minutes and put through the blender. Add the cream, heat and sprinkle with chervil.

Chop the leek greens into very small bits and simmer them in butter until tender. Add to the soup just before serving.

Stuffed Peach Halves

Standard	Metric
2 cans of peach halves, drained	2 cans of peach halves, drained
8 oz cream cheese	200 g cream cheese
2 slices lean cooked ham	2 slices lean cooked ham
1 tsp dry tarragon or	5 ml dry tarragon or
1/2 tsp fresh tarragon	2 ml fresh tarragon
4 tbsp celery, finely chopped	60 ml celery, finely chopped
Salt and pepper	Salt and pepper
Celery leaves	Celery leaves

Arrange 16 peach halves in an ovenproof baking dish. Chop the remaining peaches. Soften the cream cheese by putting it through the blender. Remove from blender. Incorporate the finely diced ham, tarragon, chopped peaches and celery into the cheese. Mix thoroughly. Add salt and pepper to taste and refrigerate for 30 minutes. Just before serving, bake the peach halves in the oven for 5 minutes; stir, and bake for another 5 minutes. Fill the peach halves with the ham and cheese mixture. Decorate with celery leaves and serve immediately.

Stuffed Peach Halves

ORANGE TERRINE WITH GRAND MARNIER

Standard	Metric
24 seedless oranges	24 seedless oranges
3/4 cup sugar	150 ml sugar
1/2 cup water	125 ml water
1 cup orange juice	250 ml orange juice
3 cups dry white wine	750 ml dry white wine
8 tbsp Grand Marnier (or Triple Sec)	120 ml Grand Marnier (or Triple Sec)
4 envelopes unflavored gelatin	4 envelopes unflavored gelatin
Juice of one lemon	Juice of one lemon
2 tbsp orange zest	30 ml orange zest

Peel oranges and separate pieces over a bowl. Save the juice. Sprinkle segments with 4 tbsp (60 ml) Grand Marnier. Arrange the oranges side by side on a cloth and refrigerate for 1 hour. Boil together the sugar and water for 2 minutes. Remove from heat and add the orange zest. Cover and let steep for 10 minutes. Add the white wine and the remaining Grand Marnier to the syrup. Pour the powdered gelatin into the cup of orange juice. Stir and add to syrup mixture. If the gelatin is not completely dissolved, heat the syrup.

Refrigerate until mixture has just begun to set.

Pour 1/4 of the gelatin into a mold. Arrange the orange slices so that they all face the same way and overlap slightly. Refrigerate until set. Cover with another 1/4 of gelatin. Add another layer of oranges. Repeat procedure until no oranges are left. Finish with a 1/2 inch (1.25 cm) layer of gelatin. Refrigerate for 4 to 5 hours.

Gently turn out of mold. To serve, slice using an electric carving knife or a very sharp knife run under hot water.

Sauce

Standard	Metric
1-1/2 cups heavy cream (35%)	375 ml heavy cream (35%)
5 tbsp sugar	75 ml sugar
1 cup fresh orange juice	250 ml fresh orange juice

Whip the cream and add the sugar as cream begins to thicken. Once cream is firm, blend in the orange juice. For best results serve immediately. If not, whip the cream once more just before pouring over terrine slices.

CHICKEN BREASTS STUFFED WITH SHRIMP

Standard	Metric
8 chicken breasts, deboned	8 chicken breasts, deboned
2 cups Matane shrimp	500 ml Matane shrimp
2 tbsp tomato paste	30 ml tomato paste
2 tbsp French shallots, chopped	30 ml French shallots, chopped
1 clove garlic, chopped	1 clove garlic, chopped
1 cup heavy cream (35%)	250 ml heavy cream (35%)
1 cup chicken or turkey stock	250 ml chicken or turkey stock
2 eggs	2 eggs
3 tbsp breadcrumbs	45 ml breadcrumbs
Pinch cayenne	Pinch cayenne
3 tbsp chopped parsley	45 ml chopped parsley
Salt and pepper	Salt and pepper

Put the shrimp, the 8 small filets found under the breasts of chicken, 1 tbsp (15 ml) tomato paste, shallots, parsley, breadcrumbs, cayenne, salt and pepper through the food processor until the ingredients form a paste. Add 1 egg and mix for 30 seconds. Add another egg and mix for 30 seconds. While still blending, slowly add 1/2 cup (125 ml) cream. Refrigerate.

Take the chicken breasts, slit and butterfly them. Stuff with the mousse and close. Place the stuffed breasts in a buttered baking dish. Pour the stock over the chicken. Cover with aluminum foil. Bake at 350°F (180°C) for 20 to 25 minutes. The chicken is cooked if an inserted toothpick comes

(Continued on page 74)

MICROWAVE METHOD

Stuffed Chicken Breasts

Place the chicken, skin side down in a glass dish. Cover with waxed paper.

Cook at HIGH for 6 minutes or until tender when pierced with a fork.

Let stand 5 to 10 minutes before serving.

Chicken Breasts Stuffed with Shrimp

out clean. To serve, cut the chicken lengthwise and arrange in a star shape on a plate.

Sauce

Save the chicken stock and juices. Boil and reduce by half. Add to this the remaining cream and tomato paste. Cook until thick and creamy. Pour over the chicken. If there is not enough sauce, simmer 3 tbsp (45 ml) shrimp in butter. Add 1 tbsp (15 ml) flour, stirring constantly. Pour the sauce into this mixture. Stir. Thin with stock if necessary.

Technique: Chicken Breasts

1 Slit the breasts without cutting all the way through and open.

2 Fill with mousse.

3 Gently fold and close without pressing.

4 Place on a buttered baking dish and cover with stock.

GLAZED CARROTS WITH ROSEMARY

Standard	Metric
2 lb diced carrots	1 kg diced carrots
1/4 cup reconstituted chicken stock	50 ml reconstituted chicken stock
2 tbsp brown sugar	30 ml brown sugar
1 tbsp chives, chopped	15 ml chives, chopped
1 tsp rosemary	5 ml rosemary
2 tbsp butter	30 ml butter

Place the carrots in a pot. Add all the ingredients to the pot except the chives. Mix thoroughly. Cover and cook over high heat for 8 to 10 minutes, or until all the liquid has evaporated and the carrots glisten. Reduce heat towards end of cooking time. Do not brown. Serve sprinkled with chives.

PIGLETS IN PASTRY

Standard	Metric
1 lb pork cocktail sausages	500 g pork cocktail sausages
3/4 cup maple syrup	170 ml maple syrup
Pastry dough	Pastry dough
Mustard and relish	Mustard and relish

Marinate the sausages in maple syrup for 3 hours. Roll out pastry into a 12 x 18 inch (30 x 44 cm) rectangle. Cut into strips 4 inches (10 cm) long and 2 inches (5 cm) wide. Spread mustard and relish on the pastry strips. Wrap each sausage in the pastry and place on a cookie sheet. Brush the tops with an egg beaten with 1 tbsp (15 ml) water. Cook at 450°F (225°C) for 15 to 20 minutes. Serve hot.

DELICIOUS BAKED POTATOES

Standard	Metric
8 potatoes	8 potatoes
4 tbsp soft butter	60 ml soft butter
4 cloves garlic, chopped	4 cloves garlic, chopped
Pinch thyme	Pinch thyme
3 tbsp chopped parsley	45 ml chopped parsley
Juice of one lemon	Juice of one lemon

Wash and dry the potatoes and wrap each one in aluminum foil. Cook at 350-375°F (180-190°C) until centers are tender when pricked with a fork. Prepare the garlic butter by blending all the remaining ingredients together. Refrigerate.

With a pointed knife, cut a cross into each potato. Place thumbs and forefingers on either side and apply pressure. The potato will open up. Place a dollop of garlic butter on each potato and serve.

NUTTY APPLE SALAD

Standard	Metric
1 bunch watercress	1 bunch watercress
4 large apples	4 large apples
2 tbsp lemon juice	30 ml lemon juice
3/4 cup chopped nuts	150 ml chopped nuts
3/4 cup chopped celery	150 ml chopped celery
2 tbsp chopped shallots	30 ml chopped shallots
3/4 cup mayonnaise	150 ml mayonnaise
1/4 cup sour cream	50 ml sour cream
1/4 tsp salt	1 ml salt
Pepper to taste	Pepper to taste

Core the apples and cut into small pieces. Place in a mixing bowl and add lemon juice. In a separate bowl, place the chopped nuts, celery and shallots. Mix the mayonnaise, sour cream and pepper and pour over the apples. Toss. Cover and refrigerate for 2 hours or more.

Prepare the watercress and place at bottom of salad bowl. Place the apple and mayonnaise mixture on top of the watercress. Sprinkle the nuts, celery and shallot mixture over the top.

For best results, use Cortland apples as they keep their color longer than other types.

Mayonnaise

Standard	Metric
1 or 2 egg yolks	1 or 2 egg yolks
1/2 tsp dry or Dijon mustard	2 ml dry or Dijon mustard
1/2 tsp salt	2 ml salt
Pinch white pepper	Pinch white pepper
1 tbsp vinegar	15 ml vinegar
1 tbsp lemon juice	15 ml lemon juice
1 cup vegetable oil	250 ml vegetable oil

Mix the egg yolks, salt, mustard and pepper with a wire whisk, electric mixer or blender. Add the vinegar and lemon juice and mix. Slowly add the oil, beating all the while. Once

Easter Custard Pie

the mayonnaise begins to thicken the oil may be added faster. Store in refrigerator. Cover with plastic wrap. Should the mayonnaise separate, follow any of the following 3 procedures. 1) Place an egg yolk in a bowl and gradually add the mayonnaise, beating constantly. 2) Same procedure using mustard instead of egg yolk. 3) Same procedure using 3-4 tbsp (40-60 ml) boiling water.

EASTER CUSTARD PIE

Shortcrust Pastry

Standard	Metric
3-1/4 cups pastry flour	800 ml pastry flour
1 tsp salt	5 ml salt
1 cup vegetable shortening	250 ml vegetable shortening
Ice water	Ice water

Sift the flour and salt. Place in a bowl. Add the shortening and work into the flour using a knife. This will prevent the dough from becoming elastic. Add water a little at a time and continue working the dough until it forms a ball and no longer sticks to the sides of the bowl.

Filling

Standard	Metric
1/2 cup sugar	125 ml sugar
1/2 cup flour	125 ml flour
1/8 tsp salt	0.5 ml salt
2 cups warm milk	500 ml warm milk
1 tsp vanilla extract	5 ml vanilla extract
2 eggs	2 eggs
Icing sugar	Icing sugar

Mix all the dry ingredients together. Gradually add the warm milk. Cook in a double boiler, stirring constantly until the mixture thickens. Add the beaten egg yolks and cook for 2 to 3 minutes. Cool and add the vanilla.

Pour contents of double boiler into prebaked pie shell. Sprinkle with icing sugar.

Variation: Mix together 5 apples cored and cubed, 1 cup (250 ml) sugar, 1/2 cup (125 ml) walnuts and the juice of one lemon. Pour into prebaked pie shell. Cover with 1 cup (250 ml) ground almonds mixed with 1 cup (250 ml) sugar. Cook at 350°F (180°C) for 45 minutes.

POPULAR CELEBRATIONS

Valentine's Day Dinner

A meal that will appeal to the romantic in everyone.

Serve with a Riesling or Chardonnay.

Menu

Serves 6 to 8

Purée of Hearts of Palm
Frogs' Legs for Lovers
Sturgeon Filets with Green Peppercorn Sauce
Buttered Broccoli and Carrots
Boston Lettuce with Mimosa Vinaigrette
Strawberry Heart

Frogs' Legs for Lovers

Standard	Metric
6 pairs frogs' legs	6 pairs frogs' legs
3 tbsp butter	45 ml butter
2 tbsp chopped shallots	30 ml chopped shallots
2 tbsp chopped parsley	30 ml chopped parsley
1 red bell pepper, diced small	1 red bell pepper, diced small
1 green bell pepper, diced small	1 green bell pepper, diced small
1 cup tomato-clam juice	250 ml tomato-clam juice
1 cup heavy cream (35%)	250 ml heavy cream (35%)
1 tbsp all-purpose flour	15 ml all-purpose flour
2 tbsp Pernod (optional)	30 ml Pernod (optional)

Cut the pairs of legs apart and dredge each leg lightly in flour seasoned with salt and pepper. Cook them gently in a skillet with 1 tbsp (15 ml) of butter until browned on all sides. Remove the legs from the pan and keep them warm on a serving platter. Discard the used butter and melt the remaining butter in the skillet. Sauté the shallots and diced peppers for 2 minutes. Add the flour and stir for 30 seconds. Pour in the tomato-clam juice, mix well, and boil vigorously for 2 minutes. Stir in the cream, chopped parsley and Pernod and cook gently until the mixture is thick and creamy. Pat the frogs' legs dry with paper towels, then top with the sauce. Decorate the plate with parsley sprigs.

Purée of Hearts of Palm

Standard	Metric
1 recipe leek soup	1 recipe leek soup
3 cups canned palm hearts	750 ml canned palm hearts
2 tbsp butter	30 ml butter
1 pinch cayenne pepper	1 pinch cayenne pepper
1 cup grated Gruyère cheese	250 ml grated Gruyère cheese
1/2 cup heavy cream (35%) (optional)	125 ml heavy cream (35%) (optional)

Make a leek soup (see recipe, page 98), and purée it in the blender. Cut up the palm hearts and sauté them in butter along with the cayenne. Purée this mixture in the blender and stir it into the leek soup. This soup should be quite well seasoned, especially if served chilled. Serve the soup in soup plates and sprinkle each serving with 1 tbsp (15 ml) grated Gruyère.

Frogs' Legs for Lovers

Sturgeon Filets with Green Peppercorn Sauce

STURGEON FILETS WITH GREEN PEPPERCORN SAUCE

Standard	Metric
3 lb sturgeon filets	1.5 kg sturgeon filets
1/4 cup butter	50 ml butter
3 tbsp chopped shallots	45 ml chopped shallots
1 cup fish stock	250 ml fish stock
1 cup heavy cream (35%)	250 ml heavy cream (35%)
3 tbsp green peppercorns	45 ml green peppercorns
1/4 cup brandy	50 ml brandy
2 tbsp flour	30 ml flour

Dredge the filets in flour and cook them in a skillet with the melted butter. Keep the filets warm on a serving platter. In the same pan, add a bit of fresh butter and sauté the shallots and peppercorns (rinsed and drained). Stir in the flour and cook for 1 minute. Add the brandy and flambé. Stir in the cream and fish stock. Correct the seasoning. Pour the sauce over the filets.

Fish Stock

Standard	Metric
1 lb fish bones	500 g fish bones
1 stalk celery	1 stalk celery
2 tbsp butter	30 ml butter
1 pinch thyme	1 pinch thyme
1 bay leaf	1 bay leaf
1 tbsp black peppercorns	15 ml black peppercorns
3 sprigs celery	3 sprigs celery
1/2 cup dry white wine	125 ml dry white wine
4 cups water	1 liter water

Melt the butter. Add the vegetables, cut into small pieces, and cook over medium heat until the liquid given off by the vegetables has evaporated. Add the fish bones, white wine, water and seasonings. Continue cooking over gentle heat for 25 minutes. Filter the broth through cheesecloth and refrigerate until use. Unused stock will keep frozen.

MICROWAVE METHOD

Sturgeon Filets

Make sure the filets are completely thawed and drain off any excess water. Arrange the filets in a single layer in a microwave-safe baking dish, with the thickest parts towards the outside. Avoid overlapping. Cook at HIGH for 10 to 12 minutes or until the flesh is opaque and flakes easily. Be sure to rotate the dish during the cooking process.

BUTTERED BROCCOLI AND CARROTS

Standard	Metric
4 medium carrots	4 medium carrots
1 medium broccoli, broken into flowerets	1 medium broccoli, broken into flowerets
Salt and pepper	Salt and pepper
Butter	Butter

Peel and cut the carrots on the bias; cook in boiling salted water for 5 minutes. Add the broccoli flowerets, and continue cooking until tender. Drain. Season with salt, pepper and butter.

BOSTON LETTUCE WITH MIMOSA VINAIGRETTE

Standard
2 or 3 heads Boston lettuce
4 hard-boiled eggs
5 tbsp chopped parsley
Juice of 1 orange
Vinaigrette

Metric
2 or 3 heads Boston lettuce
4 hard-boiled eggs
75 ml chopped parsley
Juice of 1 orange
Vinaigrette

Trim the lettuce and reserve the bright outside leaves to garnish the salad. Tear the rest into bite-sized pieces into a bowl.

Chop the hard-boiled eggs fine and add to the lettuce. Sprinkle on the chopped parsley.

Add the orange juice and some vinaigrette to taste and toss well. Arrange the salad on a bed of lettuce leaves. Decorate with fresh orange slices and slices of hard-boiled egg.

MICROWAVE METHOD

Strawberry Filling

Spread the cut strawberries evenly in a glass baking dish. Cover with sugar, water and lemon juice. Cook at HIGH uncovered for 3 minutes. Continue as with regular recipe.

STRAWBERRY HEART

Standard
1/2 cup sugar
3/4 cup water
1 tbsp lemon juice
3 cups strawberries, washed and drained
3 tbsp tapioca
1/2 cup butter
3/4 cup brown sugar
1 cup all-purpose flour
1 cup fine oatmeal
1/4 tsp cinnamon
1/4 tsp nutmeg
1 recipe puff pastry

Metric
125 ml sugar
150 ml water
15 ml lemon juice
750 ml strawberries, washed and drained
45 ml tapioca
125 ml butter
150 ml brown sugar
250 ml all-purpose flour
250 ml fine oatmeal
1 ml cinnamon
1 ml nutmeg
1 recipe puff pastry

Preheat the oven to 375°F (190°C). In a saucepan, mix the sugar, water and lemon juice and bring to a boil. Add the strawberries, cut in half, and simmer for 3 to 4 minutes.

Stir in the tapioca, butter, brown sugar, flour, oatmeal, cinnamon and nutmeg. Let cool.

Roll out the puff pastry with a rolling pin. Trim it into the shape of a heart. Lay it on a greased baking sheet and brush with beaten egg yolk. Bake in the oven for 20 minutes. Let cool.

Carefully cut a heart-shaped lid out of the pastry, leaving a rim. Hollow out the inside of the heart and fill with strawberry filling. Replace the lid.

Strawberry Heart

VALENTINE'S DAY DINNER II

A visual delight that is impressively easy to prepare.

Serve with a Vin d'Alsace, Burgundy, port and champagne.

MENU

Serves 6 to 8

Fresh Cream of Mushroom Soup
Pastry Hearts with Scampi and Clams
Pepper Steak
Scalloped Potatoes
Melon Cocktail with Port
Valentine Cake

PASTRY HEARTS WITH SCAMPI AND CLAMS

Standard	Metric
1 recipe puff pastry	1 recipe puff pastry
2 egg yolks	2 egg yolks
30 small scampi	30 small scampi
3 tbsp butter	45 ml butter
3 tbsp chopped parsley	45 ml chopped parsley
1 tsp minced garlic	5 ml minced garlic
2 tsp minced shallot	10 ml minced shallot
1 cup clams	250 ml clams
1 cup dry white wine	250 ml dry white wine
1 cup heavy cream (35%)	250 ml heavy cream (35%)
Salt and pepper	Salt and pepper

Roll out the puff pastry 1/8 inch (3 mm) thick and cut out 6 heart shapes. Brush the tops of the hearts with beaten egg yolk; be careful not to get a drop of egg on the sides or the hearts will not rise properly. Bake the hearts in a preheated oven at 350°F (180°C) for 15 minutes.

Clean and devein the scampi and sauté them in butter for 2 minutes. Remove from the pan and keep warm. In the same pan, put the shallots, garlic, parsley and clams. Cook for 3 minutes. Add the white wine and cook until reduced by half. Stir in the cream and cook until the sauce is thick and creamy.

Presentation: Split the hearts in half. Arrange the scampi around the edge of the bottom half of the heart, and spoon the clam mixture into the center. Cover with the top part of the heart.

FRESH CREAM OF MUSHROOM SOUP

Standard	Metric
2 tbsp butter	30 ml butter
2 tbsp flour	30 ml flour
1 large onion	1 large onion
1 leek, white section	1 leek, white section
1 lb mushrooms	500 g mushrooms
4 cups chicken stock	1 liter chicken stock
3/4 cup heavy cream (35%)	150 ml heavy cream (35%)
Salt and white pepper	Salt and white pepper

Chop the onion, leek and mushrooms. Sauté gently in butter, without browning, until the liquid from the vegetables has evaporated. Add the flour and stir for 30 seconds. Stir in the chicken stock and simmer for 35 minutes. Add the cream and pass the mixture through the blender. Serve with buttered toasted croutons.

Pastry Hearts with Scampi and Clams

Pepper Steak

Standard	Metric
4 lb boneless rib steak	2 kg boneless rib steak
2 tbsp crushed black peppercorns	30 ml crushed black peppercorns
2 tbsp butter	30 ml butter
1/4 cup Courvoisier cognac	50 ml Courvoisier cognac
1/2 cup dry red wine	125 ml dry red wine
1/4 cup heavy cream (35%)	50 ml heavy cream (35%)
Beurre manié (1 tsp butter kneaded together with 1 tsp flour)	Beurre manié (5 ml butter kneaded together with 5 ml flour)
Salt and pepper	Salt and pepper
2 tsp chopped parsley	10 ml chopped parsley
1 tbsp butter	15 ml butter

Press the crushed peppercorns into both sides of the steaks. Melt the butter over high heat, add the steaks and cook until desired degree of doneness. Salt to taste. Pour the cognac over the steaks and flambé. Keep the steaks warm on a serving platter.

Pour the wine into the same pan and cook rapidly until reduced by two thirds. With a fork, blend in the beurre manié and then the cream. Pour the sauce over the steaks.

Scalloped Potatoes

Standard	Metric
10 potatoes	10 potatoes
4 onions	4 onions
1 tsp thyme	5 ml thyme
1 tsp salt	5 ml salt
1 tsp pepper	5 ml pepper
3 cups chicken stock	750 ml chicken stock

Slice the potatoes into thin rounds and chop the onions. Put the potatoes and onions in a large bowl and add the salt, thyme and pepper. Mix well with your hands.

Butter a large casserole and fill with the potato mixture, packing it down well. Cover with chicken stock and bake uncovered at 350°F (190°C) until the liquid has evaporated and the potatoes are golden on top.

Melon Cocktail with Port

Standard	Standard
3 cantaloupes	3 cantaloupes
1 cup port	250 ml port
2 lemons	2 lemons
Mint leaves	Mint leaves

Cut the melons in half and remove seeds. Use a melon scoop to make small melon balls. Soak the melon balls in the port for 24 hours in the refrigerator. Rub the edges of stemmed glasses with cut lemons and roll the edges in sugar. Fill the glasses with the melon balls and decorate with mint leaves.

Valentine Cake

Valentine Cake

Standard	Standard
1 package strawberry cake mix, baked in 2 cake pans:	1 package strawberry cake mix, baked in 2 cake pans:
1 square pyrex pan (8 inch)	1 square pyrex pan (20 cm)
1 round pyrex pan (8 inch)	1 round pyrex pan (20 cm)

Bake the cakes, let cool and unmold. Cut the round cake into two semi-circles and arrange them on two sides of the square cake to make a heart shape. Use a little icing to hold the pieces together. Ice the cake on its serving platter as you cannot move it once it is frosted.

Icing

Standard	Metric
2 egg whites	2 egg whites
4 tbsp sugar	60 ml sugar
3/4 cup corn syrup	150 ml corn syrup
Red food coloring	Red food coloring

Beat the egg whites into peaks, beating in the sugar little by little. Meanwhile, boil the corn syrup for 2 or 3 minutes. Pour the corn syrup in a thin stream over the egg whites, continuing to beat all the while until the icing has a firm consistency. Add enough red food coloring to give a nice pink shade. Decorate the cake with a real rose.

VALENTINE'S DAY LUNCH BOX

A special treat for kids.

MENU

for each child

Crudités
Chips
Heart-Shaped Sandwiches
Blueberry Yogurt
Fruit Punch

CRUDITÉS

Prepare carrot and celery sticks. Add trimmed radishes and cherry tomatoes.

HEART-SHAPED SANDWICHES

Use 1 slice of brown bread and 1 slice of white bread for each sandwich. Fill them with chicken or egg salad or whatever else your child prefers and trim into heart shapes with a cookie cutter.

FRUIT PUNCH

Use either a commercial fruit punch or invent your own. Add some fresh fruit, diced small.

Crudités, Heart-Shaped Sandwiches and Fruit Punch

GROUNDHOG DAY

A celebratory meal with flavors that hint of spring.

Serve a full-bodied white wine, and perhaps a brut champagne.

MENU

Serves 6 to 8

**Velouté of Tomatoes with
Buttered Croutons
Crab-Stuffed Avocados
Veal Printanier with Vegetables
Grilled Pepper Salad
Chocolate Fondant**

VELOUTÉ OF TOMATOES WITH BUTTERED CROUTONS

Standard	Metric
2 lb tomatoes	1 kg tomatoes
2 tbsp butter	30 ml butter
1 carrot	1 carrot
1 onion	1 onion
4 tbsp chopped parsley	60 ml chopped parsley
1 garlic clove	1 garlic clove
1 tbsp sugar	15 ml sugar
1 bay leaf	1 bay leaf
1 pinch thyme	1 pinch thyme
1 pinch basil	1 pinch basil
2 tbsp all-purpose flour	30 ml all-purpose flour
4 cups cold milk	1 liter cold milk
3 tbsp tomato paste	45 ml tomato paste

Chop the carrot, onion, parsley and garlic and sauté in a saucepan with butter just until all the liquid from the vegetables has evaporated. Add the tomatoes, peeled and chopped, the sugar, herbs and tomato paste. Cook over high heat for 5 minutes. Stir in the flour well, then add the cold milk. Cook gently for 20 minutes. Remove the bay leaf and purée the mixture in the blender.

Serve with croutons browned in butter.

As a variation, you can replace the milk with chicken broth and stir in 1 cup (250 ml) of white sauce for creaminess.

CRAB-STUFFED AVOCADOS

Standard	Metric
4 ripe avocados	4 ripe avocados
8 tbsp crabmeat	120 ml crabmeat
1 minced onion	1 minced onion
1/4 cup chopped parsley	50 ml chopped parsley
Onion rings	Onion rings
Lemon rounds	Lemon rounds
1 tomato, in wedges	1 tomato, in wedges
3/4 cup mayonnaise	150 ml mayonnaise
Lettuce leaves	Lettuce leaves
Celery salt	Celery salt
Pepper	Pepper

Cut the avocados in half and cut a thin slice off the bottom of each half so it will sit flat. Scoop out most of the flesh, leaving a thin layer in each shell. Dice the flesh and the crabmeat and put into a bowl. Add the onion, parsley, mayonnaise and seasonings. Stuff the avocado shells with this mixture.

Decorate each half with a nice piece of crabmeat, a tomato wedge, onion rings, lemon rounds and a sprig of parsley.

Serve on a lettuce leaf.

VEAL PRINTANIER WITH VEGETABLES

Standard	Metric
3 lb veal shoulder, cubed large	1.5 kg veal shoulder, cubed large
1/4 cup butter or rendered veal fat	50 ml butter or rendered veal fat
4 cups light white sauce	1 liter light white sauce
1 pinch thyme	1 pinch thyme
1 pinch powdered bay leaf	1 pinch powdered bay leaf
1 pinch marjoram	1 pinch marjoram
1 cup mushrooms, sliced	250 ml mushrooms, sliced
12 small whole onions	12 small whole onions
2 carrots, peeled and diced	2 carrots, peeled and diced
1-1/2 cups green peas	375 ml green peas

Brown the veal cubes in melted butter or fat. Add the white sauce and the herbs. Cover and let simmer for 1 hour, stirring occasionally.

Add the vegetables and continue cooking another 30 minutes or until vegetables are tender.

Veal Printanier with Vegetables

GRILLED PEPPER SALAD

Standard	Metric
6 green bell peppers	6 green bell peppers
6 red bell peppers	6 red bell peppers
6 tbsp olive oil	90 ml olive oil
1 pinch thyme	1 pinch thyme
1 tsp coriander seeds	5 ml coriander seeds
1 large onion, sliced	1 large onion, sliced
5 tbsp wine vinegar	75 ml wine vinegar
Salt and pepper	Salt and pepper

Cut the peppers in half, remove seeds and white pith, and put them skin side up under the broiler until skins blacken. Wash off the charred skins and slice the peppers.

Cook the sliced onions gently in butter for 7 minutes and add to the peppers. Add the rest of the ingredients and season. Toss well.

Serve lukewarm on lettuce leaves.

Note: To make the skins easier to remove, put the charred peppers in a bowl covered with plastic wrap. Take out one pepper at a time to peel, leaving the others well covered so they retain their humidity.

CHOCOLATE FONDANT

Standard	Metric
3 squares semi-sweet chocolate	3 squares semi-sweet chocolate
1 can sweetened condensed milk	1 can sweetened condensed milk
1 pinch salt	1 pinch salt
1 tsp vanilla	5 ml vanilla
1/2 cup chopped nuts (optional)	125 ml chopped nuts (optional)

Melt the chocolate in the top of a double boiler. Remove the pan from the heat and stir in the rest of the ingredients. Pour into a pan and let cool for several hours or overnight before cutting into squares.

MICROWAVE METHOD

Chocolate Fondant

Put the chocolate in a large glass mixing bowl and heat at HIGH for 2 or 3 minutes or until the chocolate is melted. Stir in the other ingredients. Cook at medium for 4 to 6 minutes.

Technique: Grilled Pepper Salad

1 Put the pepper halves under the broiler about 3 inches (8 cm) from the element.

2 Remove them as soon as the skins are blackened.

3 Let the peppers cool but keep them humid. Remove the charred skin.

4 Slice the peppers and reserve for the salad.

Grilled Pepper Salad

SAINT PATRICK'S DAY DINNER

A comforting meal built around a traditional favorite.

Serve a white Sauvignon wine, and crème de menthe.

MENU

Serves 6 to 8

Cream of Artichoke Soup
Irish Stew
Dumplings
Cream Cheese-Stuffed Snow Peas
Red Cabbage Salad
Creamy Crème de Menthe Pie

Irish Stew

CREAM OF ARTICHOKE SOUP

Standard	Metric
1-1/2 lb canned artichokes	750 g canned artichokes
1 leek, white section	1 leek, white section
1 onion	1 onion
2 tbsp butter	30 ml butter
2 tbsp all-purpose flour	30 ml all-purpose flour
6 cups chicken stock	1.5 liters chicken stock
1 cup heavy cream (35%)	250 ml heavy cream (35%)
Salt and pepper	Salt and pepper

Rinse, drain and chop the artichokes. Melt some butter in a saucepan, and sauté the artichokes along with the chopped onion and leek for 7 to 8 minutes. Add the flour and stir for 1 minute. Pour in the chicken stock. Season and let simmer for 30 minutes. Purée in the blender. Return the artichoke mixture to the pan and stir in the cream; cook another 5 minutes.

If desired, serve garnished with diced tomato sautéed in butter for 5 minutes.

IRISH STEW

Standard	Metric
3 lb cubed lamb	1.5 kg cubed lamb
1/2 cup diced carrots	125 ml diced carrots
1/2 cup diced turnips	125 ml diced turnips
1 sliced onion	1 sliced onion
4 cups potatoes, sliced 1/4 inch thick	1 liter potatoes, sliced 5 mm thick
Salt and pepper	Salt and pepper

Dredge the cubed meat in flour and brown on all sides in a large heavy pot. Cover with boiling water, and simmer at low heat for 2 hours. After 1 hour, add the carrots, turnip and onion. Add your favorite herbs to taste.

One half hour before serving time, add the potatoes. Thicken the gravy with a little flour blended with 1/4 cup (50 ml) cold water. Season to taste.

DUMPLINGS

Standard	Metric
2 cups all-purpose flour	500 ml all-purpose flour
4 tsp baking powder	20 ml baking powder
1/2 tsp salt	2 ml salt
3/4 cup milk (a little more if you use the drop method)	150 ml milk (a little more if you use the drop method)

Sift together the dry ingredients. Stir in the milk bit by bit. Roll out the dough 1/2 inch (1.25 cm) thick and cut into rounds with a cookie cutter. Place the rounds on top of the stew (they should sit on the meat; remove a little liquid if necessary). Cover and let cook 12 minutes. Makes 12 to 15 dumplings.

Drop Method: Add a little more milk to the batter. Drop large spoonfuls of batter onto the stew. Cover and cook 12 minutes.

CREAM CHEESE-STUFFED SNOW PEAS

Standard
36 snow peas
3/4 cup Philadelphia cream cheese
1/4 cup heavy cream (35%) or milk
3 tbsp chopped chives
Juice of 1 lemon
1 tsp tomato paste
Salt and pepper

Metric
36 snow peas
150 ml Philadelphia cream cheese
50 ml heavy cream (35%) or milk
45 ml chopped chives
Juice of 1 lemon
5 ml tomato paste
Salt and pepper

Pull the stringy fibers off the edges of the peas. Blanch the peas in boiling water for 1 minute. Rinse them under cold water. Drain. With a small sharp knife, pry open the pea pods. Set aside. In the food processor, combine the cream cheese, cream, lemon juice, chives and tomato paste. Season.

Use a pastry bag with a small tip to fill the pea pods with the mixture.

Arrange in a fan shape on a serving platter.

CREAMY CRÈME DE MENTHE PIE

Standard
Shortcrust pastry
1 cup Philadelphia cream cheese
1/2 cup all-purpose flour
1 pinch cinnamon
1-1/2 cups sugar
2 eggs
1/2 cup milk
1 pinch salt
1/4 cup crème de menthe

Metric
Shortcrust pastry
250 ml Philadelphia cream cheese
125 ml all-purpose flour
1 pinch cinnamon
375 ml sugar
2 eggs
125 ml milk
1 pinch salt
50 ml crème de menthe

Put the cream cheese, sugar and flour in a large bowl and combine with an electric beater. Beat in, one at a time, the salt, cinnamon, eggs, and finally the milk. Combine well. Blend in the crème de menthe. Line a pie plate with shortcrust pastry (see recipe, page 75) and fill with the crème de menthe mixture.

Beat 1 egg together with 2 tbsp (30 ml) sugar and spread over the pie. Bake in a preheated 300°F (150°C) oven for about 40 minutes.

Garnish with mint leaves.

Variation: Add a few drops of green food coloring to the filling to enhance the mint color.

Creamy Crème de Menthe Pie

Technique: Stuffed Snow Peas

1 Pull off the stringy fibres on the edges of the peas.

2 Blanch in boiling water for 1 minute.

3 Open the peas with a small sharp knife.

4 Stuff the peas and squeeze pods gently shut.

RED CABBAGE SALAD

Standard
2 cups grated red cabbage
2 tbsp milk
2 tbsp mayonnaise
2 tbsp vinegar
2 to 4 tbsp sugar
Salt and pepper

Metric
500 ml grated red cabbage
30 ml milk
30 ml mayonnaise
30 ml vinegar
30 to 60 ml sugar
Salt and pepper

Mix together all the ingredients, with the amount of sugar to your taste. Serve the salad in stemmed glasses decorated with a tiny leaf of red cabbage.

MARDI GRAS DINNER

A menu that's guaranteed to perk up tired winter appetites.

Serve with a Chenin Blanc or Riesling wine.

MENU

Serves 6 to 8

Soup Oriental
Baked Brie and Hazelnut Fondue
Pork Chops with Apples
Glazed Lemon Mint Carrots
Caesar Salad
Queen Elizabeth Cake

SOUP ORIENTAL

Standard	Metric
2 tbsp butter	30 ml butter
3 carrots, peeled and sliced on the bias	3 carrots, peeled and sliced on the bias
4 stalks cclcry, sliced on the bias	4 stalks celery, sliced on the bias
1 head broccoli, in flowerets	1 head broccoli, in flowerets
20 snow peas, sliced on the bias	20 snow peas, sliced on the bias
6 stalks parsley, chopped	6 stalks parsley, chopped
1 tsp ginger	5 ml ginger
1-1/2 cups Chinese noodles	375 ml Chinese noodles
16 cups beef or chicken stock	4 liters beef or chicken stock
1 pinch thyme	1 pinch thyme
1 tbsp soya sauce	15 ml soya sauce
Salt and pepper	Salt and pepper

Melt the butter in a casserole and sauté the carrot and celery gently for 7 minutes. Add the stock, parsley, thyme, ginger, soya sauce and noodles. Cook over medium heat until the noodles are tender. Add the broccoli flowerets and snow peas and cook another 3 minutes. Serve.

BAKED BRIE AND HAZELNUT FONDUE

Standard	Metric
1/4 cup olive oil	50 ml olive oil
1/2 cup whole-wheat breadcrumbs	125 ml whole-wheat breadcrumbs
1/4 cup chopped parsley	50 ml chopped parsley
1/4 cup finely chopped hazelnuts	50 ml finely chopped hazelnuts
1-1/2 lb Brie	750 g Brie
Watercress or lettuce leaves	Watercress or lettuce leaves
2 green apples	2 green apples
2 red apples	2 red apples
Toast triangles	Toast triangles

Put the olive oil in a small shallow bowl.

In a second bowl, mix the breadcrumbs, parsley and chopped hazelnuts. Set aside.

Cut the Brie into wedges and dip each piece first into olive oil, then into breadcrumb nut mixture; press the mixture in firmly. Arrange the wedges on a baking pan, leaving at least 1 inch (2.5 cm) between each piece. Drizzle the remaining olive oil over the Brie. Refrigerate for 1 hour. Bake in a preheated oven at 350°F (180°C) for 10 to 15 minutcs, until golden.

Meanwhile, arrange the watercress or lettuce leaves on individual plates. Garnish each plate with pieces of apple, cut into fan shapes (see page 34, Tomato fans). Add a baked cheese wedge and hot toast triangles and serve.

Baked Brie and Hazelnut Fondue

GLAZED LEMON MINT CARROTS

Standard	Metric
1-1/2 lb carrots, julienned fine	750 g carrots, julienned fine
1 chopped onion	1 chopped onion
1 minced garlic clove	1 minced garlic clove
2 tbsp butter	30 ml butter
3 tbsp sugar	45 ml sugar
Juice of 1 lemon	Juice of 1 lemon
12 fresh mint leaves	12 fresh mint leaves
or	or
1 tbsp dried mint	15 ml dried mint
1/2 cup water	125 ml water
1 pinch salt	1 pinch salt

Melt the butter in a heavy saucepan and add the onion and garlic; cook about 3 minutes but do not let brown. Add the carrots, sugar, lemon juice, water and salt. Cover and continue cooking until the liquid has evaporated and the carrots are glazed, stirring occasionally. Add the mint just before serving.

CAESAR SALAD

Standard	Metric
2 heads romaine lettuce	2 heads romaine lettuce
1 tbsp minced garlic	15 ml minced garlic
1/2 cup olive oil	125 ml olive oil
40 fresh croutons, 1/2 inch	40 fresh croutons, 1.25 cm
Pinch of salt	Pinch of salt
Pinch of pepper	Pinch of pepper
1/2 cup olive oil	125 ml olive oil
4 egg yolks	4 egg yolks
Juice of 2 lemons	Juice of 2 lemons
1-1/4 cups grated Parmesan	300 ml grated Parmesan
3 tbsp capers	45 ml capers
Onion rings	Onion rings
12 anchovy filets (optional)	12 anchovy filets (optional)

Heat 1/2 cup (125 ml) of olive oil in a skillet and add the bread cubes; stir until the croutons are golden brown. Add more oil if necessary. Remove from the heat and stir in the minced garlic well. Drain on paper towels and set aside.

Tear the lettuce into a large salad bowl. Add the salt, pepper, egg yolks, lemon juice, capers, Parmesan, croutons and the rest of the olive oil. Toss well and garnish with onion rings and anchovy filets.

PORK CHOPS WITH APPLES

Standard	Metric
6 to 8 pork chops	6 to 8 pork chops
2 cups apple juice	500 ml apple juice
Salt, pepper and celery salt	Salt, pepper and celery salt
6 tbsp butter	90 ml butter
6 tbsp all-purpose flour	90 ml all-purpose flour
3 apples	3 apples

Season the pork chops with salt, pepper and thyme and brown them on both sides in a heavy skillet. Add the apple juice and cook over gentle heat until the chops are tender.

Put the chops on a serving platter. Knead together the butter and flour and stir it into the juice in the skillet. Let simmer a few minutes. Add a pinch of celery salt and adjust the seasoning. Serve the sauce separately.

Garnish each chop with parsley sprigs and thin slices of apple sautéed in butter and a little sugar. Alternately, sprinkle the apple slices with sugar and put them under the broiler to glaze.

QUEEN ELIZABETH CAKE

Standard	Metric
1 cup brown sugar	250 ml brown sugar
1 egg	1 egg
1/2 cup butter	125 ml butter
1 tsp vanilla	5 ml vanilla
1-1/2 cups all-purpose flour	375 ml all-purpose flour
1 tsp baking powder	5 ml baking powder
1 tsp baking soda	5 ml baking soda
1/4 tsp salt	1 ml salt
3/4 cup boiling water	150 ml boiling water
1 cup chopped nuts	250 ml chopped nuts
1 cup chopped cherries	250 ml chopped cherries
1 cup chopped dates	250 ml chopped dates

Cream together the butter, sugar and egg. Stir in the vanilla. Sift the flour, baking powder, baking soda and salt together. Mix the dry ingredients into the butter mixture. Stir in the nuts, fruit and boiling water.

Turn into a greased 9 x 9 inch (23 x 23 cm) cake pan. Bake in a preheated oven at 350°F (180°C) for 45 minutes.

Frosting

Standard	Metric
4 tbsp butter	60 ml butter
3 tbsp cream	45 ml cream
5 tbsp brown sugar	75 ml brown sugar
1/2 cup shredded coconut	125 ml shredded coconut

In a saucepan, mix the butter, cream and brown sugar and cook for 1 or 2 minutes until thick and creamy. Add the coconut and spread over the warm cake. Return the cake to the oven for a few minutes.

Pork Chops with Apples and Glazed Lemon Mint Carrots

MARDI GRAS DINNER II

Take the chill off winter with a heart-warming meal.

Serve a hearty Burgundy and a sparkling wine with dessert.

MENU

Serves 6 to 8

Onion Soup au Gratin
Escargots Bourguignonne
Swiss Steak
Onions Stuffed with Creamed Peas
Leeks à la Grecque
Carrot Cake

Escargots Bourguignonne

ESCARGOTS BOURGUIGNONNE

Standard	Metric
48 snails	48 snails
1 cup butter	250 ml butter
1/2 cup chopped parsley	125 ml chopped parsley
3 tbsp minced shallots	45 ml minced shallots
1 tbsp minced garlic	15 ml minced garlic
Juice of 2 lemons	Juice of 2 lemons
Salt and pepper	Salt and pepper

Cream the butter and work in the parsley, garlic, shallot, lemon juice, salt and pepper. Arrange snails in an escargot plate. Use a pastry tube to put butter mixture on top. Bake at 375°-400°F (190°-200°C) until butter is very hot.

If you do not have escargot plates, set each snail on a small unbaked crouton rubbed with garlic. Arrange on an oiled baking tray and bake as usual.

ONION SOUP AU GRATIN

Standard	Metric
5 cups chicken or beef stock	1.25 liters chicken or beef stock
4 tbsp butter	60 ml butter
2 tbsp vegetable oil	30 ml vegetable oil
2-1/2 lb onions, sliced thin	1.25 kg lb onions, sliced thin
1 tsp salt	5 ml salt
1 tbsp flour	15 ml flour
1 tbsp tomato paste	15 ml tomato paste
1 pinch thyme	1 pinch thyme
1-1/2 cups grated Gruyère cheese	375 ml grated Gruyère cheese
Garlic croutons	Garlic croutons

Melt the butter and oil in a large heavy saucepan. Add the onions and cook gently for 20 minutes, stirring occasionally. When the onions are browned, add the flour and tomato paste and mix well with a wooden spoon. Pour in the stock and cook at medium heat for 30 to 35 minutes.

Meanwhile, cut thin slices of crusty bread and toast them in the oven on a cookie sheet. When they are golden brown, rub them well with a garlic clove.

Put the soup in ovenproof soup bowls and float a toasted bread slice on each. Sprinkle generously with Gruyère and a bit of paprika.

Put under the broiler for 2 to 3 minutes, watching carefully so they don't burn.

Variation: Add 1 cup of white wine to the soup with the beef stock.

MICROWAVE METHOD

Onion Soup

In a large glass bowl, heat the oil and butter for 1-1/2 minutes at HIGH. Add the onions and cover. Cook at HIGH for 20 minutes or until the onions are completely tender. Stir twice during cooking. Stir in the other ingredients. Cook at HIGH for 10 minutes or until boiling point. Ladle into individual serving bowls. Garnish with croutons and sprinkle with cheese. Cook 3 or 4 bowls at a time at ROAST for 6 minutes or until cheese is melted.

Swiss Steak and Onions Stuffed with Creamed Peas

SWISS STEAK

Standard	Metric
1-3/4 to 2 lb round steak, cut in strips	750 g to 1 kg round steak, cut in strips
Flour, salt and pepper	Flour, salt and pepper
2 tbsp lard or oil	30 ml lard or oil
2 cups canned tomatoes or tomato juice	500 ml canned tomatoes or tomato juice
3 sliced onions	3 sliced onions
1 tsp mustard powder	5 ml mustard powder
1/2 tsp chili powder	2 ml chili powder
1 bay leaf	1 bay leaf
2 tsp Worcestershire sauce	10 ml Worcestershire sauce

Mix the flour, salt and pepper and dredge the beef strips well.

Melt the lard in a heavy pan. Add the beef and cook, stirring, until well seared. Add the sliced onions and tomatoes or juice. Add seasonings. Cover and cook gently over low heat about 10 minutes, or until the meat is tender. Add more tomatoes or water, if necessary.

Skim off excess fat and serve in the sauce.

ONIONS STUFFED WITH CREAMED PEAS

Standard	Metric
6 medium onions	6 medium onions
1/4 cup butter	50 ml butter
2 cups green peas	500 ml green peas
1/4 cup chopped parsley	50 ml chopped parsley
4 tbsp butter	60 ml butter
1 tbsp all-purpose flour	15 ml all-purpose flour
1 cup milk	250 ml milk
1 tsp sugar	5 ml sugar

Peel and cut the onions in half, cross-wise. Remove the inner layers and set aside, leaving a shell. Melt the first quantity of butter in a pan and brown the onion shells in it for 5 minutes. Add water to half the height of the onions and bake in the oven for 10 to 15 minutes.

Meanwhile, mince the reserved onion flesh fine and cook it gently in a pan with the second quantity of butter about 3 minutes. Add the peas, parsley, sugar and flour. Mix well and add the milk. Cook until thickened.

Remove the onion halves from the oven, drain, and stuff with creamed peas. If desired, sprinkle the stuffed onions with cheddar and brown under the broiler.

Leeks à la Grecque

Standard	Metric
8 leeks	8 leeks
1/3 cup olive oil	75 ml olive oil
Juice of 2 lemons	Juice of 2 lemons
3/4 cup dry white wine	150 ml dry white wine
1/3 cup water	75 ml water
1 tsp salt	5 ml salt
1 tsp white pepper	5 ml white pepper
1 pinch thyme	1 pinch thyme
2 tbsp chopped parsley	30 ml chopped parsley
1 bay leaf	1 bay leaf
1 tbsp coriander seeds	15 ml coriander seeds

Wash the leeks well to remove all grit and trim them to 8 inch (20 cm) lengths. Heat the olive oil and gently cook the leeks for 7 minutes, without letting them brown. Add the rest of the ingredients and cook at high heat for 10 to 12 minutes. Arrange on a serving platter, and pour the juice of 1 lemon over. Decorate with rings cut from the green part of the leek.

Carrot Cake

Standard	Metric
2 cups sugar	500 ml sugar
4 eggs, beaten	4 eggs, beaten
1/2 cup oil	125 ml oil
1 can crushed pineapple, drained	1 can crushed pineapple, drained
3 cups grated carrots	750 ml grated carrots
2 cups chopped nuts	500 ml chopped nuts
2 cups all-purpose flour	500 ml all-purpose flour
2 tsp baking powder	10 ml baking powder
2 tsp baking soda	10 ml baking soda
1 tsp salt	5 ml salt
2 tsp cinnamon	10 ml cinnamon
1 tsp vanilla	5 ml vanilla

Microwave Method

Carrot Cake

If possible, line the microwave-safe baking pan (preferably a ring mold) with wax paper rather than greasing and flouring it. Fill the pan half full and cook at HIGH for 10 to 12 minutes. Rotate the pan after 7 minutes. The cake is done when it shrinks from the edges of the pan. Let the cake stand for 5 minutes on a flat surface before unmolding.

Carrot Cake

Mix together the flour, baking powder, baking soda, salt and cinnamon. Cream together the oil, sugar, eggs and vanilla. Beat into the flour mixture. Add the carrots, pineapple, and nuts; mix well. Bake in a preheated 350°F (180°C) oven for 50 minutes.

Frosting

Standard	Metric
2-1/2 cups icing sugar	625 ml icing sugar
1/2 cup soft butter	125 ml soft butter
7 tbsp cream cheese	105 ml cream cheese
1 tsp vanilla	5 ml vanilla

Cream together the cream cheese and butter. Add the vanilla. Gradually work in the icing sugar and beat until creamy. Ice the cake and refrigerate.

Decoration Ideas

1) Cut carrot strips with a sharp knife. Cook them gently for 10 minutes in water sweetened with sugar and vanilla. Roll the strips into rings and fill the centers with nuts and frosting.

2) Cut miniature carrots into shapes and cook them in the sweetened water. Decorate the ends with parsley sprigs to suggest fresh carrot tops.

3) Trim pineapple leaves to 3 inch (7.5 cm) lengths, dip them in beaten egg white then in cherry (or other flavor) jelly powder.

MOTHER'S DAY DINNER

These delightful dishes are amazingly easy to make.

Serve with dry white Burgundy and a sparkling wine for dessert.

MENU

Serves 6 to 8

Curried Salmon Soup
Scallop Pastry Shells Vinaigrette
Breaded Veal Scallops
Buttered Rotini with Peas
Ratatouille
Banana Raspberry Tart

CURRIED SALMON SOUP

Standard	Metric
1 tbsp curry powder	15 ml curry powder
1 cup salmon, cut in strips	250 ml salmon, cut in strips
3 tbsp butter	45 ml butter
2 tbsp minced shallots	30 ml minced shallots
1 diced carrot	1 diced carrot
2 leeks, whites only, sliced	2 leeks, whites only, sliced
2 stalks celery, sliced	2 stalks celery, sliced
1/2 cup dry white wine	125 ml dry white wine
1 clove garlic, minced	1 clove garlic, minced
2 tomatoes	2 tomatoes
Juice of 1 lemon	Juice of 1 lemon
3 tbsp chopped chives	45 ml chopped chives
6 cups water	1.5 liters water

Dip the tomatoes in boiling water, peel, remove seeds and chop.

Melt 1 tbsp (15 ml) butter in a heavy pot and cook the chopped vegetables about 3 minutes or until their liquid has evaporated. Add the water, lemon juice and white wine; season and cook for 15 minutes.

Meanwhile, put the salmon strips in a small bowl and sprinkle on the curry. Melt 2 tbsp (30 ml) butter and sauté the salmon without stirring too much. Put the salmon strips in individual soup bowls and cover with hot soup. Sprinkle with chives. Serve immediately.

SCALLOP PASTRY SHELLS VINAIGRETTE

Standard	Metric
1 lb puff pastry	500 g puff pastry
6 dill pickles	6 dill pickles
1/2 lb scallops	250 g scallops
3 tbsp olive oil	45 ml olive oil
2 tbsp minced shallots	30 ml minced shallots
2 tbsp chopped parsley	30 ml chopped parsley
Juice of 3 lemons	Juice of 3 lemons

Roll out the puff pastry 1/8 inch (3 mm) thick. Turn a bowl 4 to 6 inches (7.5 to 10 cm) in diameter upside-down on the pastry and cut around with a knife to make pastry circles. Prick the circles with a fork.

Slice the pickles in rounds 1/8 inch (3 mm) thick. Slice the scallops the same thickness.

Sprinkle a little chopped shallots and parsley on each pastry circle. Starting in the centre of each circle, arrange a spiral of overlapping scallop and pickle slices to cover the pastry.

Sprinkle on a little olive oil and lemon juice and bake in a 350°F (180°C) oven for about 15 minutes. Serve the pastry rounds hot or cold, sprinkled with a little vinaigrette.

Scallop Pastry Shells Vinaigrette

BREADED VEAL SCALLOPS

Standard	Metric
6 large veal scallops	6 large veal scallops
6 slices cooked ham	6 slices cooked ham
3/4 cup grated Gruyère cheese	150 ml grated Gruyère cheese
3 eggs	3 eggs
1/2 cup milk	125 ml milk
Seasoned flour	Seasoned flour
1 cup breadcrumbs	250 ml breadcrumbs
1/2 cup butter	125 ml butter
1-1/2 cups chopped mushrooms	375 ml chopped mushrooms
1 tbsp all-purpose flour	15 ml all-purpose flour
1/2 cup heavy cream (35%)	125 ml heavy cream (35%)
1/4 cup dry white wine	50 ml dry white wine

Cut the ham slices in half. Cover the veal scallops with the ham, then with grated cheese. Fold the scallops in half, flattening well. Dip the scallops in flour seasoned with salt and pepper, then in beaten eggs, and finally in breadcrumbs.

Melt the butter in a skillet and cook the veal for one minute on both sides. Then put the veal in a 350°F (180°C) oven for 15 minutes. Turn over halfway through cooking.

Drain the scallops in paper towels before serving.

RATATOUILLE

Standard	Standard
1 large eggplant	1 large eggplant
2 zucchini	2 zucchini
2 onions	2 onions
2 green bell peppers	2 green bell peppers
1 red bell pepper	1 red bell pepper
4 tomatoes	4 tomatoes
1 tbsp tomato paste	15 ml tomato paste
1 pinch thyme	1 pinch thyme
2 garlic cloves, minced	2 garlic cloves, minced
4 tbsp olive oil or butter	60 ml olive oil or butter
1 cup tomato juice	250 ml tomato juice
1 bay leaf	1 bay leaf
1 tbsp sugar	15 ml sugar

Cut all the vegetables into 1 inch (2.5 cm) cubes. Put all ingredients in a large saucepan and cook over high heat for 20 minutes.

Can be served hot or cold.

BUTTERED ROTINI WITH PEAS

Standard	Metric
4 cups rotini pasta	1 liter rotini pasta
1-1/2 cups frozen peas	375 ml frozen peas
1/4 cup butter	50 ml butter
3 tbsp chopped tomatoes	45 ml chopped tomatoes
Water	Water
Salt	Salt

Cook the rotini and the peas in boiling salted water for 15 minutes.

Drain and arrange on a serving platter. Add the tomatoes and butter. Season well and serve.

BANANA RASPBERRY TART

Standard	Metric
5 bananas	5 bananas
2 packages frozen raspberries	2 packages frozen raspberries
1 small jar apricot jam	1 small jar apricot jam
3 tbsp icing sugar	45 ml icing sugar

Sweet Pastry Crust

Standard	Metric
2 cups all-purpose flour	500 ml all-purpose flour
3/4 cup sugar	150 ml sugar
3/4 cup soft butter	150 ml soft butter
3 eggs	3 eggs
1 tsp salt	5 ml salt
1/4 cup powdered almonds	50 ml powdered almonds

Put the eggs, butter and sugar in a bowl; mix with an electric mixer for 2 minutes at medium speed. With a table knife, work in the flour, salt and almond powder until the mixture forms a ball; the mixture should not be elastic.

Roll out a pastry circle to line a pie plate (freeze the rest of the dough for later). Prick the pastry shell and bake at 350°F (180°C) for 15 to 20 minutes. The crust should not be brown.

Slice the bananas in 1/4 inch (5 mm) rounds and spread them over the cool pastry shell. Cover with a chilled raspberry coulis (see recipe for Norwegian Omelet Cardinale, page 100).

Refrigerate for 1 hour.

Bring the apricot jam to a boil with 1/2 cup (125 ml) water, stirring constantly with a wooden spoon. When the jam reaches the consistency of heavy syrup, use a brush to spread it over the top of the pie. Decorate with whipped cream rosettes.

MOTHER'S DAY DINNER II

A very special selection of recipes to honor a special day.

Serve dry white wine and champagne or sparkling wine.

MENU

Serves 6 to 8

Potato Leek Soup
Tomato Tarts with Coulis of Zucchini
Chicken Breasts Florentine
Vegetable Medley
Broccoli Salad with Roquefort
Norwegian Omelet Cardinale

TOMATO TARTS WITH COULIS OF ZUCCHINI

Standard	Metric
10 ripe tomatoes	10 ripe tomatoes
3 tbsp butter	45 ml butter
Puff pastry or short pastry	Puff pastry or short pastry
1 tbsp tomato paste	15 ml tomato paste
1 tbsp Dijon mustard	15 ml Dijon mustard
Pinch cayenne pepper	Pinch cayenne pepper
1 large chopped onion	1 large chopped onion
3 garlic cloves, crushed	3 garlic cloves, crushed
3 tbsp chopped fresh parsley	45 ml chopped fresh parsley
3 tbsp sugar	45 ml sugar
1 tsp basil	5 ml basil
Pinch thyme	Pinch thyme
Salt and pepper	Salt and pepper

Drop the tomatoes into boiling water for 1 minute and peel. Cut in half and squeeze out the seeds. Dice the flesh large.

Melt the butter in a saucepan and add the tomatoes, chopped onion, cayenne pepper, garlic, parsley, thyme, basil, sugar, salt and pepper. Cook gently, covered, until the tomatoes have lost their liquid. Add the tomato paste and Dijon mustard. Mix and let cool.

Line the molds of a muffin tin with puff pastry or short pastry. Fill with the tomato mixture and cover the tin with aluminum foil. Bake at 350°F (180°C) for 35 minutes.

To unmold, slide a fork between the pastry and the tin. Serve with a coulis of zucchini: sauté 2 zucchini, sliced in rounds, in butter with some salt and pepper. Run the zucchini through the food processor with a little tomato juice. Decorate each plate with some of the zucchini coulis and tomato sauce; arrange the tomato tart on top.

POTATO LEEK SOUP

Standard	Metric
7 medium leeks	7 medium leeks
1-1/2 cups potatoes	375 ml potatoes
1/4 cup butter	50 ml butter
7 cups chicken stock or water	1.75 liters chicken stock or water
Salt and pepper	Salt and pepper

Trim and carefully wash the leeks, cut them in 1/2 inch (1.5 cm) lengths. Peel and wash the potatoes; cut in 1/2 inch (1.5 cm) cubes.

Melt the butter in a saucepan and add the leeks. Cook gently until they have released all their liquid. Add the chicken stock and the potatoes. Season with salt and pepper and cook 20 minutes. Serve.

Variation: Add morsels of smoked pork with the potatoes.

Tomato Tarts with Coulis of Zucchini

Chicken Breasts Florentine and Vegetable Medley

CHICKEN BREASTS FLORENTINE

Standard	Metric
4 chicken breasts, skinned and deboned	4 chicken breasts, skinned and deboned
1 cup cold water	250 ml cold water
3 tbsp butter	45 ml butter
3 tbsp flour	45 ml flour
1 dry shallot, minced	1 dry shallot, minced
1-1/4 cups mushrooms, cleaned and sliced	300 ml mushrooms, cleaned and sliced
2 bags fresh spinach, washed	2 bags fresh spinach, washed
2 cups hot chicken stock	500 ml hot chicken stock
1/2 tsp nutmeg	2 ml nutmeg
1/4 cup heavy cream (35%)	50 ml heavy cream (35%)
1 tbsp chopped parsley	15 ml chopped parsley
Paprika	Paprika
Salt and pepper	Salt and pepper

Put the cold water in a saucepan, add salt and the spinach. Cover and cook at high heat for 3 to 4 minutes. Drain the spinach and put it in a strainer. Using a spoon, press out the excess liquid. Keep warm.

Cut the chicken breasts in half and put them in a sauté pan with the shallot, mushrooms, salt and pepper. Add the chicken stock and bring to a boil. Cover and cook over gentle heat for 18 to 20 minutes, depending on the size of the chicken breasts. Remove breasts from pan and keep warm. Bring the remaining liquid to a boil and cook for 5 to 6 minutes.

Melt the butter in a saucepan. Add the flour, stir and cook for 2 minutes. Stir in the cooking liquid, nutmeg and cream. Season the sauce to taste.

Arrange the spinach on the bottom of a serving platter with the chicken on top. Pour the sauce over and sprinkle with paprika.

VEGETABLE MEDLEY

Standard	Metric
2-3/4 cups potatoes	650 ml potatoes
2 cups carrots	500 ml carrots
12 baby white onions	12 baby white onions
1 cup frozen peas	250 ml frozen peas
1/2 cup green beans	125 ml green beans
1 yellow turnip	1 yellow turnip
10 lettuce leaves	10 lettuce leaves
1 bay leaf	1 bay leaf
1/2 cup butter	125 ml butter
Thyme	Thyme

Dice the potatoes, carrots and turnips into 1/2 inch (1.25 cm) cubes. Cook them in boiling salted water. After 10 minutes, add the baby onions, the peas, and the green beans, cut in 1/2 inch (1.25 cm) lengths. Cook another 10 minutes and remove from heat. Drain. Stir in the butter, thyme, salt and pepper.

Strawberry Rhubarb Pie

LAMB BROCHETTES

Standard	Metric
2 brochettes per person	2 brochettes per person
3 cubes of lamb per brochette	3 cubes of lamb per brochette
3 red bell peppers	3 red bell peppers
3 green bell peppers	3 green bell peppers
3 onions	3 onions
1 large mushroom per brochette	1 large mushroom per brochette
1 slice bacon cut in pieces per brochette	1 slice bacon cut in pieces per brochette

Cut the peppers and bacon into cubes the same size as the lamb cubes. Cut the onions in quarters. Alternate ingredients on the brochettes, and top with a mushroom.

Baste with marinade before cooking.

You might want to serve the lamb brochettes with brochettes of quartered tomatoes and onions seasoned with thyme and celery salt.

Fines Herbes Marinade

Lay the lamb brochettes on a platter and sprinkle them with thyme, rosemary, mint, basil, and paprika. Add salt and pepper. Pour a little vegetable oil over the brochettes and turn the brochettes over until evenly coated. Cover with plastic wrap.

Refrigerate for 2 to 3 hours, turning the brochettes occasionally so that the meat is well marinated.

Drain well. Cook the brochettes under the broiler or on the barbecue over hot coals. Turn often for even cooking.

ROASTED POTATOES

Standard	Metric
6 potatoes, well scrubbed	6 potatoes, well scrubbed
1 tbsp corn oil	15 ml corn oil
Garlic powder	Garlic powder
Pepper and paprika	Pepper and paprika

Cut the potatoes in half lengthwise, score them and baste them lightly with corn oil. Season with garlic powder, pepper and paprika. Arrange the potatoes on a roasting tray and bake in a 400°F (200°C) oven for about 1 hour.

RAW VEGETABLES WITH HERBED YOGURT DIP

Standard	Metric
3 cups cauliflower, in flowerets	750 ml cauliflower, in flowerets
2 cups broccoli, in flowerets	500 ml broccoli, in flowerets
4 stalks celery, in sticks	4 stalks celery, in sticks
10 radishes	10 radishes
10 green onions	10 green onions

Herbed Yogurt Dip

Standard	Metric
1 cup plain yogurt	250 ml plain yogurt
1 cup partially skimmed milk (2%)	250 ml partially skimmed milk (2%)
3/4 cup mayonnaise	150 ml mayonnaise
4 tbsp fresh chopped herbs	60 ml fresh chopped herbs

Mix all the dip ingredients. Add salt and pepper. Refrigerate until ready to serve.

STRAWBERRY RHUBARB PIE

Standard	Metric
Shortcrust pastry for 9 inch double pie crust	Shortcrust pastry for 22 cm double pie crust
1 cup sugar	250 ml sugar
1/2 cup brown sugar	125 ml brown sugar
1/3 cup all-purpose flour	75 ml all-purpose flour
3 cups rhubarb in 1 inch lengths	750 ml rhubarb in 2.5 cm lengths
1 cup strawberries	250 ml strawberries

Preheat the oven to 450°F (230°C). Line a 9 inch (22 cm) pie plate with shortcrust pastry (see recipe, page 75).

In a bowl, combine the sugar, brown sugar and flour. Stir in the rhubarb and strawberries. Fill the pie mold with this mixture and add a few dabs of butter on top. Cover with top crust and seal and flute the edges. Cut a hole the size of a 25 cent piece in the center of the top crust. Bake at 450°F (230°C) for 15 minutes. Reduce the heat to 375°F (190°C) and bake another 40 to 45 minutes.

Remove the pie from the oven and sprinkle top with icing sugar.

Father's Day Dinner

A delight for fish fans, and for dessert lovers too.

Serve with a Gewurtztraminer or a Chardonnay.

Menu

Serves 6 to 8

Oyster Soup
Miniature Quiche with Smoked Salmon
Baked Trout en Papillote
Tian of Tomatoes and Summer Squash
Strawberry Mousse
Black Forest Cake

Miniature Quiche with Smoked Salmon

Oyster Soup

Standard	Metric
36 fresh oysters, shucked	36 fresh oysters, shucked
1/3 cup butter	75 ml butter
1/2 tsp cayenne pepper	2 ml cayenne pepper
3/4 cup clam juice	150 ml clam juice
2-1/2 cups milk	625 ml milk
3/4 cup light cream (15%)	150 ml light cream (15%)
Salt and freshly ground pepper	Salt and freshly ground pepper

Melt the butter in a saucepan. Add the clam juice and cayenne and bring to a boil. Reduce the heat and add the oysters. Cover and let simmer just until the edges of the oysters start to curl. Add the other ingredients and cook just enough to heat the cream and milk. Do not let boil. Serve the soup in soup bowls with a pat of butter on top.

Miniature Quiche with Smoked Salmon

Standard	Standard
1-1/2 cups grated cheese	375 ml grated cheese
1 cup smoked salmon, chopped	250 ml smoked salmon, chopped
2 tbsp minced onion	30 ml minced onion
2 tbsp minced celery	30 ml minced celery
2 tbsp minced parsley	30 ml minced parsley
1 tbsp flour	15 ml flour
1/2 tsp salt	2 ml salt
3 beaten eggs	3 beaten eggs
1 cup light cream (15%)	250 ml light cream (15%)

Pastry

Standard	Metric
3 cups flour	750 ml flour
1/4 tsp salt	1 ml salt
1 cup vegetable shortening	250 ml vegetable shortening
2 tbsp lemon juice	30 ml lemon juice
Ice water	Ice water

Follow the procedure for making shortcrust pastry on page 75. Refrigerate.

Roll out the pastry and cut into 4 to 5 inch (10 to 12.5 cm) rounds. Arrange the rounds gently in 3 inch (7.5 cm) muffin rings.

Combine the grated cheese, salmon, onion, celery, parsley, flour and salt. Pour into pastry molds. Beat together the eggs and cream. Pour over the salmon mixture. Bake in a preheated 375°F (190°C) oven for 30 to 35 minutes. Garnish with bits of smoked salmon.

Tian of Tomatoes and Summer Squash

Standard	Metric
3 summer squash or zucchini	3 summer squash or zucchini
3 onions	3 onions
3 tomatoes	3 tomatoes
3 minced garlic cloves	3 minced garlic cloves
Pinch of thyme	Pinch of thyme
1/3 cup olive oil	75 ml olive oil
Salt and pepper	Salt and pepper

Peel all the vegetables and slice them thin. Lightly oil a

large oval baking dish and put in a layer of summer squash. Cover with a layer of tomatoes and another of onions. Repeat layers until all vegetables are used. Sprinkle with thyme and minced garlic and season. Pour the olive oil on top and bake at 400°F (200°C) for 20 minutes.

BAKED TROUT EN PAPILLOTE

Standard
Bacon slices
Salt, pepper and parsley
Juice of 1/2 lemon
1 large trout
Julienned leeks
Julienned carrots
Julienned celery

Lay out the bacon slices on a sheet of aluminum foil. Lay the trout on top. Add salt and pepper and chopped parsley.

Baked Trout en Papillote

Squeeze on the lemon juice and add the julienned vegetables. Garnish with more bacon slices.

Seal the fish tightly in the aluminum foil.

Bake at 450°F (180°C) for about 45 minutes, or 10 minutes per inch (2.5 cm) thickness of the trout.

FROZEN STRAWBERRY MOUSSE

Standard	Metric
6 cups fresh strawberries	1.5 liters fresh strawberries
3 egg whites	3 egg whites
1 cup sugar	250 ml sugar
2 cups heavy (35%) or light (15%) cream	500 ml heavy (35%) or light (15%) cream
2 tbsp lemon juice	30 ml lemon juice
2 tsp almond extract	10 ml almond extract
1/8 tsp salt	0.5 ml salt
Whole strawberries for garnish	Whole strawberries for garnish

Wash and drain the strawberries; then remove the hulls. Crush the berries with a fork. Add the egg whites and beat until the mixture is smooth and firm (about 5 minutes at high speed).

Whip the cream just until it starts to thicken. Blend in the lemon juice, salt and almond extract. Continue beating until stiff. Fold into the berry mixture and turn into a mold. Put in the freezer until set. Garnish with whole berries.

BLACK FOREST CAKE

Standard	Metric
6 egg whites	6 egg whites
1/2 tsp cream of tartar	2 ml cream of tartar
1/2 cup sugar	125 ml sugar
6 egg yolks	6 egg yolks
1/2 cup sugar	125 ml sugar
3/4 cup water	150 ml water
3/4 cup all-purpose flour	150 ml all-purpose flour
1/2 cup cocoa	125 ml cocoa
1 tsp baking powder	5 ml baking powder

Kirsch Syrup

Standard	Metric
1/2 cup sugar	125 ml sugar
1/4 cup water	50 ml water
2 tbsp kirsch	30 ml kirsch

Boil all ingredients together for about 1 minute. Let cool.

Whipped Cream Topping

Standard	Metric
2 cups heavy cream (35%)	500 ml heavy cream (35%)
1/4 cup icing sugar	50 ml icing sugar
1 tbsp kirsch	15 ml kirsch

Beat the egg whites with the cream of tartar until they form firm moist peaks. Gradually add 1/2 cup (125 ml) sugar, beating until stiff and glossy.

In a second bowl, beat the yolks with the other 1/2 cup (125 ml) sugar for 5 minutes at high speed, until thick. Add the water.

Sift together the flour, cocoa and baking powder. Gently blend 1/4 of the flour mixture at a time into the yolk mixture. Fold in the beaten egg whites, 1/4 at a time.

Line three ungreased 8 inch (20 cm) cake pans with waxed paper. Divide the batter between the pans. Bake in a preheated 350°F (180°C) oven for 15 minutes. Let cool 5 minutes.

Unmold. Prick the cake and brush with kirsch syrup. Spread whipped cream topping between cake layers, top with cherries and garnish with chocolate curls.

Black Forest Cake

THANKSGIVING DINNER

An old-fashioned harvest meal featuring a classic rabbit dish.

Serve with a full-bodied Merlot or Cabernet wine.

POTAGE SAINT-GERMAIN

Standard	Metric
1/2 lb dried green peas	250 g dried green peas
2 leeks, white part	2 leeks, white part
1 onion	1 onion
3 tbsp butter	45 ml butter
1/4 cup salt pork	50 ml salt pork
6 cups water	1.5 liters water
1/2 bay leaf	1/2 bay leaf
1/4 cup heavy cream (35%)	50 ml heavy cream (35%)
1/3 cup croutons sautéed in butter and oil	75 ml croutons sautéed in butter and oil

Wash the peas and dice the onion and leeks in medium-size cubes. Cut the salt pork in small pieces (lardons).

Melt the butter in a saucepan and add the lardons. Add the peas and vegetables. Cook for 3 minutes over medium heat. Add the water and bay leaf. Season and cook until the peas burst their skins.

Remove the bay leaf and liquefy the soup in the food processor or blender. Reheat in the saucepan and add the cream. Serve topped with croutons.

WILD RICE

Standard	Metric
1 cup wild rice	250 ml wild rice
3 cups water	750 ml water
1/4 cup butter	50 ml butter
Salt and pepper	Salt and pepper

Carefully wash the rice in lots of water. Cook in boiling salted water. Cover and let simmer until tender, about 45 minutes. Drain. Stir in the butter and serve very hot.

POACHED STUFFED PEARS WITH SPICED APRICOTS

Standard	Metric
4 firm pears	4 firm pears
12 dried apricots	12 dried apricots
1 bottle red wine	1 bottle red wine
1 cup sugar	250 ml sugar
2 whole cloves	2 whole cloves
10 grains pepper	10 grains pepper
1 tsp cinnamon	5 ml cinnamon

Peel the pears but leave the stems attached. Sit them in a saucepan and add the rest of the ingredients. Cook for 10 minutes.

Run the apricots with a little of the cooking liquid through the food processor to make a smooth purée.

Continue cooking the pears but do not let them get too soft. Let them cool in the wine, then remove and cut the tops off the pears.

Use an apple corer to hollow out the cores. Using a pastry bag, stuff the pears with the warm apricot purée. Refrigerate for 1 hour, then cut each pear into 3 rounds.

Cover a cookie sheet with waxed paper and sprinkle with icing sugar. Arrange the stuffed pear slices on top and bake at 450°F (230°C) for 7 minutes.

Strain the leftover wine and reserve for eventual use in a sangria or punch.

JUGGED HARE

Standard	Metric
1/4 cup oil	50 ml oil
1/2 cup vinegar	125 ml vinegar
1/4 tsp thyme	2 ml thyme
1/4 tsp cloves	2 ml cloves
1/2 cup carrot rounds	125 ml carrot rounds
1 bay leaf	1 bay leaf
1 medium onion, chopped	1 medium onion, chopped
1 hare or rabbit	1 hare or rabbit
1 lb ground pork	500 g ground pork

Cut the hare or rabbit into serving pieces and marinate for at least 24 hours in the first 7 ingredients.

Remove the meat from the marinade and dry. Brown the meat on all sides in a skillet with a little oil. Put the meat in an ovenproof casserole with the marinade and enough water to cover.

Shape the ground pork into small meatballs, brown in the skillet, and add to the casserole along with the chopped onion. Simmer the dish, covered, in an 350°F (180°C) oven for 2 hours.

SCALLOP SALAD DORIA

Standard	Metric
2 cups raw scallops	500 ml raw scallops
1-1/2 English cucumbers	1-1/2 English cucumbers
2 oranges	2 oranges
1 head Boston lettuce	1 head Boston lettuce
Juice of 3 limes	Juice of 3 limes
3/4 cup olive oil	150 ml olive oil
1/4 cup chopped shallots	50 ml chopped shallots
1 minced garlic clove	1 minced garlic clove
1/4 cup chopped parsley	50 ml chopped parsley
Cooked baby onions	Cooked baby onions
Salt and pepper	Salt and pepper

Slice the scallops in rounds 1/8 inch (3 mm) thick and put in a small bowl. Add the lime juice, olive oil, shallots, garlic and 2 tbsp (30 ml) parsley. Let marinate 2 hours.

Score the cucumber peel with a fork and slice the same thickness as the scallops. Plunge into boiling salted water for 1-1/2 minutes, then into cold water. Drain.

Arrange cucumber slices in a circle on a plate with scallops on each.

Roll the baby onions in parsley and place one on top of each cucumber slice.

Wash and tear up the lettuce and heap it in the centre of the plate, dressed with the remaining marinade. Garnish with orange slices.

APPLE COCONUT SQUARES

Standard	Metric
1/2 cup soft butter	125 ml soft butter
1/2 cup brown sugar	125 ml brown sugar
1 tsp vanilla extract	5 ml vanilla extract
1-1/2 cups all-purpose flour	375 ml all-purpose flour
1-1/2 cups coconut	375 ml coconut
1 can apple pie filling	1 can apple pie filling
1/2 tsp cinnamon	2 ml cinnamon
1/4 tsp salt	1 ml salt
Vanilla ice cream	Vanilla ice cream

Preheat the oven to 375°F (190°C).

Cream together the soft butter and brown sugar. Work in the vanilla. Set aside.

Sift together the flour and salt; work into the butter mixture with a wooden spoon. Add the coconut and mix well. Press half this mixture into a buttered 8x8 inch (20x20 cm) pan. Set aside.

Mix the apple pie filling with the cinnamon, and spread on top of the coconut mixture in pan. Cover with remaining coconut mixture.

Bake for 25 to 30 minutes. Cut into squares, and serve warm topped with scoops of vanilla ice cream.

Scallop Salad Doria

THANKSGIVING DINNER II

A blend of classic and nouvelle cuisine approaches to a traditional feast.

Serve with a fruity Chardonnay and coffee with rum for dessert.

MENU

Serves 6 to 8

Lentil Soup
Escargot Turnovers with Garlic Crème
Roast Turkey with Apricots
Swiss Potato Galette
Spinach Fritters
Julienned Vegetable Salad
Rum Pie

LENTIL SOUP

Standard	Metric
2 cups dried lentils	500 ml dried lentils
4 tbsp butter	60 ml butter
1 carrot	1 carrot
1 onion	1 onion
2 celery stalks	2 celery stalks
2 garlic cloves	2 garlic cloves
5 parsley stalks	5 parsley stalks
1 pinch thyme	1 pinch thyme
1 bay leaf	1 bay leaf
2 tsp tomato paste	10 ml tomato paste
1 tbsp soya sauce	15 ml soya sauce
1 pinch cayenne pepper	1 pinch cayenne pepper
8 slices bacon	8 slices bacon
Salt and pepper	Salt and pepper
8 cups chicken stock	2 liters chicken stock

Wash the lentils and soak them in cold water for at least 5 hours. Chop the onion, carrot, celery and garlic in the food processor.

In a large saucepan, heat the butter and the bacon, cut up. Add the chopped vegetables and cook over high heat for 3 minutes. Add the drained lentils and the rest of the ingredients. Simmer for about 2 hours or until the lentils are tender.

Adjust seasoning and add more chicken stock if necessary.

SWISS POTATO GALETTE

Standard	Metric
6 to 8 large potatoes, unpeeled	6 to 8 large potatoes, unpeeled
1 cup heavy cream (35%)	250 ml heavy cream (35%)
3 tbsp butter	45 ml butter
4 tbsp oil	60 ml oil
Salt and pepper	Salt and pepper
3 eggs	3 eggs

Parboil the potatoes so that they are still firm. Let cool in the refrigerator. Peel them and cut into rounds.

Melt the butter in a heavy skillet. Add the oil and heat. Add the potatoes and brown them on both sides, making sure they do not stick to the pan. Put the potatoes in an ovenproof pan.

Mix the eggs and cream together in a bowl. Pour over the potatoes. Bake at 350°F (180°C) for 20 to 25 minutes.

Technique : Potato Galette

1 Slice the cooked potatoes into thin rounds.

2 Arrange the potatoes in an ovenproof pan.

3 Pour the egg cream mixture on top.

4 Bake in the oven.

Swiss Potato Galette

ESCARGOT TURNOVERS WITH GARLIC CRÈME

Standard	Metric
36 escargots	36 escargots
3 tbsp butter	45 ml butter
6 rounds of puff or short-crust pastry, about 5 inches across	6 rounds of puff or short-crust pastry, about 12.5 cm across
1 cup heavy cream (35%)	250 ml heavy cream (35%)
15 garlic cloves, peeled	15 garlic cloves, peeled
2 leeks, white part only, sliced thin	2 leeks, white part only, sliced thin
Salt and pepper	Salt and pepper
2 egg yolks	2 egg yolks

In a saucepan, bring the cream, garlic cloves and sliced leeks to a boil and cook until thick. Run the mixture through the food processor. Reserve this garlic crème in a small saucepan.

Sauté the escargots in hot butter for about 2 minutes. Drain and stir them into the garlic crème. Boil for 1 minute. Season to taste and refrigerate until the sauce is quite firm.

Lay 6 escargots in the center of each pastry round. Top with garlic crème. Brush the edges of the pastry with beaten egg yolk and fold the pastry over to make a turnover, sealing the edges well.

Baste the turnovers with egg yolk and use the blunt edge of a knife to score a diamond pattern in the top of each turnover.

Arrange the turnovers on a baking tray. Bake in a pre-heated oven at 375°F (190°C) for 15 minutes. Make sure the bottoms of the turnovers do not get too brown. Can be served with tomato sauce, garnished with parsley.

Escargot Turnovers with Garlic Crème

Technique : Turnovers

1 Cut out pastry circles.

2 Put escargot filling in the center of each.

3 Baste the edges with beaten egg yolk.

4 Seal the edges well with a knife.

5 Baste the top with egg yolk.

6 Score a diamond pattern with the blunt edge of a knife.

Roast Turkey with Apricots

ROAST TURKEY WITH APRICOTS

Standard	Metric
6 cups cubed toasted bread	1.5 liters cubed toasted bread
1-1/2 cups dried apricots, chopped	375 ml dried apricots, chopped
1/2 tsp salt	2 ml salt
1/2 tsp black pepper	2 ml black pepper
1/2 tsp thyme	2 ml thyme
1/2 tsp nutmeg	2 ml nutmeg
1/2 tsp ground cloves	2 ml ground cloves
1/4 cup melted butter	50 ml melted butter
2 beaten eggs	2 beaten eggs
1 turkey, 9 lb	1 turkey, 4 kg
1/2 cup butter	125 ml butter
1 small can jellied cranberries	1 small can jellied cranberries
1 tsp Worcestershire sauce	5 ml Worcestershire sauce
1/2 tsp marjoram	2 ml marjoram

Mix together the first 7 ingredients in a large bowl.

Mix the melted butter and beaten eggs in a small bowl and pour over the bread. Mix well.

Stuff the turkey with the bread mixture and sew it shut or hold shut with skewers. Put the turkey in a roasting pan and baste with soft butter. Roast at 325°F (160°C) for about 3-1/2 hours, basting from time to time.

Pour off the turkey juices into a small bowl and remove the grease. Put 4 tbsp (60 ml) of the remaining juices in a small saucepan and add the cranberries, Worcestershire and marjoram. Heat, stirring constantly, until boiling. Brush a little of this mixture over the top of the turkey, and continue baking another 30 minutes, basting frequently with more of the cranberry mixture. Serve the turkey on a heated platter.

SPINACH FRITTERS

Standard	Metric
2 lb fresh spinach	1 kg fresh spinach
2 tbsp butter	30 ml butter
Salt and pepper	Salt and pepper
1 tbsp butter	15 ml butter
1 tbsp all-purpose flour	15 ml all-purpose flour
3/4 cup milk	150 ml milk
2 eggs	2 eggs
1/2 cup grated cheddar cheese	125 ml grated cheddar cheese
Oil	Oil

Wash and drain the spinach. Heat 2 tbsp (30 ml) butter in a saucepan and add the spinach, cooking and stirring over medium heat until the spinach has lost its moisture. Chop coarsely and set aside.

In a second saucepan, melt 1 tbsp (15 ml) butter. Add the flour and stir for several minutes over low heat. Stir in the milk and cook for 5 minutes. Remove from heat and mix.

Stir in the beaten eggs, spinach and grated cheese. Mix well and refrigerate.

Drop large spoonfuls of the spinach batter carefully into hot oil. Cook for a few minutes on one side, then brown the other side.

Serve the fritters with plain yogurt or tomato sauce.

Julienned Vegetable Salad

Standard

1 head Boston lettuce
1/2 cup julienned carrots
1/2 cup julienned cucumbers, seeds removed
1/2 cup julienned white turnip
1/2 cup julienned celery
6 black olives
1/2 cup mushrooms, sliced thin
2 chopped shallots

Metric

1 head Boston lettuce
125 ml julienned carrots
125 ml julienned cucumbers, seeds removed
125 ml julienned white turnip
125 ml julienned celery
6 black olives
125 ml mushrooms, sliced thin
2 chopped shallots

Lemon Vinaigrette

Standard

4 tbsp lemon juice
1 tbsp Dijon mustard
1 cup vegetable oil
1 tbsp sugar
Salt and pepper

Metric

60 ml lemon juice
15 ml Dijon mustard
250 ml vegetable oil
15 ml sugar
Salt and pepper

For the vinaigrette, mix together the lemon juice, mustard, sugar, salt and pepper. Gradually beat in the oil. Chill.

Tear the lettuce leaves into a large bowl. Mix together the rest of the ingredients, except for the olives, and arrange on top of the lettuce. Pour on the lemon vinaigrette and garnish with black olives.

Rum Pie

Standard

1 tbsp vegetable shortening
4 tbsp semi-sweet chocolate bits
6 egg yolks
1 cup sugar
1 tbsp unflavored gelatin
1/2 cup cold water
1 cup heavy cream (35%)
3/4 cup dark rum
Pistachios and candied fruit for garnish

Metric

15 ml vegetable shortening
60 ml semi-sweet chocolate bits
6 egg yolks
250 ml sugar
15 ml unflavored gelatin
125 ml cold water
250 ml heavy cream (35%)
150 ml dark rum
Pistachios and candied fruit for garnish

Line a pie plate with aluminum foil and smooth well. Put the vegetable shortening and chocolate bits in the pie plate and heat in a 325°F (160°C) oven for 10 minutes.

Remove from the oven and use a spatula to spread the chocolate oil mixture over the entire bottom and sides of the pan to make the pie shell.

Refrigerate. When the chocolate is well chilled, carefully remove the aluminum foil. Place the chocolate shell in a chilled pie plate or serving plate.

Beat the 6 egg yolks until foamy. Beat in the sugar.

Dissolve the gelatin in 1/2 cup (125 ml) cold water and heat over low heat. Put the egg yolks in the top of a double boiler, and add the gelatin mixture, stirring rapidly until thick. Let cool, then fold in the whipped cream and the rum.

Pour the mixture into the chocolate pie shell and garnish the top with pistachios and candied fruit.

Rum Pie

Microwave Method

Melting Chocolate

Put the chocolate bits and vegetable shortening in a glass bowl. Heat uncovered at HIGH for 1-1/2 minutes, stirring halfway through.

HALLOWEEN DINNER

This stuffed pumpkin makes a beautiful presentation at the table.

Serve a rosé or sparkling rosé.

MENU

Serves 6

Cream of Carrot Soup
Entrée of Leeks
Stuffed Pumpkin
Tomato Salad with Parmesan and Fines Herbes
Raisin Pie
Pumpkin Cookies

CREAM OF CARROT SOUP

Standard	Metric
6 to 8 carrots, cut in rounds	6 to 8 carrots, cut in rounds
1 large onion, chopped	1 large onion, chopped
1 tsp butter	5 ml butter
2 cups chicken stock	500 ml chicken stock
2 cups milk	500 ml milk
Pepper	Pepper
1 tbsp parsley	15 ml parsley

Sauté the carrots and onion in the butter. Add the chicken stock and cook until carrots are tender. Purée the soup in the blender. Return to the saucepan and add the milk. Correct seasonings.

Serve garnished with croutons and thin carrot strips, blanched for 2 minutes and rolled.

MICROWAVE METHOD

Carrots

Spread the carrot rounds as evenly as possible on a glass dish. Add 1/4 cup (50 ml) water. Cover. Microwave at HIGH for 10 minutes, turning the dish after 6 minutes.

Carrots cooked this way retain their color, flavor and vitamins.

ENTRÉE OF LEEKS

Standard	Metric
3 leeks, white and tender green part sliced in 1 inch pieces	3 leeks, white and tender green part sliced in 2.5 cm pieces
3 tbsp yogurt	45 ml yogurt
3 tbsp mayonnaise	45 ml mayonnaise
Salt and pepper	Salt and pepper
Basil	Basil
Fresh chopped parsley	Fresh chopped parsley

Wash the leeks well and cook in boiling salted water until tender. Drain well. Mix together the yogurt, mayonnaise, basil, salt and pepper. Combine the leeks with the sauce and sprinkle with chopped parsley. Serve warm or chilled.

STUFFED PUMPKIN

Standard	Metric
1 small pumpkin	1 small pumpkin
2 tbsp butter	30 ml butter
1 cup chopped onion	250 ml chopped onion
1 cup chopped celery	250 ml chopped celery
1/2 cup chopped green pepper	125 ml chopped green pepper
2 garlic cloves, minced	2 garlic cloves, minced
1-1/2 lb ground beef	750 g ground beef
3 fresh or canned tomatoes, chopped	3 fresh or canned tomatoes, chopped
6 carrots, sliced in rounds	6 carrots, sliced in rounds
5 potatoes, in 1/2 inch cubes	5 potatoes, in 1.25 cm cubes
1 tsp oregano	5 ml oregano
1 tsp parsley	5 ml parsley
1 tbsp Worcestershire sauce	15 ml Worcestershire sauce
1 cup grated cheddar cheese	250 ml grated cheddar cheese
Salt and pepper	Salt and pepper

Preheat the oven to 350°F (180°C). Wash the pumpkin, cut off the top and empty out the seeds and pith. Score the pumpkin flesh on the inside, but do not pierce through the shell. Bake for 30 minutes.

Meanwhile, sauté the onions, celery and green pepper in butter until tender. Add the meat, tomatoes, carrots and potatoes. Season with oregano, parsley, pepper and Worcestershire. Simmer for 15 minutes.

Stuff the pumpkin with the meat mixture. Bake at 350°F (180°C) for 15 minutes. Sprinkle on the grated cheese and bake another 5 minutes.

Tomato Salad with Parmesan and Fines Herbes

PUMPKIN COOKIES

Standard	Metric
1/2 cup shortening	125 ml shortening
1-1/4 cups brown sugar	300 ml brown sugar
1 cup pumpkin purée	250 ml pumpkin purée
2 eggs	2 eggs
2 cups all-purpose flour	500 ml all-purpose flour
2 tsp baking powder	10 ml baking powder
1/2 tsp salt	2 ml salt
1/2 tsp ginger	2 ml ginger
1 tsp cinnamon	5 ml cinnamon
1 tsp nutmeg	5 ml nutmeg
1 cup raisins	250 ml raisins
1/2 cup chopped nuts	125 ml chopped nuts

Combine the dry ingredients in a bowl.

In a second bowl, cream the shortening and work in the brown sugar and eggs. Mix well.

Stir in the puréed pumpkin. Add the nuts and raisins. Gradually stir in the dry ingredients, mixing well. Drop spoonfuls of the batter on an ungreased cookie sheet. Bake at 375°F (180°C) for 10 to 15 minutes.

RAISIN PIE

Standard	Metric
1 cup raisins	250 ml raisins
1 cup sugar	250 ml sugar
1 tbsp melted butter	15 ml melted butter
3 tbsp breadcrumbs	45 ml breadcrumbs
Juice and zest of 1 orange	Juice and zest of 1 orange
1 beaten egg	1 beaten egg
Pinch of salt	Pinch of salt
1 recipe shortcrust pastry	1 recipe shortcrust pastry

Mix all ingredients, except pastry, in the order given. Pour mixture into unbaked pastry shell. Top with a pastry lattice. Bake at 450°F (230°C) until golden.

TOMATO SALAD WITH PARMESAN AND FINES HERBES

Standard	Metric
6 sliced tomatoes	6 sliced tomatoes
1/2 cup olive oil	125 ml olive oil
5 tbsp vinegar	75 ml vinegar
Salt and pepper	Salt and pepper
1/2 cup grated Parmesan cheese	125 ml grated Parmesan cheese
1 tbsp minced garlic	15 ml minced garlic
2 tbsp chopped shallots	30 ml chopped shallots
1 tsp basil	5 ml basil
1 tsp oregano	5 ml oregano
3 tbsp chopped fresh parsley	45 ml chopped fresh parsley

Arrange the tomatoes, sliced thin, on a large serving platter.

Mix together the rest of the ingredients, except the Parmesan, and pour over the tomatoes.

Sprinkle the Parmesan on top and serve.

Raisin Pie

Halloween Supper II

Recreate the thrill of Halloween with good old-fashioned dishes.

Serve a full-bodied red wine or a sparkling rosé.

Menu

Serves 6 to 8

Pumpkin Soup
Savory Stuffed Mushrooms
Beef and Eggplant Casserole
Paprika Rice
Bean Salad
Pumpkin Cake
Old-Fashioned Pumpkin Pie

Pumpkin Soup

Standard	Metric
1/4 cup oil or butter	50 ml oil or butter
1 sliced onion	1 sliced onion
2 celery stalks, sliced	2 celery stalks, sliced
4 leeks, white part sliced thin	4 leeks, white part sliced thin
4 cups raw pumpkin, diced	1 liter raw pumpkin, diced
2 cups potatoes, diced	500 ml potatoes, diced
2 cups chicken stock	500 ml chicken stock
1 tsp brown sugar	5 ml brown sugar
1 cup milk	250 ml milk
Salt and pepper	Salt and pepper
2 tbsp butter	30 ml butter
1 small pumpkin shell, hollowed	1 small pumpkin shell, hollowed
Croutons or toasted pumpkin seeds	Croutons or toasted pumpkin seeds

Sauté the onions, celery and leeks in 2 tbsp (30 ml) of the butter until tender. Add the diced pumpkin and potatoes. Cover and cook for 10 minutes.

Add the chicken stock and brown sugar; simmer until the potatoes and pumpkin are tender. Purée in batches in the blender. Return to the saucepan and gently reheat. Stir in the milk, salt, pepper and 2 tbsp (30 ml) of butter.

If desired, serve the soup in a hollowed pumpkin. Garnish with croutons or toasted pumpkin seeds.

Savory Stuffed Mushrooms

Standard	Metric
24 large mushrooms	24 large mushrooms
1/4 cup vegetable oil	50 ml vegetable oil
1 zucchini	1 zucchini
3 tbsp chopped shallots	45 ml chopped shallots
4 garlic cloves, minced	4 garlic cloves, minced
3 tbsp chopped parsley	45 ml chopped parsley
3 tbsp butter	45 ml butter
Pinch thyme	Pinch thyme
Breadcrumbs	Breadcrumbs
Salt and pepper	Salt and pepper

Remove the stems from the mushrooms and set aside.

Heat the oil in a skillet and sauté the mushrooms over high heat for 2 or 3 minutes. Drain and set aside.

Finely chop the mushroom stems, the zucchini, garlic, parsley and shallots. Cook in the butter over gentle heat for 8 to 10 minutes. Season and add thyme. Stuff the mushroom caps with the vegetable mixture, sprinkle with breadcrumbs and bake in a hot oven for about 5 minutes.

Savory Stuffed Mushrooms

Beef and Eggplant Casserole

BEEF AND EGGPLANT CASSEROLE

Standard	Metric
2 lb lean ground beef	1 kg lean ground beef
1 large onion, chopped	1 large onion, chopped
1/2 green pepper, chopped	1/2 green pepper, chopped
1 small can tomato sauce	1 small can tomato sauce
1 tsp salt	5 ml salt
1/2 tsp dried oregano	2 ml dried oregano
1/2 tsp dried basil	2 ml dried basil
1/4 tsp black pepper	1 ml black pepper
1 medium eggplant, cut in 2 inch cubes	1 medium eggplant, cut in 5 cm cubes
1/4 lb mozzarella, sliced	125 g mozzarella, sliced

Brown the meat in a heavy skillet. Add the chopped onion and green pepper. Cook about 2 minutes, stirring frequently. Add the tomato sauce, salt, oregano, basil, and black pepper. Mix well and cook 5 to 10 minutes.

Arrange the eggplant in a buttered ovenproof dish. Spread the meat mixture over top and bake in a 350°F (180°C) oven for 20 to 25 minutes.

Arrange the cheese slices on top of the meat and bake for another 5 to 10 minutes or until the cheese is melted.

PAPRIKA RICE

Standard	Metric
2 cups rice	500 ml rice
5 tbsp vegetable oil	75 ml vegetable oil
1 onion, chopped	1 onion, chopped
2 tsp tomato paste	10 ml tomato paste
1 tsp paprika	5 ml paprika
1 bay leaf	1 bay leaf
1 tsp salt	5 ml salt
Pinch thyme	Pinch thyme

Heat the oil in a heavy saucepan. Add the rice and onion and sauté, stirring, until golden. Add the tomato paste, thyme and paprika and mix well.

Pour in 2 cups (500 ml) of water and season. Add the bay leaf and let boil for about 20 minutes, until rice is done.

BEAN SALAD

Standard	Metric
2 cups cooked wax beans	500 ml cooked wax beans
2 cups cooked green beans	500 ml cooked green beans
1 can red kidney beans, drained	1 can red kidney beans, drained
1 cup diced celery	250 ml diced celery
1/2 cup onion, sliced in rings	125 ml onion, sliced in rings
1 cup sliced mushrooms	250 ml sliced mushrooms
1/2 tsp salt	2 ml salt
1/4 tsp pepper	1 ml pepper
1 green bell pepper, diced	1 green bell pepper, diced
1 red bell pepper, diced	1 red bell pepper, diced

Dressing

Standard	Standard
1/4 cup vinegar	50 ml vinegar
1/2 cup vegetable oil	125 ml vegetable oil
1 tsp mustard powder	5 ml mustard powder
1 tsp thyme	5 ml thyme
1 tsp sugar	5 ml sugar
Pinch garlic powder	Pinch garlic powder

Combine all the vegetables in a large salad bowl. In another bowl, mix the dressing ingredients. Pour the sauce over the salad and mix well. Garnish each salad plate with a lettuce leaf with the salad on top.

PUMPKIN CAKE

Standard	Metric
4 eggs	4 eggs
2 cups sugar	500 ml sugar
2 cups cooked pumpkin	500 ml cooked pumpkin
1 cup oil	250 ml oil
3 cups all-purpose flour	750 ml all-purpose flour
1 tsp salt	5 ml salt
2 tsp baking soda	10 ml baking soda
2 tsp baking powder	10 ml baking powder
2 tsp cinnamon	10 ml cinnamon
1 cup nuts or raisins	250 ml nuts or raisins

In the food processor, combine the eggs and sugar until smooth. Add the flour, baking powder, baking soda, salt, cinnamon and raisins or nuts. Stir in the cooked and mashed pumpkin.

Turn the batter into two round cake molds, greased and lightly floured. Bake in a preheated oven at 350°F (180°C) for 40 minutes. Unmold and stack the cakes, and ice with an orange-tinted frosting.

OLD-FASHIONED PUMPKIN PIE

Standard	Metric
2 cups steamed or baked and drained pumpkin pulp	500 ml steamed or baked and drained pumpkin pulp
1/2 tsp salt	2 ml salt
4 tbsp brown sugar	60 ml brown sugar
1 tsp ginger	5 ml ginger
1/2 tsp cinnamon	2 ml cinnamon
4 tbsp molasses	60 ml molasses
2 beaten eggs	2 beaten eggs
2 cups milk	500 ml milk
1/8 tsp mace	0.5 ml mace
1 pie crust (see page 68, Maple Syrup Pie)	1 pie crust (see page 68, Maple Syrup Pie)

Cut the pumpkin into large pieces and bake or steam until tender. Drain in a strainer and purée. Stir in the beaten eggs and milk. Add the molasses and mix well.

Stir in the sugar and spices, and turn mixture into the pastry crust. Bake at 325°F (160°C) until the center of the pie is firm.

Pumpkin Cake

116

HALLOWEEN LUNCH BOX

Kids will love this chance to start celebrating Halloween early in the day.

MENU

for each child

Half-Moon Sandwiches
Celery Stuffed with Cheese and Red Pepper
Toffee Apples
Cheese Puffs
Old-Fashioned Pull-Toffee
Milk

CELERY STUFFED WITH CHEESE AND RED PEPPER

Standard	Metric
2 celery stalks, sliced diagonally in 2 inch lengths	2 celery stalks, sliced diagonally in 5 cm lengths
1 cup Philadelphia cream cheese	250 ml Philadelphia cream cheese
1/2 red bell pepper	1/2 red bell pepper
Salt and pepper	Salt and pepper

Wash and cut the celery. Mix the cream cheese and red pepper in the food processor. Stuff the celery stalks with the aid of a pastry bag and decorate each with a celery leaf.

TOFFEE APPLES

Standard	Metric
6 apples	6 apples
2 cups sugar	500 ml sugar
1/4 cup water	50 ml water
1/4 cup butter	50 ml butter

Chill the apples in the refrigerator. In a heavy saucepan, boil 1 cup (250 ml) of water with the sugar until a golden caramel color. Remove from heat and let cool 2 or 3 minutes before stirring in 1/4 cup (50 ml) water.

Return the pan to the burner and stir in the butter with a wooden spoon. Take the apples out of the refrigerator, spear each with a wooden stick, and dunk in the caramel mixture. If the caramel does not stick to the apple, it is still too warm.

Sit each apple on a generously greased plate and refrigerate until the caramel is hard.

HALF-MOON SANDWICHES

Make sandwiches with the child's favorite filling and trim into half-moon shapes.

OLD-FASHIONED PULL-TOFFEE

See recipe, page 122.

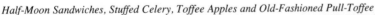

Half-Moon Sandwiches, Stuffed Celery, Toffee Apples and Old-Fashioned Pull-Toffee

THE FEAST OF SAINT CATHERINE

The celebration of the Feast of Saint Catherine is usually topped off with an old-fashioned toffee-pull.

Serve a white Bordeaux or a sparkling rosé.

MENU

Serves 6 to 8

Julienne of Vegetable Soup
Ham and Peas Vol-au-Vent
Tangy Turkey Mold
Vegetable Bouquets
Potato Salad
Molasses Cake

JULIENNE OF VEGETABLE SOUP

Standard	Metric
1 tbsp oil	15 ml oil
1/2 cup turnip	125 ml turnip
1 cup carrots	250 ml carrots
1 leek	1 leek
1 cup celery	250 ml celery
1/2 cup cabbage	125 ml cabbage
1 onion	1 onion
Salt, pepper and parsley	Salt, pepper and parsley
Rosemary to taste	Rosemary to taste
12 cups chicken stock	3 liters chicken stock

Cut the vegetables into fine julienne. Heat the oil and sauté the onion over low heat without browning. Add the rest of the vegetables and the chicken stock. Cook until vegetables are tender.

HAM AND PEAS VOL-AU-VENT

Standard	Metric
8 precooked vol-au-vent pastry shells	8 precooked vol-au-vent pastry shells
1 lb cooked ham	500 g cooked ham
2 cups frozen peas	500 ml frozen peas
2 small onions, chopped	2 small onions, chopped
2 small carrots, chopped	2 small carrots, chopped
3 tbsp butter	45 ml butter
2 tbsp all-purpose flour	30 ml all-purpose flour
1 cup heavy cream (35%)	250 ml heavy cream (35%)
2 cups chicken stock	500 ml chicken stock
3 tbsp chopped fresh parsley	45 ml chopped fresh parsley
Salt and pepper	Salt and pepper

Remove the centers from the pastry shells and keep warm on a serving platter.

Dice the ham, chop the onion, and slice the carrots on the bias. Cook the carrots in boiling salted water for 5 minutes; drain and set aside.

Melt the butter in a large heavy saucepan and sauté the diced ham, onion, carrots and peas for 7 minutes, stirring constantly. Stir in the flour. Add the chicken stock and cream. Season and cook until the sauce is thick and creamy. Add the chopped parsley.

Correct the seasoning and fill the pastry shells generously with the mixture.

Ham and Peas Vol-au-Vent

Tangy Turkey Mold with Vegetable Bouquets

TANGY TURKEY MOLD

Standard	Metric
2-1/2 cups chopped cooked turkey meat	625 ml chopped cooked turkey meat
1-1/2 cups breadcrumbs	375 ml breadcrumbs
3/4 cup turkey stock	150 ml turkey stock
1/2 cup diced celery	125 ml diced celery
1 tbsp chopped fresh parsley	15 ml chopped fresh parsley
2 tsp grated onion	10 ml grated onion
1/2 tsp Worcestershire sauce	2 ml Worcestershire sauce
1/2 tsp salt	2 ml salt
1/8 tsp pepper	0.5 ml pepper
2 tsp lemon juice	10 ml lemon juice
4 large or 6 small eggs	4 large or 6 small eggs
1 cup condensed milk	250 ml condensed milk

Combine the chopped turkey, breadcrumbs, turkey stock, celery, parsley and seasonings. Add the beaten eggs and the milk. Mix well. Turn the mixture into a 8x5x3 inch (20x13x7.5 cm) mold.

Sit the mold in a baking pan of water and bake at 350°F (180°C) for about 1 hour or until the mixture is firm and the surface golden. Unmold and serve.

VEGETABLE BOUQUETS

2 large yellow turnips
6 medium white turnips
3 large carrots
1 large leek with lots of green

Peel and cut the vegetables into 1x3 inch (2.5x7.5 cm) sticks and cook in boiling salted water until tender-crisp. Slice each vegetable stick into 9 small sticks and set the bundles aside.

Cook the green parts of the leek in boiling salted water for 1 minute, then refresh them in cold water. Slice the greens into thin strips, and wrap each with a leek strip. Steam the vegetable bundles to reheat.

Technique: Vegetable Bouquets

1 Cut the vegetables into 1x3 inch (2.5x7.5 cm) sticks.

2 Cut each stick into 9 small sticks.

3 Blanch the green part of the leek.

4 Cut into thin strips.

5 Wrap and tie the vegetable bundles.

6 Steam to reheat.

POTATO SALAD

Standard	Metric
7 unpeeled potatoes	7 unpeeled potatoes
3 tbsp chopped chives	45 ml chopped chives
3 tbsp chopped parsley	45 ml chopped parsley
3 hard-boiled eggs, chopped with a knife	3 hard-boiled eggs, chopped with a knife
1 large onion, chopped	1 large onion, chopped
1 tbsp minced garlic	15 ml minced garlic
1 cup mayonnaise	250 ml mayonnaise
Salt and pepper	Salt and pepper
7 lettuce leaves	7 lettuce leaves

Cook the potatoes in salted water. Let cool and peel; cut them into large cubes.

In a mixing bowl, combine the rest of the ingredients, except the lettuce. Mix in the potatoes and correct seasoning. Arrange the potato salad on lettuce leaves and garnish with slices of hard-boiled egg and parsley sprigs.

MOLASSES CAKE

Standard	Metric
1 tbsp shortening	15 ml shortening
1 cup maple syrup	250 ml maple syrup
1 cup brown sugar	250 ml brown sugar
1 cup milk	250 ml milk
2 eggs	2 eggs
1-3/4 cups all-purpose flour	400 ml all-purpose flour
1/8 tsp salt	0.5 ml salt
2 tsp baking powder	10 ml baking powder
1/4 tsp nutmeg	1 ml nutmeg
1 tsp ginger	5 ml ginger
Whipped cream	Whipped cream
1/4 cup molasses	50 ml molasses

Combine the shortening, syrup, brown sugar and eggs. Combine the dry ingredients and add to the syrup mixture. Stir well. Bake in a cake pan at 400°F (200°C) for 10 minutes, then adjust the heat to 350°F (180°C) for another 20 minutes.

Serve the cake with whipped cream mixed with the molasses.

Variation: Cut holes in the top of the cake and fill with the topping.

Molasses Cake

Feast of Saint Catherine Sweets

Candy Apples

Standard	Metric
6 to 8 red apples, unpeeled	6 to 8 red apples, unpeeled
1 cup sugar	250 ml sugar
1/2 cup corn syrup	125 ml corn syrup
1 can sweetened condensed milk	1 can sweetened condensed milk
1 tsp vanilla	5 ml vanilla
Wooden sticks	Wooden sticks

Insert a wooden stick in the end of each apple and chill in the refrigerator.

Put the sugar, corn syrup, vanilla and condensed milk in a heavy enamelled saucepan. Cook over gentle heat, stirring constantly, until the syrup reads 250°F (120°C) on a candy thermometer, or until a drop forms a hard ball when dropped in cold water.

Remove from heat, and dip each well-chilled apple by its handle in the syrup, turning to coat completely. Lay the apples on a buttered cake rack and let cool.

Coconut Cream Candy

Standard	Metric
1 cup sugar	250 ml sugar
1/2 cup cold water	125 ml cold water
1 cup shredded coconut	250 ml shredded coconut
1/2 tsp vanilla	2 ml vanilla
1 cup heavy cream (35%)	250 ml heavy cream (35%)

Put the sugar and water in a saucepan and cook over low heat, stirring constantly, until the syrup coats the spoon. Stir in the coconut and cream and simmer, without stirring, until the mixture reaches 235°F (115°C) on a candy thermometer or until a drop poured into cold water forms a soft ball.

Remove from the heat and stir in the vanilla. Beat until the mixture is creamy.

Use a spoon to drop small balls of the mixture about 1 inch (2.5 cm) apart on a buttered plate. Garnish with toasted almonds. Let chill.

Candy Apples

Molasses Cookies

Standard	Metric
3/4 cup shortening	150 ml shortening
3/4 cup brown sugar	150 ml brown sugar
1 egg	1 egg
3/4 cup light molasses	150 ml light molasses
3/4 cup sour milk	150 ml sour milk
3-1/2 cups all-purpose flour	875 ml all-purpose flour
1 tsp baking powder	5 ml baking powder
1 tsp baking soda	5 ml baking soda
1 tsp salt	5 ml salt
2 tsp cinnamon	10 ml cinnamon
2 tsp ginger	10 ml ginger
1/2 tsp ground cloves	2 ml ground cloves

Cream together the shortening and brown sugar.

Beat the egg for 2 minutes and combine with the shortening. Stir in the molasses and sour milk. Sift the flour together with the other dry ingredients and stir gradually into the molasses mixture until smooth. Drop by spoonfuls on a greased cookie sheet.

Bake at 450°F (230°C) for 8 to 10 minutes.

Molasses Toffee

Standard	Metric
2 cups brown sugar	500 ml brown sugar
1/2 cup water	125 ml water
1 tbsp corn syrup	15 ml corn syrup
1 cup molasses	250 ml molasses
1/3 cup butter	75 ml butter
Vanilla	Vanilla

Combine the brown sugar, water, corn syrup, molasses and butter in a saucepan. Stir well and cook until the mixture reaches 260°F (120°C) on a candy thermometer or until a drop poured into cold water forms a hard ball. Stir in the vanilla. Pour into a buttered pan and let cool. Pull and stretch the toffee, cut into pieces and twist.

Traditional Saint Catherine Pull-Toffee

Standard	Metric
1/2 cup white sugar	125 ml white sugar
1/2 cup brown sugar	125 ml brown sugar
1/2 cup molasses	125 ml molasses
1/4 cup corn syrup	50 ml corn syrup
1/4 cup water	50 ml water
1 tsp vinegar	5 ml vinegar
2 tsp butter	10 ml butter
1/2 tsp baking soda	2 ml baking soda

Combine all the ingredients except the baking soda in a large heavy saucepan. Cook over medium heat until the mixture reaches 265°F (125°C) on a candy thermometer, or until a drop poured into cold water forms a hard ball.

Remove from the heat, add the soda and stir well. Turn the mixture into a buttered pan and let cool. Pull and stretch, cut into pieces and twist.

Molasses Pie

Standard	Metric
1-1/4 cups all-purpose flour	300 ml all-purpose flour
1/2 cup sugar	125 ml sugar
1/3 cup margarine	75 ml margarine
1/2 tsp nutmeg	2 ml nutmeg
1/4 tsp cinnamon	1 ml cinnamon
3/4 cup molasses	150 ml molasses
3/4 cup water	150 ml water
1/2 tsp baking soda	2 ml baking soda
1 shortcrust pastry crust	1 shortcrust pastry crust

Arrange a layer of pastry in a 9 inch (22 cm) pie plate and flute the edges.

Sift together the flour, sugar and spices. Work in the margarine until the consistency of breadcrumbs.

Mix together the rest of the ingredients and pour the mixture into the unbaked pie shell. Sprinkle the flour mixture on top. Bake the pie at 400°F (200°C) for 15 minutes. Reduce heat to 350°F (180°C) and continue baking another 15 to 20 minutes.

Molasses Raisin Cookies

Standard	Metric
1 cup molasses	250 ml molasses
1 cup sugar	250 ml sugar
1 cup melted shortening	250 ml melted shortening
1 cup sour milk	250 ml sour milk
2 eggs	2 eggs
1-1/2 cups raisins	375 ml raisins
4 cups pastry flour	1 liter pastry flour
1 tsp ginger	5 ml ginger
1 tsp cinnamon	5 ml cinnamon
1 tsp baking soda	5 ml baking soda
1/2 tsp salt	2 ml salt
1 tsp baking powder	5 ml baking powder

Mix together the molasses, sugar and melted shortening. Add the spices, salt, the baking soda dissolved in 1 tbsp (15 ml) cold water, the raisins and sour milk.

Add the flour and baking powder. Stir. Drop by spoonfuls onto a cookie sheet and bake at 400°F (200°C) for 10 to 15 minutes.

Toffee Apple (see page 117), Coconut Cream Candy, Molasses Cookies and Traditional Saint Catherine Pull-Toffee

RECEPTIONS

CHRISTENING BRUNCH

Most of this delightful menu can be prepared in advance.

Serve with white Bordeaux or Burgundy.

MENU

Serves 6 to 8

Cheese Surprises
Orange Nut Bread
Fettuccine Salad
Seafood Quiche
Baked Tomatoes
Seasoned Asparagus and Mushrooms
Cheesy Cherry Aspic

CHEESE SURPRISES

8 small round bread rolls
8 eggs
8 slices cheese
Butter

Cut the top off each roll and butter the inside. Break an egg into each roll.

Arrange the rolls on a baking sheet. Bake in a 325°F (160°C) oven for about 25 minutes. Lay a slice of cheese on top of each roll and return to the oven for another 5 minutes.

SEAFOOD QUICHE

Standard	Metric
1/2 cup mayonnaise	125 ml mayonnaise
1 tbsp all-purpose flour	15 ml all-purpose flour
2 eggs	2 eggs
1/4 cup dry white wine	50 ml dry white wine
1 can crabmeat	1 can crabmeat
1 can shrimp	1 can shrimp
3/4 cup grated Gruyère cheese	150 ml grated Gruyère cheese
1/4 cup chopped celery	50 ml chopped celery
1/4 cup chopped shallots	50 ml chopped shallots
1 unbaked pie shell	1 unbaked pie shell

Mix all the ingredients together and pour into the unbaked pie shell. Bake at 350°F (180°C) for 30 minutes.

ORANGE NUT BREAD

Standard	Metric
1-1/2 cups all-purpose flour	375 ml all-purpose flour
1 tsp baking powder	5 ml baking powder
1 tsp salt	5 ml salt
1/3 cup butter or margarine	75 ml butter or margarine
1-3/4 cups sugar	400 ml sugar
2 eggs	2 eggs
1 tbsp grated orange peel	15 ml grated orange peel
1/2 cup chopped nuts	125 ml chopped nuts
1/2 cup milk	125 ml milk
1 tbsp orange juice	15 ml orange juice
1 tbsp honey	15 ml honey

Mix together the flour, baking powder and salt. Cream the butter, and gradually cream in the sugar until well mixed. Stir in the eggs one at a time, beating well after each addition. Stir in the orange peel, juice, honey and nuts.

Gradually stir in the dry ingredients, alternating with the milk. Mix well after each addition.

Grease a metal bread pan and pour in the batter. Bake at 350°F (180°C) for about 1 hour.

FETTUCCINE SALAD

Standard	Metric
3 cups fettuccine, broken	750 ml fettuccine, broken
2 tbsp olive oil	30 ml olive oil
4 tbsp mayonnaise	60 ml mayonnaise
1 can tuna, drained	1 can tuna, drained
2 hard-boiled eggs, chopped	2 hard-boiled eggs, chopped
2 tomatoes, peeled and chopped	2 tomatoes, peeled and chopped
1 tsp caraway seed	5 ml caraway seed
3 tbsp grated cheese	45 ml grated cheese
Salt and pepper	Salt and pepper

Cook the fettuccine and drain well. Add the olive oil while the pasta is still hot. Let cool and add the mayonnaise. Mix again.

Combine the rest of the ingredients. Add to the pasta and mix well with a fork.

Serve on a lettuce bed.

Fettuccine Salad

Seasoned Asparagus and Mushrooms

Standard	Metric
2 lb fresh asparagus	1 kg fresh asparagus
1/3 cup oil	75 ml oil
1/2 cup water	125 ml water
1/4 cup chopped shallots	50 ml chopped shallots
1 cup fresh sliced mushrooms	250 ml fresh sliced mushrooms
1 tsp salt	5 ml salt
1 cup light cream (15%)	250 ml light cream (15%)
Freshly ground pepper	Freshly ground pepper

Trim the ends off the asparagus and discard. Slice the asparagus on the bias into half inch (1 cm) lengths.

Put the oil and water in a heavy saucepan. Heat to boiling and add the asparagus, mushrooms, shallots and salt. Seal tightly (use aluminum foil if necessary) and cook over high heat, shaking the pan occasionally, about 4 minutes or until the asparagus is tender-crisp. Watch carefully and add a little water if necessary.

Add the cream and some freshly ground pepper. Reheat.

Microwave Method

Baked Tomatoes

Cut the tomatoes in half and arrange in a circle on a glass dish with space between them. Cover. Cook at HIGH for 4 minutes or until the tomatoes are tender but still firm. Rotate the dish once during cooking. Let stand a few minutes before serving.

Baked Tomatoes

Standard	Metric
6 tomatoes, cut in half	6 tomatoes, cut in half
2 tsp grated Parmesan	10 ml grated Parmesan
Basil	Basil
Pepper	Pepper

Sprinkle the tomato halves with basil, pepper and Parmesan. Arrange in a baking dish and put under the broiler until tops are golden.

Cheesy Cherry Aspic

Cheesy Cherry Aspic

Standard	Metric
1 package cherry jelly powder	1 package cherry jelly powder
1 cup boiling water	250 ml boiling water
1 cup cherry juice	250 ml cherry juice
2-1/2 cups large cherries, pitted and halved	625 ml large cherries, pitted and halved
1 package lime jelly powder	1 package lime jelly powder
1/2 tsp salt	2 ml salt
1 cup boiling water	250 ml boiling water
1 cup cold water	250 ml cold water
2 packages cream cheese	2 packages cream cheese

Dissolve the cherry jelly powder in 1 cup (250 ml) boiling water. Add the cherry juice and chill until the mixture is partially set. Mix in the cherry halves. Pour the mixture in a 9 x 5 x 3 inch (22 x 22 x 7.5 cm) mold. Chill in the refrigerator.

Meanwhile, dissolve the lime jelly powder and the salt in 1 cup (250 ml) boiling water. Add the cold water and let partially set.

Beat the cream cheese with a fork and stir it into the partially set lime jelly with the aid of a whisk. Pour on top of the cherry mixture and let set in the refrigerator until the lime mixture is firm.

Unmold. Garnish with mint leaves.

CHRISTENING BUFFET

Enjoy an elegant and leisurely meal with the family.

Serve with a dry white wine, a sparkling wine or champagne.

MENU

Serves 6 to 8

Snow Pea and Pineapple Cocktails
Bacon and Egg Sandwiches
Creamed Lobster on Rye Bread
Vol-au-Vent Neptune
Swiss Quiche
Hearts of Palm Salad
Bavarian Pears

SNOW PEA AND PINEAPPLE COCKTAILS

Standard	Metric
1 lb snow peas	500 g snow peas
1 slice lean cooked ham	1 slice lean cooked ham
2 slices fresh pineapple	2 slices fresh pineapple
4 lettuce leaves	4 lettuce leaves
1 cup mayonnaise	250 ml mayonnaise
Few drops cognac or whisky	Few drops cognac or whisky
1 lemon	1 lemon
2 firm tomatoes	2 firm tomatoes
1 or 2 hard-boiled eggs	1 or 2 hard-boiled eggs
Parsley	Parsley
Pinch cayenne pepper	Pinch cayenne pepper

Pull the strings off the snow peas and blanch them for 1 minute in boiling salted water. Rinse under cold water, drain and set aside.

Cut the ham into slices and cube the pineapple. Combine with the peas. Divide between cocktail glasses or stemmed glasses trimmed with lettuce leaves. Top each serving with a dollop of mayonnaise thinned with cognac or whisky, lemon juice and cayenne pepper.

Decorate each serving with slices of tomato and hard-boiled eggs. Sprinkle with chopped parsley and serve.

BACON AND EGG SANDWICHES

Standard	Metric
5 hard-boiled eggs, chopped	5 hard-boiled eggs, chopped
5 slices bacon, cooked and chopped	5 slices bacon, cooked and chopped
4 tsp parsley	20 ml parsley
3 tbsp mayonnaise	45 ml mayonnaise
1 to 2 tsp prepared mustard	5 to 10 ml prepared mustard

Combine all ingredients and spread on bread slices. Trim off the crusts and cut into shapes. Decorate each with parsley and a radish round.

CREAMED LOBSTER ON RYE

Standard	Metric
1 onion, minced	1 onion, minced
1 garlic clove, minced	1 garlic clove, minced
1/2 cup sliced mushrooms	125 ml sliced mushrooms
3 tbsp butter	45 ml butter
3 tbsp all-purpose flour	45 ml all-purpose flour
1-1/2 cups light cream (15%)	375 ml light cream (15%)
3/4 lb canned lobster meat	350 g canned lobster meat
1 egg yolk, lightly beaten	1 egg yolk, lightly beaten
Rye bread	Rye bread
Pieces of cooked lobster, sautéed in butter	Pieces of cooked lobster, sautéed in butter
Parsley	Parsley

Sauté the onion, garlic and mushrooms in butter until soft. Sprinkle in the flour and stir well. Add the cream and

Creamed Lobster on Rye

continue cooking, stirring constantly, until thickened.

Season with salt and pepper. Add the lobster meat and let heat for 2 to 3 minutes. Stir in the beaten egg yolk and continue cooking for 1 minute without letting boil. Serve over slices of rye bread garnished with pieces of lobster meat and parsley. The lobster can be replaced with shrimp, if desired.

VOL-AU-VENT NEPTUNE

Standard	Metric
1/2 cup butter	125 ml butter
1/2 cup diced green pepper	125 ml diced green pepper
3/4 cup diced celery	150 ml diced celery
1/2 cup chopped onion	125 ml chopped onion
1 cup sliced mushrooms	250 ml sliced mushrooms
1/2 cup all-purpose flour	125 ml all-purpose flour
3 cups milk	750 ml milk
1 lb thawed frozen lobster, chopped	500 g thawed frozen lobster, chopped
1/2 lb boiled scallops	250 g boiled scallops
1/2 lb thawed frozen large shrimp	250 g thawed frozen large shrimp
3 hard-boiled eggs, chopped	3 hard-boiled eggs, chopped
Salt and pepper	Salt and pepper
Chopped chives	Chopped chives
Chopped parsley	Chopped parsley
6 vol-au-vent shells	6 vol-au-vent shells

Melt the butter in a saucepan and sauté the onions, celery, green peppers and mushrooms.

When the vegetables are partially cooked, stir in the flour, then gradually add the milk and stir until thickened slightly.

Let simmer for about 10 minutes, then add the lobster, shrimp, scallops and hard-boiled eggs.

Season with salt and pepper and add chopped chives and parsley. Let simmer a few more minutes, stirring constantly. Fill the vol-au-vent shells with the mixture. Serve hot.

SWISS QUICHE

Standard	Metric
1-1/2 cups cooked ham, chopped fine	375 ml cooked ham, chopped fine
1 uncooked pastry shell	1 uncooked pastry shell
2 cups grated Gruyère cheese	500 ml grated Gruyère cheese
3 beaten eggs	3 beaten eggs
2 tbsp finely chopped onion	30 ml finely chopped onion
1 tbsp Dijon mustard	15 ml Dijon mustard
1/4 tsp salt	1 ml salt
1 cup light cream (15%)	250 ml light cream (15%)
1 tbsp Parmesan cheese	15 ml Parmesan cheese

Put the chopped ham in the pastry shell and press down lightly. Add the grated Gruyère.

Beat together the eggs, chopped onion, mustard and salt. Incorporate the cream gradually. Pour over the ham and cheese.

Sprinkle the Parmesan on top. Bake at 375°F (190°C) for 30 to 35 minutes or until the filling is firm.

Vol-au-Vent Neptune

Hearts of Palm Salad

HEARTS OF PALM SALAD

2 carrots sliced on the bias
8 lettuce leaves
3 hard-boiled eggs, quartered
3 cans palm hearts

Vinaigrette

Standard	Metric
2 tsp mustard	10 ml mustard
1 tbsp lemon juice	15 ml lemon juice
1 tbsp white vinegar	15 ml white vinegar
5 tbsp olive oil	75 ml olive oil
2 tsp fresh chopped parsley	10 ml fresh chopped parsley
Salt and pepper	Salt and pepper

Put the mustard, salt, pepper, lemon juice and vinegar in a bowl. Mix well. Beat in the oil bit by bit, then stir in the parsley. Let stand.

Cook the carrots for 3 minutes in boiling water. Cool under cold water and drain.

Arrange the palm hearts on a large serving platter, interspersed with the carrots and quartered eggs. Shred the lettuce finely and place in the center of the plate or around the edge.

Pour vinaigrette over top.

BAVARIAN PEARS

Standard	Metric
2 tbsp unflavored gelatin	30 ml unflavored gelatin
1/2 cup cold water	125 ml cold water
1 cup pear juice	250 ml pear juice
1 cup canned pears, crushed	250 ml canned pears, crushed
1 tbsp lemon juice	15 ml lemon juice
2 cups evaporated milk (2%)	500 ml evaporated milk (2%)
9 cut up strawberries	9 cut up strawberries
2 tbsp chopped nuts	30 ml chopped nuts

Heat the pear juice. Pour the evaporated milk into a saucepan and put in the freezer for about 30 minutes or until crystals have formed around the edge of the pan.

Put the gelatin in a large bowl, add the cold water and let sit for 5 minutes. Add the pear juice and stir to dissolve. Let stand until the mixture has set to the consistency of unbeaten egg white.

Add the crushed pears, nuts and strawberries.

Beat the chilled milk together with the lemon juice and fold this gently into the gelatin mixture.

Turn the mixture into dessert dishes and put in the refrigerator to set.

For a garnish: set quartered pears on a buttered and sugared baking sheet. Squeeze the juice of 1 lemon on top. Bake at 450°F (230°C) for 7 minutes. Let cool, then set on top of the Bavarian cream.

131

132

First Communion Brunch

This novel approach to chicken will become a family favorite.

Serve a rosé or white Bordeaux.

MENU

Serves 6 to 8

Omelet Cake
Honey Coconut French Toast
Rosy Ham Potato Salad
Chicken with Peaches
Herbed Rotini
Tarragon Peas and Carrots
Frozen Chocolate Soufflé

OMELET CAKE

Standard	Metric
14 eggs	14 eggs
1/2 cup diced ham	125 ml diced ham
1/2 cup chopped onion	125 ml chopped onion
1/2 cup diced red pepper	125 ml diced red pepper
1/2 cup sliced mushrooms	125 ml sliced mushrooms
1/2 cup grated cheese	125 ml grated cheese
1/2 cup chopped canned tomatoes	125 ml chopped canned tomatoes
1/2 cup cooked cauliflowerets	125 ml cooked cauliflowerets

Cook all the vegetables separately until the liquid has evaporated. Put each vegetable and the ham into 7 separate small bowls. Break 2 eggs into each bowl, season and mix well.

Cook each omelet separately in a nonstick 6 inch (15 cm) skillet. When each omelet is cooked, stack it on top of the preceding one.

Let cool. Cut the omelet cake into wedges and serve with a thick tomato sauce.

Omelet Cake

HONEY COCONUT FRENCH TOAST

Standard	Metric
3 eggs	3 eggs
1/2 tsp salt	2 ml salt
2 tbsp sugar	30 ml sugar
1 cup milk	250 ml milk
6 slices bread	6 slices bread
1/4 cup shredded coconut	50 ml shredded coconut

Beat the eggs. Add the salt, sugar and milk. Pour the mixture into a deep plate and dip the bread slices in until well soaked. Brown the slices on both sides in a hot well-greased skillet. Sprinkle with coconut. Serve with honey.

ROSY HAM POTATO SALAD

Standard	Metric
3 cups diced cooked ham	750 ml diced cooked ham
2 cups diced cooked potatoes	500 ml diced cooked potatoes
1 cup diced cucumber	250 ml diced cucumber
1/2 cup diced celery	125 ml diced celery
1/2 cup chopped shallots	125 ml chopped shallots
2 cups chopped lettuce	500 ml chopped lettuce

Vinaigrette

Standard	Metric
6 tbsp olive oil	90 ml olive oil
2 tbsp cider vinegar	30 ml cider vinegar
1 crushed garlic clove	1 crushed garlic clove
Chopped parsley	Chopped parsley
Pinch of thyme	Pinch of thyme
1/2 tsp strong mustard	2 ml strong mustard
1 tsp chopped fresh coriander	5 ml chopped fresh coriander
2 tsp paprika	10 ml paprika
Salt and pepper	Salt and pepper

For the vinaigrette, combine all the ingredients and mix well. Let stand a few minutes. Toss all the salad ingredients in a large salad bowl. Pour on the vinaigrette, toss well and serve.

CHICKEN WITH PEACHES

Standard	Metric
6 chicken breasts, deboned and flattened	6 chicken breasts, deboned and flattened
4 tbsp butter	60 ml butter
4 peaches, peeled and quartered	4 peaches, peeled and quartered
2 tbsp all-purpose flour	30 ml all-purpose flour
1 cup heavy cream (35%)	250 ml heavy cream (35%)
Salt and pepper	Salt and pepper
1/2 cup slivered almonds	125 ml slivered almonds

Place each chicken breast between two pieces of waxed paper and use a rolling pin to flatten to 1/4 inch (5 mm) thickness.

Brown the chicken breasts in the butter for 5 minutes on each side. Add the peaches and continue browning until the chicken is cooked, about 10 minutes. Remove the chicken and peaches from the skillet and put on an oven-proof plate; keep warm in the oven.

Add the flour to the cooking juices and stir with a whisk. Add the cream. Cook over medium heat, stirring, until the sauce starts to thicken. Season to taste. Pour over the chicken and peaches.

Sprinkle with toasted slivered almonds. Serve with pasta.

You can cut down the amount of cream to 1/2 cup (125 ml) by adding a little more flour and 1-1/2 cups (375 ml) chicken stock.

Frozen Chocolate Soufflé

HERBED ROTINI

Standard	Metric
1 lb rotini pasta	500 g rotini pasta
Boiling salted water	Boiling salted water
2 tsp olive oil	10 ml olive oil
2 tsp fines herbes	10 ml fines herbes
Salt and pepper	Salt and pepper

Cook the noodles *al dente* in plenty of boiling salted water. Drain and pass rapidly under cold running water. Drain well. Add the oil, herbs and seasoning. Mix and serve immediately.

TARRAGON PEAS AND CARROTS

Standard	Metric
4 to 6 carrots	4 to 6 carrots
1 package frozen or canned peas	1 package frozen or canned peas
1 tbsp sugar	15 ml sugar
1 tbsp tarragon	15 ml tarragon

Cut the carrots into sticks. Cook until tender in boiling salted water. Cook the frozen peas or drain the canned peas.

Combine the vegetables, add the sugar and the tarragon, and stir in a few lumps of butter. Sprinkle with chopped parsley and serve hot.

FROZEN CHOCOLATE SOUFFLÉ

Standard	Metric
1-1/4 cups semi-sweet chocolate	300 ml semi-sweet chocolate
2 cups heavy cream (35%)	500 ml heavy cream (35%)
4 whole eggs	4 whole eggs
1 tbsp sugar	15 ml sugar
1/2 cup toasted almonds	125 ml toasted almonds

In a heavy saucepan, boil the cream for 1 minute. Remove from the heat, add the chopped chocolate and stir gently with a wooden spoon until the chocolate is melted. Let cool in the refrigerator. Use a whisk to incorporate the egg yolks into the chocolate mixture.

Beat the egg whites very stiff and beat in 1 tbsp (15 ml) sugar until the whites form stiff peaks. Using a spatula, fold the egg whites gently into the chocolate mixture.

Prepare individual soufflé molds by attaching a 1-1/2 inch (3.75 cm) collar of waxed paper, fastening with string. Fill with the chocolate mixture and put in freezer for about 3 hours.

Remove the paper collars before serving. The desserts will look like little soufflés. Garnish with chopped toasted almonds.

First Communion Buffet

An impressive-looking meal that is remarkably easy to prepare.

Serve a rosé or sparkling rosé.

Menu

Serves 6 to 8

Orangy Parsnip Soup
Harlequin Ribbon Sandwiches
Quick Meat Loaf
Tomato Crown
Fresh Asparagus with Sunny Vinaigrette
Water Lily Salad
Dumplings in Maple Syrup

Harlequin Ribbon Sandwiches

Standard
1 loaf unsliced brown bread
1 loaf unsliced white bread
Choice of prepared butters

Remove the crusts from the two loaves and cut 2 lengthwise slices 1/2 inch (1.25 cm) thick from each loaf.

Butter each slice generously on one side only and stack the 4 slices, alternating the white and brown bread.

Chill in the refrigerator under a light weight until the butter is firm. Cut crosswise in thin slices. Makes about 48 sandwiches.

Prepared Butters

Olive Butter: Cream together 1/4 cup (50 ml) butter with 1 tbsp (15 ml) chopped olives and 1/2 tsp (2 ml) lemon juice.

Nut Butter: Cream together 1/4 cup (50 ml) butter with 2 tbsp (30 ml) finely chopped nuts. Add salt to taste.

Tomato Butter: Cream together 1/4 cup (50 ml) butter with 2 tbsp (30 ml) thick tomato purée or tomato paste.

Parsley Butter: Cream together 1/4 cup (50 ml) butter with 1 tbsp (15 ml) finely chopped fresh parsley and 1 tsp (5 ml) lemon juice.

Orangy Parsnip Soup

Orangy Parsnip Soup

Standard	Metric
3 cups parsnips	750 ml parsnips
1 cup potatoes	250 ml potatoes
2 large onions	2 large onions
3 tbsp butter	45 ml butter
Boiling water	Boiling water
1 cup cream	250 ml cream
2 cups milk	500 ml milk
3 tbsp butter	45 ml butter
1/2 tsp rosemary	2 ml rosemary
1/2 tsp pepper	2 ml pepper
1 tbsp grated orange rind	15 ml grated orange rind

Peel the parsnips and potatoes and cut into cubes. Peel and chop the onions. Melt the butter in a large saucepan. Add the onions, cover and let simmer for about 10 minutes over gentle heat. Add the prepared vegetables. Cover with boiling water. Add salt. Cover and let cook over medium heat for about 30 minutes until vegetables are tender. Add the remaining ingredients. Cook over low heat without boiling. Serve.

QUICK MEAT LOAF

Standard	Metric
3 lb ground veal	1.5 kg ground veal
1/2 lb ground pork	250 g ground pork
2 eggs	2 eggs
1 cup crushed soda biscuits	250 ml crushed soda biscuits
1 chopped onion	1 chopped onion
Salt and pepper	Salt and pepper

Combine all ingredients and place in a greased loaf pan. Bake at 325°F (160°C) for about 1 hour.

MICROWAVE METHOD

Vegetable Meat Loaf

Standard	Metric
1-1/2 lb ground beef	750 g ground beef
1/4 cup breadcrumbs	50 ml breadcrumbs
2 eggs	2 eggs
1 tsp Worcestershire sauce	5 ml Worcestershire sauce
1 can mixed vegetables	1 can mixed vegetables
1 can tomatoes	1 can tomatoes

Combine the ground beef, eggs, crumbs and Worcestershire. On a sheet of waxed paper, pat out the mixture into a rectangle 1/2 inch (1.25 cm) thick. Drain the mixed vegetables and spread them on top of the meat mixture, leaving a one inch (2.5 cm) border. Roll up jelly-roll fashion, and seal the ends. Place seam side down in a microwave-safe baking dish. Pour the canned tomatoes on top.

Microwave on HIGH for 5 minutes, then at MEDIUM for 22 minutes. Rotate the dish once during cooking. Let stand 5 minutes before serving.

TOMATO CROWN

Standard	Metric
1 tomato per serving	1 tomato per serving
Fine salt	Fine salt
All-purpose flour	All-purpose flour
2 tbsp vegetable oil	30 ml vegetable oil
Fresh chopped parsley	Fresh chopped parsley
Fried potato rounds	Fried potato rounds

Choose well-shaped tomatoes, and cut in half. Sprinkle with salt and let stand to draw out the moisture. Gently squeeze out the seeds and drain; dry. Dip each half in flour. Brown the tomato halves in hot oil and sprinkle with chopped parsley.

Arrange the tomatoes in the center of a crown of fried potato rounds. Reheat for a few minutes in a 325°F (160°C) oven.

FRESH ASPARAGUS WITH SUNNY VINAIGRETTE

Standard	Metric
24 asparagus	24 asparagus
Juice of 2 lemons	Juice of 2 lemons
1-1/2 cups vinaigrette	375 ml vinaigrette
Juice of 4 oranges	Juice of 4 oranges
Shredded orange peel	Shredded orange peel

Wash the asparagus carefully. Trim off the tough parts and cut to the same length.

Tie the asparagus in bunches of 10 or 12 with string.

Cook standing on end in a large pot of boiling salted water, with the tips above the water level. Cooking time will depend on the age and thickness of the asparagus; it is cooked when the tips are tender to the touch.

Untie the bundles and drain the stalks carefully to avoid breaking the tips. Arrange the stalks on individual plates. Combine the lemon and orange juices with the vinaigrette and pour over the asparagus servings.

Decorate with shreds of orange peel.

Tomato Crown

Dumplings in Maple Syrup

WATER LILY SALAD

Standard
6 hard-boiled eggs
1-1/2 cups diced celery
1-1/2 cups diced cooked
carrots
1-1/2 cups lettuce
Mayonnaise

Metric
6 hard-boiled eggs
375 ml diced celery
375 ml diced cooked
carrots
375 ml lettuce
Mayonnaise

Combine the celery, carrots and lettuce. Blend in the mayonnaise. Season.

Arrange on individual plates. Garnish with watercress or parsley and with hard-boiled eggs trimmed to resemble water lilies.

DUMPLINGS IN MAPLE SYRUP

Standard
2 cups water
1-1/4 cups maple syrup

Metric
500 ml water
300 ml maple syrup

Batter

Standard
1-1/4 cups all-purpose flour
1 tbsp baking powder
1 tbsp sugar
1/2 tsp salt
1/4 cup butter
1/2 cup milk

Metric
300 ml all-purpose flour
15 ml baking powder
15 ml sugar
2 ml salt
50 ml butter
125 ml milk

Combine all the batter ingredients well, and drop by large spoonfuls in the boiling syrup-water mixture. Cover and let simmer for about 15 minutes.

Raspberrries Bavarian

MARKET SALAD

Standard	Metric
1 head iceberg lettuce	1 head iceberg lettuce
1 head chicory	1 head chicory
1 head romaine	1 head romaine
1 bunch watercress	1 bunch watercress
1 minced egg	1 minced egg
1/2 cup French vinaigrette	125 ml French vinaigrette
Chopped parsley or chives	Chopped parsley or chives

Wash the leaves of iceberg lettuce. Wrap them gently in a towel and refrigerate for at least 2 or 3 hours before using.

Remove the green part of the chicory. Wash the white parts and refrigerate the same as the iceberg.

Remove the heart from the romaine. Tear each leaf into two. Wash and refrigerate as the iceberg lettuce.

Clean and wash the watercress. Put it in a glass like a bouquet of flowers and refrigerate.

Crush the chopped hard-boiled egg with a fork and add the vinaigrette and chopped chives or parsley. Mix well.

Arrange the greens in a salad bowl and pour the vinaigrette over. Mix well. Garnish with watercress. Serve.

French Vinaigrette

Standard	Metric
1 tsp Dijon mustard	5 ml Dijon mustard
1 tbsp salt	15 ml salt
2 tsp pepper	10 ml pepper
4 tbsp wine vinegar	60 ml wine vinegar
1/2 cup olive oil	125 ml olive oil

Put all ingredients in a bowl. Beat until mixture is well-combined and creamy. Pour over salad.

RASPBERRIES BAVARIAN

Standard	Metric
1 cup raspberries	250 ml raspberries
1/2 cup sugar	125 ml sugar
2 packages unflavored gelatin diluted in	2 packages unflavored gelatin diluted in
7 tbsp water	105 ml water
Juice 1/2 lemon	Juice 1/2 lemon
1 cup whipped cream	250 ml whipped cream
Salt	Salt

Dissolve the sugar in the raspberries, lemon juice and salt. Add the dissolved gelatin.

Let partially set. Stir in the whipped cream. Turn into individual serving dishes and refrigerate.

GRADUATION DINNER

An easy-to-make menu for a celebratory evening.

Serve with a white Burgundy, champagne.

MENU

Serves 6 to 8

Cheesy Cream Florentine
Cheese Balls
Chicken Kebabs
Herbed Rice Pilaf
Tossed Salad with Lemon Vinaigrette
Caramel Pear Puffs

CHEESY CREAM FLORENTINE

Standard	Metric
3 lb spinach	1.5 kg spinach
4 tbsp butter	60 ml butter
1 cup grated cheddar cheese	250 ml grated cheddar cheese
1 large onion, chopped	1 large onion, chopped
4 tbsp all-purpose flour	60 ml all-purpose flour
4 cups chicken or turkey stock	1 liter chicken or turkey stock
1 cup heavy cream (35%)	250 ml heavy cream (35%)
1 tbsp sugar	15 ml sugar
2 egg yolks	2 egg yolks
Salt and pepper	Salt and pepper

Wash and drain the spinach. Brown the onions in butter in a saucepan and gradually add the spinach. Cook until water has evaporated.

Add the flour, stir and pour in the stock. Season and cook for 30 minutes.

Add 3/4 of the cream and cook gently for 5 minutes. Remove from heat.

Incorporate the egg yolks into the remaining cream and pour into the stock mixture using a wire whisk. Do not boil. Add the grated cheese to the soup. Stir and serve.

CHEESE BALLS

Standard	Metric
1 cup cream cheese	250 ml cream cheese
1 tbsp fresh parsley, chopped	15 ml fresh parsley, chopped
1/4 cup shallots, chopped	50 ml shallots, chopped
2 cloves garlic, chopped	2 cloves garlic, chopped
2 tbsp green bell pepper, chopped	30 ml green bell pepper, chopped
1/4 tsp Worcestershire sauce	2 ml Worcestershire sauce
1/4 tsp paprika	2 ml paprika
1-1/2 cups grated skim milk cheese	375 ml grated skim milk cheese
1/2 cup parsley, chopped	125 ml parsley, chopped
1/2 cup walnuts, chopped	125 ml walnuts, chopped

Place the first seven ingredients in a mixing bowl. Blend with an electric mixer at low speed for 3 minutes. Incorporate the grated cheese. Shape little balls and refrigerate 15 minutes. Combine 1/2 cup (125 ml) chopped parsley, 1/2 cup (125 ml) chopped walnuts. Roll the cheese balls in the nut and parsley. You can also include little bits of shrimp or crab meat.

Serve on a bed of lettuce.

Cheesy Cream Florentine

Chicken Kebabs

CHICKEN KEBABS

Standard	Metric
1 cup vegetable oil	250 ml vegetable oil
1/4 cup soy sauce	50 ml soy sauce
1/4 cup sugar	50 ml sugar
2 tbsp lemon juice	30 ml lemon juice
Garlic salt to taste	Garlic salt to taste
6 chicken breasts, deboned	6 chicken breasts, deboned
Onion wedges	Onion wedges
Pieces of sweet peppers	Pieces of sweet peppers
Tomato wedges	Tomato wedges

Combine the first five ingredients to make a marinade.

Cut the chicken into cubes (not too small) and marinate for 2 hours, turning occasionally.

Slide the chicken pieces onto a skewer, alternating with the onions, peppers and tomatoes. Cook at 350°F (180°C) for 20 minutes. Turn the kebabs after 10 minutes cooking time.

HERBED RICE PILAF

Standard	Metric
1/4 cup butter	50 ml butter
1/2 cup chopped onion	125 ml chopped onion
1-1/2 cups long grain rice	375 ml long grain rice
1-1/4 cups chicken stock	300 ml chicken stock
2-1/2 cups water	625 ml water
1/4 tsp marjoram	1 ml marjoram
1/4 tsp thyme	1 ml thyme
2 tsp salt	10 ml salt
1/4 tsp pepper	1 ml pepper

Melt the butter in a large saucepan. Add the onion and cook over low heat, stirring occasionally.

Add the rice and cook until the grains become golden.

In a separate pot, bring the water and chicken stock to a boil. Pour this mixture onto the rice and add the thyme, marjoram, salt and pepper. Bring to a boil. Reduce the heat. Cover and simmer for 20 minutes until the rice has absorbed all the liquid.

TOSSED SALAD WITH LEMON VINAIGRETTE

1 head lettuce
1 cucumber
1 green bell pepper
1 shallot, chopped
Fresh parsley, chopped

Tear the lettuce into bite-size pieces. Slice the cucumber. Cut the pepper into very thin strips. Place vegetables in a salad bowl.

Vinaigrette

Standard	Metric
3 tbsp lemon juice	45 ml lemon juice
2 tbsp olive oil	30 ml olive oil
1 clove garlic, crushed	1 clove garlic, crushed
1 tbsp mayonnaise	15 ml mayonnaise
Salt and pepper	Salt and pepper

Combine all the ingredients. Mix well and pour required amount over the salad. Toss.

CARAMEL PEAR PUFFS

Standard	Metric
6 ripe pears	6 ripe pears
4 tbsp butter	60 ml butter
6 squares (3 x 3 inches) puff pastry, cooked	6 squares (7.5 x 7.5 cm) puff pastry, cooked
1 cup sugar	250 ml sugar
1 cup orange juice	250 ml orange juice
Juice of one lemon	Juice of one lemon
1 egg yolk	1 egg yolk

Peel, quarter, core and chop the pears.

Melt the butter in a pot. Add the pears and sugar. Cook gently until the sugar caramelizes. Add the orange and lemon juices and cook until liquid forms a syrup.

Brush the puff pastry squares with the beaten egg yolks and glaze in the oven. Cut the pastry in half (separating the top from the bottom) and fill with the pear mixture.

Top with a scoop of vanilla ice cream and raspberry sauce.

Caramel Pear Puffs

CELEBRATORY ENGAGEMENT LUNCHEON

An easy and attractive meal served buffet style.

Serve with a white Bordeaux, dry white wine or Rhine wine, iced Grand Marnier.

MENU

Serves 6 to 8

Leek and Chicken Ring Canapés
Checkerboard Sandwiches
Parmesan Fondue
Buttered Broccoli
Cauliflower and Potato Salad
Grand Marnier Fruit Whip

LEEK AND CHICKEN RING CANAPÉS

Standard	Metric
Puff or shortcrust pastry	Puff or shortcrust pastry
18 leek rings	18 leek rings
1 chicken breast, boned	1 chicken breast, boned
1/2 cup heavy cream (35%)	125 ml heavy cream (35%)
1 egg	1 egg
Salt and pepper	Salt and pepper

Wash the leeks. Trim off the green part. Cut the white part into 3/4 inch (2 cm) lengths. Push out the center of the leeks to form rings about 1/2 inch (1.25 cm) in diameter.

Roll out the pastry dough and use a cookie cutter to make 18 one inch (2.5 cm) circles. Place the leek rings in the center of the pastry. Set aside.

Put the chicken breast through the food processor. Add the egg. Blend 30 seconds. Gradually pour in the cream.

Fill the leek rings with the chicken mixture. Place on a cookie sheet.

Bake at 325°F (160°C) for 15 minutes. If the canapé stuffing starts to rise out of the pastry, simply push back in with your finger. Squares of wax paper placed over the canapés will prevent the stuffing from overflowing.

PARMESAN FONDUE

Standard	Metric
Corn oil	Corn oil
1 lb Gruyère cheese	500 g Gruyère cheese
4 eggs	4 eggs
Pinch of cayenne	Pinch of cayenne
1-1/2 cups all-purpose flour	375 ml all-purpose flour
1-1/2 cups breadcrumbs	375 ml breadcrumbs
Salt and pepper	Salt and pepper

Heat the oil in a deep-fryer to 350°F (180°C).

Grate the cheese and place in a mixing bowl. Add the salt, pepper, cayenne and 1 egg. Mix. Shape this mixture into little balls.

In three different bowls place 3 eggs, the flour and the breadcrumbs. Beat the eggs.

Take each cheese ball and dip into the flour, then into the egg and finally into the breadcrumbs.

Fry for about 2 minutes.

Serve on a plate garnished with carved radishes.

BUTTERED BROCCOLI

Standard	Metric
2 heads of broccoli broken up into flowerets	2 heads of broccoli broken up into flowerets
Lemon juice	Lemon juice
4 tbsp softened butter	60 ml softened butter
Salt and pepper	Salt and pepper

Cook the broccoli in a steamer for about 6 minutes. Add salt and pepper.

Arrange the flowerets on a serving dish and sprinkle with lemon juice. Add the softened butter and garnish with lemon slices.

Leek and Chicken Ring Canapés

CHECKERBOARD SANDWICHES

1 loaf white bread, sliced
1 loaf whole wheat bread, sliced
Sandwich filling (recipe follows)
Ham slices

Step 1

Spread generous amounts of sandwich filling on one side of the slices. Stack the slices, alternating white and whole wheat bread. Refrigerate until filling hardens.

Step 2

Take the striped loaf and trim the crusts to give it a uniform shape. Now cut the loaf lengthwise in 1/2 inch (1 cm) slices. Butter each slice and stack, alternating slices to create a checkerboard effect. Press lightly and refrigerate until filling hardens. Cut into thin slices and serve.

Sandwich Fillings

Cream 1/4 cup (50 ml) butter or cream cheese and add :
1 tbsp (15 ml) chopped parsley and 1 tbsp (15 ml) lemon juice to make parsley filling
or
1 tbsp (15 ml) finely chopped olives and 1/2 tsp (2 ml) lemon juice to make olive filling
or
1 tbsp (15 ml) tomato paste to make tomato filling.
Serve garnished with ham slices or other cold meats.

Technique: Checkerboard Sandwiches

1 Butter the slices of bread with sandwich filling.

2 Stack the slices alternating white and brown bread.

3 Trim the crusts.

4 Press lightly and refrigerate.

5 Cut into even slices.

6 Butter the slices again with sandwich filling.

7 Stack the slices alternating white and whole wheat bread.

8 Slice and serve checkerboard sandwiches.

Checkerboard Sandwiches

CAULIFLOWER AND POTATO SALAD

Standard	Metric
1 cauliflower broken up into flowerets	1 cauliflower broken up into flowerets
6 medium potatoes	6 medium potatoes
1/4 cup chopped leek or onion	50 ml chopped leek or onion
1/2 cup celery, chopped	125 ml celery, chopped
1/2 cup green bell pepper, chopped	125 ml green bell pepper, chopped
Parsley sprigs	Parsley sprigs
6 hard-boiled eggs	6 hard-boiled eggs
3/4 cup mayonnaise	150 ml mayonnaise
Salt and pepper	Salt and pepper

Cook the cauliflower in salted water. Drain. Peel the potatoes, cut into cubes and cook. Drain.

Add the chopped raw vegetables to the mayonnaise. Place the cauliflower and potatoes in a salad bowl. Stir the mayonnaise mixture into the cauliflower and potatoes. Add salt and pepper to taste. Garnish with sliced eggs and parsley sprigs.

GRAND MARNIER FRUIT WHIP

Standard	Metric
2-1/2 cups homemade fruit salad	625 ml homemade fruit salad
2 cups orange juice	500 ml orange juice
Grand Marnier to taste	Grand Marnier to taste
1 cup heavy cream (35%)	250 ml heavy cream (35%)

Prepare a fruit salad. Add sugar and a dash of lemon juice.

Add the orange juice and Grand Marnier.

Whip the cream until firm. Fold the cream into the fruit salad.

Serve in a soup tureen.

Grand Marnier Fruit Whip

ENGAGEMENT DINNER

A fashionable meal featuring delights from the sea.

Serve with a white Burgundy, champagne.

MENU

Serves 6 to 8

Ocean Fish Soup
Coquilles Saint-Jacques
Stuffed Boneless Salmon
Rice Primavera
Braised Leeks and Tomato
Salad with Bacon and Mushrooms
Peachy Cheese Cake

COQUILLES SAINT-JACQUES

Standard	Metric
2 lb scallops	1 kg scallops
1 cup sliced mushrooms	250 ml sliced mushrooms
1/2 cup dry white wine	125 ml dry white wine
3 tbsp butter	45 ml butter
3 tbsp all-purpose flour	45 ml all-purpose flour
6 French shallots, chopped	6 French shallots, chopped
1 cup heavy cream (35%)	250 ml heavy cream (35%)
2 cups grated Gruyère cheese	500 ml grated Gruyère cheese
Salt and pepper	Salt and pepper
Paprika	Paprika

Pour the wine into a large saucepan. Add the scallops, mushrooms and shallots. Boil for 6 or 7 minutes, stirring all the while.

Remove the mushrooms and scallops. Drain and set aside.

Add the cream to the contents of the pot and boil for about 2 minutes.

In the meantime, cream together the butter and flour. Slowly incorporate this mixture into the wine and cream. Continue cooking until mixture thickens.

Remove from heat. Add the scallops and mushrooms to the sauce. Season and stir. Fill scallop shells or individual gratin dishes with sauce.

Cover each serving with the grated Gruyère and sprinkle with paprika. Bake at 400°F (200°C) for 10 to 15 minutes until golden.

OCEAN FISH SOUP

Standard	Metric
1 lb fresh fish filets	500 g fresh fish filets
1 tbsp butter	30 ml butter
1 medium onion, minced	1 medium onion, minced
1/2 cup celery, chopped	125 ml celery, chopped
2 cups raw potatoes, cubed	500 ml raw potatoes, cubed
1/2 cup carrots, sliced	125 ml carrots, sliced
2 cups boiling water	500 ml boiling water
1 tsp salt	5 ml salt
1/8 tsp pepper	0.5 ml pepper
2 cups milk	500 ml milk

Cut the fish into bite-size pieces. Melt butter in a large saucepan and gently brown the onions and celery. Add the potatoes, carrots, water, salt and pepper. Cover and simmer for 10 to 15 minutes until vegetables are tender.

Add the fish and cook for 10 minutes. Add the milk, heat but do not boil.

Coquilles Saint-Jacques

STUFFED BONELESS SALMON

Standard	Metric
12 small salmon slices	12 small salmon slices
Mushroom stuffing	Mushroom stuffing
1-1/2 cups light cream (15%)	375 ml light cream (15%)
Salt and pepper	Salt and pepper
Butter	Butter

Mushroom Stuffing

Standard	Metric
1 onion, minced	1 onion, minced
Butter	Butter
Oil	Oil
2-1/2 cups breadcrumbs	625 ml breadcrumbs
Pinch parsley	Pinch parsley
Pinch mixed herbs	Pinch mixed herbs
1 lb chopped mushrooms	500 g chopped mushrooms
Lemon juice	Lemon juice
1/2 cup light cream (15%)	125 ml light cream (15%)
Salt and pepper	Salt and pepper

Place the fish in a baking dish. Set aside.

Heat a bit of oil and butter in a saucepan. Gently brown the onion. Remove from heat. Add the breadcrumbs, parsley, mushrooms, dash of lemon juice and cream. Mix thoroughly.

Place the stuffing in the center of 6 filets and cover with other slices of fish. Cover with cream. Sprinkle with salt and pepper and dot with butter. Bake at 400°F (200°C) for 20 to 30 minutes. Baste with sauce from time to time.

Stuffed Boneless Salmon

RICE PRIMAVERA

Standard	Metric
1 cup frozen peas	250 ml frozen peas
1/2 cup celery, sliced	125 ml celery, sliced
1-1/2 cups water	375 ml water
2 tbsp butter	30 ml butter
1 tsp salt	5 ml salt
1/2 tsp onion salt	2 ml onion salt
1 shallot	1 shallot
1-1/2 cups minute rice	375 ml minute rice
2 tbsp sweet red or green pepper, chopped	30 ml sweet red or green pepper, chopped

Melt the butter in a medium saucepan. Add the peas, celery, onion salt and water. Bring to a boil. Stir in the rice.

Cover and remove from heat. Let stand 5 minutes. Add the chopped pepper, stir and serve.

BRAISED LEEKS AND TOMATO

Standard	Metric
6 leeks	6 leeks
6 tomatoes	6 tomatoes
2 cups chicken broth	500 ml chicken broth
3 tbsp butter	45 ml butter
Grated Parmesan cheese	Grated Parmesan cheese
Salt and pepper	Salt and pepper

Cut the leeks lengthwise into four pieces but do not cut through the base. Excess greens may be trimmed, washed, chopped and frozen for use in soups.

Remove stems and seeds from the tomatoes and chop. Set aside.

Melt the butter in a large skillet and gently sauté the leeks. Add the tomatoes, season and cook over low heat for 5 minutes.

Add the chicken stock and stir. Place the entire contents of the skillet into a baking dish. Bake at 350°F (180°C) until only 1/2 cup (125 ml) of liquid remains.

Sprinkle with Parmesan and parsley. Serve.

Salad with Bacon and Mushrooms

PEACHY CHEESE CAKE

Standard	Metric
1 white cake	1 white cake
3/4 cup water	150 ml water
1-1/3 cups icing sugar	325 ml icing sugar
4 drops vanilla extract	4 drops vanilla extract
3 tbsp Kirsch	45 ml Kirsch
1 cup heavy cream (35%)	250 ml heavy cream (35%)
1/4 cup raspberry jam	50 ml raspberry jam
1/2 cup cottage cheese	125 ml cottage cheese
1/4 cup raspberries, fresh or frozen	50 ml raspberries, fresh or frozen
1 large can of peaches	1 large can of peaches
1/2 cup cream cheese	125 ml cream cheese

Bake the cake the night before. Cut it into two layers. Prepare a syrup using 3/4 cup (150 ml) water, the sugar, vanilla extract and the Kirsch.

Whip the cream and refrigerate.

Brush both cake layers generously with syrup. Cream the cheese until very soft and ice both layers with it. Spread raspberry jam on the bottom layer. Place the top layer on top and ice the entire cake with generous amounts of whipped cream.

Refrigerate at least two hours. Decorate with raspberries.

Peach Sauce

Drain the peaches and save the liquid. Put the peaches through a blender or food processor. Add the cottage cheese and peach syrup. Blend until smooth and creamy.

Pour the peach sauce onto each plate then top with a piece of cake. Decorate with any leftover peaches.
You can replace the peaches with canned apricots, if desired.

SALAD WITH BACON AND MUSHROOMS

Standard	Metric
1 head Chinese or Romaine lettuce	1 head Chinese or Romaine lettuce
4 cups sliced mushrooms	1 liter sliced mushrooms
12 slices bacon, chopped	12 slices bacon, chopped
1/2 cup vegetable oil	125 ml vegetable oil
1 tbsp Dijon mustard	15 ml Dijon mustard
5 tbsp red wine vinegar	75 ml red wine vinegar
1 tsp tarragon	5 ml tarragon
Salt and pepper	Salt and pepper

Wash and tear up the lettuce. Place in a large salad bowl with the mushrooms.

Fry the bacon till crisp. Drain on a paper towel to remove fat.

Add the bacon to the salad. Mix all the remaining ingredients in a small mixing bowl, using a wire whisk. Pour over the salad. Sprinkle with garlic-flavored croutons. Toss and serve.

Peachy Cheese Cake

WEDDING DAY BRUNCH

A perfect menu for starting off a perfect day.

Serve with a sparkling rosé or champagne.

MENU

Serves 6 to 8

Jam-Filled Brioche Croissants
Almond and Honey Pancakes
Quiche Royale
Grand Marnier Seafood Casserole
Lettuce and Cantaloupe Salad
Potato Salad Forestière
Orange Glazed Angel Food Cake

ALMOND AND HONEY PANCAKES

Standard	Metric
1-1/4 cups all-purpose flour	300 ml all-purpose flour
3 tbsp sugar	45 ml sugar
1-1/4 tbsp baking powder	20 ml baking powder
3/4 tsp salt	3 ml salt
4 tbsp ground almonds	60 ml ground almonds
1 handful raisins	1 handful raisins
1 beaten egg	1 beaten egg
1-1/4 cups milk	300 ml milk
2 tbsp melted butter	30 ml melted butter
1/4 tsp vanilla	1 ml vanilla
4 tbsp honey	60 ml honey

Combine the flour, sugar, baking powder, almonds and salt.

Mix the egg, milk, melted butter, vanilla extract and warm honey in a small mixing bowl. Make a well in the center of the dry ingredients and incorporate egg mixture. Use swift, vigorous strokes. Add the raisins.

Cook four pancakes at a time using about 4 tbsp (60 ml) batter for each one. Oil the skillet only once at the beginning. Cook until small bubbles appear on the surface of each pancake and the bottom is lightly browned. Turn over and cook the other side.

Serve with maple syrup, honey or jam.

JAM-FILLED BRIOCHE CROISSANTS

Brioche batter (see page 44,
Brioche with Raspberry
Topping)
Jam or marmalade
2 egg yolks beaten with milk
Sugar

Let the batter stand 24 hours in the refrigerator. Roll it out to 1/8 inch (3mm) thickness and cut into triangles, 4 inches (10 cm) at base.

At the center of each triangle, place 1 tbsp (15 ml) of jam or marmalade. Roll each triangle from the base to the point, so that the top of the triangle ends up on the top of the croissant.

Place the croissants on a cookie sheet covered with lightly greased wax paper. Cover and allow to rise for 40 minutes. Brush with the egg yolk and milk mixture, being careful not to flatten the croissants.

Sprinkle the croissants with a bit of sugar and bake at 350°F (180°C) for 35 to 40 minutes. Makes 12 croissants.

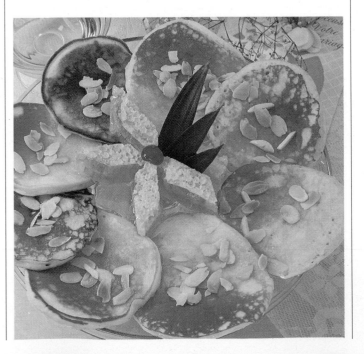

Almond and Honey Pancakes

QUICHE ROYALE

Standard	Metric
Shortcrust pastry for 1 9-inch pie shell, chilled	Shortcrust pastry for 1 22 cm pie shell, chilled
1 cup grated cheddar or mozzarella cheese	250 ml grated cheddar or mozzarella cheese
1 cup heavy cream (35%)	250 ml heavy cream (35%)
2 eggs	2 eggs
1 egg yolk	1 egg yolk
1/2 cup mushrooms, sliced	125 ml mushrooms, sliced
1/2 cup cooked ham, cubed	125 ml cooked ham, cubed
3/4 cup peppers or olives, chopped	150 ml peppers or olives, chopped
2 shallots, chopped	2 shallots, chopped
Sweet basil, salt and pepper	Sweet basil, salt and pepper
1 tbsp oil	15 ml oil

Preheat the oven to 375°F (190°C). Line a pie plate with the pastry dough. Cover the bottom with 3/4 cup (150 ml) cheese.

In a bowl beat the whole eggs and the egg yolk. Add the cream and beat again. Add the seasonings. In a skillet, heat the oil and fry the ham, shallots, mushrooms and peppers over high heat for 5 minutes.

Remove from heat. Pour this mixture into the pie shell covered with cheese. Cover with the egg and cream mixture. Sprinkle the remaining 1/4 cup (50 ml) cheese over the quiche.

Bake for 25 minutes until quiche is golden brown.

LETTUCE AND CANTALOUPE SALAD

Standard	Metric
2 heads Boston or bib lettuce	2 heads Boston or bib lettuce
Juice of one lemon	Juice of one lemon
6 tbsp sour cream	90 ml sour cream
3 tbsp chives, chopped	45 ml chives, chopped
1 cantaloupe	1 cantaloupe
Salt and pepper	Salt and pepper

Delicately tear up the lettuce. Mix the lemon juice, sour cream, salt, pepper and chives in the bottom of a salad bowl. Add the lettuce and toss gently.

Cut the cantaloupe in two, remove the seeds and cut each half into four. Peel the melon and use a potato peeler to cut the rest of the fruit into ribbons.

Arrange the cantaloupe ribbons on top of the salad.

GRAND MARNIER SEAFOOD CASSEROLE

Standard	Metric
1/2 cup butter	125 ml butter
1/2 cup all-purpose flour	125 ml all-purpose flour
2 cups milk	500 ml milk
1/4 cup orange juice	50 ml orange juice
1 lb cooked shrimp	500 g cooked shrimp
1 lb lobster or crab meat	500 g lobster or crab meat
4 tbsp Grand Marnier	60 ml Grand Marnier
Grated cheese	Grated cheese

Melt the butter in a saucepan. Add the flour, stir and cook for about 5 minutes. Remove from heat. Gradually add the milk and blend until smooth. Reheat until mixture thickens.

Add the seafood, the Grand Marnier and the orange juice. Pour into individual baking dishes.

Sprinkle each serving with grated cheese and bake at 425°F (220°C) for a few minutes. Decorate with orange quarters.

POTATO SALAD FORESTIÈRE

Standard	Metric
8 potatoes	8 potatoes
1/2 lb smoked pork	250 g smoked pork
1 carrot, grated	1 carrot, grated
1 celery stalk, diced	1 celery stalk, diced
3 shallots, chopped	3 shallots, chopped
Green pepper, chopped	Green pepper, chopped
3 tbsp parsley, chopped	45 ml parsley, chopped
2 or 3 radishes, chopped	2 or 3 radishes, chopped
3 tbsp mayonnaise	45 ml mayonnaise
Salt and pepper	Salt and pepper

Peel the potatoes and boil. Cool and cut into cubes. Place in a salad bowl. Add the carrot, celery, shallots, peppers, radishes, mayonnaise and chopped parsley. Season to taste.

Cut the pork into 1 x 1/4 inch (2.5 cm x 5 mm) pieces. Sauté over high heat, drain and add to the potato salad.

Toss and serve.

FILET MIGNON WITH STUFFED PRUNES

Standard	Metric
One 8 oz filet mignon per person	One 250 g filet mignon per person
2 tbsp butter	30 ml butter
12 prunes	12 prunes
1 tbsp liver pâté	15 ml liver pâté
1 glass Port	1 glass Port
1 tbsp all-purpose flour	15 ml all-purpose flour
Salt and pepper	Salt and pepper

Soak the prunes in warm water for several hours until plump.

Brown the filet mignon in butter in a hot skillet. Reduce heat. Add salt and pepper and sprinkle with flour. Add the Port and simmer gently for 10 minutes.

In the meantime, dry the prunes and remove the pit with a pointed knife. Stuff the prunes with the liver pâté.

Place the prunes around the filet mignon during the last 5 minutes of cooking time.

As soon as the sauce begins to thicken, place the filet mignon on a plate with the prunes. Cover with sauce and serve.

TOMATO-STUFFED ZUCCHINI

Standard	Metric
4 medium zucchini	4 medium zucchini
2 tomatoes	2 tomatoes
1/2 onion	1/2 onion
1 tbsp sugar	15 ml sugar
1 tbsp chopped parsley	15 ml chopped parsley
Pinch thyme	Pinch thyme
1 tbsp tomato paste	15 ml tomato paste
Salt and pepper	Salt and pepper

Wash and dry the zucchini and cut off both ends. Use a fork to score the sides. Slice the zucchini into 2 inch (5 cm) pieces. Boil for 4 minutes in salted water. Run the zucchini under cold water to cool.

Spoon out the inside of the zucchini. Place the pulp into a blender with all the remaining ingredients. Blend until mixture has liquefied.

Cook this sauce in a saucepan until it thickens.

Fill the zucchini with the mixture. Bake for 5 minutes at 350°F (180°C).

Grated cheese or breadcrumbs may be sprinkled over the top.

POTATOES MAÎTRE D'HÔTEL

Standard	Metric
8 unpeeled potatoes	8 unpeeled potatoes
4 tbsp melted butter	60 ml melted butter
1 tbsp chopped parsley	15 ml chopped parsley
1 tbsp chopped chives	15 ml chopped chives
Salt and pepper	Salt and pepper

Boil the potatoes in their jackets until tender. Drain and place them in a heavy pot over low heat to dry.

Peel the potatoes and place in a serving dish. Add the butter, parsley, chives, salt and pepper.

TANGY GREEN SALAD WITH GARLIC CROUTONS

Standard	Metric
1 Boston or bib lettuce	1 Boston or bib lettuce
4 shallots, chopped	4 shallots, chopped
4 tbsp plain yogurt or mayonnaise	60 ml plain yogurt or mayonnaise
2 tsp lemon juice	10 ml lemon juice
3 tbsp chopped parsley	45 ml chopped parsley
Salt and pepper	Salt and pepper

Place all the ingredients in a large salad bowl. Toss.

Take several slices of stale bread and rub them with a clove of garlic. Brush the slices with oil and vinegar and serve with the salad.

Tangy Green Salad with Garlic Croutons

Filet Mignon with Stuffed Prunes

ENCHANTED FOREST LEMON CAKE

Standard	Metric
1 cup pastry flour	250 ml pastry flour
1 tsp baking powder	5 ml baking powder
1/4 tsp salt	1 ml salt
2 egg yolks	2 egg yolks
1/2 cup cold water	125 ml cold water
1 tsp grated lemon rind	5 ml grated lemon rind
3/4 cup sugar	150 ml sugar
2 egg whites	2 egg whites
1 tsp lemon juice	5 ml lemon juice
2 tbsp sugar	30 ml sugar

Sift the flour, baking powder and salt 3 times.

Beat the egg yolks until foamy. Add the water and grated lemon rind and continue beating until mixture becomes foamier. Gradually add the sugar, stirring vigorously. Incorporate the flour, 2 tbsp (30 ml) at a time.

Beat the egg whites until stiff. Add the lemon juice and 2 tbsp (30 ml) sugar. Gently fold into the batter.

Pour the batter into two 8 inch (20 cm) well-greased cake pans. Bake at 350 °F (180°C) 25 minutes. Ice with lemon mousse and serve with lemon mousse sauce.

Lemon Mousse

Standard	Metric
1 cup sugar	250 ml sugar
5 tbsp pastry flour	75 ml pastry flour
1 beaten egg	1 beaten egg
3 tbsp butter	45 ml butter
1/3 cup lemon juice, fresh or bottled	75 ml lemon juice, fresh or bottled
1 cup water	250 ml water
1 tsp grated lemon rind	5 ml grated lemon rind
1 cup heavy cream (35%)	250 ml heavy cream (35%)

Combine the flour and sugar. Incorporate the beaten egg, lemon juice, water and butter. Mix well. Cook in a double boiler for ten minutes, stirring constantly. Remove from heat. Cool.

Once the mixture has cooled add the grated lemon rind. Whip the cream until stiff and add 1/4 cup (50 ml) to mixture. Stir.

Ice both layers with half of the lemon mousse. Add 3/4 cup (150 ml) whipped cream to what is left of the mousse and serve as sauce.

SILVER ANNIVERSARY DINNER

Featuring two elegant desserts that are remarkably easy to prepare.

Serve with a white Bordeaux, red Burgundy, sparkling rosé or champagne.

MENU

Serves 6 to 8

Tomato Consommé
Stuffed Zucchini with Cheese
Veal Pot Roast with Creamed Shallots
Potatoes in Ale
Cauliflower and Broccoli au Gratin
Rum Cake
Floating Island with Candied Fruit

Tomato Consommé

TOMATO CONSOMMÉ

Standard	Metric
4 cups chicken stock	1 liter chicken stock
4 fresh or canned tomatoes	4 fresh or canned tomatoes
1 lightly beaten egg white	1 lightly beaten egg white
1 tsp lemon juice	5 ml lemon juice
Parsley, thyme	Parsley, thyme
1 bay leaf	1 bay leaf
Salt and pepper	Salt and pepper

Place all the ingredients in a pot. Bring to a boil, stirring occasionally. Cover and simmer for about 1 hour, over low heat. Do not stir.

Pour the contents of the pot through a strainer, mashing the tomatoes.

Reheat. Garnish the consommé with parsley. Serve hot with rusks.

MICROWAVE METHOD

Stuffed Zucchini

Cut the zucchini lengthwise and arrange them in a glass dish. Cover and cook at HIGH for 4 to 6 minutes until tender. Scoop out the zucchini and add the pulp to the onion, salt, beaten eggs and breadcrumbs. Mix. Place mixture in separate dish and cook at HIGH for 12 minutes, stirring three times during cooking time. Fill the hollowed zucchini with this stuffing. Sprinkle with cheese and breadcrumbs. Cook at HIGH for 1 or 2 minutes until cheese has melted.

STUFFED ZUCCHINI WITH CHEESE

Standard	Metric
4 or 5 medium zucchini	4 or 5 medium zucchini
1 large onion, chopped	1 large onion, chopped
1 clove garlic, chopped	1 clove garlic, chopped
12 sprigs parsley or	12 sprigs parsley or
1/2 cup dried parsley	125 ml dried parsley
2 tsp olive or other oil	10 ml olive or other oil
1 tsp oregano	5 ml oregano
1 tsp salt	5 ml salt
Pinch pepper	Pinch pepper
1/2 cup Parmesan cheese	125 ml Parmesan cheese
3 beaten eggs	3 beaten eggs
1/3 cup whole wheat breadcrumbs	75 ml whole wheat breadcrumbs

Wash and cook the zucchini whole in very little boiling water for 5 minutes. Drain and cool. Cut them in half, lengthwise, and hollow out the zucchini leaving 1/4 inch (5 mm) of flesh.

Chop the pulp and sauté in oil with the onion, garlic, salt, pepper, cheese, eggs and breadcrumbs. Sprinkle salt on the hollowed out zucchini and fill with the stuffing.

Sprinkle with breadcrumbs and place on a baking dish. Cover and bake for 45 minutes at 350°F (180°C). Serve with a tomato sauce or as is with a bit of butter.

Veal Pot Roast with Creamed Shallots

POTATOES IN ALE

Standard	Metric
6 to 8 unpeeled new potatoes	6 to 8 unpeeled new potatoes
3 tbsp butter	45 ml butter
3 tbsp fresh parsley, chopped	45 ml fresh parsley, chopped
Pinch thyme	Pinch thyme
1 tbsp tarragon	15 ml tarragon
1-1/2 cups beer	375 ml beer
Juice of one lemon	Juice of one lemon
2 cloves garlic, chopped	2 cloves garlic, chopped

Partially cook the potatoes in salted water. Drain and peel. Cut into slices or cubes. Place in a pot with the beer, butter, lemon juice, thyme and tarragon.

Simmer until the liquid has evaporated. Add the parsley and garlic. Place in a serving dish.

VEAL POT ROAST WITH CREAMED SHALLOTS

Standard	Metric
1 veal roast, about 4 lb	1 veal roast, about 2 kg
6 cloves garlic	6 cloves garlic
1/2 cup butter	125 ml butter
2 tbsp all-purpose flour	30 ml all-purpose flour
30 French shallots, whole and peeled	30 French shallots, whole and peeled
1 tbsp paprika	15 ml paprika
1 onion, minced	1 onion, minced
1-1/2 cups chicken stock	375 ml chicken stock
Salt and pepper	Salt and pepper

Stick the roast with the garlic. Brush with half the butter and sprinkle with paprika, salt and pepper. Place the roast in a covered cast iron pot. Place in the oven and cook at 350°F (180°C) for 1 hour. Remove and add the chopped onion and shallots. Cook for another 30 minutes. Take out the roast and place on a serving dish. Return to oven, set at minimum. Sprinkle the onion and shallots with flour, mix well. Place the pot on the stove and add the chicken stock. Simmer until sauce becomes quite thick.

Carve the roast and serve with the creamed shallot sauce.

CAULIFLOWER AND BROCCOLI AU GRATIN

Standard	Metric
1 cauliflower	1 cauliflower
1 broccoli	1 broccoli
2 cups milk	500 ml milk
5 tbsp butter	75 ml butter
3 tbsp all-purpose flour	45 ml all-purpose flour
1 cup grated cheese	250 ml grated cheese
Salt, pepper, nutmeg, paprika and breadcrumbs	Salt, pepper, nutmeg, paprika and breadcrumbs

Break the cauliflower and broccoli into flowerets. First cook the cauliflower in a double boiler then do the broccoli the same way. Drain and arrange both vegetables in a baking dish, in alternating colors. Add salt and pepper.

Melt the butter in a saucepan. Add the flour and mix well. Gradually add the milk. Cook for 5 minutes over low heat, stirring constantly. The sauce should be very thick.

Pour the sauce over the vegetables. Cover with grated cheese and sprinkle with paprika and breadcrumbs. Place the dish under the broiler until golden brown.

Rum Cake

Standard
30 Graham crackers
2 tsp strong coffee
2 tsp sugar
3 tbsp rum
2 cups heavy cream (35%)

Metric
30 Graham crackers
10 ml strong coffee
10 ml sugar
45 ml rum
500 ml heavy cream (35%)

Place two layers of Graham crackers on a serving plate. Mix the rum, sugar and coffee and pour over the layers. Cover with a coat of cream. Add another layer of Graham crackers and cream and continue stacking these layers until all the biscuits are gone. Whip the remaining cream and use this to ice the cake.

Decorate with cherries or chopped nuts. Refrigerate for 2 hours before serving.

Floating Island with Candied Fruit

Standard
8 egg whites
1/2 cup sugar
Pinch salt
1/2 cup candied fruit

Metric
8 egg whites
125 ml sugar
Pinch salt
125 ml candied fruit

Whip the egg whites into stiff peaks, gradually adding the sugar and salt once the egg whites begin to stiffen.

Butter a pyrex cake pan and cover the bottom with the candied fruit. Cover with the beaten egg whites. Place the cake mold in a pan of water and bake at 250°F-300°F (120°C-150°C) for 30 to 40 minutes. Meringue is done when an inserted toothpick comes out clean.

Turn out of mold immediately and cover with custard sauce.

Custard Sauce

Standard
8 egg yolks
3/4 cup sugar
2 cups milk
1/2 tsp vanilla extract

Metric
8 egg yolks
150 ml sugar
500 ml milk
2 ml vanilla extract

Beat the egg yolks and sugar until creamy.

Pour the milk into a saucepan. Add the vanilla extract and bring to a boil. Cool slightly. Pour half this mixture into the eggs and sugar and mix well. Pour the milk, eggs and sugar mixture back into the saucepan. Cook over low heat, stirring constantly. The custard should thicken but not boil.

Remove from heat and pour over the fruity meringue.

Floating Island with Candied Fruit

SILVER ANNIVERSARY DINNER II

This eye-catching main course couldn't be easier.

Serve with a Chardonnay wine, and Spanish coffee with dessert.

MENU

Serves 6 to 8

Sultan's Soup
Chicken and Scallop Papillote
Salmon and Sole Trellises
Steamed Potatoes
Braised Endives
Savory Mixed Vegetable Salad
Charlotte Russe au Café

Chicken and Scallop Papillote

SULTAN'S SOUP

Standard	Metric
1 cup very fine noodles	250 ml very fine noodles
4 cups beef consommé	1 liter beef consommé
2 tbsp melted butter	30 ml melted butter
1 tbsp all-purpose flour	15 ml all-purpose flour
2 tbsp sharp cheese	30 ml sharp cheese
2 egg yolks	2 egg yolks
1 cup heavy cream (35%)	250 ml heavy cream (35%)
Salt and pepper	Salt and pepper

Bring the consommé to a boil and add the noodles. Simmer for 10 minutes until noodles are done.

In a small saucepan, melt the butter and add the flour and cheese. Mix well. Add this mixture to the consommé and continue simmering for 15 minutes, stirring often.

Beat together the cream and egg yolks. Add salt and pepper. Stir the cream and eggs into the consommé, stirring constantly. Do not boil.

Serve with a little bowl of grated sharp cheese.

MICROWAVE METHOD

Noodles

Heat water at HIGH in a covered microwave dish or container for 10 to 12 minutes, adding 1 tsp (5 ml) salt and 1 tbsp (15 ml) vegetable oil. Add the noodles and cook at LOW for 9 to 10 minutes.

CHICKEN AND SCALLOP PAPILLOTE

Standard	Metric
4 chicken breasts, boned	4 chicken breasts, boned
1-1/2 cups scallops	375 ml scallops
1 small carrot	1 small carrot
1 celery stalk	1 celery stalk
2 leeks, white part only	2 leeks, white part only
1 cup thinly sliced mushrooms	250 ml thinly sliced mushrooms
1 cup chicken stock	250 ml chicken stock
5 tbsp chopped parsley	75 ml chopped parsley
Salt and pepper	Salt and pepper

Mince the chicken and scallops and set aside in a bowl. Add salt and pepper.

Sauté the mushrooms in butter. Place with the chicken and scallops.

Cut the vegetables into julienne slices and cook for 2 minutes in boiling water. Drain and add them to the previous mixture.

Mix all the ingredients, add seasoning and place on a sheet of aluminum foil. Add a little more stock to the papillote and seal. Bake at 400°F (200°C) for 20 to 30 minutes. Use scissors to open the aluminum wrap.

SALMON AND SOLE TRELLISES

Standard	Metric
3 sole filets, 8 to 10 oz each	3 sole filets, 250 g each
3 slices of salmon, 6 oz apiece	3 slices of salmon, 175 g apiece
1/4 cup shallots, chopped	50 ml shallots, chopped
1-1/2 cups heavy cream (35%)	375 ml heavy cream (35%)
1/4 cup butter	50 ml butter
2 tsp sweet basil	10 ml sweet basil
3/4 cup dry white wine	150 ml dry white wine
Juice of half a lemon	Juice of half a lemon

Cut filets and slices into four long strips. Weave the strips together as illustrated, combining sole and salmon. Cut each trellis in half.

Butter a baking dish and sprinkle with the shallots. Place the fish trellises on the shallots and add the wine. Bake at 350°F (180°C) for 10 minutes.

Remove the fish from the baking dish and keep warm. Pour the wine and shallot and fish stock into a saucepan. Add the lemon juice and bring to a boil. Add the cream and basil and cook gently until the sauce thickens. Pour this sauce on to individual serving plates. Place the salmon and sole trellises on the plates. Serve immediately.

STEAMED POTATOES

Standard	Metric
8 potatoes	8 potatoes
Salt	Salt
1/4 cup butter	50 ml butter
Juice of one lemon	Juice of one lemon
5 tbsp chives, chopped	75 ml chives, chopped

Peel the potatoes and cut into quarters. Place in a steamer and cook for about 10 minutes.

In the meantime, melt the butter and add the lemon juice. Place the potatoes in a serving dish and top with the lemon butter. Sprinkle with chives. Add salt to taste. Mix gently and serve. May be served with any type of fish.

BRAISED ENDIVES

Standard	Metric
8 endives	8 endives
Juice of one lemon	Juice of one lemon
2 cups chicken stock	500 ml chicken stock
Salt and pepper	Salt and pepper

Braise the endives in butter until all sides are lightly browned. Add the lemon juice and chicken stock. Place the contents of the skillet in a baking dish. Bake for 45 minutes at 350°F (180°C). Drain well and serve with a bit of the cooking juices.

Salmon and Sole Trellises, Steamed Potatoes, and Braised Endives

Savory Mixed Vegetable Salad

SAVORY MIXED VEGETABLE SALAD

Standard	Metric
1/2 lb cooked green beans	250 ml cooked green beans
1/2 lb cooked wax beans	250 ml cooked wax beans
1 broccoli, cut into flowerets, cooked for 3 minutes	1 broccoli, cut into flowerets, cooked for 3 minutes
3 cooked potatoes, peeled and still warm	3 cooked potatoes, peeled and still warm
3 tomatoes, quartered	3 tomatoes, quartered
1 sweet red pepper, chopped	1 sweet red pepper, chopped
1 hollowed out cucumber, seeds removed, chopped	1 hollowed out cucumber, seeds removed, chopped
15 pitted black olives	15 pitted black olives
Chinese or Romaine lettuce leaves, washed and dried	Chinese or Romaine lettuce leaves, washed and dried
Salt and pepper	Salt and pepper

Vinaigrette

Standard	Metric
1 tbsp Dijon mustard	15 ml Dijon mustard
1 tbsp chopped parsley	15 ml chopped parsley
1 clove garlic, minced	1 clove garlic, minced
1/4 cup wine vinegar	50 ml wine vinegar
3/4 cup olive oil	150 ml olive oil
Salt and pepper	Salt and pepper
Lemon juice	Lemon juice

Place the first set of ingredients, except the lettuce, in a large salad bowl.

Using a wire whisk, mix the mustard, parsley, garlic, vinegar, salt and pepper. Continue mixing and add the oil drop by drop until mixture takes on the consistency of mayonnaise. The oil may then be poured faster. Check the seasoning and add the lemon juice. Pour this vinaigrette onto the salad; mix thoroughly. Let the salad stand for 7 to 8 minutes. Serve on a bed of lettuce leaves.

CHARLOTTE RUSSE AU CAFÉ

Standard	Metric
1 envelope unflavored gelatin	1 envelope unflavored gelatin
1/2 cup sugar	125 ml sugar
1/8 tsp salt	0.5 ml salt
2 tbsp instant coffee crystals	30 ml instant coffee crystals
1-1/4 cups milk	300 ml milk
2 egg yolks	2 egg yolks
2 egg whites	2 egg whites
1/2 tsp vanilla extract	2 ml vanilla extract
1 cup heavy cream (35%)	250 ml heavy cream (35%)
8 to 12 lady fingers	8 to 12 lady fingers

Mix together 1/4 cup (50 ml) sugar, the gelatin, salt and coffee. Place in a double boiler. Beat the egg yolks and milk and add to the first mixture. Cook for 5 minutes, stirring constantly until gelatin has dissolved. Remove from heat and add the vanilla extract. Refrigerate until mixture begins to set.

Whip the egg whites until stiff, gradually beating in 1/4 cup (50 ml) sugar. Fold gently into gelatin mixture. Fold in the whipped cream.

Line a buttered Charlotte mold, or individual molds, with lady fingers. Pour gelatin mixture into the mold.

Refrigerate for 4 to 12 hours. Serve garnished with whipped cream.

GOLDEN ANNIVERSARY BUFFET

An easy buffet with some variations on old favorites.

Serve with rosé, white Bordeaux, sparkling wine.

MENU

Serves 6 to 8

Sandwich Log
Cheese Bombe with Calvados
Veal Meatballs in Tomato Sauce
Rice Pilaf Ring with Creamed Spinach
Hearty Mironton Salad
White Chocolate Dream Cake

SANDWICH LOG

Standard	Metric
1 loaf unsliced white bread	1 loaf unsliced white bread
1/2 lb cooked ham or chicken, minced	250 g cooked ham or chicken, minced
1 tbsp prepared mustard	15 ml prepared mustard
4 tbsp mayonnaise	60 ml mayonnaise
Seasoning	Seasoning
1 package of cream cheese	1 package of cream cheese

Combine the ham or chicken, mustard and mayonnaise. This sandwich filling should have a fairly smooth consistency. Season to taste and set aside.

Cut the loaf of bread lengthwise into 5 to 7 slices. Spread the sandwich filling on each slice.

Place the slices side by side on a damp cloth. Roll the slices as if they were one large sheet of bread and form a log. Wrap this log in the damp cloth and set aside for about 30 minutes.

Unwrap and cut the ends on a slant. Ice the log with softened cream cheese mixed with a dollop of mayonnaise. Decorate with red or green pepper slices. Sprinkle with paprika.

CHEESE BOMBE WITH CALVADOS

Standard	Metric
1 lb cream cheese	500 g cream cheese
1 lb grated Gruyère	500 g grated Gruyère
4 tbsp Calvados	60 ml Calvados
1 envelope unflavored gelatin	1 envelope unflavored gelatin

Cream both cheeses and the calvados in the food processor.

Oil the sides and bottom of a plastic mold. Place the cheese mixture into the mold and refrigerate for 4 to 5 hours.

Turn out the mold by first placing it in hot water. Place the bombe on a serving plate and refrigerate.

Prepare the gelatin according to package instructions. Refrigerate until the gelatin begins to set. Use a plastic spatula to cover the bombe with the gelatin.

Decorate with shredded carrot, leek rings and parsley sprigs.

VEAL MEATBALLS IN TOMATO SAUCE

Standard	Metric
1/4 cup salt pork, diced	50 ml salt pork, diced
1/2 pound ground veal	250 g ground veal
1/2 tsp salt	2 ml salt
1 tbsp parsley	15 ml parsley
1 beaten egg	1 beaten egg
2 tbsp milk	30 ml milk
1 onion, sliced	1 onion, sliced
1/4 cup celery, chopped	50 ml celery, chopped
3 tbsp all-purpose flour	45 ml all-purpose flour
1-1/2 cups canned tomatoes	375 ml canned tomatoes
1 tbsp sugar	15 ml sugar

Sauté the salt pork. Drain and save the fat. Combine the veal, salt, parsley, beaten egg, milk and salt pork.

Mix thoroughly and shape into small meatballs. Dredge the meatballs in flour.

Brown the meatballs in pork fat. Add the onion and celery and the flour. Mix well. Add the tomatoes and sugar. Cook over medium heat for 25 minutes.

Cheese Bombe with Calvados

RICE PILAF RING WITH CREAMED SPINACH

Standard	Metric
1-1/2 cups long grain rice	375 ml long grain rice
2 tbsp butter	30 ml butter
2 tbsp onion, finely chopped	30 ml onion, finely chopped
2 cups chicken stock, hot	500 ml chicken stock, hot
1/2 tsp chervil	2 ml chervil
Pinch thyme	Pinch thyme
1 bay leaf	1 bay leaf
10 oz spinach	280 g spinach
Salt and pepper	Salt and pepper

Heat the oven to 350°F (180°C). Place the rice in a strainer and rinse under cold running water for a few minutes. Drain and set aside.

Melt the butter in a heavy casserole dish. Over medium heat, sauté the onions. Add the rice and herbs and cook for 2 to 3 minutes stirring frequently. Do not brown the rice.

Pour in the chicken stock and bring to a boil. Cover and place the casserole in the oven. Bake for 18 to 20 minutes until the rice has absorbed all the liquid. Place the rice pilaf in a tube mold. Pack firmly and turn out onto a serving plate.

Garnish the inside of the ring with spinach cooked in butter. Pour a cheese béchamel sauce over the spinach (see section on sauces).

WHITE CHOCOLATE DREAM CAKE

Standard	Metric
6 egg yolks	6 egg yolks
6 egg whites	6 egg whites
1 tbsp sugar	15 ml sugar
2 cups white chocolate	500 ml white chocolate
7 tbsp sugar	105 ml sugar
1 cup butter	250 ml butter
Pinch salt	Pinch salt
3 tbsp all-purpose flour	45 ml all-purpose flour
Dark chocolate shavings	Dark chocolate shavings
Custard sauce	Custard sauce

Cut the white chocolate into small pieces. Place in the top of a double boiler with the butter and melt.

Whip the egg yolks and sugar for 6 minutes with an electric mixer. Incorporate the flour and the melted chocolate mixture. Stir well.

Whip the egg whites until stiff, adding the salt and 1 tbsp (15 ml) sugar as the whites begin to foam. Fold the egg whites into previous mixture.

Pour this mixture into a greased and floured cake pan. Bake at 325°F (160°C) for 35 minutes. Decorate with dark chocolate shavings and serve with custard sauce (see page 160, Fruity Meringue with Custard Sauce).

HEARTY MIRONTON SALAD

Standard	Metric
8 unpeeled potatoes	8 unpeeled potatoes
3 carrots, diced	3 carrots, diced
1-1/2 lb stewing beef (blade cut)	750 g stewing beef (blade cut)
1/4 cup parsley	50 ml parsley
1 onion, chopped	1 onion, chopped
2 cloves garlic, chopped	2 cloves garlic, chopped
3 cups beef stock	750 ml beef stock
1/4 cup pickles, sliced	50 ml pickles, sliced
3 tbsp Dijon mustard	45 ml Dijon mustard
3/4 cup oil	150 ml oil
1/4 cup vinegar	50 ml vinegar

Boil the beef cubes in the stock, until meat is well done. Add water if necessary. Cook the potatoes in salted boiling water. Drain, peel and cut into cubes.

Cook the carrots in the leftover beef stock. Remove and drain. Place the potatoes, carrots, onion and pickles in a salad bowl. Shred the beef and add to the salad.

Mix together the mustard, garlic, parsley and vinegar. Gradually add the oil, using a wire whisk. Pour the vinaigrette over the salad. Toss and serve.

White Chocolate Dream Cake

GOLDEN ANNIVERSARY DINNER

This Beef Stroganoff recipe is unbelievably tasty.

Serve with a full-bodied red wine and champagne.

Asparagus Feuilleté

CREAM OF ZUCCHINI SOUP

Standard	Metric
1-1/2 lb zucchini, cubed	750 g zucchini, cubed
1 onion, chopped	1 onion, chopped
1 carrot, diced	1 carrot, diced
1 small celery stalk, diced	1 small celery stalk, diced
1/4 cup parsley, chopped	50 ml parsley, chopped
2 tbsp all-purpose flour	30 ml all-purpose flour
2 cups cold milk	500 ml cold milk
1 cup chicken stock	250 ml chicken stock
2 tbsp butter	30 ml butter
Salt and pepper	Salt and pepper

Melt the butter in a large saucepan. Add the onion, carrot, celery and zucchini. Cover and cook over low heat for 7 minutes. Add the flour and stir for 1 minute. Gradually add the milk and the chicken stock and bring to a boil, stirring frequently. Simmer for 30 minutes.

Pour the contents of the saucepan into a blender and liquefy. Season and reheat if necessary. Sprinkle with parsley and serve.

SNOW PEAS AND CORN

Standard	Metric
3 cups snow peas	350 g snow peas
1 cup canned corn kernels, drained	125 g canned corn kernels, drained
1 onion, chopped	1 onion, chopped
1/4 cup butter	50 ml butter

Boil the snow peas in salted water for 3 minutes. Run under cold water to cool. Drain.

Melt the butter in a saucepan, add the corn and chopped onion and sauté for 5 minutes. Add the snow peas. Stir, heat and serve.

ASPARAGUS FEUILLETÉ

Standard	Metric
1 lb puff pastry	500 g puff pastry
2 lb asparagus	1 kg asparagus
1 cup mayonnaise	250 ml mayonnaise
3 tbsp chopped parsley	45 ml chopped parsley

Cut and discard tough ends of asparagus. Boil or steam the asparagus until tender. Run them under cold water to cool. Drain and set aside.

Roll out the pastry dough. Cut equal lengths of: one strip 3 inches (7.5 cm) wide and two strips 1/2 inch (1.25 cm) wide. Prick the dough with a fork and brush with a beaten egg yolk. Place the wide strip on a cookie sheet; lay the two thin strips on the edges of the wide one to form sides (as shown in photo). Bake at 350°F (180°C) for 25 minutes.

Remove from the oven. Press down the center of the wide strip to make room for the asparagus. Spread a layer of mayonnaise on the pastry and arrange the asparagus in the center, propped up by the side strips.

Refrigerate for 2 hours and cut the feuilleté into 2 inch (5 cm) pieces.

A shortcrust pastry may be used instead of puff pastry.

BEEF STROGANOFF

Standard	Metric
1-3/4 lb beef round, cut into strips	750 g beef round, cut into strips
2 chopped onions	2 chopped onions
1/2 lb mushrooms	250 g mushrooms
1/4 cup butter	50 ml butter
4 tbsp chopped pickles	60 ml chopped pickles
4 tomatoes, peeled and chopped	4 tomatoes, peeled and chopped
2 tbsp tomato paste	30 ml tomato paste
2 tbsp tomato ketchup	30 ml tomato ketchup
1 tbsp Worcestershire sauce	15 ml Worcestershire sauce
1 cup light cream	250 ml light cream
1/2 cup dry white wine	125 ml dry white wine
1 tbsp paprika	15 ml paprika
1 tbsp all-purpose flour	15 ml all-purpose flour
4 tbsp parsley	60 ml parsley
1 tbsp Dijon mustard	15 ml Dijon mustard

Melt the butter in a skillet and sauté the onions, mushrooms, tomatoes and pickles until liquid has evaporated. Remove from heat and set aside.

Melt more butter in another skillet and brown the meat over high heat. Season. Add the paprika, tomato paste, parsley, Worcestershire sauce and mustard. Stir. Add the white wine and cook over high heat for 1 minute. Reduce the heat to low and add the cream.

When the sauce has thickened, add the sautéed vegetables. Stir, season to taste and serve.

FANCY MASHED POTATOES

Standard	Metric
4 cups mashed potatoes	1 liter mashed potatoes
5 tbsp heavy cream (35%)	75 ml heavy cream (35%)
4 tbsp butter	60 ml butter
1 tbsp finely chopped celery	15 ml finely chopped celery
1 tbsp finely chopped parsley	15 ml finely chopped parsley
1 tbsp finely chopped shallot	15 ml finely chopped shallot
1 tsp finely chopped green pepper	5 ml finely chopped green pepper
1 tbsp finely chopped red pepper	15 ml finely chopped red pepper
2 beaten egg yolks	2 beaten egg yolks
Salt and pepper	Salt and pepper

Combine all the ingredients. Mix thoroughly. Reheat if necessary and serve.

Beef Stroganoff

SPICY CARROT SALAD

Standard	Metric
6 carrots	6 carrots
1 onion, chopped	1 onion, chopped
2 tomatoes, quartered	2 tomatoes, quartered
1/4 cup wine vinegar	50 ml wine vinegar
3 tbsp sugar	45 ml sugar
1 tsp ground ginger	5 ml ground ginger
1 tsp paprika	5 ml paprika
1 tbsp crushed black peppercorns	15 ml crushed black peppercorns
3 tbsp chopped parsley	45 ml chopped parsley
1/2 cup olive oil	125 ml olive oil

Cut the carrots on a slant to make the thinnest possible slices. Cook them in boiling water for 3 minutes. Drain and place in a salad bowl. Add all the other ingredients, except tomatoes. Toss. Marinate for at least 1 hour, stirring occasionally.

Serve garnished with tomato quarters.

BLACK FOREST CHEESE CAKE

Standard	Metric
1-1/4 cups chocolate wafer crumbs	300 ml chocolate wafer crumbs
1/3 cup melted butter	75 ml melted butter
2 envelopes unflavored gelatin	2 envelopes unflavored gelatin
2 tbsp hot water	30 ml hot water
1 can cherry pie filling	1 can cherry pie filling
1 tsp almond extract	5 ml almond extract
1 lb softened cream cheese	500 g softened cream cheese
1/3 cup sugar	75 ml sugar
3 squares semi-sweet chocolate	3 squares semi-sweet chocolate
2 tbsp hot water	30 ml hot water
2 tbsp cherry brandy	30 ml cherry brandy
1 cup sour cream	250 ml sour cream

Filling

Whipped cream
Chocolate rose buds
Maraschino cherries

Combine the chocolate wafer crumbs and the butter. Work well and line the bottom of a spring-form mold. Refrigerate.

Dissolve 1 envelope of gelatin in 2 tbsp (30 ml) hot water. Combine the cherry pie filling, almond extract and dissolved gelatin. Pour into the mold and refrigerate.

Melt the chocolate in a double boiler. Beat the cream cheese and sugar and add to the melted chocolate. Mix well and keep warm. Dissolve the other packet of gelatin in 2 tbsp (30 ml) hot water. Add the dissolved gelatin, cherry brandy and sour cream to the chocolate and cream cheese mixture. Use a spoon to spread this mixture over the cherry filling in the mold.

Refrigerate the cake for 3 to 4 hours to allow it to set. Turn out of the mold. Decorate with whipped cream, chocolate rose buds and Maraschino cherries.

MICROWAVE METHOD

Chocolate Cream Sauce

Standard	Metric
6 oz chocolate	175 g chocolate
1/4 cup butter	50 ml butter
6 tbsp light cream (15%)	90 ml light cream (15%)
6 tbsp heavy cream (35%)	90 ml heavy cream (35%)

Break up the chocolate in a bowl. Add the butter. Cook at MEDIUM for 3 minutes or until chocolate melts. Gradually incorporate the cream. Heat at MEDIUM for 1 minute 30 seconds. Stir after 45 seconds have elapsed.

Black Forest Cheese Cake

BIRTHDAYS

Child's Birthday
Ages 5 to 8

Iced Raspberry Milkshakes

Standard	Metric
6 cups milk	1.5 liters milk
1 cup raspberries, fresh or frozen	250 ml raspberries, fresh or frozen
Juice of one lemon	Juice of one lemon
Juice of one orange	Juice of one orange
1 cup honey	250 ml honey
2 tsp vanilla extract	10 ml vanilla extract
2 eggs	2 eggs

Place all the ingredients in a blender and mix at high speed for about 3 minutes.

Pour into fancy glasses that have been in the freezer for at least one hour. Serve with a straw.

Bacon Sticks and Cheesies

Preheat the oven to broil.

Take 4 or 5 slices of bacon and cut in two, lengthwise. Wrap each strip of bacon, spiral fashion, around a bread stick. Place the breadsticks on a cookie sheet and place 6 inches (15 cm) from the element. Cook until bacon is crisp.

Drain on a paper towel and place on a serving plate with 'cheesies'.

Fiesta Sloppy Joes

Standard	Metric
12 small dinner rolls	12 small dinner rolls
1 lb lean ground beef	500 g lean ground beef
1/4 cup finely chopped onion	50 ml finely chopped onion
1/4 cup finely chopped green pepper	50 ml finely chopped green pepper
2 tbsp chili sauce	30 ml chili sauce
1 tbsp mustard	15 ml mustard
1 can cream of chicken soup	1 can cream of chicken soup
Salt and pepper	Salt and pepper

Sauté the meat, onions and green pepper. Add salt and pepper. When the meat is done, incorporate the cream of chicken, mustard and chili sauce.

Cut the dinner rolls in half and fill with the beef and chicken mixture.

Crunchy Vegetable Dip

Standard	Metric
1/2 cup mayonnaise	125 ml mayonnaise
1/2 cup yogurt	125 ml yogurt
1 tbsp minced onion	15 ml minced onion
Assorted vegetables	Assorted vegetables

Thoroughly mix the mayonnaise, yogurt and onion. Add salt and pepper to taste. Cut vegetables into sticks. Use carrots, cucumber, green peppers, cauliflower, etc.

Microwave Tip

Bacon Sticks

Line a microwave dish with 3 layers of paper towel. Arrange the prepared bacon sticks on the paper and cover with another sheet. Cook at HIGH for 9 minutes or until the bacon is crisp.

Iced Raspberry Milkshakes, Bacon Sticks and Cheesies, Fiesta Sloppy Joes, and Crunchy Vegetable Dip

Birthday Clock Cake

BIRTHDAY CLOCK CAKE

Standard	Metric
1/4 cup butter or margarine	50 ml butter or margarine
2/3 cup corn syrup	150 ml corn syrup
3 beaten eggs	3 beaten eggs
1 cup mashed bananas	250 ml mashed bananas
1/3 cup milk	75 ml milk
1 tsp vanilla extract	5 ml vanilla extract
1 tsp salt	5 ml salt
2 tsp baking powder	10 ml baking powder
1 tsp baking soda	5 ml baking soda
2 cups whole wheat flour	500 ml whole wheat flour
1 cup raisins	250 ml raisins

Heat the oven to 325°F (175°C). Mix the butter and corn syrup in a bowl. Continue mixing until creamy. Add the eggs, bananas, milk and vanilla extract. Blend until smooth. Set aside.

In another bowl, sift the flour, baking powder and baking soda.

Gradually add the flour to the banana mixture. Stir vigorously until smooth then add the raisins.

Pour this mixture into a greased and floured 9 inch (23 cm) cake pan. Bake for 1 hour.

Icing

Standard	Metric
1/4 cup butter	50 ml butter
2-1/2 cups sifted icing sugar	625 ml sifted icing sugar
1/4 cup milk	50 ml milk
1/2 tsp vanilla extract	2 ml vanilla extract

Cream the butter and alternately add the sugar and milk, a little at a time. Stir vigorously until mixture is smooth. Add extra amounts of sugar or milk as needed. Add the vanilla extract. Ice the cake.

Decoration: Save a bit of the icing and add food coloring. Using a pastry bag with a fluted tip, draw the face of a clock with the hands pointing to the child's age.

MICROWAVE TIP

To prepare the icing, place the butter in a bowl and soften at HIGH for 30 seconds.

CHILD'S BIRTHDAY
AGES 5 TO 8

MENU

Serves 8 children

Sparkling Fruit Punch
Cheese and Tuna Balls
Sloppy Joes
Pink Yogurt Surprise
Lemon Marshmallow Cake

SPARKLING FRUIT PUNCH

Standard	Metric
6 cups pineapple juice	1.5 liters pineapple juice
2-1/2 cups orange juice	625 ml orange juice
2 cups lemonade	500 ml lemonade
2 cups grapefruit juice	500 ml grapefruit juice
5 cups water	1.25 liters water
1 cup sugar	250 ml sugar

Pour all the ingredients into a punch bowl. Place in the freezer until the juices begin to set. Stir occasionally and just before serving.

Fill each glass half full of punch, top up with Seven-Up and a drop or two of grenadine. Serve with straws.

CHEESE AND TUNA BALLS

Standard	Metric
1-1/4 cups cream cheese	300 ml cream cheese
1 can tuna or flakes of ham	1 can tuna or flakes of ham
3/4 tsp salt	3 ml salt
3 tbsp onion soup mix	45 ml onion soup mix
1 tsp Worcestershire sauce	5 ml Worcestershire sauce
Chopped nuts	Chopped nuts

Drain the tuna. Thoroughly mix all the ingredients except the nuts. Shape the mixture into balls and roll in the nuts.

Serve with vegetable sticks and potato chips.

Sparkling Fruit Punch and Cheese and Tuna Balls

Sloppy Joes

LEMON MARSHMALLOW CAKE

Standard	Metric
3 eggs	3 eggs
1 cup sugar	250 ml sugar
1/2 cup butter	125 ml butter
1/2 cup lemon juice	125 ml lemon juice
2 cups miniature marshmallows	500 ml miniature marshmallows
1 cup whipped cream	250 ml whipped cream
1 sponge cake mix baked in a tube mold	1 sponge cake mix baked in a tube mold

Beat the eggs thoroughly. Gradually beat in the sugar until the mixture becomes thick.

Melt the butter in a double boiler; stir in the eggs and the lemon juice. Cook for a few minutes, stirring until mixture becomes thick and smooth. Remove from heat and add the marshmallows. Stir and cool. Fold in the whipped cream.

Cut the sponge cake into 3 layers and ice each layer with the marshmallow cream. Decorate with miniature marshmallows and candied lemon peel, if desired. Refrigerate for a few hours before serving.

Slice the cake using a moist knife.

Lemon Marshmallow Cake

SLOPPY JOES

Standard	Metric
1 tbsp vegetable oil	15 ml vegetable oil
1/2 lb ground beef	250 g ground beef
1 can meat sauce	1 can meat sauce
1/4 cup relish	50 ml relish
1 tbsp vinegar	15 ml vinegar
1 small can tomato paste	1 small can tomato paste
1/8 tsp pepper	0.5 ml pepper
1/4 tsp salt	1 ml salt
8 hamburger buns	8 hamburger buns
1/2 cup chopped green pepper	125 ml chopped green pepper

Heat the oil in a skillet and sauté the beef and the peppers. Add the rest of the ingredients. Stir and simmer uncovered for 20 minutes.

Serve on hamburger buns.

PINK YOGURT SURPRISE

Standard	Metric
4 cups plain yogurt	1 liter plain yogurt
2 cups mashed strawberries, unsweetened	500 ml mashed strawberries, unsweetened
1/4 cup honey (optional)	50 ml honey (optional)

Mix all the ingredients. Makes 8 individual servings.

CHILD'S BIRTHDAY AGES 9 TO 14

MENU

Serves 6 to 8 children

Tomato Chicken Noodle Soup
Fancy Grapes
Chicken Timbales
Creamy Carrots
Gourmet Salad
Millionaire Cake

FANCY GRAPES

Standard	Metric
40 seedless green grapes	40 seedless green grapes
2 cups cream cheese	500 ml cream cheese
2 to 3 tbsp heavy cream (35%)	30 to 45 ml heavy cream (35%)
Salt and white pepper	Salt and white pepper
Finely chopped parsley	Finely chopped parsley

Wash and dry the grapes and separate.

Put the cream cheese through the blender and add the cream to make a smooth mixture. Place creamed cheese in a pastry bag with a fluted tip. Dot each grape with the cheese mixture. Sprinkle with parsley. Refrigerate until time to serve.

TOMATO CHICKEN NOODLE SOUP

Standard	Metric
1 tbsp butter	15 ml butter
3 tbsp chopped onion	45 ml chopped onion
1 celery stalk, chopped	1 celery stalk, chopped
4 tomatoes, peeled and chopped	4 tomatoes, peeled and chopped
6 cups hot chicken stock	1.5 liters hot chicken stock
1/4 tsp oregano	1 ml oregano
1 cup noodles (shell pasta)	250 ml noodles (shell pasta)
Grated cheese	Grated cheese
Salt and pepper	Salt and pepper

Heat the butter in a saucepan and sauté the onion and celery. Cover and cook for 2 to 3 minutes. Add the tomatoes and oregano. Add salt and pepper, cover and simmer for 3 minutes.

Add the chicken stock and bring to a boil.

Add the noodles and boil for about 12 minutes. Add a generous handful of grated cheese and serve with garlic bread.

Variation: Ladle the soup into oven-proof bowls and add the grated cheese. Place under broiler for soup au gratin.

Tomato Chicken Noodle Soup

CHICKEN TIMBALES

Standard	Metric
4 cups sliced mushrooms	1 liter sliced mushrooms
1/2 cup chopped green peppers	125 ml chopped green peppers
1/2 cup butter	125 ml butter
5 tbsp all-purpose flour	75 ml all-purpose flour
Pinch cayenne	Pinch cayenne
2-1/2 cups chicken stock	625 ml chicken stock
2-1/2 cups milk	625 ml milk
1/2 cup chopped sweet red peppers	125 ml chopped sweet red peppers
5 cups cooked chicken, cubed	1.25 liters cooked chicken, cubed
Salt and pepper	Salt and pepper

Heat the butter in a large saucepan. Sauté the mushrooms and green peppers until water has evaporated. Add the flour and seasonings. Mix well. Add the milk, chicken stock, red peppers and chicken.

Bring to a boil, stirring constantly.

Fill heated timbales with the sauce, or serve on a bed of rice.

CREAMY CARROTS

Standard	Metric
10 carrots	10 carrots
1 cup water	250 ml water
3 tbsp butter	45 ml butter
2 tsp sugar	10 ml sugar
2 fresh tomatoes	2 fresh tomatoes
3 egg yolks	3 egg yolks
1/2 cup milk	125 ml milk

Peel and slice the carrots. Place them in a pot and add the water, butter and sugar. Cover and simmer over low heat for 20 minutes. Towards the end of the cooking time, remove the lid and allow water to evaporate. Remove seeds from the tomatoes, chop and add to the carrots. Remove from heat.

In a bowl, beat the egg yolks and the milk until mixture is completely smooth. Add to the carrots and tomatoes. Heat but do not boil.

MICROWAVE METHOD

Carrots

Arrange the sliced carrots evenly in a glass dish. Add 1/4 cup (50 ml) water. Cover and cook at HIGH for 10 minutes. Let stand awhile and add to the remaining prepared ingredients.

Chicken Timbales and Creamy Carrots

Millionaire Cake

GOURMET SALAD

Standard	Metric
4 medium carrots	4 medium carrots
2 cups sliced mushrooms	500 ml sliced mushrooms
2 cans asparagus	2 cans asparagus
or	or
2 bunches asparagus	2 bunches asparagus
1 cantaloupe	1 cantaloupe

Slice the carrots lengthwise into thin sticks. Add a little salad dressing to the mushrooms and mix. Arrange the carrots, mushrooms and cooked asparagus on individual plates. Place a slice of melon on each serving.

Cover the servings with vinaigrette to which 1 tsp (15 ml) of sugar has been added for every 1/2 cup (125 ml) of dressing.

MICROWAVE TIP

Millionaire Cake

Soften the cheese by heating it at MEDIUM for 3 to 4 minutes.

MILLIONAIRE CAKE

Standard	Metric
14 oz can crushed pineapple (save the juice)	400 ml can crushed pineapple (save the juice)
2 cups flour	500 ml flour
1 tsp baking soda	5 ml baking soda
2 cups sugar	500 ml sugar
2 eggs	2 eggs

Place all the ingredients, one after the other into a bowl and mix thoroughly. Pour into a greased 9 x 13 inch (23 x 33 cm) cake pan. Bake at 350°F (180°C) for 35 to 40 minutes.

Icing

Standard	Metric
1 package cream cheese	1 package cream cheese
2-1/2 cups icing sugar	625 ml icing sugar
1 tsp vanilla extract	5 ml vanilla extract
1 tsp melted butter	5 ml melted butter

Beat all the ingredients together until smooth. Ice the cake while still warm. Garnish with whipped cream and pineapple chunks.

CHILD'S BIRTHDAY AGES 9 TO 14

MENU

Serves 6 to 8

Best Chicken Soup
Sweet n' Sour Vegetable Dip
Club Sandwiches
Poutine with Mini Sausages
Coleslaw in a Cabbage Leaf
Yogurt and Berry Cake

BEST CHICKEN SOUP

Standard	Metric
4 cups chicken stock	1 liter chicken stock
1 cup hot milk	250 ml hot milk
2 grated carrots	2 grated carrots
3/4 cup cooked rice	150 ml cooked rice
Parsley	Parsley

Bring the chicken stock to a boil. Add the carrots and boil for a few minutes. Add the cooked rice. Pour in the hot milk. Add salt and pepper to taste and sprinkle with parsley. Serve.

CLUB SANDWICHES

6 slices cooked bacon
6 slices white cheese
6 slices cooked chicken
6 lettuce leaves
18 slices toast
2 sliced tomatoes
Mayonnaise

Spread mayonnaise on each slice of toast. Cover with a slice each of bacon, tomato and cheese. Cover with another piece of toast. Place a slice of chicken and a lettuce leaf and another slice of toast.

Cut each three-decker sandwich into four pieces and secure with a toothpick. Serve.

SWEET N' SOUR VEGETABLE DIP

Standard	Metric
3/4 cup icing sugar	150 ml icing sugar
1/2 cup vinegar	125 ml vinegar
1 finely chopped onion	1 finely chopped onion
1/2 tsp finely chopped pepper	2 ml finely chopped pepper
1 cup ketchup	250 ml ketchup
1/2 cup vegetable oil	125 ml vegetable oil
1 clove finely chopped garlic	1 clove finely chopped garlic
Salt and pepper	Salt and pepper

Combine all the ingredients and mix well. Serve with raw vegetables such as cherry tomatoes, radishes, cauliflower, broccoli, carrots, snow peas, celery, etc...

Club Sandwiches

Poutine with Mini Sausages

POUTINE WITH MINI SAUSAGES

Standard	Metric
8 potatoes cut into French fries	8 potatoes cut into French fries
18 cocktail sausages	18 cocktail sausages
1-1/2 cups tomato sauce	375 ml tomato sauce
3/4 cup grated Parmesan or Gruyère cheese	150 ml grated Parmesan or Gruyère cheese
Salt and pepper	Salt and pepper

Cook the French fries in a deep fryer. Cut the sausages into three short pieces. Brown them on all sides. Drain and place in a saucepan containing the heated tomato sauce. Place the French fries into individual bowls, add the tomato and sausages and generous amounts of cheese. Serve.

COLESLAW IN A CABBAGE LEAF

Standard	Metric
2 tbsp milk	30 ml milk
2 tbsp vinegar	30 ml vinegar
2 tbsp mayonnaise	30 ml mayonnaise
2 tbsp sugar	30 ml sugar
1 small shredded cabbage	1 small shredded cabbage
1 finely chopped onion	1 finely chopped onion
Salt and pepper	Salt and pepper

Place the cabbage and onion in a mixing bowl. In another bowl combine the remaining ingredients and blend until smooth. Pour onto the cabbage and onion. Toss. Serve individual servings in large attractive cabbage leaves.

YOGURT AND BERRY CAKE

Standard	Metric
2 cups all-purpose flour	500 ml all-purpose flour
1 tsp baking soda	5 ml baking soda
1/2 tsp baking powder	2 ml baking powder
1/2 cup butter or margarine	125 ml butter or margarine
1 cup brown sugar	250 ml brown sugar
1 egg	1 egg
1 tsp vanilla extract	5 ml vanilla extract
1 cup raspberry or strawberry yogurt	250 ml raspberry or strawberry yogurt
Icing sugar	Icing sugar

Sift together the flour, baking soda and baking powder.

Cream the butter or margarine. Gradually add the brown sugar, egg and vanilla extract. Mix thoroughly.

Alternately blend in the flour and yogurt. Pour the batter into a greased 9 inch (23 cm) cake pan. Bake at 350°F (180°C) for 50 minutes.

Turn out of the mold and sprinkle with icing sugar.

Yogurt and Berry Cake

TEENAGER'S BIRTHDAY AGES 15 TO 18

MENU

Serves 6 to 8 teenagers

Red Radish Soup
Zesty Vegetable Dip
Chicken Croque-Mitaines
Baked Potatoes with Tomato Butter
Chef's Salad Dressing
Coconut Volcano Cake

RED RADISH SOUP

Standard	Metric
2 bunches radish	2 bunches radish
4 potatoes	4 potatoes
1 bunch parsley, chopped	1 bunch parsley, chopped
4 cups chicken stock	1 liter chicken stock
3 tbsp all-purpose flour	45 ml all-purpose flour
3 tbsp butter	45 ml butter
1 tbsp tomato paste	15 ml tomato paste
3 egg yolks	3 egg yolks
1/2 cup heavy cream (35%)	125 ml heavy cream (35%)
Salt	Salt

Melt the butter in a saucepan. Sauté the potatoes and sliced radishes until liquid has evaporated.

Add the flour and mix well. Pour in the chicken stock and add the tomato paste. Stir and simmer 30 minutes.

Put the contents of the pot through the blender until smooth.

Pour the contents back into the pot. Add the cream and boil for a few minutes. Remove from heat.

Beat the egg yolks in a small mixing bowl with a bit of soup. Gradually stir this mixture into the soup. Reheat if necessary. Add the salt and parsley just before serving. Do not add pepper.

ZESTY VEGETABLE DIP

Standard	Metric
1 cup cottage cheese	250 ml cottage cheese
1/2 cup sour cream	125 ml sour cream
1 cup mayonnaise	250 ml mayonnaise
1 cup cooked ham, diced fine	250 ml cooked ham, diced fine
2 tbsp grated onion	30 ml grated onion
1/4 tsp Tabasco sauce	1 ml Tabasco sauce
1/2 tsp Worcestershire sauce	2 ml Worcestershire sauce
Salt and pepper	Salt and pepper

Blend the cottage cheese and the sour cream until smooth. Add the remaining ingredients. Arrange raw vegetables around serving plate and place the dip in the center.

Red Radish Soup

Chicken Croque-Mitaine and Baked Potato with Tomato Butter

Chicken Croque-Mitaines

Standard	Metric
8 slices cooked bacon	8 slices cooked bacon
8 slices bread	8 slices of bread
8 slices white cheese	8 slices white cheese
3 cups shredded cooked chicken	750 ml shredded cooked chicken
2 thinly sliced tomatoes	2 thinly sliced tomatoes
3 tbsp butter	45 ml butter
1-1/2 cups white sauce (see section on sauces)	375 ml white sauce (see section on sauces)

Lightly butter the bread slices and add the following, in order: chicken pieces, seasoned tomato slices, cold white sauce, pieces of bacon and cheese slices.

Place the croque-mitaines on a cookie sheet and bake at 350°F (180°C) for 20 minutes. If the cheese begins to bubble prematurely, cover with a sheet of aluminum foil.

Chef's Salad Dressing

Standard	Metric
1/4 cup vinegar	50 ml vinegar
1 cup sugar	250 ml sugar
1 can tomato soup	1 can tomato soup
1 tsp prepared mustard	5 ml prepared mustard
1 tbsp salt	15 ml salt
1 tbsp pepper	15 ml pepper
1 cup vegetable oil	250 ml vegetable oil
2 tbsp HP sauce	30 ml HP sauce
4 cloves garlic, crushed	4 cloves garlic, crushed

Thoroughly mix all the ingredients. Store in a bottle in the refrigerator. Recommended especially as a dressing for Romaine lettuce.

Baked Potatoes with Tomato Butter

6 potatoes
Tomato paste
Butter
Chives

Wash and dry the potatoes. Wrap individually in aluminum foil and prick with a fork. Bake at 325°F (160°C) for 1 hour.

When the potatoes are done, cut a cross on the top and press with thumbs and forefingers on either side to open up the incision. Mix the butter with a touch of tomato paste and chives and place a dollop of this mixture on each potato.

Coconut Volcano Cake

Coconut Volcano Cake

Standard	Metric
2 egg yolks	2 egg yolks
3/4 cup sugar	150 ml sugar
2 tbsp butter	30 ml butter
1/2 cup milk	125 ml milk
1 cup all-purpose flour	250 ml all-purpose flour
1 tsp baking powder	5 ml baking powder

Meringue

Standard	Metric
2 egg whites	2 egg whites
2 cups brown sugar	500 ml brown sugar
1/2 tsp maple or vanilla extract	2 ml maple or vanilla extract
Coconut	Coconut

Cream the butter and add the egg yolks and sugar. Blend until creamy. Sift the flour with the baking powder and gradually add to the butter mixture, alternating with the milk. Stir vigorously until smooth.

Pour this batter into a round cake pan. Bake at 325°F (160°C) for 30 minutes.

In the meantime, whip the egg whites until stiff, gradually adding the brown sugar and flavoring extract. Cover the cake with the meringue and sprinkle with shredded coconut.

Place the cake under the broiler for 2 minutes. Decorate with half a coconut filled with raspberry topping.

Teenager's Birthday Ages 15 to 18

Menu

Serves 6 teenagers

Avocado Soup Aurora
Mini Croque-Monsieur with Bacon
Chinese Fondue
Vegetable Rice
Cucumber and Watercress Salad
Fresh Pineapple Chantilly

Avocado Soup Aurora

Standard	Metric
8 oz chopped onions	250 g chopped onions
4 whole cloves garlic	4 whole cloves garlic
5 egg yolks	5 egg yolks
3 ripe avocados	3 ripe avocados
6 tomatoes, seeds removed	6 tomatoes, seeds removed
1/3 cup butter	75 ml butter
8 cups water	2 liters water
Salt, pepper and cayenne	Salt, pepper and cayenne

Melt the butter in a heavy saucepan. Sauté the onions, garlic and tomatoes and add the water. Boil for 20 minutes and add salt, pepper and cayenne.

In the meantime, peel the avocados and put them through the food processor or food mill. Mix the avocados and the egg yolks.

Put the contents of the saucepan through the blender and pour back into the pot. Heat but do not boil.

Add a bit of soup to the avocado and egg mixture and mix, using a wire whisk. Gradually whip this mixture into the soup.

Serve very hot but without bringing to a boil.

Mini Croque-Monsieur with Bacon

Cut slices of bread into 4 triangles. Spread with mayonnaise, cover with a slice of cheese and bacon. Bake at 350°F (180°C) for about 20 minutes. Serve.

Avocado Soup Aurora

VEGETABLE RICE

Standard	Metric
1-1/2 cups cooked rice	375 ml cooked rice
1/4 cup vegetable oil	50 ml vegetable oil
1 can sliced mushrooms with liquid	1 can sliced mushrooms with liquid
3 cups water	750 ml water
1 cup chopped celery	250 ml chopped celery
1 cup diced carrots	250 ml diced carrots
1 cup diced green peppers	250 ml diced green peppers
1 package onion soup mix	1 package onion soup mix
3 tbsp soy sauce	45 ml soy sauce
2 tbsp beef bouillon concentrate	30 ml beef bouillon concentrate

Mix all the ingredients together. Place in a baking dish and bake for 1 hour and 30 minutes at 350°F (180°C).

CHINESE FONDUE

Standard	Metric
3 lb beef or turkey, in paper-thin slices	1.5 kg beef or turkey, in paper thin slices
1 tbsp beef soup base	15 ml beef soup base
1 tsp chicken soup base	5 ml chicken soup base
3 bay leaves	3 bay leaves
1/2 tsp thyme	2 ml thyme
1/2 tsp marjoram	2 ml marjoram
1 tsp Kitchen Bouquet™	5 ml Kitchen Bouquet™
Raw vegetables	Raw vegetables

Place all the ingredients, except meat and vegetables, in a fondue pot. Fill to 3/4 with boiling water. Stir and boil for a few minutes. Do not add salt.

Arrange the meat slices on a serving plate. Place vegetables, such as broccoli, cauliflower, mushrooms, peppers, etc, in separate bowls. Fondue sauces may be prepared by flavoring mayonnaise with any of the following: curry, ketchup, chili sauce, chopped garlic and Worcestershire.

When ready to serve, place the fondue pot on its stand with the burner below in the center of the table. Make sure everyone has a long-handled fondue fork for cooking their own meat and vegetables.

CUCUMBER AND WATERCRESS SALAD

Standard	Metric
1 bunch watercress, stems removed	1 bunch watercress, stems removed
1-1/4 cups sour cream or plain yogurt	300 ml sour cream or plain yogurt
4 tsp lemon juice	20 ml lemon juice
2 tsp Dijon mustard	10 ml Dijon mustard
2 English cucumbers, peeled and sliced into 1/4 inch rounds	2 English cucumbers, peeled and sliced into 5 mm rounds
1 tbsp salt	15 ml salt
5 finely chopped radishes	5 finely chopped radishes
2 finely chopped small shallots	2 finely chopped small shallots
Salt and pepper	Salt and pepper

Blanch the watercress for 30 seconds in boiling water. Drain and run under cold water. Dry and chop (not too fine).

In a large bowl, combine the sour cream or yogurt, lemon juice and Dijon mustard. Mix well and add salt and pepper.

Add 1 tbsp (15 ml) salt to the cucumber. Toss lightly and let stand 15 minutes to extract water. Drain.

Add the cucumber to the sour cream and mix. Add the watercress, radishes and shallots.

Refrigerate or serve immediately. Toss before serving.

Cucumber and Watercress Salad

Fresh Pineapple Chantilly

FRESH PINEAPPLE CHANTILLY

Standard	Metric
1 to 2 pineapples	1 to 2 pineapples
Maraschino cherries	Maraschino cherries
1-1/2 cups heavy cream (35%)	375 ml heavy cream (35%)
4 tbsp sugar	60 ml sugar
1 tsp vanilla extract	5 ml vanilla extract

Whip the cream until firm, gradually adding the sugar and vanilla extract.

Refrigerate.

Cut the pineapple, top to bottom, into 6 pieces without cutting off the leaves. Use a sharp knife to cut the fruit away from the skin, leaving the core uncut (see technique). Cut the long pieces of flesh horizontally into seven. Offset each piece of pineapple as shown.

Using a pastry bag fitted with a fluted tip, pipe whipped cream down the center of each serving.

Technique: Pineapple

1 Cut the pineapple into six long wedges.

2 Detach the flesh from the skin.

3 Slice the flesh into seven segments.

4 Arrange each segment slightly off-center.

Adult's Birthday

Serve with a Cabernet or Medoc and a sparkling wine.

MENU

Serves 6 to 8

Cream of Green Pea Soup
Ham and Asparagus au Gratin
Roast Beef with Sauce Albert
Old-Fashioned French Fries
Brussels Sprouts Créole
Designer Salad
Honeydew Melon Romanoff

Ham and Asparagus au Gratin

CREAM OF GREEN PEA SOUP

Standard	Metric
2 cups fresh or frozen peas	500 ml fresh or frozen peas
2 cups water	500 ml water
1 onion, chopped	1 onion, chopped
2 cups milk	500 ml milk
2 tsp butter or margarine	10 ml butter or margarine
1 tbsp all-purpose flour	15 ml all-purpose flour
Salt and pepper	Salt and pepper
Croutons	Croutons

Cover the fresh or frozen peas with water and cook with the chopped onion until water evaporates.

Add the milk to the peas and onions and simmer over low heat.

Melt the butter in a saucepan and add the flour. Stir well. Incorporate this mixture into the peas and milk, stirring constantly.

Run the soup through the blender to liquefy. Reheat and serve with the garlic rye bread croutons.

This soup can also be made with canned peas. Cook the chopped onion in the liquid from the peas until tender. Add the peas and continue as above.

Croutons

Toast slices of French bread in the oven. Rub each slice with cut cloves of garlic and brush with olive oil.

HAM AND ASPARAGUS AU GRATIN

Standard	Metric
1 can asparagus	1 can asparagus
1-1/2 cups heavy cream (35%)	375 ml heavy cream (35%)
4 slices cooked ham	4 slices cooked ham
4 slices mozzarella	4 slices mozzarella
1 tbsp mixed spices	15 ml mixed spices
Salt and pepper	Salt and pepper

Thoroughly drain the asparagus. Add the spices, salt and pepper to the cream. Dip the asparagus in this mixture and then place in a buttered square baking dish.

Cover the asparagus with the ham slices and the mozzarella cheese. Place in a 400°F (200°C) oven until golden brown.

In the meantime whip the seasoned cream until firm.

Serve the whipped cream as a topping with the asparagus. (Also delicious with baked potatoes or string beans.)

ROAST BEEF WITH SAUCE ALBERT

Standard

1 round roast, about 3 lb
2 cloves garlic, quartered
2 tbsp Dijon mustard
Butter
1 onion, chopped
1 tbsp margarine
1 cup beef stock, hot
Salt and pepper

Imperial

1 round roast, about 1.5 kg
2 cloves garlic, quartered
30 ml Dijon mustard
Butter
1 onion, chopped
15 ml margarine
250 ml beef stock, hot
Salt and pepper

Heat the oven to 450°F (230°C). Place the roast in a roasting pan. Make deep cuts in the roast and insert the pieces of garlic. Sprinkle a generous amount of pepper but do not add salt until beef has been seared. Brush the roast with the butter and Dijon mustard, and place in the oven for 20 minutes. Now sprinkle with salt. Continue cooking at 350°F (180°C), calculating 15 minutes per pound (500 g) including first twenty minutes for searing the beef.

Place the roast on a serving plate and cover with aluminum foil. Place the roasting pan on the stove-top, over high heat. Add the chopped onion, margarine, salt and pepper. Pour in the beef stock and continue boiling until liquid has been reduced to 2/3. Correct the seasoning and pour into a gravy boat.

Sauce Albert

Standard

1 cup mayonnaise
1 tbsp Dijon mustard
1 cup artichoke hearts
1 onion, chopped
1/2 cup chopped parsley
1 cup chicken stock
Salt and pepper

Metric

250 ml mayonnaise
15 ml Dijon mustard
250 ml artichoke hearts
1 onion, chopped
125 ml chopped parsley
250 ml chicken stock
Salt and pepper

Drain the artichokes and simmer together with the onion and chicken stock. Cool. Add seasoning and put through the blender or food processor. Combine the mustard and mayonnaise and incorporate into artichoke mixture. Add the parsley and blend. Serve in a gravy boat.

Roast Beef with Sauce Albert

OLD-FASHIONED FRENCH FRIES

8 small potatoes
Salt

Peel and quarter the potatoes. Cook the potatoes in a deep fryer set at 250°F (120°C) for 8 to 10 minutes. Remove and let stand awhile.

Set the deep fryer at 325°F (160°C) and cook the potatoes a second time until golden brown. Drain, add salt to taste and serve.

BRUSSELS SPROUTS CRÉOLE

Standard	Metric
1-1/2 lb Brussels sprouts	750 g Brussels sprouts
3 tbsp butter	45 ml butter
1 large onion, minced	1 large onion, minced
1 clove garlic, crushed	1 clove garlic, crushed
1 green pepper, chopped	1 green pepper, chopped
1 lb tomatoes, blanched, peeled and chopped	500 g tomatoes, blanched, peeled and chopped
1/2 tsp pepper	2 ml pepper
1/4 tsp dried sweet basil	1 ml dried sweet basil
1 tsp salt	5 ml salt

Remove any limp or damaged leaves from the Brussels sprouts. Wash in cool water and cut a cross at the base of each sprout.

Melt the butter in a large skillet and add the onion, garlic and green pepper. Cook for about 8 minutes over medium heat, stirring occasionally. Add the remaining ingredients. Reduce the heat and simmer for 15 to 20 minutes or until Brussels sprouts are tender.

DESIGNER SALAD

2 bunches watercress
1 can hearts of palm, sliced
4 endives, quartered
4 tomatoes, quartered

Arrange bouquets of watercress, hearts of palm, quartered endives and tomatoes on a large serving plate. Cover lightly with a vinaigrette. The idea is to be as creative as possible when arranging the components of the salad. See the photo for some ideas.

HONEYDEW MELON ROMANOFF

Standard	Metric
2 honeydew melons	2 honeydew melons
4 tbsp lemon juice	60 ml lemon juice
4 tbsp orange juice	60 ml orange juice
1 cup heavy cream (35%)	250 ml heavy cream (35%)
4 tbsp icing sugar	60 ml icing sugar
1 tsp vanilla extract	5 ml vanilla extract
1/3 cup Curaçao	75 ml Curaçao

Cut the melons in half and remove seeds. Peel and cut the fruit into pieces. Place all the ingredients in the food processor. Serve in soup bowls that have been chilled in the freezer for about one hour.

Designer Salad

ADULT'S BIRTHDAY II

Serve with a Riesling or white Graves, and of course, champagne.

MENU

Serves 6 to 8

Cauliflower Soup
Scallop and Bacon Cocktail
Santa Fausta Vegetable Paella
Watercress Salad with Anchovy Vinaigrette
Peach Cup with Iced Almond Milk
Strawberries in Champagne

SCALLOP AND BACON COCKTAIL

Standard	Metric
1 lb scallops	500 g scallops
Salt	Salt
Bacon slices	Bacon slices

Salt the scallops. Cut slices of bacon in half crosswise and wrap each scallop in a bacon piece, fastening with a toothpick.

Bake at 450°F (220°C) for about 5 minutes, until bacon is browned.

Cocktail Sauce

Standard	Metric
3 tbsp catsup or chili sauce	45 ml catsup or chili sauce
Lemon juice	Lemon juice
1 cup tomato or vegetable juice	250 ml tomato or vegetable juice
Salt and pepper	Salt and pepper
1/4 tsp sugar	1 ml sugar
1 tbsp finely chopped fresh parsley	15 ml finely chopped fresh parsley
Few drops Tabasco sauce	Few drops Tabasco sauce

In a small saucepan, combine all ingredients except the parsley. Heat for a few minutes, stirring occasionally, without bringing to a boil. Use the sauce on the scallops. This dish looks best arranged in scallop shells or stemmed glasses. Garnish with parsley.

CAULIFLOWER SOUP

Standard	Metric
1/4 lb diced salt pork	125 g diced salt pork
1 diced onion	1 diced onion
2 celery stalks, diced	2 celery stalks, diced
2 potatoes, peeled and diced	2 potatoes, peeled and diced
6 cups chicken stock, hot	1.5 liters chicken stock, hot
2 stalks parsley	2 stalks parsley
1 bay leaf	1 bay leaf
1/2 head cauliflower, broken into flowerets	1/2 head cauliflower, broken into flowerets
Salt and pepper	Salt and pepper

Put the diced salt pork in a heavy saucepan and render for a few minutes over medium heat. Add the onions, celery and potatoes. Season with salt and pepper.

Cover and cook for 4 to 5 minutes. Add the heated chicken stock. Correct seasoning, add parsley and bay leaf, and cook uncovered for about 30 minutes. Add the cauliflowerets and continue simmering about 10 minutes.

Serve with small buttered rolls.

Cauliflower Soup

Santa Fausta Vegetable Paella

SANTA FAUSTA VEGETABLE PAELLA

Standard	**Metric**
1/2 cup olive oil	125 ml olive oil
2 large chopped onions	2 large chopped onions
2 crushed garlic cloves	2 crushed garlic cloves
1 large red bell pepper, seeds and white parts removed, sliced	1 large red bell pepper, seeds and white parts removed, sliced
2 cups long-grain rice, washed and soaked in cold water for 30 minutes	500 ml long-grain rice, washed and soaked in cold water for 30 minutes
2 cups vegetable stock	500 ml vegetable stock
4 large tomatoes, blanched, peeled, seeds removed and chopped	4 large tomatoes, blanched, peeled, seeds removed and chopped
1 cup frozen green beans	250 ml frozen green beans
1/2 cup frozen peas	125 ml frozen peas
2 celery stalks, pared and sliced	2 celery stalks, pared and sliced
18 black olives, halved and pitted	18 black olives, halved and pitted
2 tsp salt	10 ml salt
1 tsp grey pepper	5 ml grey pepper
1 tsp saffron, soaked in	5 ml saffron, soaked in
2 tsp hot water	10 ml hot water
1/2 cup slivered almonds	125 ml slivered almonds
2 cooked carrots	2 cooked carrots
10 cooked Brussels sprouts	10 cooked Brussels sprouts
1 cup fried mushrooms	250 ml fried mushrooms

Heat the olive oil over medium heat in a large heavy saucepan. Add the onions, garlic and red pepper and sauté 5 to 7 minutes, stirring occasionally, until the onions are tender and translucent but not browned. Drain the soaking water from the rice and add the rice to the pan, stirring to coat each grain with oil. Sauté for about 5 minutes, stirring occasionally. Add the vegetable stock and turn up the heat until the liquid boils.

Reduce the heat and add the chopped tomatoes, green beans, peas, celery, olives, salt, pepper and saffron with its soaking water. Cover the pan and cook gently for 30 to 35 minutes, or until the rice is tender and has absorbed all the liquid.

Remove the pan from the burner and turn the contents into a heated serving dish.

Decorate with the carrots, Brussels sprouts, mushrooms and almonds, which should all be hot. Serve.

Watercress Salad with Anchovy Vinaigrette

2 bunches watercress,
coarsely chopped
Grated Parmesan cheese
1/4 red bell pepper, sliced
Tomato quarters
Black olives

Anchovy Vinaigrette

Standard	Metric
1 tbsp grated onion	15 ml grated onion
1 tsp chopped parsley	5 ml chopped parsley
1 tbsp Dijon mustard	15 ml Dijon mustard
2 oz chopped anchovy filets	50 ml chopped anchovy filets
3 tbsp wine vinegar	45 ml wine vinegar
7 tbsp olive oil	105 ml olive oil
1 tbsp lemon juice	15 ml lemon juice
Salt and pepper	Salt and pepper

Combine all the vinaigrette ingredients except olive oil and lemon juice. Add the olive oil gradually, beating constantly. Stir in the lemon juice. Pour the vinaigrette over the watercress salad and sprinkle with Parmesan cheese.

Peach Cup with Iced Almond Milk

Watercress Salad with Anchovy Vinaigrette

Strawberries in Champagne

Standard	Metric
2 cups fresh unsweetened strawberries	500 ml fresh unsweetened strawberries
1 bottle champagne or sparkling white or rosé wine	1 bottle champagne or sparkling white or rosé wine
Dash of freshly ground black pepper	Dash of freshly ground black pepper
1 tsp sugar	5 ml sugar

Wash the strawberries and prick them all with a fork. Twist on a little black pepper. Put the champagne in a large jar with a tight-fitting lid. Add the sugar, then the strawberries. Let marinate in the refrigerator a few hours at least.

Serve the strawberries in champagne flutes.

You can drink the wine, or use it for another batch of strawberries.

Peach Cup with Iced Almond Milk

Standard	Metric
1 can peach halves	1 can peach halves
2 cups milk	500 ml milk
1 cup sugar	250 ml sugar
3/4 cup powdered almonds	150 ml powdered almonds
1 tsp vanilla extract	5 ml vanilla extract

Drain the peaches and put them on paper towels in a bowl. Refrigerate. Combine the milk, sugar, vanilla and powdered almonds in a saucepan and bring to a boil. Remove from heat, cover, and let stand for 20 minutes.

Pour the almond milk through several layers of cheesecloth, squeezing well to retrieve all the milk. Return the liquid to the saucepan and cook over gentle heat until the mixture thickens slightly. Chill the almond milk.

Pour the almond milk over the peach halves. You can also add vanilla ice cream to this dish, pouring the almond milk over all.

Macaroni Salad

Queen Elizabeth Cake

Standard	Metric
1/4 cup butter	50 ml butter
1 cup sugar	250 ml sugar
1-1/2 cups all-purpose flour	375 ml all-purpose flour
1 egg	1 egg
3/4 tsp baking soda	3 ml baking soda
1 tsp vanilla extract	5 ml vanilla extract
1/4 tsp salt	1 ml salt
1 cup boiling water	250 ml boiling water
1 cup chopped nuts	250 ml chopped nuts
1/2 cup shredded coconut	125 ml shredded coconut
1 cup pitted dates	250 ml pitted dates

Soak the dates in boiling water. Set aside. Combine the remaining ingredients, except the flour, and beat vigorously until fluffy.

Add the dates and boiling water to egg mixture, alternating with the flour. Use swift strokes until batter is smooth.

Pour into a greased and floured cake pan and bake at 350°F (180°C) for 35 to 40 minutes.

Turn out of the mold and cool for about 10 minutes.

Icing

Standard	Metric
3 tbsp butter	45 ml butter
2 tbsp light cream (15%)	30 ml light cream (15%)
5 tbsp brown sugar	75 ml brown sugar
1/2 cup shredded coconut	125 ml shredded coconut

Boil all the ingredients in a saucepan for 3 minutes. Pour over the cooled cake. Place in 350°F (180°C) oven for 15 minutes.

Macaroni Salad

Standard	Metric
2 cups elbow macaroni	500 ml elbow macaroni
1/2 cup mayonnaise	125 ml mayonnaise
1/2 cup chopped shallots	125 ml chopped shallots
2 tbsp chopped parsley	30 ml chopped parsley
1/2 cup chopped celery	125 ml chopped celery
Salt and pepper	Salt and pepper

Cook the pasta according to package instructions. Run under cold water to cool quickly. Drain well. Add the mayonnaise, shallots, parsley, celery, salt and pepper. Mix well. Line a serving dish with lettuce leaves. Place the macaroni salad on top of the lettuce.

BRUNCH II

Serve with rosé or Alsatian wine.

VEGETABLE QUICHE

Standard	Metric
1 unbaked 10 inch pastry shell	1 unbaked 25 cm pastry shell
1-1/2 cups grated cheese	375 ml grated cheese
1-1/2 cups chopped onion	375 ml chopped onion
1-1/2 cups assorted chopped vegetables	375 ml assorted chopped vegetables
3 beaten eggs	3 beaten eggs
3/4 cup milk	150 ml milk
2 tbsp soy sauce	30 ml soy sauce
1/4 tsp thyme	1 ml thyme
1/4 tsp sweet basil	1 ml sweet basil
1/4 tsp savory	1 ml savory
1/4 tsp sea salt	1 ml sea salt
Cayenne pepper	Cayenne pepper

Steam the vegetables of your choice for about 10 minutes until tender-crisp.

In the meantime cover the pie crust with half the grated cheese. Add the chopped onion to the cooked vegetables and place on top of the grated cheese. Add the rest of the cheese.

Whip the eggs, milk, herbs and cayenne. Pour this mixture into the pastry shell. Place on the lower rack of the oven and bake at 375°F (190°C) for 30 minutes, or until the quiche has set and is quite firm.

CRABMEAT CROISSANTS

Standard	Metric
1 chopped hard-boiled egg	1 chopped hard-boiled egg
1/4 cup mayonnaise	50 ml mayonnaise
1/2 cup chopped celery	125 ml chopped celery
Red or green sweet pepper to taste	Rred or green sweet pepper to taste
1 can crabmeat	1 can crabmeat
1 package prepared croissant dough	1 package prepared croissant dough
1 cup grated mozzarella	250 ml grated mozzarella

Dice the pepper fine and flake the crabmeat with a fork.

Combine the egg, mayonnaise, celery, pepper and crabmeat. Place a heaping spoonful of this mixture into the pastry triangles and shape into croissants.

Sprinkle with grated mozzarella and bake on a cookie sheet at 350°F (180°C) for 15 to 20 minutes.

Crabmeat Croissants

199

CRETONS

Standard
1 lb ground pork
3 slices stale bread, crumbled
1/2 onion, finely chopped
1/2 tsp cinnamon
1/4 tsp ground cloves
1/4 tsp ground nutmeg
1 tsp salt
Pepper
3/4 cup milk

Metric
500 g ground pork
3 slices stale bread, crumbled
1/2 onion, finely chopped
2 ml cinnamon
1 ml ground cloves
1 ml ground nutmeg
5 ml salt
Pepper
150 ml milk

Combine all the ingredients, mixing thoroughly. Place in a baking dish.

Bake at 300°F (150°C) for about 60 minutes. Cool. Reverse onto a plate. Serve as you would a pâté.

Cretons

RED AND GREEN COLESLAW

1 red cabbage, shredded
1 green cabbage, shredded
1 onion, finely chopped
3 grated carrots

Herbed Vinaigrette

Standard
5 tbsp vegetable oil
1 tsp fresh chopped parsley
Pinch sweet basil
Salt and pepper
2 tbsp wine vinegar
1 tsp chopped chives
1 tsp prepared or Dijon mustard

Metric
75 ml vegetable oil
5 ml fresh chopped parsley
Pinch sweet basil
Salt and pepper
30 ml wine vinegar
5 ml chopped chives
5 ml prepared or Dijon mustard

Place the cabbage, onion and carrots in a large salad bowl.

In a separate bowl, thoroughly mix the remaining ingredients. Pour over the coleslaw and toss.

HEAD CHEESE

Standard
3 lb pork hocks
6 cups water
1/2 cup chopped celery leaves
1/4 cup chopped parsley
2 onions, sliced
1 carrot, sliced
2 cloves garlic, chopped
1/4 tsp salt
6 peppercorns
1 tsp allspice
1 tsp thyme
2 cloves
1 bay leaf
2 tsp caraway seeds

Metric
1.5 kg pork hocks
1.5 liters water
125 ml chopped celery leaves
50 ml chopped parsley
2 onions, sliced
1 carrot, sliced
2 cloves garlic, chopped
1 ml salt
6 peppercorns
5 ml allspice
5 ml thyme
2 cloves
1 bay leaf
10 ml caraway seeds

Place all the ingredients, except caraway seeds, in a pot. Cover and simmer for about 3 hours, until the meat is tender. Remove the pork hocks and save the stock. Remove skin and bones from the meat and chop. Add caraway seeds to the stock and simmer until only 2 cups (500 ml) of liquid is left.

Strain the contents of the pot and degrease. Combine the stock and the meat and pour into a greased loaf pan.

Refrigerate for 4 hours before turning out the mold.

CARROT AND ALMOND MUFFINS

Standard
1/3 cup margarine
1 cup sugar
2 eggs
1 cup grated carrots
Lemon juice
1 cup raisins
1-1/2 cups all-purpose flour
1 tsp baking soda
2 tsp baking powder
1/2 tsp salt
1/2 cup ground almonds

Metric
75 ml margarine
250 ml sugar
2 eggs
250 ml grated carrots
Lemon juice
250 ml raisins
375 ml all-purpose flour
5 ml baking soda
10 ml baking powder
2 ml salt
125 ml ground almonds

Cream the margarine in a mixing bowl and add half the sugar. Mix well. Incorporate the eggs one at a time and add the rest of the sugar. Add the carrots, raisins, almonds and a dash of lemon juice. Mix thoroughly using short swift strokes.

In a separate bowl, combine the flour, baking soda, baking powder and salt. Gradually add to the previous mixture, stirring with a wooden spoon. Do not overbeat as the muffins will be heavy. Pour batter into muffin tins.

Bake at 350°F (180°C) for 25 to 30 minutes.

Carrot and Almond Muffins

BUFFET

Prepare this meal almost completely ahead of time and enjoy your guests.

Serve with rosé or Alsatian wine.

MENU

Serves 6 to 8

Tomato Aspic
Ham Canapés
Seafood Salad
Baked Ham Rolls
Mixed Salad
Fruit Salad Cake

HAM CANAPÉS

Standard	Metric
6 ham slices	6 ham slices
1/4 cup cream cheese	50 ml cream cheese
6 dill pickles	6 dill pickles
6 olives	6 olives
Salt and pepper	Salt and pepper
Parsley sprigs	Parsley sprigs

Add salt and pepper to softened cream cheese. Spread the cheese on the ham slices. Place the pickle on the edge of the slice and roll. Secure with a toothpick. Stick the olive onto the toothpick and garnish with a sprig of parsley.

TOMATO ASPIC

Standard	Metric
2 cups tomato juice	500 ml tomato juice
1/4 tsp salt	1 ml salt
1 envelope lemon-flavored gelatin	1 envelope lemon-flavored gelatin
3/4 tsp cinnamon	3 ml cinnamon
Pinch pepper	Pinch pepper
1/4 tsp ground cloves	1 ml ground cloves
1/4 tsp chopped onion	1 ml chopped onion
1 tbsp chopped olives	15 ml chopped olives
1 tbsp chopped celery	15 ml chopped celery
1 tbsp chopped sweet pickles	15 ml chopped sweet pickles

Heat the tomato juice in a saucepan. Add the gelatin, salt, pepper, cinnamon and cloves.

Let the mixture cool until it has the consistency of raw egg white. Stir in the last four ingredients.

Pour into a tube mold and refrigerate until gelatin has set.

Turn out the mold and garnish with olives and celery leaves.

Tomato Aspic

Baked Ham Rolls

SEAFOOD SALAD

Standard	Metric
2 cups shrimp, cooked or canned	500 ml shrimp, cooked or canned
1 cup chopped celery	250 ml chopped celery
1/4 cup stuffed olives, sliced	50 ml stuffed olives, sliced
1/4 cup green peppers, chopped	50 ml green peppers, chopped
1/2 cup mayonnaise	125 ml mayonnaise
or	or
1/2 cup salad dressing	125 ml salad dressing
or	or
1/2 cup plain yogurt	125 ml plain yogurt
1 tbsp lemon juice	15 ml lemon juice
1/2 tsp onion salt	2 ml onion salt
Pepper	Pepper
Tomato Aspic ring mold	Tomato Aspic ring mold

Mix the shrimp with olives, celery and chopped peppers. In a separate bowl, combine the mayonnaise (salad dressing or yogurt), lemon juice, onion salt and pepper.

Pour this mixture over the shrimp and toss gently. Refrigerate.

Place the seafood salad in the center of the Tomato Aspic mold and garnish with eggs and watercress.

BAKED HAM ROLLS

Standard	Metric
1/4 lb grated cheese	125 g cheese grated
1 medium onion, chopped	1 medium onion, chopped
1/4 lb ground ham	125 g ground ham
1/4 cup ketchup	50 ml ketchup
1/2 tsp salt	2 ml salt
1/2 tsp Worcestershire sauce	2 ml Worcestershire sauce
1/4 tsp pepper	1 ml pepper
1/4 cup vegetable oil	50 ml vegetable oil
2 tsp chopped parsley	10 ml chopped parsley
8 dinner rolls	8 dinner rolls

Combine the ham and cheese. Incorporate remaining ingredients and mix well. Stuff the dinner rolls with this mixture and bake at 350°F (180°C) for 20 minutes. Serve.

Fruit Salad Cake

MIXED SALAD

Standard	Metric
1 cabbage, shredded	1 cabbage, shredded
3 grated carrots	3 grated carrots
4 hard-boiled eggs	4 hard-boiled eggs
Salt and pepper	Salt and pepper
1 medium onion, finely chopped	1 medium onion, finely chopped
1 red apple	1 red apple
Parsley sprigs	Parsley sprigs
1/3 cup vinaigrette	75 ml vinaigrette

Vinaigrette

Standard	Metric
3/4 cup vegetable oil	150 ml vegetable oil
1/4 cup white vinegar	50 ml white vinegar
1 tbsp sugar	15 ml sugar
1/2 tsp thyme	2 ml thyme
1/2 tsp oregano	2 ml oregano
1/2 tsp paprika	2 ml paprika
1/4 tsp dry mustard	1 ml dry mustard
1 tsp garlic salt	5 ml garlic salt
1 tsp garlic powder	5 ml garlic powder

Place all the salad ingredients except eggs in a large salad bowl. Pour the vinaigrette onto the salad. Add salt and pepper to taste. Toss and garnish with egg slices. Serve.

FRUIT SALAD CAKE

Standard	Metric
2 cups all-purpose flour	500 ml all-purpose flour
2 cups sugar	500 ml sugar
2 tsp baking soda	10 ml baking soda
2 eggs	2 eggs
1 can fruit salad	1 can fruit salad

Frosting

Standard	Metric
1/2 cup butter	125 ml butter
1/2 cup brown sugar	125 ml brown sugar
1/2 cup condensed milk	125 ml condensed milk

Heat the oven to 350°F (180°C). Combine the flour, sugar and baking soda in a large mixing bowl. In a separate bowl, mix the eggs, fruit salad and juice. Crush the fruit. Fold the fruit mixture into the flour; do not use a mixer. Pour the batter into a greased pan and bake for 45 to 50 minutes.

Prepare the frosting in a saucepan. Mix the ingredients thoroughly and bring to a boil. Remove from heat and stir. Make small holes in the cake and pour the frosting. Cool, garnish with fruit and serve.

BUFFET II

These dishes are easy to double for a larger group.

Serve a white Bordeaux, red Bordeaux and sparkling wine.

VEGETARIAN PIZZA

Standard	Metric
5 unbaked pizza crusts, 9 inch	5 unbaked pizza crusts, 22 cm
1/2 can cream of mushroom or cream of celery soup	1/2 can cream of mushroom or cream of celery soup
6 broccoli flowerets	6 broccoli flowerets
6 cauliflower flowerets	6 cauliflower flowerets
1 cup chopped celery	250 ml chopped celery
1 chopped onion	1 chopped onion
12 fresh or canned mushrooms	12 fresh or canned mushrooms
1 tomato	1 tomato
1/2 green pepper, sliced	1/2 green pepper, sliced
1 grated carrot	1 grated carrot
mozzarella cheese	mozzarella cheese

Cook the broccoli and cauliflower in salted boiling water for 8 minutes. Drain and cool, then cut into thin slices.

Sauté the onion and celery in 1 tbsp (15 ml) butter. Add sliced mushrooms and cook for 3 minutes.. Spread 2 tbsp (30 ml) of cream of mushroom or celery soup on each pizza crust. Sprinkle on the onion and celery and garnish with broccoli, cauliflower and mushrooms. Cover with grated carrot, sliced peppers and mozzarella cheese. Bake at 450°F (230°C) for 12 to 15 minutes.

STUFFED SALAD ROLLS

Standard	Metric
1 clove garlic	1 clove garlic
1 onion	1 onion
1-1/2 lb ground pork	750 g ground pork
1 tsp dry mustard	5 ml dry mustard
1 tbsp Worcestershire sauce	15 ml Worcestershire sauce
1 can chicken gumbo soup	1 can chicken gumbo soup
2 tbsp chili sauce	30 ml chili sauce

Place all the ingredients in a large pot and boil for about 45 minutes. Cool. Reheat in a 350°F (180°C) oven for 5 minutes, just before serving.

Stuff 4 dozen salad rolls with this mixture and serve.

May also be stored in the freezer.

Vegetarian Pizza

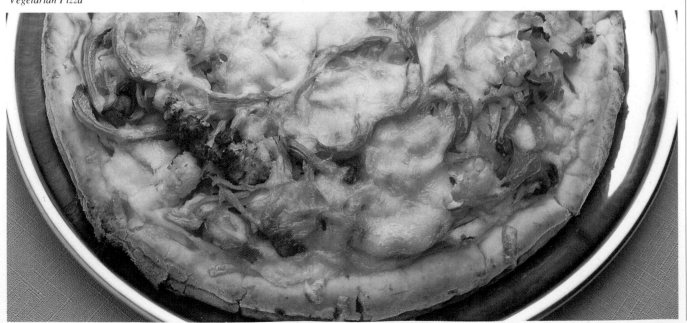

205

CHEESE AND CRAB CANAPÉS

Standard	Metric
1 can crabmeat, drained	1 can crabmeat, drained
1/2 cup grated Edam cheese	125 ml grated Edam cheese
1/2 cup grated carrot	125 ml grated carrot
1/3 cup mayonnaise	75 ml mayonnaise
1 tbsp lemon juice	15 ml lemon juice
1/4 tsp sugar	1 ml sugar
1/4 tsp curry powder	1 ml curry powder
18 slices of bread	18 slices of bread

Lightly toast the pieces of bread and trim the crust. Butter a muffin tin (for 18 muffins) and line the molds with the toast, pressing into place. Set aside.

Mix all the remaining ingredients and fill the muffin molds. Brush lightly with butter and bake for 10 minutes at 375°F (190°C) until golden brown.

CHICKEN SALAD

Standard	Metric
4 cups cooked chicken, cubed	1 liter cooked chicken, cubed
2 cups diced celery	500 ml diced celery
1/2 cup sliced olives	125 ml sliced olives
1/4 cup lemon vinaigrette	50 ml lemon vinaigrette
1/2 cup mayonnaise	125 ml mayonnaise
Lettuce	Lettuce
Tomatoes	Tomatoes
Parsley	Parsley

Place the chicken, celery and olives in a salad bowl. Add the lemon vinaigrette, toss and let stand for 1 hour. Arrange the salad on a bed of lettuce. Cover with mayonnaise. Garnish with tomato wedges and chopped parsley.

Lemon Vinaigrette

Standard	Metric
2 tbsp lemon juice	30 ml lemon juice
1 tbsp olive oil	15 ml olive oil
1 crushed clove garlic	1 crushed clove garlic
Salt and pepper	Salt and pepper
Chopped parsley	Chopped parsley

Combine the lemon juice, salt, pepper, garlic and parsley. Mix with a wire whisk and gradually add the oil. The vinaigrette should be thick and creamy.

Cheese and Crab Canapés

Ham Tarts

HAM TARTS

Standard
1 lb shortcrust pastry
3 tbsp butter
1/2 lb cooked ham, cubed
12 small sour pickles, chopped
1/4 cup chopped fresh parsley
1 onion, chopped
2 celery stalks, chopped
3 hard-boiled eggs, chopped
1 cup milk
3 eggs
1/2 cup grated cheddar
Salt and pepper

Metric
500 g shortcrust pastry
45 ml butter
250 g cooked ham, cubed
12 small sour pickles, chopped
50 ml chopped fresh parsley
1 onion, chopped
2 celery stalks, chopped
3 hard-boiled eggs, chopped
250 ml milk
3 eggs
125 ml grated cheddar
Salt and pepper

Line muffin tins with the shortcrust pastry. Melt the butter in a large saucepan and sauté the ham, pickles, onion and celery for about 5 minutes.

Add the parsley and the hard-boiled eggs. Remove from heat. Season to taste and fill muffin tins to 3/4 capacity.

In a separate bowl, beat the eggs, milk and cheese. Pour this mixture into the muffin molds and bake at 375°F (190°C) for 20 to 25 minutes.

STRAWBERRY SQUARES

Standard
3/4 cup pastry flour
1/8 tsp salt
1 tbsp sugar
1/4 cup butter
1 tbsp milk
1 egg
1/2 cup brown sugar
1/4 tsp baking powder
1 tsp vanilla extract
1 cup strawberry jam
3/4 cup slivered almonds

Metric
150 ml pastry flour
0.5 ml salt
15 ml sugar
50 ml butter
15 ml milk
1 egg
125 ml brown sugar
1 ml baking powder
5 ml vanilla extract
250 ml strawberry jam
150 ml slivered almonds

Sift the flour, salt, sugar and baking powder twice. Add the butter and the milk; mix thoroughly. Pour this batter into a greased 9 x 14 inch (22 x 35 cm) cake pan. Bake at 350°F (180°C) for 15 minutes.

In the meantime, lightly beat the egg and add the brown sugar, vanilla extract and almonds. Spread the strawberry jam on top of the cooked batter and cover with the egg and brown sugar mixture.

Place the pan back in the oven at the same temperature and bake for 10 minutes. If the surface begins to brown too quickly, cover the pan with a sheet of aluminum foil.

Cool before serving.

OYSTER PARTY

For oyster enthusiasts.

Serve with a semi-dry white wine, sparkling wine.

MENU

Serves 6

Oysters Rockefeller
Oyster Soup
Pâté de Foie and Oyster Nibbles
Cucumber Dip
Oyster-Stuffed Doré
Cauliflower au Gratin
Raspberry or Blueberry Cake

OYSTERS ROCKEFELLER

Standard	Metric
3 dozen oysters	3 dozen oysters
1 cup light white sauce (see section on sauces)	250 ml light white sauce (see section on sauces)
10 oz fresh spinach, washed and dried	300 g fresh spinach, washed and dried
1/2 cup grated Gruyère	125 ml grated Gruyère
3 egg yolks	3 egg yolks
Salt, pepper and nutmeg	Salt, pepper and nutmeg

Wash, brush and open the oysters. Place them on a bed of coarse salt on a large serving plate.

Prepare the white sauce and pour into the food processor or blender. Add the remaining ingredients and blend for 2 minutes.

Cover each oyster with this mixture and place under the broiler until golden.

Serve with buttered rye bread.

OYSTER SOUP

See page103.

PÂTÉ DE FOIE AND OYSTER NIBBLES

Standard	Metric
24 one-inch puff pastry shells	24 2.5 cm puff pastry shells
1 small tin pâté de foie	1 small tin pâté de foie
24 fresh oysters	24 fresh oysters
Freshly ground pepper	Freshly ground pepper

Heat the pastry shells and place a small amount of pâté de foie at the bottom of each one.

Drop a shucked oyster into each shell, add pepper and serve.

CUCUMBER DIP

Standard	Metric
1 cup sliced cucumbers	250 ml sliced cucumbers
1 cup sour cream or plain yogurt	250 ml sour cream or plain yogurt
3 tbsp chives or shallots	45 ml chives or shallots

Mix all the ingredients together and put through the blender until creamy.

Pour this cucumber dip over oysters on the half shell.

Serve immediately.

Oyster Soup

Oyster-Stuffed Doré

CAULIFLOWER AU GRATIN

1 cauliflower
Béchamel sauce
Breadcrumbs
Grated cheese

Break up the cauliflower into flowerets. Soak in cold, salted water. Cook for 8 to 10 minutes in boiling water. Drain and place in a baking dish.

Cover the cauliflower with a béchamel sauce (see section on sauces). Sprinkle with breadcrumbs and grated cheese. Bake at 350°F (180°C) for 15 to 20 minutes until the surface is golden brown. Serve.

OYSTER-STUFFED DORÉ

Standard	Metric
2 lb doré filets	1 kg doré filets
1 cup oysters	250 ml oysters
1/4 cup melted butter	50 ml melted butter
2 cups toasted breadcrumbs	500 ml toasted breadcrumbs
1 tsp lemon juice	5 ml lemon juice
1 lightly beaten egg	1 lightly beaten egg
2 tbsp chopped parsley	30 ml chopped parsley
Salt and pepper	Salt and pepper

Dry the filets on a paper towel. Place half the filets in a buttered baking dish. Add salt and pepper.

Drain the oysters and chop them if they are large. Combine the remaining ingredients and add the oysters. Mix gently and spread over the filets in the dish. Cover the oyster stuffing with the other half of the filets.

Bake at 450°F (230°C), calculating 10 minutes for each 1 inch (2.5 cm) thickness.

RASPBERRY OR BLUEBERRY CAKE

Standard	Metric
2 beaten eggs	2 beaten eggs
1 cup sugar	250 ml sugar
1/2 cup vegetable oil	125 ml vegetable oil
1/4 cup orange juice	50 ml orange juice
1-3/4 cups all-purpose flour	400 ml all-purpose flour
2 tsp baking powder	10 ml baking powder
1 tsp vanilla extract	5 ml vanilla extract
1 small package of frozen raspberries or blueberries	1 small package of frozen raspberries or blueberries
1/4 tsp cinnamon	1 ml cinnamon

Combine the eggs, 1/2 cup (125 ml) sugar, oil and orange juice. Mix well. Sift the flour and baking powder and incorporate into previous mixture. Add the raspberries or blueberries along with the vanilla extract. Mix.

Pour this mixture into a greased pyrex dish, measuring 9 x 13 inches (22 x 34 cm).

Combine the rest of the sugar and the cinnamon, and sprinkle over the batter. Bake at 350°F (180°C) for approximately 45 to 50 minutes.

Mixed Vegetables Vinaigrette

CARROT AND CRANBERRY CAKE

Standard
1-1/2 cups all-purpose flour
1 cup brown sugar
1 tsp baking powder
1 tsp baking soda
1/2 tsp salt
1/2 tsp cinnamon
1/2 tsp nutmeg
1 cup grated carrots
1 cup chopped cranberries
2 eggs
3/4 cup vegetable oil
Icing sugar

Metric
375 ml all-purpose flour
250 ml brown sugar
5 ml baking powder
5 ml baking soda
2 ml salt
2 ml cinnamon
2 ml nutmeg
250 ml grated carrots
250 ml chopped cranberries
2 eggs
150 ml vegetable oil
Icing sugar

Combine the flour, brown sugar, baking powder, baking soda, salt, cinnamon and nutmeg. Add the carrots and cranberries and mix thoroughly.

Beat the eggs and vegetable oil and incorporate into the previous mixture. Mix until ingredients are perfectly blended.

Pour the batter into a square mold with a 10 cup (2.5 liter) capacity. Bake at 350°F (180°C) for 40 to 45 minutes. The cake is done when an inserted toothpick comes out clean.

Cool and sprinkle with icing sugar.

MIXED VEGETABLES VINAIGRETTE

Standard
4 cups cooked mixed vegetables
3 hard-boiled eggs, quartered
1 tsp vinegar
1/2 cup vegetable oil
1 tsp Dijon mustard
Salt and pepper
Chopped parsley

Metric
1 liter cooked mixed vegetables
3 hard-boiled eggs, quartered
5 ml vinegar
125 ml vegetable oil
5 ml Dijon mustard
Salt and pepper
Chopped parsley

Combine the salt, pepper, mustard, parsley and vinegar. Gradually add the oil, stirring constantly. Pour over the eggs and vegetables. Toss and serve on a bed of lettuce.

COTTAGE GET-TOGETHER II

Prepare these dishes at home; just heat them up while you make the salad.

Serve with a hearty red Burgundy.

MENU

Serves 6 to 8

Fondue Parmesan
Barley Soup
Beef Bourguignon
Caesar Salad with Tomato
Pineapple Squares

BARLEY SOUP

Standard	Metric
1/4 cup barley	50 ml barley
1 cup diced carrots	250 ml diced carrots
1/2 cup chopped celery	125 ml chopped celery
1/4 cup chopped onion	50 ml chopped onion
1/2 cup Chinese cabbage	125 ml Chinese cabbage
1/2 cup chopped leeks	125 ml chopped leeks
1 cup fresh or frozen peas	250 ml fresh or frozen peas
2 tbsp oil	30 ml oil
3 tbsp soy sauce	45 ml soy sauce
Salt and thyme	Salt and thyme
Chopped parsley	Chopped parsley

Cook the barley in 6 cups (1.5 liters) water for 1 hour. Add the remaining vegetables and simmer until tender. Season with oil, soy sauce, salt and thyme. Garnish with parsley.

FONDUE PARMESAN

Standard	Metric
1/2 cup margarine	125 ml margarine
3/4 cup all-purpose flour	150 ml all-purpose flour
1/2 tsp salt	2 ml salt
1-3/4 cups milk	400 ml milk
3/4 cup grated Parmesan	150 ml grated Parmesan
1/2 cup grated cheddar cheese	125 ml grated cheddar cheese
2 beaten eggs	2 beaten eggs
1 cup breadcrumbs	250 ml breadcrumbs
Cooking oil	Cooking oil

Melt the margarine in a medium saucepan. Add the flour and salt and cook for 3 to 5 minutes, stirring constantly. Gradually add the milk and continue stirring until mixture thickens.

Add the cheese and stir until sauce is smooth.

Pour this mixture into a buttered 8 inch (20 cm) pan and freeze.

When ready to serve, thaw partially and cut into cubes. Dip the cubes in the beaten eggs, dredge in the breadcrumbs and fry in the cooking oil.

Fondue Parmesan

Beef Bourguignon

BEEF BOURGUIGNON

Standard	Metric
2 lb cubed beef	1 kg cubed beef
1/4 cup vegetable oil	50 ml vegetable oil
4 tbsp all-purpose flour	60 ml all-purpose flour
4 tbsp butter	60 ml butter
4 or 5 sliced carrots	4 or 5 sliced carrots
12 small onions	12 small onions
1 clove garlic	1 clove garlic
2 celery stalks, diced	2 celery stalks, diced
Bay leaf	Bay leaf
1/2 tsp thyme	2 ml thyme
2 cups dry red wine	500 ml dry red wine
2 cups apple juice	500 ml apple juice
1/2 lb salt pork	250 g salt pork
1 can beef consommé	1 can beef consommé
1 cup water	250 ml water
2 tbsp beef concentrate	30 ml beef concentrate
2 tbsp tomato paste	30 ml tomato paste
1 leek, sliced	1 leek, sliced
Parsley	Parsley
1 cup fresh mushrooms, sliced	250 ml fresh mushrooms, sliced

Pour all the liquids into a bowl except for the tomato paste. Add all the vegetables except the mushrooms. Marinate the beef in this mixture for 24 hours.

Remove the beef and vegetables and keep them separate. Reserve the marinade.

Sauté the beef cubes in a large heavy saucepan. Degrease, add the flour and mix well. Pour in the marinade to make a thick broth, then add the tomato paste.

Sauté the vegetables in a skillet and transfer to the pot when tender. Sauté the mushrooms and add to the beef bourguignon. Simmer over low heat for 2 hours.

CAESAR SALAD WITH TOMATO

Standard	Metric
1/2 cup olive oil	125 ml olive oil
2 tbsp tomato paste	30 ml tomato paste
24 cubes of bread	24 cubes of bread
1 tsp finely chopped garlic	5 ml finely chopped garlic
2 heads Romaine lettuce	2 heads Romaine lettuce
2 eggs	2 eggs
1/4 cup lemon juice	50 ml lemon juice
1 cup grated Parmesan	250 ml grated Parmesan
6 to 8 anchovy filets, chopped	6 to 8 anchovy filets, chopped
Salt and pepper	Salt and pepper

Pour a bit of olive oil into a skillet and sauté the cubes of bread on all sides until golden brown. Add more oil if necessary. Remove from heat and add the garlic. Mix well. Remove from the skillet and drain on paper towels.

Wash, dry and break up the lettuce. Place in a large salad bowl. Mix the tomato paste, olive oil, salt and pepper. Pour over the lettuce and toss.

Place the eggs in boiling water for 10 seconds and break over the salad. Add the lemon juice and toss well. Add the grated Parmesan, chopped anchovies and garlic croutons. Toss once again and serve immediately.

PINEAPPLE SQUARES

Standard	Metric
2-1/2 cups Graham cracker or vanilla wafer crumbs	625 ml Graham cracker or vanilla wafer crumbs
1 cup butter	250 ml butter
1-1/2 cups icing sugar	375 ml icing sugar
2 eggs	2 eggs
1 can crushed pineapple, drained	1 can crushed pineapple, drained
1 cup whipped cream	250 ml whipped cream

Set aside a few crackers or wafers to decorate. Work together half the butter and the remaining cracker or wafer crumbs. Line an 8 x 8 inch (20 x 20 cm) pan with this mixture.

Mix the rest of the butter with the icing sugar and the eggs and pour into the crust. Top with the drained pineapple.

Spread the whipped cream over the pineapple. Decorate with Graham crackers or vanilla wafers and chopped cherries. Refrigerate until firm and cut into squares.

Caesar Salad with Tomato

Seafood Casserole and Noodles

Standard	Metric
1 lb shelled shrimp	500 g shelled shrimp
1 lb scallops	500 g scallops
1 cup of canned mushroom pieces, drained	250 ml of canned mushroom pieces, drained
1/4 cup butter	50 ml butter
1 tbsp shallot, minced	15 ml shallot, minced
1 tsp rosemary	5 ml rosemary
1/4 cup all-purpose flour	50 ml all-purpose flour
4 cups egg noodles, cooked	1 liter egg noodles, cooked
Salt and pepper	Salt and pepper

Place all the ingredients, except noodles and flour, in an ovenproof casserole dish. Mix well.

Bake at 400°F (200°C) for 15 minutes. Remove from the oven and sprinkle evenly with flour. Mix thoroughly.

Return to the oven for another 15 minutes or until the sauce has thickened. Correct the seasoning.

Serve on a bed of hot egg noodles.

Endive and Scallop Salad

Standard	Metric
6 endives	6 endives
2 shallots, chopped	2 shallots, chopped
1/4 cup parsley, chopped	50 ml parsley, chopped
1 small Boston lettuce	1 small Boston lettuce
1/4 cup radishes, sliced	50 ml radishes, sliced
1 clove garlic, minced	1 clove garlic, minced
1 lb scallops, chopped and sautéed	500 g scallops, chopped and sautéed
1/2 cup chopped hazelnuts	125 ml chopped hazelnuts

Vinaigrette

Standard	Metric
1 cup vegetable oil	250 ml vegetable oil
1/4 cup vinegar	50 ml vinegar
1 tsp sugar	5 ml sugar
1 tsp salt	5 ml salt
1/2 tsp paprika	2 ml paprika
1/2 tsp dry mustard	2 ml dry mustard
1/4 tsp garlic powder	1 ml garlic powder
1/4 tsp pepper	1 ml pepper
2 tbsp lemon juice	30 ml lemon juice

Mix together all the vinaigrette ingredients in a jar with a tight-fitting lid. Shake thoroughly to blend. Chill in the refrigerator for a few hours.

Meanwhile, wash the endives carefully. Separate into leaves, or cut them in four lengthwise, then into 1 inch (2.5 cm) pieces. Tear the lettuce into bite-size pieces, and put in a deep salad bowl. Add the endives, shallots, parsley, garlic and radishes. Top with the scallops and chopped hazelnuts.

Shake the vinaigrette again and pour over the salad.

Lemon Pineapple Mousse

Lemon Pineapple Mousse

Standard	Metric
3 eggs	3 eggs
1 tsp grated lemon rind	5 ml grated lemon rind
6 tbsp sugar	90 ml sugar
1 package unflavored gelatin	1 package unflavored gelatin
1 can pineapple chunks (reserve 3/4 cup juice)	1 can pineapple chunks (reserve 150 ml juice)
3 tbsp lemon juice	45 ml lemon juice
3/4 cup heavy cream (35%)	150 ml heavy cream (35%)

Separate the eggs. In a small bowl, add the lemon rind and sugar to the yolks. Beat until thick and creamy.

Heat the pineapple juice in the top of a double boiler and dissolve the gelatin in it. Stir this into the egg yolk mixture. Mix in the lemon juice and the drained and chopped pineapple. Chill the mixture until it stiffens slightly.

Beat the egg whites stiff and whip the cream. Fold them into the pineapple mixture.

Turn the mixture into a soufflé dish or individual serving dishes. Chill for several hours before serving.

Après-Ski

A hearty meal to serve after a day of winter sports.

Serve with a full-bodied red wine.

Menu

Serves 6 to 8

Ham and Onion Soup au Gratin
Cabbage Rolls
Potato Cakes
Apricot Upside-Down Cake

Cabbage Rolls

1 medium cabbage

Sauce

Standard	Metric
3 cups tomato juice	750 ml tomato juice
3 tbsp lemon juice	45 ml lemon juice
1/4 cup brown sugar	50 ml brown sugar
1 tsp salt	5 ml salt
1/8 tsp pepper	0.5 ml pepper
1 clove garlic, crushed	1 clove garlic, crushed

Filling

Standard	Metric
1/2 lb ground pork	250 g ground pork
1/2 lb ground lamb **or**	250 g ground lamb **or**
1/2 lb ground veal	250 g ground veal
1/4 cup grated onion	50 ml grated onion
1/4 cup uncooked rice	50 ml uncooked rice
1 tsp salt	5 ml salt
1/8 tsp pepper	0.5 ml pepper
1 beaten egg	1 beaten egg
1/4 cup water	50 ml water

Discard the tough outside leaves of the cabbage. Place the cabbage in a large bowl and pour in enough boiling water to cover the vegetable. Allow to soak for 15 to 20 minutes. Drain and separate the leaves.

Place all the sauce ingredients in a saucepan and simmer for 15 to 20 minutes. In the meantime, combine the filling ingredients and place 2 or 3 tbsp (30 to 45 ml) of this mixture on a large cabbage leaf. Roll the leaves into fat cigars and tuck in the ends to keep the filling inside.

Arrange the cabbage rolls in a greased baking dish and cover with sauce. Cover and bake at 325°F (160°C) for 2-1/2 to 3 hours. Baste frequently.

Ham and Onion Soup au Gratin

Standard	Metric
1/3 cup corn oil	75 ml corn oil
6 medium onions, thinly sliced	6 medium onions, thinly sliced
1-1/2 cups cooked ham, cubed	375 ml cooked ham, cubed
1 tsp sugar	5 ml sugar
1/2 tsp pepper	2 ml pepper
6 cups beef stock	1.5 liters beef stock
6 thin slices toast	6 thin slices toast
1/2 cup grated Gruyère or Parmesan cheese	125 ml grated Gruyère or Parmesan cheese

Heat the oil in a heavy pot, over medium heat. Add the onions, ham, sugar and pepper. Sauté for about 20 minutes or until the onions are lightly browned. Add the beef stock and bring to a boil. Remove from heat and pour into oven-safe soup bowls. Place a slice of toast on the soup, sprinkle with grated cheese and grill until golden.

Cabbage Rolls

Apricot Upside-Down Cake

POTATO CAKES

Standard	Metric
2 cups sifted all-purpose flour	500 ml sifted all-purpose flour
1 tbsp baking powder	15 ml baking powder
1 tsp salt	5 ml salt
2 cups mashed potatoes	500 ml mashed potatoes
3/4 cup milk	150 ml milk

Combine the first four ingredients and work together well. Gradually add the milk and mix well until smooth. Use a rolling pin to spread out the mixture about 1/2 inch (1.25 cm) thick. Cut into squares and bake on a greased cookie sheet at 400°F (200°C) for 10 minutes. Serve with butter.

APRICOT UPSIDE-DOWN CAKE

Standard	Metric
3 tbsp butter	45 ml butter
1 can apricots, sliced	1 can apricots, sliced
1/4 cup cherries	50 ml cherries
1/2 cup slivered almonds	125 ml slivered almonds
1/2 cup shredded coconut	125 ml shredded coconut
1/2 cup brown sugar	125 ml brown sugar
3 tbsp milk	45 ml milk
1/4 cup candied ginger	50 ml candied ginger
1/3 cup butter	75 ml butter
1 cup sugar	250 ml sugar
2 eggs	2 eggs
2 cups all-purpose flour	500 ml all-purpose flour
1 tbsp baking powder	15 ml baking powder
Pinch salt	Pinch salt
3/4 cup milk	150 ml milk

Melt the butter in a mold and line with the apricots, candied cherries and almonds. In a separate bowl, combine the coconut, brown sugar, milk and ginger. Mix well, pour over the fruit and set aside.

Cream the butter and gradually add sugar. Incorporate the eggs one at a time, stirring after each addition. Combine the baking powder, salt and flour; add to the egg mixture alternating with the milk. Mix thoroughly and pour batter over the fruit.

Bake at 350°F (180°C) for about 50 minutes. Turn out the mold while still warm. Cool and serve.

MICROWAVE METHOD

Apricot Upside-Down Cake

Standard	Metric
1/2 cup butter	*125 ml butter*
1/2 cup sugar	*125 ml sugar*
2 eggs	*2 eggs*
1-1/4 cups all-purpose flour	*300 ml all-purpose flour*
1/2 tsp baking powder	*2 ml baking powder*
3 tbsp milk	*45 ml milk*
10 oz apricot jam	*275 g apricot jam*
1 tbsp apricot brandy	*15 ml apricot brandy*
Canned apricots, quartered	*Canned apricots, quartered*

Blend together the butter, sugar and eggs. Sift the flour and the baking powder together. Add the flour and milk alternately to the egg mixture and mix well. Line a microwave-safe cake mold with greased wax paper. Cook at HIGH for 4-1/2 minutes or until the cake no longer sticks to the sides of the mold. Cover with a paper towel and let stand for 5 minutes before turning out. Mix the jam and brandy and spread on the cake. Garnish with apricots.

APRÈS-SKI II

Prepare this meal early; just heat up the soup and stew when you come home from a day outside.

Serve with a hearty red or rosé wine.

CREAM OF POTATO AND BROCCOLI

Standard	Metric
2 cups chicken stock	500 ml chicken stock
2 cups broccoli flowerets	500 ml broccoli flowerets
2 medium onions, minced	2 medium onions, minced
3 potatoes, peeled and sliced	3 potatoes, peeled and sliced
2 cups milk	500 ml milk
1/4 tsp salt	1 ml salt
Pepper	Pepper
1/4 tsp thyme	1 ml thyme
2 tbsp chives, chopped	30 ml chives, chopped

Bring the chicken stock to a boil. Add the broccoli, onions and potatoes to the boiling stock. Reduce heat, cover and simmer for 10 to 15 minutes.

Put the soup through the blender until smooth. Pour contents back into the pot. Stir in the milk and add salt and thyme. Reheat without boiling. Add pepper to taste and garnish with chives. Serve hot.

MICROWAVE TIP

How to Dry Fresh Herbs

Remove the leaves from their stems. Arrange the leaves on a paper towel placed on a sheet of cardboard. Cover with plastic wrap. Heat at HIGH for 20 seconds. Some herbs may require an additional 10 seconds of drying time. Let stand 10 minutes before storing.

DOWN HOME STEW

Standard	Metric
1 chicken, about 3 lb	1 chicken, about 1.5 kg
3 lb pork, cubed	1.5 kg pork, cubed
2 pig knuckles	2 pig knuckles
1 lb ground beef meatballs	500 g ground beef meatballs
1 lb ground pork meatballs	500 g ground pork meatballs
1 clove garlic, minced	1 clove garlic, minced
1 onion, minced	1 onion, minced
3 tbsp toasted flour	45 ml toasted flour
1 cup green peas	250 ml green peas
1 cup diced carrots	250 ml diced carrots
1 cup diced potatoes	250 ml diced potatoes
1 tbsp beef concentrate	15 ml beef concentrate
Parsley	Parsley

Brown the cubed pork and the meatballs in a heavy skillet. Reserve. Place the chicken and pig knuckles in a large cooking pot. Add 4 cups (1 liter) water and boil until the meat falls from the bone. Debone and return to the pot, adding the garlic, parsley and onion. Sift the toasted flour over the stew and stir. Add the pork cubes, meatballs, vegetables and beef concentrate. Simmer for another 30 minutes or until tender and serve with Potato Cakes (see page 225).

Cream of Potato and Broccoli

Cheese-Stuffed Pepper Slices

CHEESE-STUFFED PEPPER SLICES

3 sweet green peppers
3 sweet red peppers
Cheese Bombe with Calvados
(see page 165)

Cut the tops off the peppers and empty carefully using a spoon. Plunge them in salted boiling water and cook for 3 to 4 minutes. Run under cold water to cool. Drain.

Stuff the peppers with the Cheese Bombe recipe.

Refrigerate for about 3 hours. Slice and serve with a cold tomato sauce.

PRINCESS SALAD

Standard	Metric
2 heads Boston or Bib lettuce	2 heads Boston or Bib lettuce
3 dozen asparagus spears (cooked or canned)	3 dozen asparagus spears (cooked or canned)
3 large tomatoes	3 large tomatoes
3/4 cup French dressing	150 ml French dressing
2 sweet red peppers	2 sweet red peppers
6 tbsp chopped parsley	90 ml chopped parsley

Make sure the lettuce is free of sand and dirt. Cut each head of lettuce into 1/2 inch (1.25 cm) slices.

On each plate, overlap the following: 1 slice of lettuce, 2 slices tomato, 3 asparagus spears. Slice the peppers into long, thin ribbons and place around the lettuce, tomato and asparagus. Sprinkle with parsley.

Serve with French dressing or favorite vinaigrette.

RICE PUDDING PIE

Standard	Metric
4 cups milk	1 liter milk
3/4 cup uncooked rice	150 ml uncooked rice
Pinch salt	Pinch salt
1/2 tsp cinnamon	2 ml cinnamon
3/4 cup sugar	150 ml sugar
3 egg yolks	3 egg yolks
2 tbsp custard powder	30 ml custard powder
1/4 cup cold milk	50 ml cold milk
3 egg whites	3 egg whites, whipped
1 egg beaten with	1 egg beaten with
1 tbsp icing sugar	15 ml icing sugar

Line two 8 inch (20 cm) pie plates with a 1/8 inch (3 mm) layer of shortcrust pastry (see Easter Custard Pie page 75).

Pour the milk into a heavy pot and bring to a boil. Add the rice and salt and continue boiling, stirring constantly with a wooden spoon. Once the milk begins to froth and bubble over, add the cinnamon and the sugar. Reduce the heat, cover and cook gently until the rice is done.

In the meantime, dissolve the custard in the cold milk. Blend in beaten egg yolks and add this to the hot rice mixture. Stir the contents of the pot with a wire whisk until very thick. Remove from heat and gently fold in the egg whites. Pour this mixture into the lined pie plates.

Brush the pies with the egg and icing sugar mixture.

Bake at 350°F (180°C) for approximately 30 minutes.

Rice Pudding Pie

MIDNIGHT MEAL

When you feel like celebrating for no reason at all.

Serve with a white Sauvignon or Bordeaux wine.

MENU

Serves 6 to 8

Red Cabbage and Apple Soup
Curried Artichoke Hearts
Roast Veal with Apples
Scalloped Potatoes
Custard Pie

RED CABBAGE AND APPLE SOUP

Standard	Metric
1 red cabbage, shredded	1 red cabbage, shredded
6 apples, peeled, cored and diced	6 apples, peeled, cored and diced
6 cups chicken stock	1.5 liters chicken stock
1/4 cup vinegar	50 ml vinegar
1 cup cooked ham, diced	250 ml cooked ham, diced
1/2 cup smoked pork, diced	125 ml smoked pork, diced
3 tbsp butter	45 ml butter
1 onion, minced	1 onion, minced
2 tbsp sugar	30 ml sugar

Melt the butter in a large saucepan and fry the pork. Add the red cabbage, ham and onion and braise for 10 minutes or until the cabbage has lost all its liquid.

Add the apples, vinegar, sugar and chicken stock. Bring to a boil and cook for 30 minutes. Serve.

MICROWAVE METHOD

Cooking Artichokes

Remove bottom leaves and cut the points off the remaining leaves.

Brush artichokes with lemon and wrap individually in plastic. Cook at HIGH for 10 to 12 minutes or until lower leaves are easily pulled off. Let stand 3 to 5 minutes.

CURRIED ARTICHOKE HEARTS

Standard	Metric
1 cup light cream (15%)	250 ml light cream (15%)
1-1/4 cups mayonnaise	300 ml mayonnaise
2 tbsp curry	30 ml curry
1/2 tsp dry mustard	2 ml dry mustard
1/4 cup dry white wine	50 ml dry white wine
1 tsp garlic powder	5 ml garlic powder
3 cans artichoke hearts, drained	3 cans artichoke hearts, drained
1 tsp salt	5 ml salt

Beat all the ingredients together, except artichokes, until smooth.

Arrange the artichokes on a serving dish garnished with lettuce leaves. Pour the sauce over the artichokes and serve.

Red Cabbage and Apple Soup

Roast Veal with Apples

ROAST VEAL WITH APPLES

Standard	Metric
1 tsp salt	5 ml salt
1/2 tsp pepper	2 ml pepper
2 tsp prepared mustard	10 ml prepared mustard
Veal roast, about 4 lb	Veal roast, about 2 kg
1/2 lb bacon, sliced	250 g bacon, sliced
3/4 cup vegetable oil	150 ml vegetable oil
3 apples, quartered	3 apples, quartered
1/2 cup carrots, chopped	125 ml carrots, chopped
1/2 cup onion, chopped	125 ml onion, chopped
1/2 cup celery, chopped	125 ml celery, chopped
1/2 cup all-purpose flour	125 ml all-purpose flour
2-1/2 cups beef stock	625 ml beef stock

Rub the veal with salt and pepper. Brush with the mustard and cover with the bacon slices. Tie with string to keep the bacon slices in place. Braise the roast on all sides in the vegetable oil. Place the veal in a roasting pan and cook for 45 minutes at 350°F (180°C). Remove from the oven and place the apples, carrots, celery and onion around the roast. Return to the oven for 20 minutes. Remove the roast and set aside.

Degrease the drippings and gradually add the flour to the sauce. Simmer the sauce on the stovetop for a few minutes. Add the beef stock and simmer until sauce is reduced by half. Correct the seasoning and put the sauce through a strainer.

Carve the roast into slices and place these on a serving plate (or individual plates). Add the sauce and garnish with raw or sautéed apple quarters.

SCALLOPED POTATOES

Standard	Metric
6 to 8 potatoes	6 to 8 potatoes
1 onion, thinly sliced	1 onion, thinly sliced
3 cups hot milk	750 ml hot milk
2 tbsp butter	30 ml butter
All-purpose flour	All-purpose flour
Salt and pepper	Salt and pepper

Peel and cut the potatoes into thin slices. Line a baking dish with a layer of potatoes. Between each layer sprinkle flour, salt and pepper; add a few onion slices and dot with butter. Continue until potatoes are used.

Cover the potatoes with hot milk.

Bake uncovered at 375°F (190°C) for 30 to 35 minutes, until potatoes are tender and golden.

CUSTARD PIE

Standard	Metric
3 eggs	3 eggs
1/2 tsp vanilla extract	2 ml vanilla extract
Pinch nutmeg	Pinch nutmeg
1-1/3 cups warm milk	325 ml warm milk
3/4 cup sugar	150 ml sugar
1 shortcrust pastry shell	1 shortcrust pastry shell

Beat the eggs and add the sugar, milk, vanilla and nutmeg.

Line a pie plate with shortcrust pastry and bake at 450°F (230°C) for 10 minutes. Remove from the oven. Pour the custard into the pie shell and bake at 350°F (180°C) for about 30 minutes, or until firm.

229

HUNTER'S BANQUET

Wild game is featured in this classic and substantial menu.

Serve with a semi-dry white wine, red Bordeaux, or sparkling rosé.

MENU

Serves 6 to 8

Cream of Chicken and Quail Soup
Baked Beans with Partridge
Stuffed Shoulder of Venison
Vegetable Bacon Casserole
Maple Chiffon Pie

CREAM OF CHICKEN AND QUAIL SOUP

Standard	Metric
2 tbsp butter	30 ml butter
2 tbsp all-purpose flour	30 ml all-purpose flour
6 cups chicken stock	1.5 liters chicken stock
1-1/2 cups cooked chicken, in small cubes	375 ml cooked chicken, in small cubes
1 cup baked quail meat, in small cubes	250 ml baked quail meat, in small cubes
2 shallots, chopped	2 shallots, chopped
2 tbsp tarragon	30 ml tarragon
2 tbsp heavy cream (35%)	30 ml heavy cream (35%)

Cream of Chicken and Quail Soup

Melt the butter in a heavy saucepan and add the flour. Cook briefly to form a paste. Gradually add the chicken stock and cream. Bring to a boil, stirring constantly and continue simmering for 20 minutes. Add the chicken, quail, tarragon and shallots. Once hot, serve immediately.

Variation: For a creamier soup, add the cream just before serving. Leeks may be substituted for shallots.

BAKED BEANS WITH PARTRIDGE

Standard	Metric
2 cups Navy beans	500 ml Navy beans
1/4 to 1/2 lb salt pork, in large cubes	125 to 250 g salt pork, in large cubes
1 medium onion	1 medium onion, whole
1/4 cup molasses	50 ml molasses
1/4 cup brown sugar	50 ml brown sugar
1/4 cup ketchup	50 ml ketchup
1 tsp mustard	5 ml mustard
3 partridge	3 partridge
Salt	Salt

Soak the beans in cold water for 12 hours. Boil them gently in the soaking water, until plump. Place the beans in a crock pot or a bean pot. Stir in the salt pork, onion, salt, molasses, brown sugar, ketchup and mustard.

Cut each partridge into six pieces and place in the pot. Add just enough water to cover the contents. Bake at 250°F (120°C) for 5 to 6 hours, adding liquid as necessary. Uncover for the last hour.

Variation: Hare or chicken may be used instead of partridge.

STUFFED SHOULDER OF VENISON

Standard	Metric
3 lb venison, shoulder cut	1.5 kg venison, shoulder cut
Salt pork	Salt pork
1 onion, chopped	1 onion, chopped
2 cups boiling water	500 ml boiling water
2 cups stale bread soaked in	500 ml stale bread soaked in
1 cup beef stock	250 ml beef stock
1 onion, chopped	1 onion, chopped
1 egg	1 egg
Nutmeg	Nutmeg
Salt and parsley	Salt and parsley

Baked Beans with Partridge

Maple Chiffon Pie

Standard	Metric
1/2 cup maple syrup	125 ml maple syrup
1/4 cup milk	50 ml milk
1/4 tsp salt	1 ml salt
1 tbsp unflavored gelatin	15 ml unflavored gelatin
2 tbsp cold water	30 ml cold water
2 eggs	2 eggs
1-1/2 cups whipping cream	375 ml whipping cream
1 tsp vanilla extract	5 ml vanilla extract
1 shortcrust pie shell, cooked	1 shortcrust pie shell, cooked

Dissolve the gelatin in cold water. Separate the egg yolks from the whites and set aside. Heat the beaten egg yolks over hot water.

Heat the milk, maple syrup and salt in a double boiler. Carefully add the egg yolks and stir. Add warmed gelatin and stir until mixture is smooth. Remove from heat and cool.

Beat the egg whites until firm. Whip the cream and add vanilla extract. Fold the egg whites and half the cream into the milk and maple syrup mixture. Pour this filling into the pie shell. Decorate with the rest of the whipped cream and refrigerate.

Sprinkle with chopped nuts or shredded coconut.

Prepare stuffing by combining the bread, beef stock, onion and egg. Debone the roast and fill the cavity with the stuffing.

Sew the opening to prevent the stuffing from falling out. Place the meat in a large covered baking dish lined with salt pork and onions. Add the boiling water and cook at 350°F (180°C) for about 2 hours. Add water if necessary.

Keep the roast warm in a low oven. Place the pan or casserole on the stovetop and reduce the stock. Correct the seasoning. Serve the roast with the gravy and with apple sauce.

Vegetable Bacon Casserole

Standard	Metric
1/2 lb smoked bacon	250 g smoked bacon
2 potatoes, sliced	2 potatoes, sliced
1 cup carrots, sliced	250 ml carrots, sliced
1 cup celery, sliced	250 ml celery, sliced
1 cup onions, sliced	250 ml onions, sliced
2 tomatoes, sliced	2 tomatoes, sliced
Thyme and paprika	Thyme and paprika
Salt and pepper	Salt and pepper

In a buttered baking dish, arrange all the ingredients in layers in the above order. A layer of bacon may be added at the halfway mark. Sprinkle with salt, pepper, thyme and paprika. Bake at 350°F (180°C) for 1 hour. Serve warm.

Vegetable Bacon Casserole

231

Hunter's Banquet II

Nature's bounty in one satisfying meal.

Serve a light-bodied red wine, and chilled rum.

Menu

Serves 6 to 8

Rice and Partridge Soup
Forest Tourtière
Wild Goose Stew
Vegetable Macedoine with Onion Marmalade
Rum Fritters

Rice and Partridge Soup

Standard	Metric
1 partridge	1 partridge
1 small onion	1 small onion
3/4 cup rice	150 ml rice
Fine herbes	Fine herbes
Parsley and savory	Parsley and savory
Salt and pepper	Salt and pepper

Cook the partridge in 6 cups (1.5 liters) boiling water for about 1 hour. Add salt, pepper and chopped onion. Remove the partridge and strain the stock. Bring the stock to a boil and add rice and herbs. Simmer for 30 minutes.

In the meantime debone the partridge and cut the meat into bite-size pieces. Place the meat in with the stock; add parsley and savory to taste.

Rice and Partridge Soup

Forest Tourtière

Standard	Metric
Shortcrust pastry	Shortcrust pastry
1 or 2 hares	1 or 2 hares
12 cups chicken stock	3 liters chicken stock
1 lb ground pork	500 g ground pork
1 lb ground beef	500 g ground beef
3 large onions	3 large onions
2 large potatoes, diced	2 large potatoes, diced
Thyme and chopped parsley	Thyme and chopped parsley
Cinnamon and cloves	Cinnamon and cloves
Salt and pepper	Salt and pepper

Season and roast the hare in a 400°F (200°C) oven for 30 minutes. Remove and place in the chicken stock. Bring to a boil and simmer for 1 hour and 30 minutes.

In a separate saucepan, sauté the pork, beef, onions and potatoes in a small amount of water.

Debone the hare and add to the ground meat mixture; cook for about 10 minutes.

Line a deep pie plate with the shortcrust and add the tourtière filling. Add spices and seasoning and cover with the second pastry crust. Seal the edges and prick the surface of the pie with a fork. Bake at 300°F (150°C) for 1 hour.

Wild Goose Stew

Standard	Metric
2 wild geese	2 wild geese
1/3 lb salt pork, sliced	150 g salt pork, sliced
2 medium onions	2 medium onions
1/2 cup diced celery	125 ml diced celery
2/3 cup all-purpose flour	150 ml all-purpose flour
3 tbsp parsley	45 ml parsley
1/2 cup butter	125 ml butter

Clean the geese and cook in salted boiling water for 1 hour. Drain and cut each goose into eight pieces. Place in a large casserole with the salt pork. Add the onion and half the celery and sauté until all ingredients are lightly browned. Degrease and cover with boiling water. Simmer for about one hour or until the meat is tender (drumsticks require longer cooking time).

In the meantime, work the butter and flour together. Add to the stew and stir until sauce thickens. Add the rest of the celery.

Serve with vegetables or brown rice.

Forest Tourtière and Vegetable Macedoine with Onion Marmalade

VEGETABLE MACEDOINE WITH ONION MARMALADE

Standard	Metric
1 cup carrots, diced	250 ml carrots, diced
1 cup wax or green beans, diced	250 ml wax or green beans, diced
1 cup peas	250 ml peas
1 tbsp roast drippings	15 ml roast drippings
1 cup chicken stock	250 ml chicken stock
Fresh parsley or dried fines herbes	Fresh parsley or dried fines herbes
5 to 6 tbsp of onion marmalade (see chapter on canapés)	75 to 90 ml onion marmalade (see chapter on canapés)
Salt and pepper	Salt and pepper

Cook all the vegetables separately in boiling water. This will help them retain their color and flavor. Drain and run under cold water to cool. Drain once more.

Melt the roast drippings in a skillet and sauté the vegetables, stirring gently. Add the chicken stock and herbs. Add salt and pepper to taste. Simmer for several minutes.

Add the onion marmalade, mix and serve.

RUM FRITTERS

Standard	Metric
3/4 cup raisins	150 ml raisins
2/3 cup rum	150 ml rum
1-1/2 envelopes dry yeast	1-1/2 envelopes dry yeast
1/2 cup warm water	125 ml warm water
4 cups all-purpose flour	1 liter all-purpose flour
1/4 cup sugar	50 ml sugar
Pinch salt	Pinch salt
Grated lemon rind	Grated lemon rind
5 tbsp chopped nuts	75 ml chopped nuts
Pinch cinnamon	Pinch cinnamon
1/3 cup candied fruit peel	75 ml candied fruit peel
Cooking oil	Cooking oil
Sugar	Sugar

Soak the raisins in the rum until plump. Dissolve the yeast in the warm water. Sift the flour into a warm mixing bowl and make a well in the center. Add the yeast, sugar, salt, lemon rind, nuts, raisins, rum, cinnamon and candied fruit. Mix thoroughly with a wooden spoon. Add a bit of water if necessary.

Cover the bowl with a warm cloth and stand in a warm place for 4 hours or until batter has doubled in volume.

Punch the dough down and knead until very smooth. Add water to make the dough easier to work.

Heat the cooking oil in a deep-fryer. Gently drop in small balls of dough. Remove when golden brown. Drain on a paper towel and sprinkle with sugar or icing sugar. Serve.

Rum Fritters

COUNTRY BRUNCH

Invite friends over Sunday morning for an easy relaxed meal.

Serve with dry white wine or sparkling rosé.

MENU

Serves 6 to 8

Kir Ticklers
Grapefruit and Salmon
Cream of Endive Soup
Merguez and Spinach Salad
Cretons
Strawberry and Banana Mousse

KIR TICKLERS

Standard
4 cups dry white wine
1 bottle ginger ale
6 oz cassis

Metric
1 liter dry white wine
1 bottle ginger ale
175 ml cassis

Combine the ingredients and serve in iced wine glasses.

GRAPEFRUIT AND SALMON

Standard
6 small grapefruit
3 tbsp mayonnaise
1 tsp capers
Juice of half a lemon
2 cans of salmon

Metric
6 small grapefruit
45 ml mayonnaise
5 ml capers
Juice of half a lemon
2 cans of salmon

Cut the tops off the grapefruit. Empty the fruit and cut the top edge into a sawtooth pattern.

Combine the pulp and the other ingredients and season to taste. Mix well and stuff the grapefruit with this filling. Serve on plates decorated with lettuce leaves. Garnish with fresh parsley.

Grapefruit and Salmon

CREAM OF ENDIVE SOUP

Standard	Metric
10 endives, chopped	10 endives, chopped
2 potatoes, chopped	2 potatoes, chopped
1 onion, minced	1 onion, minced
6 cups chicken stock	1.5 liters chicken stock
1/2 cup heavy cream (35%)	125 ml heavy cream (35%)
1 tbsp lemon juice	15 ml lemon juice
1 tsp Dijon mustard	5 ml Dijon mustard
1 tsp thyme	5 ml thyme
2 tbsp butter	30 ml butter
Handful croutons	Handful croutons
Salt and pepper	Salt and pepper

Sprinkle the lemon juice over the chopped endives. Mix. Melt the butter in a large skillet and sauté the endives, potatoes, onion and thyme. Cook for 7 minutes over low heat, stirring occasionally. Add the chicken stock and simmer for an additional 20 minutes. Put the contents of skillet through the blender to liquefy. While running the blender, add the cream and Dijon mustard. Add salt and pepper to taste and heat for 3 minutes before serving. Garnish with croutons.

MICROWAVE TIP

How to Cook Merguez Sausage

Place the sausage links on several sheets of paper towels. Cover with another paper towel and cook at HIGH for 3 to 4 minutes. Let stand several minutes before serving.

MERGUEZ AND SPINACH SALAD

Standard	Metric
5 merguez sausages, cooked and sliced	5 merguez sausages, cooked and sliced
2 bags (20 oz) spinach, chopped	2 bags (625 g) spinach, chopped
2 tomatoes, sliced	2 tomatoes, sliced
3 hard boiled eggs, chopped	3 hard boiled eggs, chopped
1/2 cup yogurt	125 ml yogurt
4 tsp lemon juice	20 ml lemon juice
3 shallots, chopped	3 shallots, chopped
Salt and pepper	Salt and pepper

Combine the yogurt, lemon juice, shallots and seasonings. Mix well and set aside. Place the merguez, spinach and eggs in a large salad bowl. Decorate with tomato slices. Pour the yogurt dressing over the salad.

CRETONS

Standard	Metric
2 lb pork, cubed	1 kg pork, cubed
2 onions, chopped	2 onions, chopped
Pepper	Pepper
2 cups water	500 g water
2 cloves garlic	2 cloves garlic
1/2 cup oatmeal	125 ml oatmeal
1 tbsp salt	15 ml salt
1/2 tsp mixed spice	2 ml mixed spice
1 cup milk	250 ml milk

Place all the ingredients in a cooking pot and braise for approximately one hour or until the pork can easily be cut with a fork. Put through the blender using short pulses.

Refrigerate in a glass dish.

Makes 3 lb (1.5 kg) of cretons.

STRAWBERRY AND BANANA MOUSSE

Standard	Metric
1-1/2 cups ripe strawberries, fresh or frozen	375 ml ripe strawberries, fresh or frozen
3 bananas	3 bananas
1/4 cup orange juice	50 ml orange juice
3 tbsp plain yogurt	45 ml plain yogurt

Put all the ingredients through the blender until mousse becomes smooth and creamy. Serve in dessert bowls or parfait glasses. Decorate with chopped walnuts. Serve with tea biscuits, if desired.

Strawberry and Banana Mousse

COUNTRY BRUNCH II

A light brunch with an elegant version of pizza.

Serve with a white Bordeaux or sparkling wine.

MENU

Serves 6 to 8

Marinated Chicken and Avocado Pizza
Celery Hearts Vinaigrette
Scrambled Eggs with Shrimp Sauce
Tossed Salad with Low-Cal Dressing
Iced Tea
Orange Cake

MARINATED CHICKEN AND AVOCADO PIZZA

Standard	Metric
1 frozen pizza crust	1 frozen pizza crust
4 boneless chicken breasts	4 boneless chicken breasts
Juice of 3 limes	Juice of 3 limes
Juice of one lemon	Juice of one lemon
1 tbsp parsley	15 ml parsley
1 tsp thyme	5 ml thyme
1 tsp oregano	5 ml oregano
1 tsp sweet basil	5 ml sweet basil
1 tsp salt	5 ml salt
1 tsp pepper	5 ml pepper
1 tsp cayenne	5 ml cayenne
2 tbsp butter	30 ml butter
1/2 cup olive oil	125 ml olive oil
2 avocados, coarsely chopped	2 avocados, coarsely chopped
2 onions, thinly sliced	2 onion, thinly sliced
2 tomatoes, sliced	2 tomatoes, sliced
2 hard-boiled eggs, sliced	2 hard-boiled eggs, sliced
1 cup sour cream	250 ml sour cream

Mince the chicken and place in a bowl with the lemon and lime juices. Add the parsley, thyme, oregano, sweet basil, salt, pepper, cayenne and olive oil. Marinate in the refrigerator for 2 hours, stirring occasionally.

Sauté the onions in butter until golden. Set aside.

Place the chicken on the pizza crust, along with a bit of the marinade. Then add the sautéed onions, eggs and tomatoes. Garnish with the avocados.

Bake at 350°F (180°C) for about 35 minutes. Serve with a dollop of sour cream.

Variation: Halfway through the cooking time, cover the pizza with ricotta cheese.

Celery Hearts Vinaigrette

CELERY HEARTS VINAIGRETTE

Standard	Metric
2 celery hearts	2 celery hearts
2 chicken bouillon cubes	2 chicken bouillon cubes
2 cups lemon-flavored water	500 ml lemon-flavored water
3/4 cup white vinegar	150 ml white vinegar
1/3 cup vegetable oil	75 ml vegetable oil
1/3 cup green pepper, chopped	75 ml green pepper, chopped
3 tbsp green peppercorns	45 ml green peppercorns
1 tsp sugar	5 ml sugar
1 tsp salt	5 ml salt
3/4 tsp pepper	3 ml pepper
1 tsp dry mustard	5 ml dry mustard
Romaine lettuce	Romaine lettuce

Quarter each celery heart and remove the leaves. Place the celery in a saucepan filled with lemon water. Add bouillon cubes and bring to a boil. Simmer for one hour.

Vinaigrette

Combine vinegar, vegetable oil, green peppers, green peppercorns, sugar, salt, pepper and mustard. Mix well with a wire whisk.

Drain the celery and place in a long dish. Cover with vinaigrette and refrigerate for 4 hours. Serve on a bed of Romaine lettuce.

Scrambled Eggs with Shrimp Sauce

SCRAMBLED EGGS WITH SHRIMP SAUCE

Standard	Metric
8 eggs	8 eggs
1/2 lb shrimp, chopped	250 g shrimp, chopped
1-1/2 cups white sauce	375 ml white sauce
1/4 cup dry white wine	50 ml dry white wine
4 tbsp butter	60 ml butter
1 shallot, chopped	1 shallot, chopped
2 tsp parsley	10 ml parsley
1 tsp paprika	5 ml paprika
Salt and pepper	Salt and pepper

Sauté the shrimp, shallot and parsley in 2 tbsp (30 ml) butter. Cook for 4 minutes. Add the wine and continue to simmer for 2 minutes. Add the white sauce and paprika. Keep warm.

Beat the eggs lightly, adding salt and pepper to taste. Cook the eggs quickly over high heat, stirring constantly with a wooden spoon. Place the scrambled eggs on a warm dish and cover with shrimp sauce. Serve immediately.

ICED TEA

Standard	Metric
4 cups hot tea	1 liter hot tea
1 lemon	1 lemon
7 tbsp icing sugar	105 ml icing sugar
Ice cubes	Ice cubes

Wash the lemon and cut into very thin slices. Place the slices at the bottom of a carafe or juice container. Add the ice cubes, icing sugar and hot tea. Stir and refrigerate. Serve very cold, over ice.

TOSSED SALAD WITH LOW-CAL DRESSING

Standard	Metric
2 to 3 heads leaf or Boston lettuce	2 to 3 heads leaf or Boston lettuce
2 tsp corn starch	10 ml corn starch
3/4 cup water	150 ml water
1/2 tsp salt	2 ml salt
1/2 tsp onion powder	2 ml onion powder
1/2 tsp celery seed	2 ml celery seed
1/2 tsp paprika	2 ml paprika
1/2 tsp dry mustard	2 ml dry mustard
1/4 cup lemon juice	50 ml lemon juice
1/2 cup ketchup	125 ml ketchup
1 tbsp vegetable oil	15 ml vegetable oil
1 tsp Worcestershire sauce	5 ml Worcestershire sauce
1 tbsp sugar	15 ml sugar

Boil the corn starch and water until mixture thickens. Add to the remaining salad dressing ingredients and mix well. Pour over lettuce leaves or favorite uncooked vegetables. Unused salad dressing should be stored in the refrigerator.

ORANGE CAKE

Standard	Metric
1/2 cup butter	125 ml butter
1 cup sugar	250 ml sugar
2 eggs	2 eggs
Juice and grated rind of one orange	Juice and grated rind of one orange
3/4 cup hot water	150 ml hot water
1 cup raisins	250 ml raisins
1 cup nuts	250 ml nuts
1 tsp vanilla extract	5 ml vanilla extract
2 cups all-purpose flour	500 ml all-purpose flour
2 tsp baking soda	10 ml baking soda

Cream the butter and incorporate the sugar and eggs. Mix well. Add the grated orange rind. Put the peeled orange (seeds removed) through the food processor and add to egg mixture. Alternately add the flour and water, stirring constantly. Add raisins, nuts and vanilla extract. Mix thoroughly. Pour batter into a cake mold and bake at 350°F (180°C) for 30 to 45 minutes.

Decorate with thin slices of orange.

Orange Cake

Country Buffet

Combining old favorites and some new twists.

Serve with a semi-dry white wine and a sparkling wine.

Stuffed Mushrooms

Standard	Metric
24 large mushrooms	24 large mushrooms
3/4 cup grated Emmenthal	150 ml grated Emmenthal
3/4 cup cretons	150 ml cretons
(see page 236, Cretons)	(see page 236, Cretons)
1 tbsp butter	15 ml butter
Salt and pepper	Salt and pepper

Remove and finely chop the mushroom stems. Add salt and pepper.

Sauté the stems in butter until all the liquid has evaporated. Remove and place in a bowl.

Add the cretons to the mushrooms and mix well. Use this filling to stuff the mushroom caps. Place the stuffed mushrooms on a greased cookie sheet, sprinkle with Emmenthal and place under the broiler for 3 to 5 minutes. Serve immediately.

Home-Baked Bread

Standard	Metric
1 envelope dry yeast	1 envelope dry yeast
1 cup warm water	250 ml warm water
1 cup milk	250 ml milk
1 cup cold water	250 ml cold water
2 tsp salt	10 ml salt
3 tbsp sugar	45 ml sugar
4 tsp shortening	20 ml shortening
5 cups all-purpose flour	1.5 liters all-purpose flour

Dissolve the yeast in warm water. Let stand for 20 minutes. Set aside. Heat the milk but do not boil. Pour the milk into a large mixing bowl. Add cold water, salt, sugar, shortening and yeast. Gradually add the flour and work with both hands. Place on a greased surface and let stand for 30 minutes.

Knead the dough and let stand for another 30 minutes.

In the meantime, grease 2 loaf pans. Knead the dough and place in the pans. Let stand in a warm place for about 3 hours, until dough has doubled in volume.

Bake at 350°F (180°C) for 30 minutes. Remove from oven and brush with butter.

Pâté de Foie

Standard	Metric
1 lb calf's liver or chicken livers	500 g calf's liver or chicken livers
1 lb salt pork	500 g salt pork
1 tsp salt	5 ml salt
1/2 tsp pepper	2 ml pepper
1 tsp dry mustard	5 ml dry mustard
4 bay leaves	4 bay leaves

Line the top of a double-boiler with strips of salt pork. Place the bay leaves on the strips. Rinse and dry remaining

Stuffed Mushrooms

240

Pâté de Foie

lard slices and put through the blender or food processor along with the liver. Add salt, pepper and dry mustard.

Turn the liver paste into the double-boiler. Cover and cook for 4 hours. Refrigerate for 24 hours before removing the pâté from the pan.

Oven Method: Line a pyrex dish with the strips of lard and 4 bay leaves. Turn the liver paste into the dish. Place the dish in a pan of water and bake at 350°F (180°C) for 2 hours. Refrigerate for 24 hours before turning out of the mold.

SWEDISH MEATBALLS

Standard	Metric
1-1/2 lb ground beef	750 g ground beef
2 cups fresh breadcrumbs	500 ml fresh breadcrumbs
1/2 lb ground pork	250 g ground pork
2 mashed potatoes	2 mashed potatoes
2 beaten eggs	2 beaten eggs
1 small onion, finely chopped	1 small onion, finely chopped
7 tbsp all-purpose flour	105 ml all-purpose flour
2 tsp salt	10 ml salt
Pinch pepper	Pinch pepper
1/4 to 1/3 cup butter or margarine	50 to 75 ml butter or margarine

Combine the beef, breadcrumbs, pork, potatoes, eggs and onion. Mix thoroughly and shape into meatballs 1 inch (2.5 cm) in diameter. Coat each meatball in flour seasoned with salt and pepper. Melt the butter or margarine in a skillet and brown the meatballs quickly on all sides. Remove from heat.

Sauce

Standard	Metric
1/4 cup butter or margarine	50 ml butter or margarine
1/4 cup all-purpose flour	50 ml all-purpose flour
3 cups beef consommé	750 ml beef consommé
3/4 cup light cream (15%)	150 ml light cream (15%)
Salt and pepper	Salt and pepper
Few drops beef concentrate	Few drops beef concentrate

Melt the butter in a saucepan. Add the flour and cook for several minutes, stirring constantly. Gradually add the consommé, cream, salt and pepper, stirring all the while. Add enough beef concentrate to give color to the sauce. Simmer for about 5 minutes and pour over the meatballs in the skillet. Simmer over low heat for 40 to 50 minutes or until the meatballs are cooked.

Makes 6 dozen meatballs.

Salmon Salad

FRUIT SALAD WITH CHEDDAR CHEESE

Standard	Metric
3/4 cup sour cream	150 ml sour cream
1/2 cup pineapple, chopped and drained	125 ml pineapple, chopped and drained
1/4 cup honey	50 ml honey
1/4 cup chopped nuts	50 ml chopped nuts
2 cups cheddar, cubed	500 ml cheddar, cubed
1 cup strawberries	250 ml strawberries
1 cup cherries	250 ml cherries
1 cup red or green grapes	250 ml red or green grapes
1 cup blueberries	250 ml blueberries
1 orange, peeled and sliced	1 orange, peeled and sliced
1 kiwi, peeled and sliced	1 kiwi, peeled and sliced

Combine all the ingredients except chopped nuts. Mix well, cover and refrigerate for at least 3 hours. Add the nuts just before serving.

Fruit Salad with Cheddar Cheese

SALMON SALAD

Standard	Metric
12 to 14 oz salmon, fresh or canned	350 to 500 g salmon, fresh or canned
2 red apples, diced with peel	2 red apples, diced with peel
3 tbsp lemon juice	45 ml lemon juice
2 celery stalks, diced	2 celery stalks, diced
4 tbsp plain yogurt	60 ml plain yogurt
6 to 8 lettuce leaves	6 to 8 lettuce leaves
2 tbsp chopped parsley	30 ml chopped parsley

Drain the salmon and break into pieces.

In a mixing bowl, combine the apples, lemon juice, salmon, celery and yogurt. Mix well and season to taste. Make individual servings placed on a lettuce leaf. Sprinkle with parsley.

Variation: If using fresh salmon, cut the filets into strips and place in a buttered dish. Add a few dashes of dry white wine. Cover and bake at 400°F (200°C) for about 10 minutes. Arrange on lettuce leaves with other ingredients and sprinkle with parsley.

COUNTRY PARTY

The ideal meal for a casual celebration.

Serve with a dry white wine or dry sparkling rosé.

MENU

Serves 6 to 8

Hearty Vegetable Soup
Chicken Cretons
Veal Paupiettes
Tossed Green Salad Italian Style
Broccoli and Carrots au Gratin
Matilda's Maple Cake

CHICKEN CRETONS

Use the recipe for Cretons on page 236, but add 1-1/2 lb (750 g) chopped chicken.

Prepare Herbed Bread (see page 25) at the same time to serve with the Chicken Cretons.

Variation: Cook small chunks of chicken separately from the cretons. Add them at the end.

HEARTY VEGETABLE SOUP

Standard	Metric
3 tbsp butter	45 ml butter
2 chopped leeks, white part only	2 chopped leeks, white part only
1 medium onion, chopped	1 medium onion, chopped
2 potatoes, cubed	2 potatoes, cubed
1 large carrot, sliced	1 large carrot, sliced
2 tsp salt	10 ml salt
1/4 tsp pepper	1 ml pepper
1 bay leaf	1 bay leaf
6 cups water	1.5 liters water
1/4 cup brown rice	50 ml brown rice
2 asparagus spears, 1 inch slices	2 asparagus spears, 2.5 cm slices
1-1/2 bags (15 oz) fresh spinach, chopped	1-1/2 bags (450 g) fresh spinach, chopped
2 cups milk	500 ml milk
1/2 cup light cream (15%)	125 ml light cream (15%)
Salt and pepper	Salt and pepper

Heat the butter in a large cooking pot. Sauté the onion and leeks for 5 minutes, stirring occasionally. Add the potatoes,

Hearty Vegetable Soup

carrots, salt, pepper, bay leaf, water and brown rice. Bring to a boil. Reduce heat, cover and simmer for 35 minutes.

Add the asparagus and simmer for 5 minutes. Add the spinach and cook for another 5 minutes until all the vegetables are tender. Heat the milk in a separate saucepan and add to the soup.

Correct the seasoning and remove the bay leaf. Add the cream and stir. Do not boil. Serve hot.

VEAL PAUPIETTES

Standard	Metric
1-1/2 lb veal scaloppine, fairly large	750 g veal scaloppine, fairly large
1 tbsp butter	15 ml butter
1 small onion, finely chopped	1 small onion, finely chopped
1/2 celery stalk, finely chopped	1/2 celery stalk, finely chopped
1 cup cooked rice	250 ml cooked rice
or	or
1 cup packed breadcrumbs	250 ml packed breadcrumbs
1 beaten egg	1 beaten egg
Thyme and marjoram	Thyme and marjoram
2 thin slices salt pork	2 thin slices salt pork
2 cups chicken stock	500 ml chicken stock
Salt and pepper	Salt and pepper

Pound the scaloppine until flat and thin. Heat the butter in a skillet and sauté the onion and celery. Add the rice or breadcrumbs. Stir and cool. Add the beaten egg and seasoning.

Spread this filling on the scaloppine. Roll, secure with string and lightly coat with flour.

Heat the salt pork in a skillet and sauté the veal until golden. Place the scaloppine in a baking dish. Add the chicken stock and correct the seasoning.

Cover and bake at 350°F (180°C) for 1 hour. Remove the string and serve.

BROCCOLI AND CARROTS
AU GRATIN

Standard	Metric
1 broccoli	1 broccoli
1 lb carrots	500 g carrots
Grated cheese	Grated cheese

Prepare the broccoli and break up into flowerets. Peel and cut the carrots. Steam both vegetables until tender-crisp. Drain and place the vegetables in a baking dish. Prepare a béchamel sauce (see chapter on sauces) and pour over the carrots and broccoli. Sprinkle with grated cheese.

Bake at 400°F (200°C) for 10 minutes until golden.

Veal Paupiettes, Broccoli and Carrots au Gratin

TOSSED GREEN SALAD
ITALIAN-STYLE

Standard	Metric
2 to 3 heads Boston lettuce	2 to 3 heads Boston lettuce
1/2 cup each spinach and celery	125 ml each spinach and celery
1 onion chopped	1 onion chopped
2 small cloves garlic, crushed	2 small cloves garlic, crushed
2 tbsp lemon juice	30 ml lemon juice
1 tbsp corn oil	15 ml corn oil
1 tbsp mayonnaise	15 ml mayonnaise
3/4 tsp Dijon mustard	3 ml Dijon mustard
1/3 cup grated Parmesan	75 ml grated Parmesan
1 tsp oregano	5 ml oregano
Salt and pepper	Salt and pepper

Wash and dry the lettuce, spinach and celery. Combine the remaining ingredients and mix thoroughly. Pour the dressing over the lettuce, spinach and celery. Toss and serve.

MATILDA'S MAPLE CAKE

Standard	Metric
6 eggs	6 eggs
1 cup sugar	250 ml sugar
1 tbsp cold water	15 ml cold water
1 tbsp lemon juice	15 ml lemon juice
1 cup pastry flour	250 ml pastry flour
Pinch salt	Pinch salt

Separate the yolks from the egg whites. Beat the egg whites into stiff peaks while gradually adding 1/2 cup (125 ml) sugar. In a separate bowl, combine the yolks and the remaining amount of sugar and beat until smooth. Add the water and lemon juice. Mix. Gently fold in the egg whites. Add the flour and salt. Mix thoroughly and pour into a rectangular cake pan.

Bake at 325°F (169°C) for about 1 hour.

Maple Cream

Standard	Metric
1 cup maple syrup	250 ml maple syrup
3 tbsp sugar	45 ml sugar
2 cups heavy cream (35%)	500 ml heavy cream (35%)
1 cup milk	250 ml milk
4 egg yolks	4 egg yolks
3 tbsp cornstarch	45 ml cornstarch
1 tbsp unflavored gelatin	15 ml unflavored gelatin
1/2 cup unsalted butter	125 ml unsalted butter

In a saucepan heat the maple syrup, cream and half the sugar without boiling. Dissolve the gelatin in a bit of warm water. Dissolve the cornstarch in the milk. Combine the egg yolks, cornstarch, gelatin and the rest of the sugar. Mix well. Add this mixture to the cream and maple syrup. Add the softened butter and beat with a wire whisk until smooth. Bring to a boil and remove from heat. Cool. Serve with the cake.

HIGH TEA

Revive the genteel art of entertaining with afternoon tea.

BANANA AND COCONUT BREAD

Standard	Metric
2-1/4 cups shredded coconut	550 ml shredded coconut
1/3 cup butter	75 ml butter
3/4 cup sugar	150 ml sugar
2 cups all-purpose flour	500 ml all-purpose flour
1 cup puréed bananas	250 ml puréed bananas
2 eggs	2 eggs
3 tbsp milk	45 ml milk
2 tbsp sugar	30 ml sugar
1/2 tsp almond extract	2 ml almond extract
1/4 tsp vanilla extract	1 ml vanilla extract
1 tsp baking powder	5 ml baking powder
1 tsp baking soda	5 ml baking soda
1/2 tsp salt	2 ml salt

Heat the oven to 350°F (180°C) and grease a 9 x 5 x 3 inch (23 x 12.5 x 7.5 cm) loaf pan.

Toast 1 cup (250 ml) of shredded coconut on a cookie sheet, stirring occasionally. Cool and set aside.

Cream the butter and add the sugar and eggs. Mix until smooth. Incorporate the milk and the almond and vanilla extracts. Mix.

Sift the flour, baking powder, salt and baking soda. Incorporate into the butter and egg mixture. Add the banana and toasted coconut. Mix.

Place the dough in the greased loaf pan. Combine the sugar and leftover coconut and sprinkle over the dough.

Bake for about 50 minutes or until an inserted toothpick comes out clean.

Remove the loaf from the pan and place on a cooling rack.

ALMOND LOAF

Standard	Metric
1/2 cup slivered almonds	125 ml slivered almonds
1/2 cup softened butter	125 ml softened butter
1 cup sugar	250 ml sugar
2 cups all-purpose flour	500 ml all-purpose flour
1/2 cup light cream (15%)	125 ml light cream (15%)
1 egg	1 egg
1/4 tsp baking powder	1 ml baking powder
1/4 tsp baking soda	1 ml baking soda
1/4 tsp salt	1 ml salt
1/2 tsp almond extract	2 ml almond extract
1 tsp grated lemon rind	5 ml grated lemon rind

Heat the oven to 350°F (180°C) and grease a 9 x 5 x 3 inch (23 x 12.5 x 7.5 cm) loaf pan.

Toast the almonds on a cookie sheet, stirring occasionally. Cool and set aside.

Cream the butter and gradually add the sugar and the egg. Mix thoroughly.

Sift the flour, baking powder, salt and baking soda. Alternately add the sifted ingredients, cream and almond extract to the egg mixture. Mix thoroughly. Add the grated lemon rind and toasted almonds. Stir.

Place the dough into the greased loaf pan and bake for 50 to 60 minutes until an inserted toothpick comes out clean. Cool for 10 minutes and turn out onto a cooling rack.

SCONES

Standard	Metric
1-1/4 cups all-purpose flour	300 ml all-purpose flour
1/4 cup butter	50 ml butter
3/4 cup heavy cream (35%)	150 ml heavy cream (35%)
1 tsp baking powder	5 ml baking powder
1/2 tsp salt	2 ml salt
2 tsp white vinegar	10 ml white vinegar
1 egg	1 egg
Butter	Butter
Jam	Jam
3 tbsp breadcrumbs	45 ml breadcrumbs

Sift the flour, baking powder and salt. Work in the butter with a fork and mix thoroughly.

In a separate bowl, whip the cream, egg and vinegar. Make a well in the center of the dry ingredients and pour in the cream and egg mixture. Mix gently as the dough must not become tough.

Roll out the dough on a floured surface until 1/2 inch

Special Tea Biscuits and Three-Fruit Preserve

(2.5 cm) thick. Prick with a fork and cut out 3 inch (7.5 cm) circles.

Sprinkle a cookie sheet with flour. Place the scones on the cookie sheet and sprinkle with breadcrumbs. Bake at 300°F (150°C) for 15 minutes until golden brown. Serve hot with jam or butter.

SPECIAL TEA BISCUITS

Standard	Metric
2 cups all-purpose flour	500 ml all-purpose flour
1/4 cup butter	50 ml butter
3/4 cup milk	150 ml milk
1/3 cup melted butter	75 ml melted butter
1/3 cup sugar	75 ml sugar
2 tbsp sugar	30 ml sugar
1 tbsp baking powder	15 ml baking powder
1 tsp salt	5 ml salt
1/4 tsp nutmeg	1 ml nutmeg
1 egg	1 egg
1/2 tsp mace	2 ml mace

Heat the oven to 450°F (230°C).

In a mixing bowl, sift the flour, 2 tbsp (30 ml) sugar, baking powder, salt and nutmeg. Work in the butter with a fork.

In a separate bowl, whip the egg and milk. Add this to the dry ingredients and mix well to form a ball of dough. Knead gently on a floured surface.

Roll out the dough until it is 1/2 inch (1 cm) thick. Use a cookie cutter to cut out circles about 1 inch (2.5. cm) in diameter. Place on a cookie sheet and bake for about 7 minutes until slightly golden.

Dip half of each biscuit in the melted butter, then in a mixture of sugar and mace. Serve warm.

Variation: to make plain biscuits, omit the sugar and nutmeg from the dough and eliminate final step.

THREE-FRUIT PRESERVE

Standard	Metric
2 cups frozen strawberries	500 ml frozen strawberries
1 medium orange	1 medium orange
1 cup pineapple, finely chopped (juice & pulp)	250 ml pineapple, finely chopped (juice & pulp)
3-3/4 cups fruit sugar	925 ml cups fruit sugar
3/4 cup water	150 ml water
1 envelope jelly powder (any flavor)	1 envelope jelly powder (any flavor)
1/2 tsp grated orange rind	2 ml grated orange rind

Thaw the strawberries. In the meantime, peel the orange, separate pieces and remove seeds and membrane. Crush the strawberries and add the chopped orange.

Place 1 cup (250 ml) of this mixture into a large bowl. Add the pineapple and fruit sugar. Set aside.

In a saucepan, mix the water and jelly powder. Bring to a boil and continue boiling for 1 minute, stirring constantly. Add the jelly to the fruit and stir for 3 minutes. Refrigerate for 24 hours or until the jam has set.

This jam will keep for 2 to 3 weeks in the refrigerator and longer if frozen.

BRIDGE PARTY

A lovely light luncheon or evening meal.

You might serve a light dry wine wine with the sandwiches.

MENU

Serves 6 to 8

Stuffed Mushroom Caps
Sausage Rolls
Ham Sandwich Rolls
Chicken Sandwich Ribbons
Camembert Dip
Gingerbread
Mulled Wine

STUFFED MUSHROOM CAPS

Standard	Metric
18 large mushrooms	18 large mushrooms
1 cup sharp cheddar cheese	250 ml sharp cheddar cheese
1 tbsp softened butter	15 ml softened butter
1 clove garlic, finely chopped	1 clove garlic, finely chopped

Clean the mushrooms. Remove and chop the stems. Place the mushroom caps on a cookie sheet. Set aside.

Combine the grated cheddar, butter, garlic and mushroom stems. Mix well. Stuff the mushroom caps with this filling.

Broil for 3 minutes until slightly golden. Serve hot.

Sausage Rolls

SAUSAGE ROLLS

Standard	Metric
1-1/2 lb small sausages	750 g small sausages
Puff pastry	Puff pastry
1 egg yolk	1 egg yolk
1 tbsp water	15 ml water

Simmer the sausages for 5 minutes in boiling water. Drain and set aside.

Puff Pastry

Standard	Metric
2 cups all-purpose flour	500 ml all-purpose flour
1 tsp salt	5 ml salt
3/4 cup cold butter	150 ml cold butter
1/2 tsp lemon juice	2 ml lemon juice
1/2 cup ice water	125 ml ice water

Sift the flour and salt. Add the butter in small pieces and work by hand to coat every piece. Make a well in the center of the ingredients. Add the lemon juice and 1 tbsp (15 ml) of water. Mix with a fork without crushing the butter. Continue adding water and work the dough until firm. Shape the dough into a ball and refrigerate for several minutes.

Roll out the dough to make a sheet of pastry measuring 16 x 8 inches (40 x 20 cm). Fold into three to make a 5 x 8 inch (12.5 x 20 cm) rectangle. Turn the pastry 180° and work with a rolling pin to make a sheet of pastry measuring 16 x 8 inches (40 x 20 cm). Once again fold the pastry into three and turn 180°. Roll out the dough and repeat the operation twice. Wrap the pastry in wax paper and refrigerate for 1 hour.

Heat the oven to 375°F (190°C). Roll out the pastry until 1/8 inch (3 mm) thick. Cut into 3-1/2 inch (8 cm) squares. Brush each square with mustard and wrap around the sausages. Moisten the edge of the pastry and seal well. Leave the sausage rolls open at both ends. Place on a cookie sheet, seam side down. Brush the rolls with the beaten egg yolk.

Bake for 30 minutes until golden brown. Serve hot.

Note : Ready to use puff pastry is also available commercially.

Ham Sandwich Rolls

Standard	Metric
7 cups cooked ham	1.75 liters cooked ham
12 oz of corn relish with mustard,	375 g of corn relish with mustard,
or	or
1-1/2 cups chopped sweet pickles with mustard	375 ml chopped sweet pickles with mustard
1 cup mayonnaise	250 ml mayonnaise
1/2 cup sweet salad dressing (see following recipe)	125 ml sweet salad dressing (see following recipe)
4 loaves bread, unsliced	4 loaves bread, unsliced
2 cups softened butter	500 ml softened butter
Olives and small pickles	Olives and small pickles

Put the ham through the meat grinder. Add the relish or chopped pickles and mix thoroughly.

Add enough mayonnaise and salad dressing to the ham to make a sandwich spread. Refrigerate.

Cut the crust from the four loaves. Cut each loaf lengthwise into 7 thin slices. Butter each slice and cover with the sandwich spread. Place a row of chopped olives or sliced pickles on one of the short edges of each slice. Roll each slice lengthwise and secure and cover with a sheet of plastic wrap. Refrigerate.

Cut each roll into 6 slices and serve as you would canapés.

Chicken Sandwich Ribbons

Standard	Metric
6 cups cooked chicken, finely chopped	1.5 liters cooked chicken, finely chopped
1 onion, finely chopped	1 onion, finely chopped
2 cups celery, finely chopped	500 ml celery, finely chopped
1 cup toasted almonds, finely chopped	250 ml toasted almonds, finely chopped
1/2 cup sweet salad dressing	125 ml sweet salad dressing
4 cups softened butter	1 liter softened butter
2 cups mayonnaise	500 ml mayonnaise
1 tsp salt	5 ml salt
1/4 tsp pepper	1 ml pepper
2 sandwich loaves, white	2 sandwich loaves, white
2 sandwich loaves, whole wheat	2 sandwich loaves, whole wheat

Combine the onions and the chicken. Add the celery, almonds, mayonnaise, salt and pepper and just enough sweet salad dressing to make a sandwich spread. Correct the seasoning and refrigerate.

Butter the white slices and spread with sandwich filling. Top with a slice of whole wheat bread. Cut off the crusts. Wrap and secure the sandwiches with plastic wrap and refrigerate.

Cut the sandwiches into 6 fingers just before serving.

Sweet Salad Dressing

Standard	Metric
3/4 cup sugar	150 ml sugar
3/4 cup white vinegar	150 ml white vinegar
2 cups milk	500 ml milk
2 eggs	2 eggs
3 tbsp all-purpose flour	45 ml all-purpose flour
1 tbsp dry mustard	15 ml dry mustard
1 tsp salt	5 ml salt

Place the milk, sugar, eggs, flour, mustard and salt in a saucepan. Stir with a wooden spoon until mixture is smooth. Gradually add the vinegar and bring to a boil, stirring constantly. Boil over medium heat for 1 minute, stirring all the while. Cool.

Chicken Sandwich Ribbons

Camembert Dip

Standard	Metric
1 cup creamed cottage cheese	250 ml creamed cottage cheese
1/2 cup cream cheese	125 ml cream cheese
1/4 cup heavy cream (35%)	50 ml heavy cream (35%)
1/4 lb Camembert cheese	125 g Camembert cheese
1/2 tsp seasoned salt	2 ml seasoned salt
1/8 tsp pepper	0.5 ml tsp pepper
1/2 tsp dried dill	2 ml dried dill

Drain the cottage cheese. Put the cheeses and cream through the blender until smooth. Place in a serving bowl, add the seasonings and stir. Refrigerate for 1 hour. Serve with chips, crackers or raw vegetables.

GINGERBREAD

Standard	Metric
1/3 cup shortening	75 ml shortening
1/2 cup brown sugar	125 ml brown sugar
3/4 cup molasses	175 ml molasses
2 cups all-purpose flour	500 ml all-purpose flour
1 cup boiling water	250 ml boiling water
1 beaten egg	1 beaten egg
1-1/4 tsp powdered ginger	6 ml powdered ginger
1/4 tsp cinnamon	1 ml cinnamon
1/4 tsp ground cloves	1 ml ground cloves
1/2 tsp salt	2 ml salt
2 tsp baking soda	10 ml baking soda
Sweetened whipped cream	Sweetened whipped cream

Heat the oven to 350°F (180°C) and grease a 9 x 9 x 2 inch (23 x 23 x 5 cm) cake pan.

Thoroughly mix the shortening and brown sugar. Incorporate the molasses and egg.

Sift together the flour, ginger, cinnamon, cloves and salt. Add to previous mixture. Mix.

Dissolve the baking powder in boiling water. Add to the batter and mix well.

Pour the batter into the cake pan and bake for about 30 minutes. Serve warm or cold with whipped cream.

MULLED WINE

Standard	Metric
4 cups water	1 liter water
1/4 cup sugar	50 ml sugar
1/2 cup raisins	125 ml raisins
1/2 cup almonds	125 ml almonds
2 bottles dry red wine	2 bottles dry red wine
1/4 tsp Angostura bitters	1 ml Angostura bitters
8 cloves	8 cloves
1 tsp allspice	5 ml allspice
1/2 tsp ground nutmeg	2 ml ground nutmeg
1/2 tsp powdered ginger	2 ml powdered ginger
Cinnamon sticks	Cinnamon sticks

Combine all the ingredients except the wine and cinnamon sticks. Place in a saucepan and bring to a boil. Reduce the heat and simmer for 30 minutes. Strain. Bring to a boil once more. Add the wine and heat without boiling.

Serve hot with cinnamon sticks to be used as stirrers.

Mulled Wine

251

OUTDOOR DINING

Corn Roast

Everybody's favorite meal during the sweet corn season.

Serve with beer or semi-dry wine, sparkling wine.

Corn on the Cob

12 to 18 ears of fresh-picked corn
Salt
Butter

Plunge the corn with husk in boiling water. Boil for 15 to 20 minutes. Drain, shuck and dredge in butter. Sprinkle with salt.

Variation: Garlic added to the water will make the corn more tender.

Barbecued Brie Burgers

Standard	Metric
3 lb medium ground beef	1.5 kg medium ground beef
2 eggs	2 eggs
4 tbsp breadcrumbs	60 ml breadcrumbs
4 tbsp milk	60 ml milk
1 tsp salt	5 ml salt
1 tsp pepper	5 ml pepper
1 tbsp fresh parsley	15 ml fresh parsley
1 small onion, chopped	1 small onion, chopped
6 pickles, chopped	6 pickles, chopped
1 tbsp Worcestershire sauce	15 ml Worcestershire sauce
1/2 lb sliced Brie	250 g sliced Brie

Combine all the ingredients except the Brie. Mix well and shape a dozen hamburger patties with a slice of Brie tucked inside. Cook the patties over the barbecue and brush frequently with barbecue sauce, or beef or vegetable stock. Serve on toasted hamburger buns. The Brie should be melted inside the burgers.

Cabbage in Aspic

Standard	Metric
1 envelope lemon-flavored jelly powder	1 envelope lemon-flavored jelly powder
3/4 cup boiling water	150 ml boiling water
2 cups finely shredded cabbage	500 ml finely shredded cabbage
4 tsp finely chopped onion	20 ml finely chopped onion
2 tbsp vinegar	30 ml vinegar
2 celery stalks	2 celery stalks
1/2 cup grated carrots	125 ml grated carrots
3/4 cup mayonnaise	150 ml mayonnaise
Salt and pepper	Salt and pepper

Dissolve the gelatin in boiling water and refrigerate until it begins to set. Add mayonnaise, stir and refrigerate for 15 minutes. Combine the remaining ingredients in a separate bowl. Mix well and incorporate into the first mixture. Pour into a greased mold and refrigerate until aspic is firm.

Miracle Dip

Standard	Metric
2 cups heavy cream (35%)	500 ml heavy cream (35%)
or	or
2 cups plain yogurt	500 ml plain yogurt
1 envelope onion soup mix	1 envelope onion soup mix
1/2 cup red chili sauce	125 ml red chili sauce

Put all the ingredients through the blender. Serve with water biscuits, crackers or raw vegetables.

Pear and Raisin Dessert

Standard	Metric
2 cans of pear halves (reserve the juice)	2 cans of pear halves (reserve the juice)
2 tbsp butter	30 ml butter
2 tbsp sugar	30 ml sugar
3 tbsp Tia Maria	45 ml Tia Maria
3/4 cup raisins	150 ml raisins
4 tbsp slivered almonds	60 ml slivered almonds

Cut the pear halves in two.

Heat the butter and sugar over medium heat until caramelized. Stir every 2 or 3 minutes. Add the pear juice and pears. Pour in the Tia Maria and flambé. Boil over low heat for 2 to 3 minutes.

Add the raisins and almonds. Simmer for another 3 minutes and serve with ice cream.

Corn on the Cob and Barbecued Brie Burgers

BARBECUE

A terrific summer menu for indoors or out.

Serve with a white Bordeaux, iced Kirsch.

MENU

Serves 6 to 8

Lettuce Soup
Fruit and Cheddar Kebabs
Baked Salmon Steaks
Stuffed Cherry Tomatoes with Smoked Oysters
Tropical Cucumber Salad
Blueberries with Kirsch

LETTUCE SOUP

Standard	Metric
2 medium potatoes, diced	2 medium potatoes, diced
7 tbsp chopped onion	105 ml chopped onion
2 heads of lettuce	2 heads of lettuce
1 tbsp chives	15 ml chives
5 cups chicken stock	1.25 liters chicken stock
Salt and pepper	Salt and pepper

Chop the lettuce. Combine and sauté all the ingredients, except for chicken stock, for 5 minutes. Add the stock, bring to a boil and simmer for 20 minutes. Put the soup through the blender until completely smooth. Reheat and serve.

FRUIT AND CHEDDAR KEBABS

Orange cheddar
White cheddar
Apples
Oranges
Green seedless grapes
Pitted cherries
or
Fresh strawberries
Lettuce leaves
Bamboo skewers

Cut the cheese into fairly large even cubes. Wash and core the apples but do not peel. Cut them into cubes. Wash the grapes. Peel and slice the oranges. Cut each slice in half.

Slide the skewers through the cheese and fruit. Alternate the fruit with the different colored cheddar. Serve on lettuce leaves.

BAKED SALMON STEAKS

1 salmon steak per person
Salt, pepper, parsley
Butter
Lemon
Onion slices
Dry white wine

Place each steak on a sheet of aluminum foil. Sprinkle with salt and pepper. Add a bit of chopped parsley, butter, thin slice of onion, thin slice of lemon and a tablespoon (15 ml) of wine.

Seal the steak in the foil and bake at 350°F (180°C) for 20 minutes.

Variation: Double the amount of wine and cook the salmon steaks sealed in foil on the barbecue.

Lettuce Soup

Tropical Cucumber Salad

STUFFED CHERRY TOMATOES WITH SMOKED OYSTERS

Standard	Metric
15 cherry tomatoes	15 cherry tomatoes
1 tin smoked oysters	1 tin smoked oysters
8 oz cream cheese	250 g cream cheese
Salt and pepper	Salt and pepper
Chopped parsley	Chopped parsley

Gently scoop out the tomatoes with a grapefruit knife. Stuff each tomato with a smoked oyster.

Whip the cream cheese and season to taste. Fill the tomatoes with the cheese, sprinkle with parsley and serve.

TROPICAL CUCUMBER SALAD

Standard	Metric
2 cucumbers	2 cucumbers
1 cup mandarin segments	250 ml mandarin segments
3 tbsp chives	45 ml chives

Peel and cut the cucumbers into very thin slices. Place in a strainer and sprinkle with salt. Let stand for 1 hour to eliminate water. Place the cucumber in a salad bowl. Add the mandarins and chives. Cover with Tropical Dressing. Garnish with mango or avocado slices.

Tropical Dressing

Standard	Metric
1 cup vegetable oil	250 ml vegetable oil
1/4 cup brown sugar	50 ml brown sugar
1/4 cup lemon juice	50 ml lemon juice
1/4 cup orange juice	50 ml orange juice
1 tbsp shredded coconut	15 ml shredded coconut
1 tbsp wine vinegar	15 ml wine vinegar
1 tsp salt	5 ml salt

Mix all the ingredients. May be served with any salad containing fruit. Makes about 1-1/2 cups (375 ml).

BLUEBERRIES WITH KIRSCH

Standard	Metric
6 cups fresh blueberries or 2 packages frozen blueberries	1.5 liters fresh blueberries or 2 packages frozen blueberries
1/2 cup sugar	125 ml sugar
2 cups heavy cream (35%)	500 ml heavy cream (35%)
1/3 cup Kirsch or white rum	75 ml Kirsch or white rum
Vanilla extract	Vanilla extract

Place the blueberries in a bowl with the Kirsch and 1/3 cup (75 ml) of sugar. Refrigerate for 1 hour.

In the meantime, whip the cream and gradually add the rest of the sugar and a dash of vanilla extract. Mix the cream and blueberries. Serve very cold in iced fruit cups.

Technique : Spit-Roasted Lamb

1   Place the lamb on a table covered with aluminum foil.

2   Rub the inside of the carcass with salt.

3   Rub the outside of the lamb with salt.

4   Pierce through the legs using a sharp pointed knife.

5   Skewer the lamb on the spit.

6   Slide a metal wire through the leg slits and fasten to the spit.

7   Place a metal brace just above the hindquarters.

8   Put the spit into place and begin cooking.

GLAZED CITRUS KEBABS

Standard	Metric
2 grapefruit	2 grapefruit
4 oranges	4 oranges
2 lemons	2 lemons
2 cups citrus fruit marmalade	500 ml citrus fruit marmalade
1/2 cup brown sugar	125 ml brown sugar
1/2 cup orange juice	125 ml orange juice

Cut the fruit into segments and thread on skewers. Do not stack too tightly. Set aside.

Bring the marmalade, brown sugar and orange juice to a boil. Continue boiling until mixture turns into a syrup.

Place the fruit kebabs on the barbecue grill, over low heat. Turn frequently and cook gently for 20 minutes. Baste frequently with the marmalade glaze.

Place the kebabs on individual plates. Cover with the glaze and serve hot with vanilla ice cream or raspberry sauce. Decorate with shredded coconut.

Glazed Citrus Kebabs

POOL PARTY

A delicious meal for summer entertaining.

Serve with dry white wine and red Burgundy.

MENU

Serves 6 to 8

Tropical Punch
Galantine of Salmon
Boiled Beef
Stuffed Zucchini with Shrimp
Spaghetti with Creamy Shrimp Sauce
Cantaloupe Surprise

TROPICAL PUNCH

Standard	Metric
2 cups sugar	500 ml sugar
1/2 cup lemon juice	125 ml lemon juice
3 large bottles ginger ale	3 large bottles ginger ale
3 cups tea	750 ml tea
1 can of sweetened orange and grapefruit juice	1 can of sweetened orange and grapefruit juice

Boil the tea and sugar for 5 minutes. Cool. Add the fruit juices and stir. Add the 3 bottles of ginger ale just before serving. Garnish with fruit slices.

GALANTINE OF SALMON

Standard	Metric
2 envelopes unflavored gelatin	2 envelopes unflavored gelatin
1 tbsp sugar	15 ml sugar
1/4 tsp salt	1 ml salt
1 tsp dry mustard	5 ml dry mustard
1/4 cup cold water	50 ml cold water
1/4 cup vinegar	50 ml vinegar
1 cup whipped cream	250 ml whipped cream
1/2 cup mayonnaise	125 ml mayonnaise
2 cups cooked or canned salmon	500 ml cooked or canned salmon
1 cup celery, chopped	250 ml celery, chopped
1 tbsp lemon juice	15 ml lemon juice

Combine the powdered gelatin, sugar, salt and mustard. Set aside.

Pour the water and vinegar into the upper part of a double-boiler. Heat and add the gelatin mixture. Stir and cool until mixture has the consistency of beaten egg.

Fold in the whipped cream, mayonnaise, diced salmon. celery and lemon juice.

Pour into a greased mold and refrigerate until firm.

Tropical Punch

Stuffed Zucchini with Shrimp

BOILED BEEF

Standard	Metric
3 lb beef brisket	1.5 kg beef brisket
1 cabbage, quartered	1 cabbage, quartered
3 potatoes, cut in half	3 potatoes, cut in half
2 carrots	2 carrots
4 onions, cut in half	4 onions, cut in half
1 leek cut in half	1 leek cut in half
Salt and pepper	Salt and pepper
1 bouquet garni: parsley, basil and thyme	1 bouquet garni: parsley, basil and thyme
2 onions, chopped	2 onions, chopped
Parsley, chopped	Parsley, chopped

Place the beef into a pot. Cover with cold water and bring to a boil. Remove the scum from the surface and set the beef aside.

Rinse the pot and put back the beef. Cover with cold water and add the bouquet garni, salt and pepper. Bring to a boil. Reduce the heat and simmer for 2 hours and 15 minutes.

Thirty minutes before the end of the cooking period, add all the vegetables except the chopped onions. Season to taste and remove the various vegetables when done. Place the vegetables in a serving dish. Cover with a bit of stock to keep them warm.

When all vegetables are done, discard the bouquet garni and place the beef and stock in the serving dish. Garnish with parsley and chopped onions.

STUFFED ZUCCHINI WITH SHRIMP

Standard	Metric
4 medium zucchini	4 medium zucchini
7 cherry tomatoes cut in half	7 cherry tomatoes cut in half
3/4 cup green or red pepper, diced	150 ml green or red pepper, diced
3 tbsp red onion or shallot, chopped	45 ml red onion or shallot, chopped
3 tbsp rice vinegar	45 ml rice vinegar
3 tbsp olive oil	45 ml olive oil
2 tsp salt	10 ml salt
1 clove garlic, crushed	1 clove garlic, crushed
1 tsp oregano	5 ml oregano
Pinch freshly ground pepper	Pinch freshly ground pepper
2 cans shrimp or	2 cans shrimp or
1/2 lb fresh cooked shrimp	250 g fresh cooked shrimp

Wash the zucchini and pierce the skin in several places with a fork. Cook in salted boiling water for 15 minutes, or until tender. Run under cold water to cool.

Cut the zucchini in half, lengthwise. Scoop out the flesh and place in a bowl with the cherry tomatoes, shrimp, peppers and onions. Mix well. Stuff the zucchini with this filling. Cover and refrigerate for at least 2 hours. Prepare a vinaigrette with the remaining ingredients and serve with the stuffed zucchini.

SPAGHETTI WITH CREAMY SHRIMP SAUCE

Standard	Metric
1 lb spaghetti	500 g spaghetti
1 lb shrimp	500 g shrimp
3 tbsp butter	45 ml butter
2 tbsp tomato paste	30 ml tomato paste
1 clove garlic, chopped	1 clove garlic, chopped
Pinch cayenne	Pinch cayenne
1/4 cup chives, chopped	50 ml chives, chopped
1 cup heavy cream (35%)	250 ml heavy cream (35%)
3 tbsp onion, chopped	45 ml onion, chopped
3 beaten egg yolks	3 beaten egg yolks
Salt	Salt

Cook and drain the spaghetti. Return to the pot and set aside.

In a separate pot, melt the butter and sauté the shrimp, garlic, onion, cayenne and tomato paste for 7 minutes. Add the cream and and bring to a boil. Continue boiling for 3 minutes. Remove from heat and add the chives. Pour the sauce onto the spaghetti. Gently reheat for several minutes.

Remove from heat and incorporate the beaten egg yolks. Mix thoroughly and serve.

CANTALOUPE SURPRISE

Standard	Metric
1 cantaloupe	1 cantaloupe
1/4 lb green or red grapes	125 g green or red grapes
1/3 cup strawberries	75 ml strawberries
2 canned peaches, chopped	2 canned peaches, chopped
2 tbsp strawberry juice	30 ml strawberry juice
1 kiwi peeled and sliced	1 kiwi peeled and sliced
1 tbsp Kirsch	15 ml Kirsch
Juice of half an orange	Juice of half an orange

Cut the cantaloupe in half and remove seeds. Use a melon spoon to scoop out the flesh or carefully remove the flesh using a grapefruit knife. Then cut into small cubes. Save the empty halves.

Place the melon balls or cubes in a salad bowl. Add the remaining ingredients. Mix well and let stand for 2 hours. Serve the fruit salad in the empty cantaloupe halves.

Variation: Cut off the top of the cantaloupe and carefully scoop out the flesh. Prepare the fruit salad and add one envelope of cherry-flavored gelatin.

Pour this mixture into the empty cantaloupe. Refrigerate until the gelatin has set. Cut into slices and serve.

Cantaloupe Surprise

POOL PARTY II

This menu is so easy you'll have lots of time to sit around the pool with your friends.

Serve with iced vodka and fruit juice, or rum punch.

MENU

Serves 6 to 8

Sunburst Salad
Carrot Sherbet
Glazed Ham
Green and Wax Bean Salad
Smoked Sausage Salad
Hawaiian Dessert

CARROT SHERBET

Standard	Metric
3/4 cup sugar	150 ml sugar
3/4 cup water	150 ml water
2 cups cooked, drained and puréed carrots	500 ml cooked, drained and puréed carrots
4 tbsp lemon juice	60 ml lemon juice
2 tbsp frozen orange juice concentrate	30 ml frozen orange juice concentrate
1 tbsp Cognac	15 ml Cognac
1 tbsp chives, chopped	15 ml chives, chopped
1 tsp chervil	5 ml chervil

Place the sugar and water in a saucepan. Dissolve the sugar over low heat and then bring to a boil. Remove from heat immediately and cool until liquid is at room temperature.

Combine the carrot purée, lemon juice, orange juice, Cognac and chervil. Mix well. Stir in the syrup. Add salt and pepper to taste and mix thoroughly. Place in an ice cream maker. Freeze or refrigerate, churning often as the sherbet begins to set.

When ready to serve, place the sherbet on flat plates which have been kept in the freezer. Sprinkle with chopped chives.

SUNBURST SALAD

Standard	Metric
3 grapefruit	3 grapefruit
4 oranges	4 oranges
2 avocados	2 avocados
3/4 cup lemon juice	150 ml lemon juice
1/2 tsp salt	2 ml salt
1 tsp sugar	5 ml sugar

Peel the avocados and cut into bite-size pieces. Place in a

Carrot Sherbet

bowl and sprinkle with lemon juice.

Peel and slice the oranges and grapefruit. Arrange them around the border of a serving dish, alternating the orange and grapefruit.

Use a slotted spoon to remove the avocado from the bowl of lemon juice and place in the center of the dish.

Add the salt and sugar to the lemon juice. Sprinkle this mixture over the salad. Serve.

GLAZED HAM

Standard	Metric
1 slice ready-to-serve ham about 2 inches thick	1 slice ready-to-serve ham about 5 cm thick
1 can sliced pineapple, drained	1 can sliced pineapple, drained
Ice	Ice
1/2 cup prepared mustard	125 ml prepared mustard
1/2 cup orange marmalade	125 ml orange marmalade
2 tbsp brown sugar	30 ml brown sugar
Pinch ground cloves	Pinch ground cloves

Cut off any excess fat around the ham. Make small cuts at 1 inch (2.5 cm) intervals around the edge of the ham. Stick a few cloves between the fat and lean parts of the ham. Place the slice on an ovenproof platter resting on an upside down

Smoked Sausage Salad

saucer. Cover with aluminum foil. Bake at 350°F (175°C), calculating 10 minutes per pound (500 g).

In the meantime, combine the mustard, marmalade, brown sugar and ground cloves. Dredge the pineapple slices in this mixture.

Halfway through the cooking time, remove the ham and cover with the remaining glaze. Decorate the ham with the pineapple slices. Cover with the foil and return to the oven for the duration of cooking time.

Let stand 15 minutes before serving.

Green and Wax Bean Salad

Standard	Metric
1 cup green beans, cooked and cut into 1 inch pieces	250 ml green beans, cooked and cut into 2.5 cm pieces
1 cup wax beans, cooked and cut into 1 inch pieces	250 ml wax beans, cooked and cut into 2.5 cm pieces
1 onion, finely chopped	1 onion, finely chopped
1/4 cup celery, finely chopped	50 ml celery, finely chopped
2 tbsp parsley, chopped	30 ml parsley, chopped

Combine all the ingredients and place in a salad bowl.

Vinaigrette

Standard	Metric
1/2 tsp salt	2 ml salt
1/2 tsp pepper	2 ml pepper
1 tsp dry mustard	5 ml dry mustard
1 tbsp vegetable oil	15 ml vegetable oil
1/2 tsp vinegar	2 ml vinegar

Combine the vinaigrette ingredients a few minutes before serving time and pour over salad ingredients.

Smoked Sausage Salad

Standard	Metric
5 tbsp vegetable oil	75 ml vegetable oil
4 tsp vinegar	20 ml vinegar
Salt and pepper	Salt and pepper
2 tbsp mayonnaise	30 ml mayonnaise
3/4 tsp prepared mustard	3 ml prepared mustard
6 smoked sausages, sliced	6 smoked sausages, sliced
1/4 cup shallots, chopped	50 ml shallots, chopped
1/2 cup green peas, cooked and drained	125 ml green peas, cooked and drained
1/2 cup cucumber, peeled and cubed	125 ml cucumber, peeled and cubed
Lettuce leaves	Lettuce leaves

Place salt, pepper, mustard and mayonnaise into a small bowl. Add the vinegar and mix well. Gradually add 4 tbsp (60 ml) oil and beat with a wire whisk. Refrigerate.

Sauté the sausage slices in the the remaining 1 tbsp (15 ml) oil. Drain on a paper towel and set aside.

Sauté the shallots in the same skillet for 1 minute, stirring frequently. Add to the sausages and cool. Transfer the sausages and shallots to a salad bowl.

Add the cucumber and green peas. Refrigerate.

When ready to serve, add the vinaigrette and garnish with lettuce. Toss and serve.

Variation: Add a few boiled potatoes cut into cubes.

Hawaiian Dessert

Standard	Metric
8 slices white cake	8 slices white cake
8 slices canned pineapple (save the juice)	8 slices canned pineapple (save the juice)
2 egg whites	2 egg whites
1/4 tsp cream of tartar	1 ml cream of tartar
1/4 cup sugar	50 ml sugar
1/2 tsp vanilla extract	2 ml vanilla extract
1/8 tsp almond extract	0.5 ml almond extract
8 walnuts, shelled	8 walnuts, shelled

Place the slices of white cake on a greased cookie sheet. Place a pineapple slice on each piece.

Whip the egg whites into firm peaks while adding the sugar and cream of tartar. Add the almond and vanilla extracts. Cover the cake and pineapple with the meringue mixture and top with walnuts.

Broil for 2 to 3 minutes until meringue is golden brown. Serve immediately.

Green and Wax Bean Salad

CATCH OF THE DAY

Fresh-caught fish and a deliciously off-beat cake.

Serve with a dry white wine or sparkling rosé.

MENU

Serves 6 to 8

Abitibi Bouillabaisse
Stuffed Trout with Tangy Rice
Tartar Sauce
Leaf Lettuce with Walnut Oil Dressing
Red Beet Cake

ABITIBI BOUILLABAISSE

Standard	Metric
2 cups raw potatoes, cubed	500 ml raw potatoes, cubed
1/2 cup raw celery, cubed	125 ml raw celery, cubed
1/4 cup raw carrots, cubed	50 ml raw carrots, cubed
2 cups water	500 ml water
1 tsp salt	5 ml salt
1/8 tsp pepper	0.5 ml pepper
1/3 cup onion, chopped	75 ml onion, chopped
1 tbsp butter or margarine	15 ml butter or margarine
1-1/2 lb fish filets (doré, pike, cod, haddock, flounder)	750 g fish filets (doré, pike, cod, haddock, flounder)
2 cups milk	500 ml milk

Place the water in a soup pot. Add the vegetables and seasoning. Cover and simmer until vegetables are tender.

Melt the butter in a skillet and sauté the onion. Add to the soup pot. Cut the fish into bite-size pieces and also add to the pot. Simmer for 15 minutes. Add the milk. Heat but do not boil. Serve.

Note: 2 or 3 varieties of fish may be combined. Make sure that all bones have been removed from the fish.

STUFFED TROUT WITH TANGY RICE

Standard	Metric
2-1/2 cups cooked rice	625 ml cooked rice
6 trout about 6 inches long	6 trout about 15 cm long
3 tomatoes	3 tomatoes
1/3 cup soy sauce	75 ml soy sauce
1/4 cup chili sauce	50 ml chili sauce

Brush the trout with the soy sauce. Cut the tomatoes into wedges.

Abitibi Bouillabaisse

Stuffing

Standard	Metric
1 sweet red pepper, finely chopped	1 sweet red pepper, finely chopped
1 sweet green pepper, finely chopped	1 sweet green pepper, finely chopped
3/4 cup mushrooms, finely chopped	150 ml mushrooms, finely chopped
2 shallots, finely chopped	2 shallots, finely chopped
2 tsp melted butter or margarine	10 ml melted butter or margarine
1 tbsp parsley	15 ml parsley
1 tbsp lemon juice	15 ml lemon juice

Combine all the stuffing ingredients and mix well. Stuff the trout and wrap each fish in a sheet of aluminum foil. Bake at 350°F (180°C) for about 35 minutes.

Unwrap each fish and place on a bed of rice sprinkled with the soy and chili sauces. Garnish with tomatoes.

TARTAR SAUCE

Standard	Metric
2 tbsp butter	30 ml butter
2 tbsp all-purpose flour	30 ml all-purpose flour
1 cup milk	250 ml milk
1 tbsp mayonnaise	15 ml mayonnaise
10 green olives, chopped	10 green olives, chopped
10 pickles, chopped	10 pickles, chopped
1 tsp finely chopped parsley	5 ml finely chopped parsley
1 tsp vinegar	5 ml vinegar
Salt and pepper	Salt and pepper

Melt the butter in the upper part of a double-boiler. Add the flour and mix well. Add all the cold milk at once. Stir constantly until thickened. Season to taste and add the olives, pickles, parsley, mayonnaise and vinegar. Serve warm.

LEAF LETTUCE WITH WALNUT OIL DRESSING

Standard	Metric
1 head curly leaf lettuce	1 head curly leaf lettuce
1 tbsp Dijon mustard	15 ml Dijon mustard
1 tsp salt	5 ml salt
3 tbsp wine vinegar	45 ml wine vinegar
2 tbsp shallots, chopped	30 ml shallots, chopped
1/4 cup walnut oil	50 ml walnut oil

Wash and dry the lettuce. Place in a salad bowl. Combine the remaining ingredients and mix well. Pour over the salad. Toss and serve.

Chopped walnuts may also be added to the salad at the last minute.

RED BEET CAKE

Standard	Metric
1-1/2 cups sugar	375 ml sugar
3/4 cup oil	150 ml oil
1/4 cup hot water	50 ml hot water
1 tsp vanilla extract	5 ml vanilla extract
3 egg yolks	3 egg yolks
2 cups all-purpose flour	500 ml all-purpose flour
1 tbsp baking powder	15 ml baking powder
1 tsp cinnamon	5 ml cinnamon
1/2 tsp allspice	2 ml allspice
Pinch salt	Pinch salt
2 cups beets, par-boiled and finely grated	500 ml beets, par-boiled and finely grated
3 egg whites, beaten stiff	3 egg whites, beaten stiff

Combine the sugar, oil, water, vanilla extract and the egg yolks. Beat thoroughly. Sift the dry ingredients together. Add to the yolk mixture, stirring all the while. Add the grated beets; mix well. Fold in the egg whites.

Pour the batter into a greased cake pan. Bake at 350°F (180°C) for about 50 minutes. Cake is done when an inserted toothpick comes out clean.

Cool before serving.

Stuffed Trout with Tangy Rice

272

CATCH OF THE DAY II

Fresh pike plays the starring role in this easy menu.

Serve with a Chardonnay or Riesling.

MENU

Serves 6 to 8

Meaty Vegetable Soup
Fresh Lake Pike Filets
Stuffed Baked Potatoes
Leek and Mushroom Salad
Pumpkin Chiffon Pie

MEATY VEGETABLE SOUP

Standard	Metric
One piece salt pork, about 1/2 lb	One piece salt pork, about 250 g
1 chicken drumstick	1 chicken drumstick
1/2 beef knuckle, about 1 inch thick	1/2 beef knuckle, about 2.5 cm thick
1 thinly sliced onion	1 thinly sliced onion
4 to 5 carrots	4 to 5 carrots
1/2 turnip	1/2 turnip
4 to 5 celery stalks	4 to 5 celery stalks
1 parsnip	1 parsnip
2 medium potatoes	2 medium potatoes
1 cup shredded cabbage	250 ml shredded cabbage
2 bay leaves	2 bay leaves
2 tbsp parsley	30 ml parsley
8 cups stock	2 liters stock
or	or
8 cups hot water	2 liters hot water
Salt and pepper	Salt and pepper

Dice all the vegetables, except for the cabbage.

Melt the salt pork in a heavy cooking pot and sauté the onions for 5 minutes until golden.

Add the remaining ingredients except for the cabbage and stock. Cover and cook over medium heat until the vegetables are almost done. Add the cabbage and the stock; continue cooking over low heat for 10 minutes.

Serve with warm dinner rolls.

FRESH LAKE PIKE FILETS

Standard	Metric
2 pike filets, about 1-1/2 to 2 lb	2 pike filets, about 750 g to 1 kg
1 small onion, minced	1 small onion, minced
1/2 cup milk	125 ml milk
3/4 cup breadcrumbs	150 ml breadcrumbs
1/2 cup grated cheddar cheese	125 ml grated cheddar cheese
2 sprigs parsley, finely chopped	2 sprigs parsley, finely chopped
Salt, pepper and thyme	Salt, pepper and thyme

Cut the filets into four. Dip each piece in milk and then in the breadcrumbs. Place in a buttered baking dish. Add the milk and breadcrumbs, then sprinkle with cheese. Place in a 400°F (200°C) oven and bake for 20 minutes until the fish flakes easily with a fork. Sprinkle with salt, pepper and thyme. Garnish with parsley.

Serve with baked potatoes, green beans and tomato slices.

Note: May be cooked in a microwave oven at HIGH for 6 minutes.

Fresh Lake Pike Filets

Leek and Mushroom Salad

STUFFED BAKED POTATOES

Standard	Metric
6 - 8 medium potatoes	6 - 8 medium potatoes
3 very crisp bacon slices	3 very crisp bacon slices
3/4 cup softened butter	150 ml softened butter
1/2 cup sour cream	125 ml sour cream
1 tsp salt	5 ml salt
Pinch paprika	Pinch paprika
Salt and pepper	Salt and pepper

Bake the potatoes at 350°F (180°C) for 1 hour. Cut the top off the potatoes and carefully scoop out the inside with a spoon. Place pulp in a bowl with crumbled bacon, butter, sour cream salt and pepper. Mix well.

Stuff the potato skins with the potato filling. Reheat in the oven for 10 to 12 minutes. Sprinkle with paprika and serve.

LEEK AND MUSHROOM SALAD

Standard	Metric
1 lb fresh mushrooms	500 g fresh mushrooms
1 leek, white part only	1 leek, white part only
3 tbsp sunflower oil	45 ml sunflower oil
3 tbsp water	45 ml water
Salad seasonings	Salad seasonings
Juice of one lemon	Juice of one lemon
Salted herbs	Salted herbs

Clean and thinly slice the mushrooms. Wash and thinly slice the leeks. Add the remaining ingredients and toss.

Let stand for at least 15 minutes before serving. Serve with toasted slices of French bread.

PUMPKIN CHIFFON PIE

Standard	Metric
1 envelope unflavored gelatin	1 envelope unflavored gelatin
1/2 cup sugar	125 ml sugar
1/2 tsp salt	2 ml salt
1/2 tsp cinnamon	2 ml cinnamon
1/2 tsp allspice	2 ml allspice
1/4 tsp powdered ginger	1 ml powdered ginger
1/4 tsp nutmeg	1 ml nutmeg
3/4 cup milk	150 ml milk
2 egg yolks, beaten lightly	2 egg yolks, beaten lightly
1 cup puréed pumpkin	250 ml puréed pumpkin
2 egg whites	2 egg whites
1/2 cup heavy cream (35%)	125 ml heavy cream (35%)
1 baked pie shell	1 baked pie shell

Combine the first 7 ingredients in a large saucepan. Add the milk, egg yolks and pumpkin. Cook over medium heat and bring to a boil, stirring constantly until the gelatin has dissolved. Remove from heat and refrigerate until mixture begins to set.

Whip the egg whites into firm peaks while adding the sugar. Whip the cream until stiff. Fold the egg whites and the whipped cream into the pumpkin mixture. Pour the pie filling into the pastry shell and refrigerate until firm.

Garnish with whipped cream and walnuts.

CHILDREN'S PICNIC

These recipes are easy for kids to carry on a picnic, and even easy enough to make themselves.

MENU

Serves 6 to 8 children

Vegetable Dip
Sausage Kebabs
Potato Salad with Radishes
Creamy Coleslaw
Caramel Squares

VEGETABLE DIP

Standard	Metric
1 cup mayonnaise	250 ml mayonnaise
1 cup sour cream	250 ml sour cream
1 tsp parsley	5 ml parsley
1 tsp monosodium glutamate	5 ml monosodium glutamate
1/2 tsp minced onion	2 ml minced onion
1/2 tsp garlic powder	2 ml garlic powder
3 drops Tabasco sauce	3 drops Tabasco sauce
1 tsp crushed coriander seeds	5 ml crushed coriander seeds
1 tbsp beef concentrate	15 ml beef concentrate

Combine all the ingredients and mix thoroughly. Serve with chips, pickles or a variety of uncooked vegetables.

SAUSAGE KEBABS

Standard	Metric
24 cocktail sausages	24 cocktail sausages
2 sweet red peppers cut into 1 inch squares	2 sweet red peppers cut into 2.5 cm squares
2 tomatoes, in wedges	2 tomatoes, in wedges
1 cube of cheese, 1 inch, per brochette	1 cube of cheese, 2.5 cm, per brochette
1 piece of pickle per brochette	1 piece of pickle per brochette

Cook the sausages and place on skewers alternating with the vegetables. Top each with a piece of cheese and pickle. Wrap the kebabs in aluminum foil. Serve cold with the vegetable dip.

POTATO SALAD WITH RADISHES

Standard	Metric
6 potatoes	6 potatoes
12 radishes, sliced	12 radishes, sliced
4 tbsp parsley	60 ml parsley
1/2 cup mayonnaise	125 ml mayonnaise

Cook the potatoes, in their jackets, in salted boiling water. Cool, peel and cut into cubes. Add the radishes. Incorporate the mayonnaise and parsley.

Mix well and serve.

Sausage Kebabs

CREAMY COLESLAW

Standard	Metric
1 medium cabbage	1 medium cabbage
1/2 cup relish	125 ml relish
2 tsp vinegar	10 ml vinegar
1 cup mayonnaise	250 ml mayonnaise
1/4 cup milk	50 ml milk
1 tbsp sugar	15 ml sugar

Shred the cabbage. Combine all the ingredients. Mix well and refrigerate.

CARAMEL SQUARES

Standard	Metric
35 caramels	35 caramels
1 small tin condensed milk	1 small tin condensed milk
1 cup all-purpose flour	250 ml all-purpose flour
3/4 cup brown sugar	150 ml brown sugar
1/2 tsp baking soda	2 ml baking soda
1/4 tsp salt	1 ml salt
3/4 cup margarine	150 ml margarine
1 bag chocolate chips	1 bag chocolate chips

Place the caramels and condensed milk in a saucepan. Cook over low heat until caramels have melted. Stir frequently.

Combine the dry ingredients in a bowl. Work the margarine into the dry ingredients. Mix thoroughly. Set aside 1 cup (250 ml) of this mixture. Pour the rest into a greased rectangular cake pan. Bake at 325°F (160°C) for 10 to 12 minutes. Remove from the oven and add a layer of chocolate chips and a layer of melted caramel.

Spread the reserved flour mixture on top of the caramel. Return to the oven for another 15 to 20 minutes.

MICROWAVE METHOD

Caramel Sauce

Standard	Metric
1-1/4 cups brown sugar	300 ml brown sugar
1 cup light cream	250 ml light cream
2 tsp corn syrup	10 ml corn syrup
1/4 cup butter	50 ml butter
Pinch salt	Pinch salt
1 tsp vanilla	15 ml vanilla
Pinch nutmeg	Pinch nutmeg

Combine the brown sugar, cream, corn syrup, butter and salt in a bowl. Cook at HIGH for 4 minutes or until contents begin to boil. Mix well. Add the vanilla and nutmeg. Stir until mixture becomes smooth.

Caramel Squares

PICNIC

These elegant picnic dishes are easy to make and transport.

Serve with a dry white wine.

MENU

Serves 6 to 8

Crab Dip
Stuffed Tomatoes with Mussels
Ham and Veal Meat Loaf
Spinach Salad
Marinated Vegetables
Coffee Squares
Crème Charlotte

CRAB DIP

Standard	Metric
1/2 lb cream cheese	250 g softened cream cheese
1/3 lb crab meat, drained and flaked	170 g crab meat, drained and flaked
1 shallot, minced	1 shallot, minced
Dash Tabasco sauce	Dash Tabasco sauce
Dash lemon juice	Dash lemon juice
Parsley, chopped	Parsley, chopped

Combine all the ingredients and mix well. Serve with crackers, raw vegetable sticks and bread rolls.

STUFFED TOMATOES WITH MUSSELS

Standard	Metric
4 large tomatoes	4 large tomatoes
1/2 cup cooked rice	125 ml cooked rice
30 mussels	30 mussels
1 cup mayonnaise	250 ml mayonnaise
1 cup canned mixed vegetables	250 ml canned mixed vegetables

Cut the tomatoes in two. Gently scoop out the flesh and put through the food processor. Pour the processed tomato into a large pot. Clean the mussels and place in the pot. Cover and cook over high heat for 5 to 10 minutes until mussels open.

Remove the mussels from the shells and set aside. Strain the mussel and tomato juice through a paper towel. Use this stock to cook the rice. Add water if necessary. Cool.

Combine all the ingredients and fill the tomatoes.

Stuffed Tomatoes with Mussels

Variation for Stuffed Tomatoes: Grated Gruyère may be used instead of mayonnaise; then bake at 375°F (190°) for 10 minutes.

SPINACH SALAD

Standard	Metric
2 cups spinach, chopped	500 ml spinach, chopped
2 tomatoes, sliced	2 tomatoes, sliced
2 hard-boiled eggs	2 hard-boiled eggs
1/3 cup plain yogurt	75 ml plain yogurt
1 tbsp lemon juice	15 ml lemon juice
1 shallot, chopped	1 shallot, chopped
Onion slices	Onion slices
Pepper and marjoram	Pepper and marjoram

Combine the yogurt, lemon juice, shallot and seasonings. Mix. Place the spinach in a salad bowl and sprinkle with crumbled hard-boiled egg; decorate with onion and tomato slices. Pour the yogurt dressing over the salad. Toss and serve.

HAM AND VEAL MEAT LOAF

Standard	Metric
1 lb ground veal	500 g ground veal
1 lb ground ham	500 g ground ham
2 eggs	2 eggs
4 tbsp ketchup	60 ml ketchup
3 tbsp green peppercorns, chopped	45 ml green peppercorns, chopped
3/4 can cream of mushroom soup	3/4 can cream of mushroom soup
1/4 to 1/2 cup breadcrumbs	50 to 125 ml breadcrumbs

Combine all the ingredients and place in a pyrex loaf pan. Bake at 350°F (180°C) for 1 hour.

Turn out the meat loaf onto a sheet of aluminum foil and discard any juices. Cool and then refrigerate. Serve cold.

Variation: Place a layer of sliced mushrooms in the center of the meat loaf mixture before baking.

MARINATED VEGETABLES

Standard	Metric
1 cauliflower, cut into flowerets	1 cauliflower, cut into flowerets
3 carrots, cut into 3 inch sticks	3 carrots, cut into 7.5 cm sticks
2 celery stalks, cut into 1 inch cubes	2 celery stalks, cut into 2.5 cm cubes
1 sweet green pepper, cut into strips	1 sweet green pepper, cut into strips
1 jar of pickled peppers	1 jar of pickled peppers
1 cup green beans, cut into 2 inch pieces	250 ml green beans, cut into 5 cm pieces
1/2 cup stuffed olives	125 ml stuffed olives
3/4 cup vinegar	150 ml vinegar
3/4 cup water	150 ml water
1/2 cup oil	125 ml oil
2 tbsp sugar	30 ml sugar
1 tsp salt	5 ml salt
1/4 tsp pepper	1 ml pepper
1/2 tsp oregano	2 ml oregano

Place all the ingredients in a large saucepan. Bring to a boil, stirring occasionally. Reduce the heat, cover and simmer for 8 to 10 minutes (vegetables will be tender-crisp). Cool. Refrigerate for 24 hours, stirring every now and then.

Keeps for about 1 month in the refrigerator.

Marinated Vegetables

COFFEE SQUARES

Standard	Metric
1 cup all-purpose flour	250 ml all-purpose flour
1/2 tsp baking powder	2 ml baking powder
1 tbsp instant coffee crystals	15 ml instant coffee crystals
1/2 tsp salt	2 ml salt
1/2 cup butter or margarine	125 ml butter or margarine
1/2 cup brown sugar	125 ml brown sugar
1 tsp vanilla extract	5 ml vanilla extract
1/4 cup walnuts, chopped	50 ml walnuts, chopped
1/2 cup chocolate chips	125 ml chocolate chips

Sift together the flour, baking powder, instant coffee and salt. Set aside. Mix the butter, brown sugar and vanilla extract until smooth and creamy. Incorporate into flour mixture. Add the walnuts and chocolate chips. Mix well.

Pour into a 8 x 8 inch (20 x 20 cm) pan. Bake at 350°F (180°C) for 25 to 30 minutes until golden brown.

Immediately cut into squares.

Coffee Squares

CRÈME CHARLOTTE

Standard	Metric
1 can condensed milk	1 can condensed milk
1-1/2 envelopes unflavored gelatin	1-1/2 envelopes unflavored gelatin
1/2 cup sugar	125 ml sugar
1/2 tsp vanilla extract	2 ml vanilla extract
1/2 cup cold water	125 ml cold water
1/2 cup boiling water	125 ml boiling water

Place the can of condensed milk in the freezer until almost frozen (at least 2 to 3 hours). Dissolve the gelatin in cold water. Stir in the boiling water as soon as the gelatin begins to set.

Mix the condensed milk with the sugar and vanilla extract. When the mixture begins to thicken, add the gelatin and beat vigorously. Refrigerate until ready to serve.

INTERNATIONAL AND REGIONAL CUISINE

German Cuisine

Serve with a dry white Riesling or Gewurtztraminer.

Menu

Serves 6 to 8

Heisse Biersuppe
(Beer Soup)
Sausage and Potato Cakes
Köningsberger Klopse
(German-Style Meatballs with Lemon Sauce)
Rhine Wine Sauerkraut
Bohnensalat
(Green Bean Salad)
Sachertorte

Heisse Biersuppe

Standard	Metric
3 bottles beer	3 bottles beer
3/4 cup sugar	150 ml sugar
4 egg yolks	4 egg yolks
6 tbsp heavy cream (35%)	90 ml heavy cream (35%)
with a dash of lemon juice	with a dash of lemon juice
1/2 tsp cinnamon	2 ml cinnamon
1/2 tsp salt	2 ml salt
Black pepper, freshly ground	Black pepper, freshly ground

Place the beer in a large pot. Add sugar. Bring to a boil at high, stirring constantly until sugar is dissolved. Remove from heat.

Beat egg yolks in a bowl, using a whisk. Add cream gradually. Stir in 4 tbsp (60 ml) beer. Pour mixture into pot. Add cinnamon, salt and pepper. Cook over medium heat stirring constantly until soup thickens. Do not boil. Adjust seasoning and serve.

Sausage and Potato Cakes

Standard	Metric
3 large potatoes, unpeeled	3 large potatoes, unpeeled
6 German sausages	6 German sausages
3 eggs	3 eggs
4 tbsp butter	60 ml butter
Salt and pepper	Salt and pepper

Parboil the potatoes in salted water. Cool, then grate. Cut the sausages in 3 inch (7.5 cm) slices.

Melt butter in a non-stick pan and sauté sausages for about 7 minutes. Add potatoes and press lightly onto sausages. Cook over medium heat about 10 minutes.

Meanwhile, beat eggs. Pour over potatoes and continue cooking for 5 minutes or until eggs are just cooked.

Turn onto a platter. Serve.

Sausage and Potato Cakes

Rhine Wine Sauerkraut

KÖNINGSBERGER KLOPSE

Standard	**Metric**
1 lb ground beef	500 g ground beef
1/2 cup seasoned bread-crumbs	125 ml seasoned bread-crumbs
1 egg	1 egg
1 tsp lemon zest	5 ml lemon zest
1 cup water	250 ml water
2 tbsp beef broth	30 ml beef broth
1 tbsp lemon juice	15 ml lemon juice
1 tsp corn starch	5 ml corn starch
4 tsp cold water	20 ml cold water
1 egg yolk	1 egg yolk

Mix the ground beef, breadcrumbs, egg and lemon zest until well blended. Shape into balls (about 12). Bring water to a boil in a medium-sized pot. Dissolve beef broth. Add meat balls to the bubbling broth.

Cook 8 to 10 minutes. Remove meat balls and keep warm.

Add lemon juice to the broth. Mix corn starch with cold water. Pour into hot broth stirring constantly. Continue cooking until broth thickens. Add a small amount of this mixture to the egg yolk. Beat well, and add to the hot broth. Remove from heat and pour over meat balls.

RHINE WINE SAUERKRAUT

Standard	**Metric**
2 lb sauerkraut	1 kg sauerkraut
12 German sausages, cut in two	12 German sausages, cut in two
1 lb onions	500 g onions
2 tbsp pork fat	30 ml pork fat
2 apples	2 apples
1/2 lb smoked slab bacon	250 g smoked slab bacon
1/2 cup white Rhine valley wine	125 ml white Rhine valley wine

Place salted sauerkraut, onions, pork fat, pared apples and bacon in an earthenware pot. Add the wine and an equal quantity of water.

Simmer over low heat for at least 3 hours. Add sausages about an hour before cooking is completed.

BOHNENSALAT

Standard	Metric
3 tbsp wine vinegar	45 ml wine vinegar
3 tbsp vegetable oil	45 ml vegetable oil
1/2 cup chicken consommé	125 ml chicken consommé
1 tsp fresh fennel	5 ml fresh fennel
1 tsp minced parsley	5 ml minced parsley
1 lb fresh green beans	500 g fresh green beans
1 sprig fresh savory or	1 sprig fresh savory or
1/4 tsp dried savory	1 ml dried savory
2 tsp salt	10 ml salt
Black pepper	Black pepper

Mix vinegar, vegetable oil, consommé, 1 tsp (5 ml) of the salt, and pepper in a bowl until well blended. Add fennel and parsley. Cover.

Trim green beans and cut into 2 inch (5 cm) pieces. Place in boiling water salted with 1 tbsp (15 ml) salt and the savory. Let boil 15 minutes. Drain. Run cold water over beans, then dry with paper towel.

Arrange on a platter. Add vinaigrette. Refrigerate 1 hour prior to serving.

SACHERTORTE

Standard	Metric
1 cup bitter chocolate	250 ml bitter chocolate
8 egg yolks	8 egg yolks
1/2 cup melted butter	125 ml melted butter
10 egg whites	10 egg whites
Pinch of salt	Pinch of salt
3/4 cup sugar	150 ml sugar
1/2 cup pastry flour	125 ml pastry flour
1/2 cup apricot jam	125 ml apricot jam

Preheat oven to 350°F (180°C).

Melt chocolate in a double boiler over hot water. Butter and flour two 8 inch (20 cm) cake pans.

Beat egg yolks. Add melted butter and chocolate.

Whip the egg whites with a pinch of salt until foamy. Add sugar and whip into firm peaks. Add a third of the beaten whites to the first mixture.

Gradually fold in the rest of the beaten egg whites. Sprinkle flour on the mixture and fold in gently, maintaining the egg white volume.

Bake 30 minutes or until cake rises and a toothpick comes out clean. Remove from pans. Let cool.

Frosting

Standard	Metric
3/4 cup semi-sweet chocolate	150 ml semi-sweet chocolate
1 cup heavy cream (35%)	250 ml heavy cream (35%)
3/4 cup sugar	150 ml sugar
1 egg	1 egg

Melt chocolate in a heavy pot over low heat, stirring constantly. Add cream and sugar. Boil gently for 5 minutes without stirring. Beat egg. Add to mixture. Cook for 4 minutes. Let cool.

To Assemble

Insert apricot jam between the two layers and cover cake with chocolate frosting mixture. Refrigerate 3 hours until frosting hardens. Remove from refrigerator 30 minutes before serving.

Sachertorte

CHINESE CUISINE

Serve with a red wine, white Bordeaux, or dry sparkling rosé.

BEATEN EGG SOUP

Standard	Metric
6 cups beef broth	1.5 liters beef broth
4 beaten eggs	4 beaten eggs
1/2 tsp ginger	2 ml ginger
4 tbsp chopped parsley	60 ml chopped parsley
Salt and pepper	Salt and pepper

Bring the broth to a boil. Add the ginger, then the beaten eggs, stirring constantly. Cook over low heat until eggs separate into filaments. Season. Pour into warmed bowls. Sprinkle with parsley. Serve.

CANTONESE SPARERIBS

Standard	Metric
3 lb spareribs	1.5 kg spareribs
1 small onion, finely chopped	1 small onion, finely chopped
1 tsp salt	5 ml salt
3/4 cup beef broth	150 ml beef broth
2 tbsp corn starch	30 ml corn starch
1/4 cup cider vinegar	50 ml cider vinegar
2 tbsp soy sauce	30 ml soy sauce
3/4 cup brown sugar	150 ml brown sugar
1/2 tsp ginger, garlic powder and curry powder, mixed	2 ml ginger, garlic powder and curry powder, mixed
1/4 tsp cloves	1 ml cloves

Cut spareribs into 2 inch (5 cm) lengths. Place in a heavy pot. Add the small, finely chopped onion and l tsp (5 ml) salt. Cover with water. Simmer covered for 45 minutes. Drain.

Mix the corn starch with the vinegar. Stir into broth. Add the other ingredients, stirring constantly until broth thickens. Add spareribs and cook until they are glazed and very hot. Serve with plum sauce.

Variation: Glaze spareribs cooking them in the oven at 350ºF (180ºC) for 30 minutes.

Beaten Egg Soup

286

ALMOND CHICKEN

Standard	Metric
3 tbsp vegetable oil	45 ml vegetable oil
2 tsp salt	10 ml salt
3 chicken breasts, deboned and cut in pieces	3 chicken breasts, deboned and cut in pieces
2 tbsp soy sauce	30 ml soy sauce
1 cup celery, cut in 2 inch julienne	250 ml celery, cut in 5 cm julienne
1 small green pepper, cut in 1 inch dice	1 small green pepper, cut in 2.5 cm dice
1 small onion, finely chopped	1 small onion, finely chopped
1 can sliced mushrooms	1 can sliced mushrooms
1 can bamboo shoots, drained and sliced	1 can bamboo shoots, drained and sliced
1 cup chicken broth	250 ml chicken broth
2 tbsp corn starch	30 ml corn starch
1/4 cup almonds, hulled and toasted	50 ml almonds, hulled and toasted

Heat oil with salt in a pot. Add chicken and brown for 3 minutes. Remove fat from pot. Add the soy sauce. Put in the vegetables and broth. Cover and simmer about 5 minutes.

Mix corn starch with a small amount of cold water and add to pot, stirring. Cook until sauce thickens and becomes clear. Add the almonds. Serve with white rice.

BLACK BEAN EGGPLANT

Standard	Metric
2 small eggplants, diced	2 small eggplants, diced
1/2 onion, sliced	1/2 onion, sliced
4 tsp black bean purée	20 ml black bean purée
2 garlic cloves, minced	2 garlic cloves, minced
1/2 tsp sugar	2 ml sugar
1 tbsp soy sauce	15 ml soy sauce
1/2 tsp salt	2 ml salt
1/2 tsp corn starch mixed in a little water	2 ml corn starch mixed in a little water
4 tsp vegetable oil	20 ml vegetable oil

Blanch eggplant for 3 to 4 minutes. Remove, drain and put aside.

Place 4 tsp (20 ml) vegetable oil in a wok and heat. Add garlic and black bean purée. Stir for 1/2 minute. Add blanched eggplant, then the remaining ingredients. Mix together. Cook until thickening occurs. Serve.

Left: A few ingredients of Chinese cuisine
Below: Almond Chicken

Marinated Cucumber Salad

MARINATED CUCUMBER SALAD

Standard	Metric
2 or 3 medium cucumbers	2 or 3 medium cucumbers
1/2 lb cooked shrimp	250 g cooked shrimp
1 tbsp sugar	15 ml sugar
1 tbsp salt	15 ml salt

Marinade

Standard	Metric
1 tsp soy sauce	5 ml soy sauce
3/4 tsp sesame oil	3 ml sesame oil
3 to 4 tbsp vinegar	45 to 60 ml vinegar
3 to 4 tbsp sugar	45 to 60 ml sugar
1/2 tsp ginger juice	2 ml ginger juice
2 red chili peppers	2 red chili peppers
1/2 tsp ground Szechuan pepper	2 ml ground Szechuan pepper
A few drops Tabasco sauce	A few drops Tabasco sauce

Peel the cucumbers and cut into thin slices. Mix the sugar and salt together. Dip cucumber slices in this and set aside for 30 minutes.

Gently rinse, drain and place in a bowl. Prepare the marinade and pour over cucumbers. Garnish with the cooked shrimp. Refrigerate before serving.

ALMOND JELLY

Standard	Metric
1 package unflavored gelatin	1 package unflavored gelatin
1 cup milk powder	250 ml milk powder
1 cup sugar	250 ml sugar
1 tbsp almond extract	15 ml almond extract
4 cups water	1 liter water

Bring the water to a boil. Add the sugar and gelatin, and stir until dissolved. Add the milk powder and almond extract. Mix well.

Pour into a mold and place in refrigerator. Allow to set before serving.

CHINESE CUISINE

Serve with hot sake.

MENU

Serves 6 to 8

Chinese Vegetable Soup
Chicken with Rice
Chinese Calf Liver
Broccoli, Chinese-Style
Chinese Fan Salad
Litchis on Ice

CHICKEN WITH RICE

Standard	Metric
2 cups water	500 ml water
3/4 tsp salt	3 ml salt
2-1/2 cups Minute rice	625 ml Minute rice
(follow directions on the	(follow directions on the
package)	package)

Bring salted water to a boil. Add the rice, cover and remove from heat. Let stand 5 minutes. Fluff rice gently using a fork.

Chicken

Standard	Metric
4 tbsp vegetable oil	60 ml vegetable oil
1-1/2 cups chopped green pepper	325 ml chopped green pepper
1 cup finely chopped onions	250 ml finely chopped onions
1/3 cup corn starch	75 ml corn starch
3 cups chicken broth	750 ml chicken broth
3 tbsp soy sauce	45 ml soy sauce
3 cups chicken slices or large pieces	750 ml chicken slices or large pieces
2 large celery stalks, diced	2 large celery stalks, diced
1-1/2 cups fresh or tinned mushrooms	375 ml fresh or tinned mushrooms

Preheat oven to 325°F (160°C).
Heat oil in a heavy pot. Brown vegetables lightly. (They should remain slightly crispy). Add broth and bring to a boil. Add 1/4 cup (50 ml) corn starch. Allow to thicken. Add chicken. Mix gently. Cook in oven for about 10 minutes.
Arrange on a platter and surround with rice.

CHINESE VEGETABLE SOUP

Standard	Metric
8 shallots	8 shallots
1/2 package frozen broccoli	1/2 package frozen broccoli
1 can bamboo shoots	1 can bamboo shoots
or	or
1 can water chestnuts	1 can water chestnuts
1 cup celery cut in 1 inch pieces	250 ml celery cut in 2.5 cm pieces
6 cups chicken broth	1.5 liters chicken broth
1/2 cup vermicelli	125 ml vermicelli
1 cup diced chicken	250 ml diced chicken
1/2 cup fresh mushrooms, sliced	125 ml fresh mushrooms, sliced
1 tbsp soy sauce	15 ml soy sauce
Salt and pepper	Salt and pepper

Slice shallots lengthwise and cut in four. Cut broccoli into large pieces. Drain the bamboo shoots and cut into cubes or slice the water chestnuts.

In a large pot, bring water to a boil over high heat. Add vermicelli, vegetables and chicken. Bring to a boil again and cook for about 6 minutes.

Add soy sauce and season.

Chinese Vegetable Soup

Chinese Calf Liver

BROCCOLI, CHINESE-STYLE

Standard	Metric
3 to 4 cups broccoli pieces (flowerets and stalk)	750 ml to 1 liter broccoli pieces (flowerets and stalk)
1 tbsp sunflower oil	15 ml sunflower oil
1 to 2 tsp freshly ground ginger	5 to 10 ml freshly ground ginger
1 to 2 cloves garlic, minced	1 to 2 cloves garlic, minced
1 tbsp sugar	15 ml sugar
1/2 tsp salt	2 ml salt

Steam broccoli in a small quantity of salted water for 3 to 4 minutes. Drain and run under cold water. Drain again and let stand.

Heat oil in a wok, over low heat. Add the ginger and garlic and cook for about 30 seconds. Add the broccoli, water, sugar and salt. Stir constantly, using a wooden spatula, for about 2 minutes. Serve.

CHINESE FAN SALAD

Standard	Metric
2 tomatoes, cut in fan shape (See page 34, Fan Shape Tomatoes)	2 tomatoes, cut in fan shape (See page 34, Fan Shape Tomatoes)
2 medium cucumbers	2 medium cucumbers
2 medium zucchini	2 medium zucchini
2 carrots	2 carrots
3 tbsp chopped parsley	45 ml chopped parsley
Choice of vinaigrette	Choice of vinaigrette

Cook the zucchini in boiling, salted water for 3 to 4 minutes. Run under cold water to cool them. Trim and cut into strips lengthwise, keeping one end intact.

Follow the same procedure for the raw cucumbers.

Pare the carrots and cut into thin slices, on the slant. Cook in boiling, salted water for about 5 minutes. Run under cold water to preserve their color.

On a large serving platter, arrange the zucchini, tomatoes and cucumber in the shape of a fan.

Add the carrots and parsley. Dress with vinaigrette of your choice.

CHINESE CALF LIVER

Standard	Metric
3 tbsp vegetable oil	45 ml vegetable oil
1/2 cup chopped onion	125 ml chopped onion
1/2 cup celery, cut slantwise	125 ml celery, cut slantwise
1/2 cup red or green pepper, cut in strips	125 ml red or green pepper, cut in strips
3 cloves crushed garlic	3 cloves crushed garlic
2 lb calf liver, cut in strips	1 kg calf liver, cut in strips
3 to 4 tbsp soy sauce	45 to 60 ml soy sauce

Heat oil in a heavy pot. Sauté the vegetables until tender. Remove and keep hot.

Quickly fry the strips of liver. Add the vegetables, and the soy sauce. Mix well. Serve with rice.

LITCHIS ON ICE

Standard	Metric
1 can litchis, drained and chilled	1 can litchis, drained and chilled
4 cups crushed ice	1 liter crushed ice
or	or
4 cups ice cream	1 liter ice cream
8 to 12 strawberries or cherries	8 to 12 strawberries or cherries

Fill tall whiskey glasses with crushed ice or ice cream. Place strawberries or cherries in the center. Surround with litchi nuts. Serve.

Chinese Fan Salad

CREOLE CUISINE

Serve with a dry white wine, or sparkling rosé.

MENU

Serves 6 to 8

Touloulou or Small Crab Bisque
Sweet Potato Pie
Ham Creole
Cream of Corn Meal
Creole Salad
Chocolate Pineapple

TOULOULOU OR SMALL CRAB BISQUE

Standard	Metric
1 lb small crabs	500 g small crabs
1 carrot	1 carrot
1 large onion, chopped	1 large onion, chopped
Thyme	Thyme
Bay leaves	Bay leaves
2 or 3 hot peppers	2 or 3 hot peppers
7 tbsp white rum	105 ml white rum
7 tbsp dry white wine	105 ml dry white wine
1/2 cup rice	125 ml rice
1/3 cup heavy cream (35%)	75 ml heavy cream (35%)
Croutons	Croutons

Brown peppers, carrot and onion in butter with thyme and bay leaves. Add the well-cleaned crabs. When they are very red, add the white rum. Flambé. Cover with equal parts of water and white wine. Let bubble gently for 30 minutes. Strain and save the liquid. Cook the rice in it.

Meanwhile, mash vegetables and touloulous. Pass the purée and the rice through a fine sieve. Moisten with rice cooking water. Cook over high heat for 10 minutes, stirring well. Pass through sieve again. Add the cream.

Fry the croutons in butter. Serve with the touloulou bisque.

SWEET POTATO PIE

Standard	Metric
2 lb sweet potatoes	1 kg sweet potatoes
2 egg yolks	2 egg yolks
3 tbsp all-purpose flour	45 ml all-purpose flour
4 tsp butter	20 ml butter
3 tbsp almonds	45 ml almonds
1 drop vanilla	1 drop vanilla

Cook sweet potatoes in a steamer. Purée them. Add egg yolks, flour, butter and ground almonds. Mix well. Add vanilla.

Place in a buttered pie plate and brown in the oven.

Touloulou or Small Crab Bisque

Cream of Corn Meal

HAM CREOLE

Standard	Metric
1 ham butt	1 ham butt
1 banana per person	1 banana per person
Cloves	Cloves
2-1/2 cups brown sugar	625 ml brown sugar
1 cup wine vinegar	250 ml wine vinegar
2 tins sliced pineapple	2 tins sliced pineapple
1 cup butter or margarine	250 ml butter or margarine
Pepper	Pepper
Bouquet garni (herb bouquet)	Bouquet garni (herb bouquet)
Cognac	Cognac

Place ham, bouquet garni and cloves in a large pot. Cook 15 minutes per pound (500 g) of ham. Drain. Let cool. Remove the ham rind and some of the fat. Cut diagonal gashes across the fat crisscross fashion to make diamond shapes. Insert a whole clove in each section. Bake the ham in the oven at 325ºF (160ºC) for 2-1/2 hours.

Prepare a syrup mixture with the vinegar, brown sugar and 3 crushed cloves. Baste the ham every 15 minutes. Add pineapple juice from time to time to prevent the sauce from caramelizing. Heat the pineapple in the butter. Add the bananas. Pepper.

Serve the ham on a platter surrounded with the peppered pineapple and bananas. Pour 3 tbsp (45 ml) cognac on the fruit and flambé.

CREAM OF CORN MEAL

Standard	Metric
6 cups milk	1-1/2 liters milk
3 tbsp sugar	45 ml sugar
1 drop vanilla	1 drop vanilla
1 cup corn meal	250 ml corn meal
4 egg yolks	4 egg yolks
4 egg whites, beaten into stiff peaks	4 egg whites, beaten into stiff peaks
1 cup heavy cream (35%)	250 ml heavy cream (35%)

Heat milk, half the sugar and vanilla. Meanwhile, place egg yolks in a bowl. Add sugar and beat for 3 minutes. Mix in the corn meal using a wooden spatula.

When milk begins to boil, add half of this mixture. Beat with a whisk, scraping mixture from side of bowl. Add to milk.

Cook over low heat and beat with a whisk or work with a wooden spatula tracing tracing figure 8's. Remove from heat, add the cream and beaten egg whites. Fold together gently. Serve.

Chocolate Pineapple

CREOLE SALAD

Standard
2 heads of lettuce
2 green peppers, diced small
2 red peppers, diced small
3 tomatoes, cut in quarters
1-1/2 cups mushrooms, thinly sliced
2 minced cloves garlic
1-1/2 cups cooked rice
Vinaigrette

Metric
2 heads of lettuce
2 green peppers, diced small
2 red peppers, diced small
3 tomatoes, cut in quarters
375 ml mushrooms, thinly sliced
2 minced cloves garlic
375 ml cooked rice
Vinaigrette

Wash lettuce and cut into pieces. Drain well and place in a bowl. Add peppers, mushrooms, garlic, tomatoes, rice and vinaigrette. Mix and serve.

CHOCOLATE PINEAPPLE

Standard
2 or 3 bananas
1/2 cup heavy cream (35%), whipped with vanilla
1 pineapple
1/3 cup rum
1 tbsp sugar
Grated chocolate

Metric
2 or 3 bananas
125 ml heavy cream (35%), whipped with vanilla
1 pineapple
75 ml rum
15 ml sugar
Grated chocolate

Mash the bananas and add the cream and vanilla.

Cut pineapple into thick slices. Soak in the rum and sugar. Place a small amount of the banana cream in the center of individual slices. Cover with grated chocolate. Refrigerate. Serve very cold.

Danish Cuisine

Serve with a red Burgundy, dry white wine, or sparkling wine.

Menu

Serves 6 to 8

Brunkaalsuppe
(Danish-Style Cabbage Soup)
Meat Smorrebrod
Danish Fondue
Brunede Kartofler
(Caramelized Potatoes)
Hummersalat
(Danish Curried Lobster Salad)
Aeblekage
(Apple Cake)

Meat Smorrebrod

Take buttered rye bread and garnish with: sliced roast beef, tomato slices and fried onions topped with fried egg; liver paté spread, garnished with sautéed mushroom slices and 2 strips of bacon.

Serve with tomato quarters and 2 cucumber slices; tartar sauce with sliced onions and pickles, capers and fresh grated horse radish.

Brunkaalsuppe

Standard	Metric
1/2 cup butter or margarine	125 ml butter or margarine
1 small cabbage, shredded	1 small cabbage, shredded
1 tbsp sugar	15 ml sugar
2 cans beef consommé	2 cans beef consommé
2 cans water	2 cans water
1 tsp salt	5 ml salt
1/2 tsp pepper	2 ml pepper
1 tbsp chopped parsley	15 ml chopped parsley

Melt the butter or margarine in a large pot. Add the cabbage and stir until well coated. Sprinkle with the sugar. Brown lightly for 3 minutes over low heat, stirring occasionally.

Add the beef consommé, water, salt and pepper. Cover. Simmer over low heat for about 20 minutes, or until the cabbage is tender. Sprinkle with parsley. Serve.

Brunkaalsuppe

DANISH FONDUE

Standard	Metric
1 clove garlic, cut in two	1 clove garlic, cut in two
1-1/2 cups Danish beer	375 ml Danish beer
1 lb grated Havarti cheese	500 g grated Havarti cheese
2 tsp dry mustard	10 ml dry mustard
1 loaf crusty bread, cut into cubes	1 loaf crusty bread, cut into cubes
Salt and pepper	Salt and pepper

Rub the garlic around the inside of an enamel fondue pot. Place over low heat, pour in beer and bring to a boil.

Mix the cheese and mustard. Add to the beer a handful at a time. Stir, tracing out figure 8's, until the mixture is smooth. Add the salt. Place on the warmer.

MICROWAVE METHOD

Cooking the Fondue

Rub garlic around inside of glass casserole. Add the beer and heat at HIGH for 2-1/2 minutes or until boiling begins. Remove from the oven. Add the mustard and half the cheese. Stir, tracing out figure 8's.

Cook at MEDIUM for 2 minutes. Add the rest of the cheese and stir. Cook at MEDIUM for 2 minutes. Stir until mixture is a smooth consistency. Pour into the fondue dish.

Danish Fondue

HUMMERSALAT

Standard	Metric
2 tins lobster	2 tins lobster
1/2 cup mayonnaise	125 ml mayonnaise
1/2 cup sour cream	125 ml sour cream
2 tsp lemon juice	10 ml lemon juice
1 tsp curry powder	5 ml curry powder
3 stalks celery, chopped	3 stalks celery, chopped
1 apple, cored and diced	1 apple, cored and diced
3 hard-boiled eggs, cut in quarters	3 hard-boiled eggs, cut in quarters
Lettuce leaves	Lettuce leaves

Drain lobster thoroughly and remove the membranes. Mix together the mayonnaise, sour cream, lemon juice and curry powder to give a smooth sauce. Add the celery, apple and lobster. Stir together gently.

Place the mixture on lettuce leaves. Garnish with the hard-boiled eggs.

BRUNEDE KARTOFLER

Standard	Metric
2 lb potatoes (unpared)	1 kg potatoes (unpared)
1/2 cup sugar	125 ml sugar
3 tbsp butter or margarine	45 ml butter or margarine

Cook potatoes in boiling water. Pare them while they are still hot.

In a heavy pot, brown the sugar and add the butter or margarine, stirring constantly. Add the potatoes. Turn them lightly until they are well coated with the caramelized sugar.

AEBLEKAGE

Standard	Metric
2 tbsp sugar	30 ml sugar
1/2 tsp vanilla	2 ml vanilla
1 can apple sauce	1 can apple sauce
1-1/4 cups breadcrumbs	300 ml breadcrumbs
1/2 cup melted butter or margarine	125 ml melted butter or margarine
1 cup heavy cream (35%), whipped	250 ml heavy cream (35%), whipped

Preheat oven to 450°F (230°C).

Butter a baking dish. Mix sugar, vanilla and apple sauce. Alternate layers of bread crumbs and sauce mixture, finishing with bread crumbs. Pour melted butter or margarine over top.

Bake for 30 minutes. Garnish with whipped cream. Serve hot.

Spanish Cuisine

Serve with a semi-dry white wine, red Bordeaux, or Spanish champagne.

Menu

Serves 6 to 8

Gazpacho
Aranjuez Eggs-Asparagus
Spanish Pork Chops
Galicia-Style Artichokes
Andalusian Salad
Natillas
(Light English Custard)

Gazpacho

Standard	Metric
1/2 cup chopped chives	125 ml chopped chives
1 cup chopped parsley	250 ml chopped parsley
1/2 cup chopped chervil	125 ml chopped chervil
1 clove crushed garlic	1 clove crushed garlic
1 green pepper, diced	1 green pepper, diced
2 large tomatoes, peeled and seeded	2 large tomatoes, peeled and seeded
1 cup olive oil	250 ml olive oil
3/4 cup lemon juice	150 ml lemon juice
1 large Spanish onion, thinly sliced	1 large Spanish onion, thinly sliced
1 cucumber, diced	1 cucumber, diced
3 slices dry bread	3 slices dry bread
1 tsp Tabasco	5 ml Tabasco
Salt and pepper	Salt and pepper
Ice cubes	Ice cubes

Crush and mix the chives, parsley, chervil and garlic. Add the green pepper and tomato. Mix. Add olive oil in a fine stream, stirring constantly. Add the lemon juice, onions and cucumber. Salt and pepper. Add Tabasco. Break up the dry bread and mix together.

Refrigerate for 3 to 4 hours. Adjust seasonings. Serve.

Aranjuez Eggs-Asparagus

Standard	Metric
1-3/4 cups asparagus	400 ml asparagus
1-3/4 cups fresh dainty green peas	400 ml fresh dainty green peas
1 clove minced garlic	1 clove minced garlic
5 tbsp vegetable oil	75 ml vegetable oil
1 tbsp all-purpose flour	15 ml all-purpose flour
6 eggs	6 eggs
Parsley	Parsley
Salt and pepper	Salt and pepper
Croutons	Croutons

Trim asparagus and cut into pieces. Add the peas.

Fry garlic with oil, remove it, and add the asparagus and peas to the pan. Cover. Simmer for about 5 minutes. Salt and pepper.

Lightly sprinkle in the flour, mix and add a little water. Put the garlic back in and cook until liquid begins to bubble.

Meanwhile, beat the eggs and pour over the asparagus and peas mixture. Cook. Sprinkle with parsley. Garnish with croutons. Serve.

Gazpacho

Spanish Pork Chops

SPANISH PORK CHOPS

Standard
4 pork chops
1 green pepper, chopped
3 onions, chopped
1 lb fresh mushrooms
1/2 cup catsup
1/4 cup Worcestershire sauce
1/2 cup chicken broth

Metric
4 pork chops
1 green pepper, chopped
3 onions, chopped
500 g fresh mushrooms
125 ml catsup
50 ml Worcestershire sauce
125 ml chicken broth

Heat oil and butter in a skillet and brown the pork chops. Set aside. Lightly fry the vegetables.

Put pork chops and vegetables together in a pot. Add the Worcestershire sauce, catsup and chicken broth. Cook for 3 to 5 minutes or until meat and vegetables are tender.

GALICIA-STYLE ARTICHOKES

Standard
6 to 8 small artichokes
1 bouillon cube
2 cups dry white wine
Onions, chopped
Garlic, chopped
Parsley, chopped
1 tbsp all-purpose flour
Salt and pepper
Lard

Metric
6 to 8 small artichokes
1 bouillon cube
500 ml dry white wine
Onions, chopped
Garlic, chopped
Parsley, chopped
15 ml all-purpose flour
Salt and pepper
Lard

Cook the artichokes in boiling, salted water for 20 minutes. Drain. In a pot, cover artichokes with equal parts of bouillon and wine. Continue cooking for about 20 minutes.

Fry the onions, garlic and parsley in the lard. Sprinkle with flour, and brown. Salt and pepper. Spoon over artichokes.

Natillas

ANDALUSIAN SALAD

Standard

1/3 cup olive oil
1/4 cup lemon juice
Black pepper, freshly ground
2 Boston or Romaine lettuces
A few endive leaves, cut into small pieces
1 bunch watercress
2 large tomatoes, thinly sliced
1 large red onion, thinly sliced and separated into rings
8 black olives
Salt

Metric

75 ml olive oil
50 ml lemon juice
Black pepper, freshly ground
2 Boston or Romaine lettuces
A few endive leaves, cut into small pieces
1 bunch watercress
2 large tomatoes, thinly sliced
1 large red onion, thinly sliced and separated into rings
8 black olives
Salt

Mix oil and lemon juice together and add seasoning.

Put lettuce, endives and watercress in a bowl. Pour vinaigrette over and stir gently.

Place in center of a cold serving platter. Surround with alternate slices of tomato and onion rings. Serve.

NATILLAS

Standard

4 cups milk
2 cinnamon sticks
5 eggs
3 egg yolks
3/4 cup sugar
12 ladyfingers
Powdered cinnamon to taste

Metric

1 liter milk
2 cinnamon sticks
5 eggs
3 egg yolks
150 ml sugar
12 ladyfingers
Powdered cinnamon to taste

In a heavy pot, heat milk and cinnamon sticks just to the point of boiling. Remove cinnamon sticks.

Beat the eggs, egg yolks and sugar in a bowl until the mixture thickens slightly. And the milk in a fine stream, stirring gently. Return mixture to the pot. Cook over low heat, stirring constantly. Do not boil. Cool to room temperature.

Pour into small bowls and sprinkle with powdered cinnamon. Serve with ladyfingers.

Greek Cuisine

Serve with a Greek red wine and Ouzo with ice.

Lemon Soup

Standard	Metric
4 cups chicken broth	1 liter chicken broth
1/2 cup rice	125 ml rice
4 eggs	4 eggs
2 lemons	2 lemons

Bring chicken broth to a boil. Add rice. Cook over low heat for 20 minutes.

In a pot, beat the eggs until foamy. Add the lemon juice and a quarter of the hot broth.

Gradually add the remaining broth to the soup, stirring constantly. Cook for 3 to 5 minutes until the soup thickens slightly.

Attention: Do not let boil or the eggs will coagulate.

Tarato

Standard	Metric
1 lb eggplant	500 g eggplant
3 red peppers, diced	3 red peppers, diced
Vegetable oil	Vegetable oil
2 containers of plain yogurt	2 containers plain yogurt
6 tbsp olive oil	90 ml olive oil
1 lemon	1 lemon
3 cloves garlic	3 cloves garlic
Salt and pepper	Salt and pepper

Cook the diced peppers and the eggplant in oil. Remove skin. Mash the pulp.

Mix this purée with the yogurt. Add salt, pepper, minced garlic, olive oil and lemon juice. Cover with 4 cups (1 liter) boiling water and stir well. Let cool. Serve chilled.

Lemon Soup

Greek Stew

GREEK STEW

Standard	Metric
1-1/2 lb lean beef, cut into 1 inch cubes	750 g lean beef, cut into 1 inch cubes
2 tbsp butter or margarine	30 ml butter or margarine
2 cups water	500 ml water
1 cup onions, sliced	250 ml onions, sliced
1/2 cup tomato paste	125 ml tomato paste
2 tbsp white vinegar	30 ml white vinegar
2 tsp red wine	10 ml red wine
1 tsp brown sugar	5 ml brown sugar
1 clove garlic	1 clove garlic
1 bay leaf	1 bay leaf
1 cinnamon stick	1 cinnamon stick
1/4 tsp ground cloves	1 ml ground cloves
1/4 tsp ground saffron	1 ml ground saffron

Melt butter or margarine in a pot. Lightly fry the beef cubes for about 20 minutes. Add the remaining ingredients. Mix well.

Cover and simmer for 2-1/2 hours, stirring occasionally. Remove the garlic, bay leaf and cinnamon stick.

GREEN BEANS WITH RINGS OF ONION

Standard	Metric
1 cup water	250 ml water
1 onion, thinly sliced	1 onion, thinly sliced
2 lb green beans, with ends trimmed	1 kg green beans, with ends trimmed
1/2 cup butter	125 ml butter
Lemon juice	Lemon juice
Salt and pepper	Salt and pepper

Bring water to a boil in a pot. Add the onion slices separated into rings. Mix in the green beans, butter, salt, pepper and lemon juice.

Boil for about 20 minutes or until the green beans are tender.

PATATOSALATA

Standard	Metric
1/2 cup olive oil	125 ml olive oil
3 tbsp wine vinegar	45 ml wine vinegar
1 tsp ground oregano	5 ml ground oregano
2 tbsp chopped parsley	30 ml chopped parsley
1 medium onion, thinly sliced	1 medium onion, thinly sliced
5 large red-skinned potatoes	5 large red-skinned potatoes
Salt and pepper	Salt and pepper

Mix together thoroughly the olive oil, vinegar, oregano, parsley and onion and let marinate.

Wash the unpeeled potatoes. Cook in salted water for about 40 minutes or until tender. Remove and run under cold water. Peel them while still warm, and cut into equal slices.

Pour the marinade over the potatoes. Stir well. Salt and pepper.

ANISE SOUFFLÉ

Standard	Metric
4 tbsp butter	60 ml butter
2 tbsp all-purpose flour	30 ml all-purpose flour
1/3 cup milk	75 ml milk
Pinch of anise	Pinch of anise
2 tbsp sugar	30 ml sugar
4 egg yolks	4 egg yolks
4 egg whites, beaten to stiff peaks	4 egg whites, beaten to stiff peaks
3 tbsp anisette (Ouzo)	45 ml anisette (Ouzo)

Preheat oven to 375°F (190°C).

In a pot, melt 2 tbsp (30 ml) of the butter. Add flour, milk flavored with anise and the sugar. Heat at very low temperature.

Remove from stove at first sign of boiling. Add the egg yolks and 2 tbsp (30 ml) butter. Fold in the stiffly beaten egg whites. Pour into a greased and sugared soufflé mold.

Bake for 30 minutes. Remove from oven. Pour 1 tbsp (15 ml) of the liqueur (Ouzo) over the soufflé.

Anise Soufflé

GREEK CUISINE

Serve with a dry white wine, or rosé.

MENU

Serves 6 to 8

Fassoulatha
(White Bean Soup)
Saganaki
(Fried Cheese)
Moussaka
Karota me Anitho
(Carrots with Fennel)
Tsatziki
(Cucumber Salad with Yogurt)
Kourkourti
(Thick Soup with Almonds and Currants)

FASSOULATHA

Standard	Metric
1 cup large white beans	250 ml large white beans
4 cups water	1 liter water
1 cup celery, cut in 1/2 inch pieces	250 ml celery, cut in 1.25 cm pieces
2 cups chopped onions	500 ml chopped onions
4 medium carrots, cut in 1/2 inch pieces	4 medium carrots, cut in 1.25 cm pieces
1/2 cup chopped parsley	125 ml chopped parsley
1 tbsp tomato paste	15 ml tomato paste
1 cup olive oil	250 ml olive oil
1 tbsp minced oregano	15 ml minced oregano
3 tbsp wine vinegar	45 ml wine vinegar
Salt and pepper	Salt and pepper

Put water and beans in a pot and bring to the boil. Reduce heat and simmer for an hour.

Add all the other ingredients. Continue cooking for 2 hours. Salt and pepper.

Serve with toast.

SAGANAKI

Standard	Metric
Cheese slices Kefalotyri or Kasseri, 1/4 inch thick (about 1.5 lb for 6 people)	Cheese slices Kefalotyri or Kasseri, 0.65 cm thick (about 750 g for 6 people)
2 egg yolks	2 egg yolks
2 tbsp water	30 ml water
All-purpose flour	All-purpose flour
Olive oil	Olive oil
2 lemons, cut in quarters	2 lemons, cut in quarters

Mix egg yolks and water. Dip the cheese slices in this mixture, then in the flour.

Heat oil in a skillet. Lightly fry the cheese slices. Drain and serve on a platter. Sprinkle with lemon juice.

MOUSSAKA

Standard	Metric
1 eggplant, peeled and cut in round slices	1 eggplant, peeled and cut in round slices
1 lb ground beef (or ground lamb)	500 g ground beef (or ground lamb)
1 medium onion, chopped	1 medium onion, chopped
1 clove minced garlic	1 clove minced garlic
1 can tomatoes	1 can tomatoes
1/2 tsp oregano	2 ml oregano
1 tsp salt	5 ml salt
1/8 tsp pepper	0.5 ml pepper
1 tbsp olive oil	15 ml olive oil
1/2 cup feta cheese	125 ml feta cheese
2 eggs, slightly beaten	2 eggs, slightly beaten
Nutmeg	Nutmeg

Preheat oven to 350°F (180°C).

Lightly fry the meat, onion and garlic in a large skillet until the meat is golden brown. Drain. Add the tomatoes, oregano, salt and pepper. Simmer for 10 minutes. Brush the eggplant rounds with olive oil and brown both sides, cooking for 5 minutes. In a greased baking dish, alternate layers of eggplant rounds and meat sauce, topping with a mixture of feta cheese and beaten eggs. Sprinkle with nutmeg.

Bake for 2 hours.

Moussaka and Karota me Anitho

Karota me Anitho

Standard	Metric
1 cup water	250 ml water
1/4 cup wine vinegar	50 ml wine vinegar
1 medium onion, cut in quarters	1 medium onion, cut in quarters
1/2 tsp salt	2 ml salt
1 tbsp fennel	15 ml fennel
6 large carrots, pared and cut into thick slices	6 large carrots, pared and cut into thick slices

Bring water and vinegar to the boil in a pot. Add the onion, salt, fennel and carrots. Reduce heat and simmer for 10 minutes. Let cool. Refrigerate. When the liquid is very cold, drain and serve.

Tsatziki

Standard	Metric
2 cups plain yogurt	500 ml plain yogurt
1 shallot, chopped	1 shallot, chopped
1 tsp mint	5 ml mint
1/2 tsp salt	2 ml salt
Black pepper, freshly ground	Black pepper, freshly ground
Pinch of fennel	Pinch of fennel
1 clove crushed garlic	1 clove crushed garlic
4 cucumbers	4 cucumbers

Mix the yogurt, shallots, mint, salt, pepper, fennel and garlic.

Peel the cucumbers and cut into thin strips. Add to the first mixture. Stir carefully. Refrigerate for 1 hour. Serve with slices of toast.

Kourkourti

Standard	Metric
2-1/2 cups whole wheat grains	625 ml whole wheat grains
Water	Water
Salt, sugar and cinnamon	Salt, sugar and cinnamon
1 cup almonds, blanched and chopped large	250 ml almonds, blanched and chopped large
1/2 cup dried currants	125 ml dried currants

The night before, put whole wheat in a large pot. Cover with cold water and let stand.

The next day, drain the wheat. Cover again with fresh, cold water. Bring to a boil and simmer for about 4 hours, until the wheat is tender. Stir often and add more water as needed. The contents should be very thick. Drain and save the broth.

Pour the broth, salt, sugar and cinnamon into a casserole. Stir in the almonds, currents and 1 cup (250 ml) of the boiled wheat. Serve hot.

Tsatziki

306

GREEK CUISINE

Serve with a semi-dry white wine, red wine, or Greek wine.

MENU

Serves 6 to 8

Faki
(Lentil Soup)
Salata Melitzana
(Eggplant Entrée)
Greek-Style Tournedos
Garlic Zucchini
Roseiki Salad
Figs in Greek Wine

SALATA MELITZANA

Standard	Metric
1 large eggplant	1 large eggplant
1 medium onion, chopped	1 medium onion, chopped
1 crushed clove garlic	1 crushed garlic clove
1 tsp parsley	5 ml parsley
1/2 tsp dried mint	2 ml dried mint
1/2 cup olive oil	125 ml olive oil
1 tbsp wine vinegar	15 ml wine vinegar
Juice of a large lemon	Juice of a large lemon
Salt and pepper	Salt and pepper

Place eggplant in an oven ware pot and prick with a fork in 5 or 6 places. Cook at 360ºF (180ºC) for about 45 minutes or until the skin is wrinkled.

Cool the eggplant slightly and cut in two lengthwise. Remove the flesh and put into a blender. Add onion, garlic, parsley and mint. Mix well.

Mix together the olive oil, vinegar and lemon juice. Add to the eggplant mixture. Blend well. Salt and pepper. Refrigerate. Serve with small pita breads.

MICROWAVE TIP

How to get more juice from a lemon . . .

Place a lemon in the microwave oven at HIGH for 30 seconds prior to squeezing. This technique also works for other citrus fruits.

FAKI

Standard	Metric
1 package (16 oz) of lentils	1 package (500 g) of lentils
8 cups water	2 liters water
1/2 cup olive oil	125 ml olive oil
1 cup chopped celery	250 ml chopped celery
1/2 cup grated carrots	125 ml grated carrots
1 onion, cut in quarters	1 onion, cut in quarters
1 tbsp tomato paste	15 ml tomato paste
3 garlic cloves	3 garlic cloves
2 bay leaves	2 bay leaves
Salt and pepper	Salt and pepper
Vinegar	Vinegar

Rinse the lentils several times and drain thoroughly. Place all ingredients in a heavy pot. Bring to a boil. Reduce heat. Cover and simmer for 2 hours. Adjust seasoning.

Put vinegar in a cruet. Serve with the faki.

Faki

GREEK-STYLE TOURNEDOS

Standard	Metric
6 slices beef filet (1-1/2 inch thick)	6 slices beef filet (3.5 cm thick)
1/2 cup butter	125 ml butter
1/4 cup all-purpose flour	50 ml all-purpose flour
3/4 cup dry white wine	150 ml dry white wine
1/2 cup chopped parsley	125 ml chopped parsley
Juice of a lemon	Juice of a lemon
Salt and pepper	Salt and pepper

Melt the butter in a heavy pot. Quickly brown the meat. Remove and place on a platter.

Add the flour to the pot and stir constantly over low heat for 2 minutes. Add the wine. Stir. Cover. Simmer for 5 minutes.

Return the meat to the pot. Add the parsley and lemon juice and simmer for another 5 minutes. Serve.

Greek-Style Tournedos

MICROWAVE METHOD

Cooking Diced Beets

Evenly arrange beets in a container with cover. Add a little water. Cook at HIGH for 15 minutes or until tender. Let stand for a few minutes. Drain before adding the rest of the ingredients in the recipe.

ROSEIKI SALAD

Standard	Metric
1/3 cup olive oil	75 ml olive oil
3 tbsp vinegar	45 ml vinegar
1 cup carrots, cooked and diced	250 ml carrots, cooked and diced
1 cup beets, cooked and diced	250 ml beets, cooked and diced
2 potatoes, cooked and diced	2 potatoes, cooked and diced
1 cup green beans, diced	250 ml green beans, diced
1 cup green peas	250 ml green peas
1/4 cup chopped parsley	50 ml chopped parsley
2 tsp capers	10 ml capers
Mayonnaise	Mayonnaise
Salt and pepper	Salt and pepper

Place all the vegetables in a bowl. Mix the oil and vinegar and add to vegetables. Marinate about 1 hour 30 minutes. Drain.

Add the parsley and mix in about 1 cup (250 ml) of mayonnaise. Season. Garnish with capers. Serve.

GARLIC ZUCCHINI

Standard	Metric
6 zucchini cut into thick slices	6 zucchini cut into thick slices
1 cup water	250 ml water
1/2 cup olive oil	125 ml olive oil
1/4 cup wine vinegar	50 ml wine vinegar
Fresh parsley	Fresh parsley
1 garlic clove	1 garlic clove
Salt and pepper	Salt and pepper

Mix all the ingredients in a pot. Bring to a boil, then reduce heat. Simmer for about 8 minutes. Adjust seasoning. Cool.

Serve hot or cold.

FIGS IN GREEK WINE

Standard	Metric
24 ripe figs	24 ripe figs
2 cups Mavrodaphne wine	500 ml Mavrodaphne wine
2 cups heavy cream (35%)	500 ml heavy cream (35%)
1/4 cup walnuts	50 ml walnuts

Peel the figs and prick with a fork in 3 or 4 places. Place in a bowl and pour wine over. Refrigerate for 2 hours, stirring occasionally.

Drain the figs, reserving the wine. Arrange the figs on a serving plate. Whip the cream and place around the figs. Garnish with nuts. Serve the wine as accompaniment.

HUNGARIAN CUISINE

Serve with a white wine, red Bordeaux, or rosé.

GREEN PEA SANDWICHES

Standard	Metric
1 cup dainty green peas	250 ml dainty green peas
3/4 cup plain yogurt (firm)	150 ml plain yogurt (firm)
8 slices brown or white bread, buttered and cut in two	8 slices brown or white bread, buttered and cut in two
2 tbsp chopped onion	30 ml chopped onion
1 tsp chopped garlic	5 ml chopped garlic
Cayenne pepper	Cayenne pepper
Salt and pepper	Salt and pepper

Cook the peas to a purée. Salt and pepper generously. Cool. Mix in the yogurt, onion, garlic and cayenne pepper. Spread on bread and roll up. Hold with toothpicks.

Makes 16 sandwiches.

HARCHO

Standard	Metric
1 lb boneless lamb breast, cut in small cubes	500 g boneless lamb breast, cut in small cubes
6 cups water	1.5 liters water
1 tsp salt	5 ml salt
1/2 cup onion, finely chopped	125 ml onions, finely chopped
4 tbsp butter	50 g butter
2 tbsp tomato purée	30 ml tomato purée
7 tbsp rice	105 ml rice
1 garlic clove, crushed	1 garlic clove, crushed
1/4 cup celery, finely chopped	50 ml celery, finely choppcd
2 tbsp fennel, finely chopped	30 ml fennel, finely chopped

Put meat and water in a pot. Bring to the boil and skim off at regular intervals. Salt. Add the onions. Cover and simmer for 1 hour.

Melt butter in another pot. Add the tomato purée. Mix and add to the soup.

Add the rice, garlic and celery. Simmer for about 20 minutes or until the rice is cooked. Sprinkle with the fennel. Serve.

Green Pea Sandwiches

GOULASH

Standard	Metric
3 lb beef, cut in cubes	1.5 kg beef, cut in cubes
3 tbsp fat or margarine	45 ml fat or margarine
4 onions, sliced	4 onions, sliced
1 tbsp salt	15 ml salt
1/2 tsp pepper	2 ml pepper
1/2 tsp garlic powder	2 ml garlic powder
2 tsp paprika	10 ml paprika
1 tbsp lemon juice	15 ml lemon juice
1 beef bouillon cube	1 beef bouillon cube
1 green pepper, diced	1 green pepper, diced
1 can of tomatoes	1 can of tomatoes
1/2 to 1 tsp saffron	2 to 5 ml saffron
2 to 3 cups water	500 to 750 ml water
Pastry for 2-crust pie	Pastry for 2-crust pie

Brown the beef cubes in the fat (or margarine). Add the onions. Salt and pepper. Fry, stirring constantly for about 5 minutes. Cover. Reduce the heat. Continue cooking for 20 to 30 minutes. Add a little water, if necessary. Add the water, lemon juice, garlic, paprika and simmer for 40 minutes.

When the meat is tender, add the rest of the ingredients and continue cooking for 20 minutes.

Press one portion of pastry into pie plate. Pour mixture into it. Cover with remaining pastry. Cook in the oven at 475°F (240°C) until golden.

PAPRIKA ASPARAGUS

Standard	Metric
2 lb asparagus	1 kg asparagus
7 tbsp sour cream	105 ml sour cream
1 slice of bread, crumbled	1 slice of bread, crumbled
Pinch of salt	Pinch of salt
Pinch of sugar	Pinch of sugar
Paprika	Paprika
Butter	Butter

Cook the asparagus in water with pinch of salt and sugar, for 30 minutes. Drain. Butter a baking dish. Spread the bottom with sour cream and a spoonful of the bread, crumbled.

Place the asparagus on this. Cover with a mixture of the sour cream, bread and paprika. Brown the top.

FRIED PEPPERS SALAD

Standard	Metric
1 lb green peppers	500 g green peppers
1 large onion, chopped	1 large onion, chopped
Oil and vinegar	Oil and vinegar
Chopped parsley	Chopped parsley
Chopped tarragon	Chopped tarragon
Salt and pepper	Salt and pepper

Cut and seed the peppers. Fry them in oil for a few minutes. Skin them. Mix the onion, parsley, tarragon, oil, vinegar, salt and pepper. Marinate peppers in this mixture for several hours. Serve.

Goulash

310

Croissants with Nuts

CROISSANTS WITH NUTS

Standard
1 tsp yeast
7 tbsp milk
2 cups all-purpose flour
3/4 cup butter
6 tbsp sugar
1 egg

Metric
5 ml yeast
105 ml milk
500 ml all-purpose flour
150 ml butter
90 ml sugar
1 egg

Pastry Preparation

Standard
1 cup water
1 cup sugar
1-1/4 cups crushed walnuts
1 tsp cinnamon powder
Zest of grated lemon
1/4 cup dry, crushed biscuits
2 eggs

Metric
250 ml water
250 ml sugar
300 ml crushed walnuts
5 ml cinnamon powder
Zest of grated lemon
50 ml dry, crushed biscuits
2 eggs

Warm the milk. Add salt. Dissolve yeast in it. Mix the flour, butter, sugar, the dissolved yeast and eggs. Knead and place in the refrigerator for several hours. Divide the pastry into 6. Shape into balls, then roll into oval shapes as thin as possible, using a rolling pin.

Filling

Mix the nuts, cinnamon, lemon zest and the crushed biscuits. Reserve. Cook the water and sugar together, creating a syrup. Combine with the first mixture. Let cool. Divide into 6 portions and spread on the pastry ovals. Roll them up into small croissants.

Place on a buttered cookie sheet. Beat together one egg and one egg yolk. Baste the croissants and bake at 325°F (160°C) for 30 minutes. Baste again. Let dry. Return to the oven for 30 minutes.

Makes 8 to 10 croissants.

Technique: Croissants

1 Divide pastry into 6 balls.

2 Roll each ball into an oval.

3 Spread the nut filling on the pastry.

4 Roll up the croissants.

5 Place on a buttered cooking sheet and brush with beaten egg.

6 Sprinkle the remaining filling on top and bake.

INDIAN CUISINE

Serve with a red Burgundy.

MENU

Serves 6 to 8

Shrimp Soup
Indian-Style Rice with Peppers
Chamignon
(Lamb Meat Balls with Mint)
Fried Eggplant
Curried Tomato and Pepper Salad
Small Indian Cakes

SHRIMP SOUP

Standard	Metric
1 cup onions, chopped	250 ml onions, chopped
2 tbsp vegetable oil	30 ml vegetable oil
1/2 lb shrimp, shelled and deveined	250 g shrimp, shelled and deveined
1 tsp vegetable concentrate	5 ml vegetable concentrate
3 cups chicken stock	750 ml chicken stock
2 tbsp corn starch	30 ml corn starch
1 tbsp curry powder	15 ml curry powder
Salt and pepper	Salt and pepper

Heat oil in a pot. Brown the onions. Add the shelled, deveined shrimp, the stock mixed with the corn starch and the curry powder. Bring to a boil and cook until thickening occurs. Adjust seasoning.

MICROWAVE METHOD

To Cook Rice

Put oil, onions, parsley, garlic and peppers in a glass dish. Cook at HIGH for 2-1/2 to 3 minutes. Stir mid-way through cooking.

Add the stock. Cover and cook at MEDIUM for 14 minutes or until rice is cooked. Stir every 5 minutes. Let stand 5 minutes before serving.

Indian-Style Rice with Peppers

INDIAN-STYLE RICE WITH PEPPERS

Standard	Metric
1-1/2 cups rice	375 ml rice
Olive oil	Olive oil
2 onions, chopped	2 onions, chopped
3 tbsp chopped parsley	45 ml chopped parsley
2 cloves minced garlic	2 cloves minced garlic
3 green peppers, chopped	3 green peppers, chopped
4 cups chicken stock	l liter chicken stock
Cayenne pepper	Cayenne pepper
Salt	Salt

Sauté the peppers in butter. Set aside. Brown the rice, onions, parsley and garlic in the olive oil. Add the peppers. Stir. Season with cayenne pepper. Lightly moisten with the stock and cook over low heat for about 20 minutes.

CHAMIGNON

Standard	Metric
1-1/2 lb ground lean lamb	750 g ground lean lamb
4 tbsp grated almonds	60 ml grated almonds
4 tbsp grated pistachios	60 ml grated pistachios
2 tbsp chick pea flour	30 ml chick pea flour
2 tbsp all-purpose flour	30 ml all-purpose flour
1 tbsp curry powder	15 ml curry powder
2 tbsp butter	30 ml butter
Parsley	Parsley
Mint leaves, chopped	Mint leaves, chopped
Salt and pepper	Salt and pepper

Combine the meat, parsley, mint leaves, almonds, pistachios, salt, pepper and chick pea flour. Shape into balls. Fry in the butter over low heat until golden brown. Sprinkle with flour and mix. Add a glass of water and the curry powder. Cover. Cook slowly.

CURRIED TOMATO AND PEPPER SALAD

Standard	Metric
3 large tomatoes, cut in quarters	3 large tomatoes, cut in quarters
2 green peppers, chopped	2 green peppers, chopped
1 red pepper, chopped	1 red pepper, chopped
1 onion, chopped	1 onion, chopped
1 small, hot yellow pepper, finely chopped	1 small, hot yellow pepper, finely chopped
1 tbsp curry powder	15 ml curry powder
1 cup chick peas	250 ml chick peas
Vinaigrette	Vinaigrette

In a salad bowl, combine the tomatoes, peppers, onion, hot pepper and chick peas.

Add the curry powder to the vinaigrette. Pour over the salad. Serve well-seasoned.

FRIED EGGPLANT

Standard	Metric
2 lb eggplants	1 kg eggplants
2 or 3 onions	2 or 3 onions
3 tbsp butter	45 ml butter
1 egg	1 egg
Stale bread, crumbled	Stale bread, crumbled
Curry powder	Curry powder
Salt	Salt

Wash the eggplant and cut in two lengthwise. Soak in cold water. Scoop out, leaving 1/2 inch (1.25 cm) flesh. Fry the onions in the butter. Chop the scooped out eggplant. Mix in the onions, salt and curry powder. Stuff the eggplant. Top with the egg and bread. Fry.

SMALL INDIAN CAKES

Standard	Metric
1 cup wheat flour	250 ml wheat flour
1 cup corn flour	250 ml corn flour
1 cup butter	250 ml butter
1 tbsp yeast	15 ml yeast
1 cup milk	250 ml milk
1 egg yolk	1 egg yolk
Grated nutmeg	Grated nutmeg
Vanilla	Vanilla
Powdered cinnamon	Powdered cinnamon
Salt	Salt

Warm the milk. Mix yeast with a small amount of the milk in a bowl. Stir until dissolved.

To the remaining warm milk, add salt, vanilla, nutmeg, cinnamon and butter. Stir milk mixture into yeast. Add the flours. Knead.

Roll out the dough to a thickness of 1/4 inch (1/2 cm). Cut out rounds. Brush with beaten egg yolk. Place on a greased cookie sheet and bake at 325ºF (160ºC) for about 15 minutes.

Chamignon

313

ITALIAN CUISINE

Serve with a red Italian wine, white Bordeaux, and champagne.

MENU

Serves 6 to 8

Italian Vegetable Soup
Cannelloni Stuffed with Shrimp
Chicken Cacciatore
Baked Artichoke Lasagna
Mushroom Salad
Fruit Cup with Honey and Lime

Cannelloni Stuffed with Shrimp

ITALIAN VEGETABLE SOUP

Standard	Metric
2 tbsp olive oil	30 ml olive oil
or	or
2 tbsp vegetable oil	30 ml vegetable oil
2 tbsp butter	30 ml butter
1 large onion, chopped	1 large onion, chopped
1 crushed garlic clove	1 crushed garlic clove
1/2 cup celery, chopped	125 ml celery, chopped
1/2 cup carrots, chopped or sliced	125 ml carrots, chopped or sliced
1/2 green pepper, chopped	1/2 green pepper, chopped
2 tbsp chopped parsley	30 ml chopped parsley
1 tsp basil	5 ml basil
1 can Italian or plain tomatoes	1 can Italian or plain tomatoes
2 tbsp tomato paste	30 ml tomato paste
1 can beef broth	1 can beef broth
3 cups water	750 ml water
1/2 cup shell noodles or other small noodles	125 ml shell noodles or other small noodles
1 cup red or white beans, cooked, preserved	250 ml red or white beans, cooked, preserved
2 cups chopped cabbage	500 ml chopped cabbage
Salt and pepper	Salt and pepper

Heat oil and butter in a large pot. Add the onion, garlic, celery, carrots and green pepper and braise without browning the vegetables. Add the parsley, basil, salt and pepper. Mix in the tomatoes, tomato paste, beef broth and water. Bring to a boil, then reduce heat, cover and simmer for 20 minutes.

Add the pasta, cover and cook until tender. Add the beans and cabbage. Cover and simmer for another 30 minutes.

If the soup is too thick, dilute with water to the desired consistency. Taste and adjust seasonings.

CANNELLONI STUFFED WITH SHRIMP

Standard	Metric
32 cannelloni	32 cannelloni
1-1/2 cups shrimp	375 ml shrimp
1/2 cup breadcrumbs	125 ml breadcrumbs
2 cloves chopped garlic	2 cloves chopped garlic
4 tbsp chopped parsley	60 ml chopped parsley
1 tsp fresh basil, chopped	5 ml fresh basil, chopped
1 tbsp tomato paste	15 ml tomato paste
2 tbsp butter	30 ml butter
1 cup chicken broth	250 ml chicken broth
2 eggs	2 eggs
Salt and pepper	Salt and pepper
House vinaigrette, slightly warmed	House vinaigrette, slightly warmed

Cook the cannelloni in boiling, salted water. Run under cold, running water, drain and reserve.

Dry the shrimp in a towel to remove all the water. Place in the blender with all the other ingredients except the butter and vinaigrette. Mix to a smooth, fluffed consistency. Using a pastry bag, fill the cannelloni. Place side by side in a lightly buttered baking dish. Add the chicken broth and sprinkle the top with the breadcrumbs. Dot with butter.

Place in the oven at 350°F (180°C) for about 30 minutes. Remove from the oven and drain. Dress with the slightly warmed vinaigrette. Garnish with fresh, chopped basil.

CHICKEN CACCIATORE

Standard	Metric
1 green pepper	1 green pepper
1 red pepper	1 red pepper
2 onions, chopped	2 onions, chopped
2 cans mushrooms	2 cans mushrooms
1 tbsp chopped garlic	15 ml chopped garlic
1 can large tomatoes	1 can large tomatoes
1/2 can tomato sauce	1/2 can tomato sauce
1 tsp sugar	5 ml sugar
2 tbsp tomato paste	30 ml tomato paste
12 chicken legs	12 chicken legs
2 tbsp oil	30 ml oil
2 tbsp butter	30 ml butter
1 tsp thyme	5 ml thyme
Salt and pepper	Salt and pepper

Heat the butter and oil in a heavy pot. Lightly brown the chicken on all sides. Skim off some of the fat, leaving chicken legs in the pot.

Add the chopped onions, the mushrooms, green and red peppers, tomatoes and chopped garlic. Cook for about 10 minutes.

Add the tomato paste and mix. Add the remaining ingredients and simmer for 1 hour over low heat.

MUSHROOM SALAD

Standard	Metric
1-1/2 lb mushrooms, chopped	750 g mushrooms, chopped
7 tbsp olive oil	105 ml olive oil
2 tbsp parsley, chopped	30 ml parsley, chopped
6 anchovy fillets, washed, dried and chopped	6 anchovy fillets, washed, dried and chopped
1 lemon, squeezed	1 lemon, squeezed
Salt and pepper	Salt and pepper

Place the mushrooms in a large salad bowl. Add all the other ingredients and mix. Let marinate 30 minutes before serving.

FRUIT CUP WITH HONEY AND LIME

Standard	Metric
2 peaches	2 peaches
or	or
2 nectarines	2 nectarines
1 small cantaloupe	1 small cantaloupe
1 cup blueberries	250 ml blueberries
1/3 cup honey	75 ml honey
3 tbsp fresh lime juice	45 ml fresh lime juice
12 peppercorns, ground	12 peppercorns, ground

Chicken Cacciatore

Cut the peaches and nectarines into quarters. Dice the canteloupe. Combine the fruit, adding the blueberries, honey and fresh lime juice. Cover and refrigerate for 1 hour. Garnish with a few grains of ground peppercorns.

BAKED ARTICHOKE LASAGNA

Standard	Metric
1 box lasagna	1 box lasagna
2 cups tinned artichokes, cut into pieces	500 ml tinned artichokes, cut into pieces
2 tomatoes, sliced	2 tomatoes, sliced
2 onions, finely chopped	2 onions, finely chopped
2 cups tomato juice	500 ml tomato juice
1 tsp thyme	5 ml thyme
1/3 cup olive oil	75 ml olive oil
1/2 cup breadcrumbs	125 ml breadcrumbs
1/2 cup mozzarella cheese	125 ml mozzarella cheese
1 tbsp paprika	15 ml paprika
Salt and pepper	Salt and pepper

Cook the lasagna in boiling, salted water. Set aside.

Heat the oil in a pot. Add the artichokes and onions and cook for about 8 minutes over low heat. Season and set aside.

In a baking dish, alternate layers of lasagna, artichokes and tomatoes. End with the cheese, breadcrumbs and sprinkled paprika. Bake at 350ºF (180ºC) for 40 minutes.

Fruit Cup with Honey and Lime

ITALIAN CUISINE

Serve with a white Burgundy, and William Pear liqueur on ice.

MINESTRONE

Standard	Metric
4 to 5 garlic cloves, finely chopped	4 to 5 garlic cloves, finely chopped
1 cup onions, chopped	250 ml onions, chopped
3 tbsp oil (olive or other)	45 ml oil (olive or other)
1 tsp salt	5 ml salt
1 cup carrots, in small dice	250 ml carrots, in small dice
1 cup celery, finely diced	250 ml celery, finely diced
1 cup eggplant or zucchini, diced	250 ml eggplant or zucchini, diced
1 tsp oregano	5 ml oregano
1/4 tsp freshly ground black pepper	1 ml freshly ground black pepper
1 tsp dried basil	5 ml dried basil
or	or
1 tbsp fresh basil	15 ml fresh basil
1 cup green pepper, in small dice	250 ml green pepper, in small dice
3-1/2 cups water or beef stock	875 ml water or beef stock
2 cups tomato purée	500 ml tomato purée
1-1/2 cups cooked split peas or chick peas	375 ml cooked split peas or chick peas
3 tbsp dry red wine	45 ml dry red wine
1 cup crushed fresh tomatoes	250 ml crushed fresh tomatoes
1/2 cup fresh pasta noodles	125 ml fresh pasta noodles
1/2 cup fresh parsley, chopped	125 ml fresh parsley, chopped
1/2 cup grated Parmesan cheese	125 ml grated Parmesan cheese

In a 16 cup (4 liter) pot, sauté the onions and garlic in oil until tender and transparent. Add half the salt, and the carrots, celery and eggplant (if using zucchini, add at the same time as

Roasted Chick Peas

the green pepper), oregano, black pepper and basil. Cover. Simmer for 5 to 8 minutes. Add the green pepper (and zucchini, if applicable), water or beef stock, tomato purée, cooked peas and wine. Continue cooking for 15 minutes. Add tomatoes and the rest of the salt. Continue cooking, bubbling gently, for about 10 minutes. Add the noodles and cook for another 10 minutes, approximately.

Garnish with parsley and freshly grated Parmesan. Serve immediately.

ROASTED CHICK PEAS

Standard	Metric
1 garlic clove, peeled	1 garlic clove, peeled
3 tbsp olive oil	45 ml olive oil
1 lb dried chick peas	500 g dried chick peas
1/2 tsp salt	2 ml salt

Crush the garlic clove with the flat of a knife. Add to the olive oil.

Cover chick peas generously with water. Bring to a boil. After 2 minutes, remove from heat and let them soak for an hour. Drain and dry them.

Heat the oven to 350°F (180°C). Place the peas on a large cooking sheet. Take out the garlic clove and pour the oil over the chick peas. They should be well coated. Salt and let cook in the oven for 40 minutes. Remove from the oven and wipe the chick peas.

These are served as appetizer or entrée with radishes.

PORK CHOPS À LA MILANAISE

Standard
8 lean pork chops
All-purpose flour
2 eggs, lightly beaten
1-1/4 cups breadcrumbs
3/4 cup grated Parmesan cheese
6 tbsp oil and butter
1 tsp thyme
Salt and pepper

Metric
8 lean pork chops
All-purpose flour
2 eggs, lightly beaten
300 ml breadcrumbs
150 ml grated Parmesan cheese
90 ml oil and butter
5 ml thyme
Salt and pepper

Season the chops with salt, pepper and thyme. Coat them lightly with flour and dip into the beaten egg and breadcrumbs making an even coating. Brown in the skillet with the oil and butter for 5 to 6 minutes, over medium heat, turning once. Place on a baking sheet, cover with grated Parmesan and continue cooking in the oven at 350°F (180°C) for 10 to 15 minutes.

Serve with lemon quarters or slices.

BAKED FLORENTINE POTATOES

Standard
6 potatoes
1/2 lb spinach
1 tbsp butter
Salt and pepper
2 tbsp mozzarella cheese, grated

Metric
6 potatoes
250 g spinach
15 ml butter
Salt and pepper
30 ml mozzarella cheese, grated

Scrub the potatoes and bake in the oven at 350°F (180°C) for about 1 hour.

Meanwhile, cook the spinach in boiling water, and chop.

Scoop out the potatoes. Mix with salt, pepper, butter and spinach. Heap into the potato shells. Sprinkle with the cheese and brown in the oven.

Pork Chops à la Milanaise

Broccoli all'Olio e Limone

Standard
1 large broccoli
7 tbsp olive oil
Juice of one lemon
Salt and pepper

Metric
1 large broccoli
105 ml olive oil
Juice of one lemon
Salt and pepper

Divide the broccoli into flowerlets and cut the stalk to 3-1/4 inch (8 cm) length. Place in a pot and cover with boiling salted water.

Cook "al dente" for 5 minutes. Drain and arrange on a serving platter. Mix the lemon juice, oil, salt and pepper. Dress the broccoli. Serve hot or cold.

Microwave Method

To Cook Broccoli

Place flowerlets in the center of a dish. Moisten with 4 tsp (20 ml) water. Cover with plastic wrap, partly open. Cook at HIGH for 8 minutes. Let stand for 2 to 4 minutes. Drain.

Poirissimo

Standard
6 fresh pears
3/4 cup almond powder
3/4 cup sugar
Juice of one lemon
1/2 cup raspberry jam
1 cup raspberry purée (see page 100, Norwegian Omelette Cardinale)
Vanilla ice cream

Metric
6 fresh pears
150 ml almond powder
150 ml sugar
Juice of one lemon
125 ml raspberry jam
250 ml raspberry purée (see page 100, Norwegian Omelette Cardinale)
Vanilla ice cream

Peel the pears. Cut a slice from the top of the pear and set aside for decoration. Scoop out the pears vertically, using an apple corer. Cook in water with sugar and lemon. They should remain slightly firm.

Combine the raspberry jam and the powdered almond, making a medium thick mixture. Fill the pears using a pastry bag. Replace the pear tops. Refrigerate for 2 to 3 hours.

Place each pear in a dish and add raspberry purée. Garnish with vanilla ice cream.

Poirissimo

ITALIAN CUISINE

Serve with a white Burgundy and rosé.

MENU

Serves 6 to 8

Minestra with Cucumbers and Cream
Fritata
(Italian Omelette)
Italian-Style Scallops
Fettuccine with Butter
Village Caesar Salad
Sicilian Cheese Cake

MINESTRA WITH CUCUMBERS AND CREAM

Standard	Metric
2 large cucumbers, peeled and diced	2 large cucumbers, peeled and diced
3 pickles with fennel	3 pickles with fennel
1 cup heavy cream (35%)	250 ml heavy cream (35%)
3 tbsp lemon juice	45 ml lemon juice
4 tbsp grated onion	60 ml grated onion
1 tbsp chopped fennel	15 ml chopped fennel
Salt and pepper	Salt and pepper
Chives	Chives

Place cucumbers, pickles and fennel in a mixer. Blend to a smooth consistency.

Pour into a chilled bowl. Add salt, pepper, grated onion and lemon juice. Blanch thick slices of cucumber in boiling water for 1 minute. Run under cold water and use them to garnish the minestra. Sprinkle with chives. Add a few sprigs of fennel.

MICROWAVE METHOD

To Cook Omelet

Melt 1 tbsp (15 ml) butter in a pie plate at HIGH for 30 seconds. Beat 2 eggs with 3 tbsp (45 ml) milk. Season. Pour into plate and cover with plastic wrap. Cook at MEDIUM for 2 to 3 minutes or until the eggs just begin to set. Stir after 1 minute. Let stand, covered, for 2 minutes.

FRITATA

Standard	Metric
10 eggs	10 eggs
1 cup cottage cheese (2%), well mashed	250 ml cottage cheese (2%), well mashed
2 tbsp fresh parsley, chopped	30 ml fresh parsley, chopped
3 tbsp water	45 ml water
1/2 tsp salt	2 ml salt
1/4 tsp oregano	1 ml oregano
2 medium zucchini	2 medium zucchini
All-purpose flour	All-purpose flour
1/3 cup vegetable oil	75 ml vegetable oil
2 small garlic cloves, finely chopped	2 small garlic cloves, finely chopped

Combine the eggs, cottage cheese, parsley, water, salt and oregano in a bowl. Chop the zucchini into 1/4 inch (0.65 cm) slices and sprinkle with flour.

In a non-stick pan, heat the oil and garlic. Add the zucchini slices and brown lightly on both sides.

Pour the egg mixture over the zucchini slices. Cook for 1 minute. Cover and continue cooking over medium heat for 4 to 5 minutes.

Cut the omelette into 6 pie-shaped pieces. Serve on warmed plates, with crackers.

Minestra with Cucumbers and Cream

ITALIAN-STYLE SCALLOPS

Standard	Metric
2 tbsp butter	30 ml butter
2 tbsp shallots	30 ml shallots
1 lb scallops	500 g scallops
1 cup sliced mushrooms	250 ml sliced mushrooms
1 cup chicken broth	250 ml chicken broth
Juice of 1/2 lemon	Juice of 1/2 lemon
1/4 tsp salt	1 ml salt
1/8 tsp pepper	0.5 ml pepper
3 tbsp butter	45 ml butter
2 tsp all-purpose flour	10 ml all-purpose flour
1/4 cup heavy cream (35%)	50 ml heavy cream (35%)
1 tbsp chives	15 ml chives
1/2 cup hot, buttered noodles per serving	125 ml hot, buttered noodles per serving

Melt the 2 tbsp (30 ml) butter in a heavy skillet. Add the shallots, scallops, mushrooms, broth and lemon juice. Salt and pepper.

Heat until boiling. Reduce heat and continue cooking over low heat for 5 minutes or until the scallops are tender. Do not over cook or they will become tough. Remove the scallops and mushrooms with a slotted spoon and keep hot. Continue cooking over high heat to reduce the liquid to half.

Mix 1 tbsp (15 ml) butter and the flour. Gradually add to the hot mixture, stirring constantly until the sauce is thick and glossy.

Add the cream and bring to the boiling point. Do not let boil.

Remove from heat. Add the scallops and mushrooms. Add the chives and adjust seasoning.

Serve immediately on hot, buttered noodles.

FETTUCCINE WITH BUTTER

Standard	Metric
3-1/2 cups cooked fettuccine	875 ml cooked fettuccine
1/2 cup butter	125 ml butter
Juice of 1/2 lemon	Juice of 1/2 lemon
2 garlic cloves, finely chopped	2 garlic cloves, finely chopped
Salt and pepper	Salt and pepper

Cook the fettuccine in rapidly boiling, salted water, until tender.

In another dish, melt sufficient butter to coat the fettuccine. Add the garlic. Add the lemon juice and mix.

Pour over the fettuccine.

Italian-Style Scallops

Village Ceasar Salad

VILLAGE CAESAR SALAD

Standard	Metric
1/2 tsp anchovy fillets	2 ml anchovy fillets
1 tbsp capers	15 ml capers
3 tbsp vegetable oil	45 ml vegetable oil
1 tsp wine vinegar	5 ml wine vinegar
Pinch of sugar	Pinch of sugar
1 garlic clove	1 garlic clove
1 egg yolk	1 egg yolk
2 French shallots	2 French shallots
1 tsp Dijon mustard	5 ml Dijon mustard
A few drops of lemon juice	A few drops of lemon juice
Parmesan cheese	Parmesan cheese
Bacon bits	Bacon bits
Parsley	Parsley
Croutons	Croutons
Pepper	Pepper
Romaine lettuce	Romaine lettuce
1 cup pepperoni, finely sliced	250 ml pepperoni, finely sliced
2 tbsp butter	30 ml butter

Crush the anchovies, capers and garlic. Mix with the egg yolk, vinegar, sugar, shallots, mustard and lemon juice. Add the oil slowly, stirring constantly.

Fry the pepperoni in hot butter, over high heat. Add to the first mixture. Add the rest of the ingredients. Serve immediately.

SICILIAN CHEESE CAKE

Standard	Metric
1-3/4 cups ricotta cheese	400 ml ricotta cheese
1-3/4 cups sugar	400 ml sugar
Pinch of cinnamon	Pinch of cinnamon
3/4 cup bitter chocolate, grated	150 ml bitter chocolate, grated
2 cups candied fruit	500 ml candied fruit
3 tbsp chopped pistaschios	45 ml chopped pistaschios
1 sponge cake	1 sponge cake
4 tbsp maraschino liqueur	60 ml maraschino liqueur

In a large bowl, beat the ricotta to a smooth consistency. Dissolve the sugar in 4 tbsp (60 ml) water over low heat and cook until it changes color. Add the ricotta. Add the cinnamon and chocolate and mix well. Chop half the candied fruit and combine with the mixture. Add the pistachios. Mix together.

Cut the sponge cake in two and allow to absorb the maraschino liqueur. Line a round bowl with waxed paper. Place a slice of the cake in it. Fill with ricotta mixture. Cover with the other slice. Press down lightly, using the blade of a knife. Refrigerate for several hours. Remove from bowl. Sprinkle with icing sugar and decorate with the candied fruit.

JAPANESE CUISINE

Serve with hot sake.

FISH SOUP

Standard	Metric
8 cups fish broth (very spicy)	2 liters fish broth (very spicy)
1 lb salt water fish	500 g salt water fish
1/2 lb cooked shrimp (shelled and deveined)	250 g cooked shrimp (shelled and deveined)
12 oysters	12 oysters
2 white onions	2 white onions
3 to 4 leeks, chopped	3 to 4 leeks, chopped
4 eggs	4 eggs

Heat the broth. Debone the fish, cut into 1 inch (2.5 cm) pieces, and add to the broth. Run oysters under water and add to the broth along with the shrimp, white onions and leeks. When the soup is boiling, use it to poach 1 egg per person.
Serve.

SHIRO BAI

Standard	Metric
Vegetable oil	Vegetable oil
1 can snails	1 can snails
1 tsp sake	5 ml sake
1/2 tsp Japanese soy sauce	2 ml Japanese soy sauce
Pinch of salt	Pinch of salt
1 tsp fresh ginger, crushed	5 ml fresh ginger, crushed
2 cups cooked rice	500 ml cooked rice

Lightly oil and heat a skillet. Add the snails. Cover and brown for 2 minutes, stirring often. Still stirring, add the sake, soy sauce and the pinch of salt. Cover and cook at high for 20 seconds. Remove from heat.
Wrap the ginger in cheese cloth. Squeeze its juice on the snails. Stir gently. Cut the snails in two and serve hot on a bed of rice.

Shiro Bai

Sukiyaki

SUKIYAKI

Standard
4 lb beef, cut in strips
2 cups chicken stock
or
1 can beef consommé
3/4 can water
5 tbsp Japanese soy sauce
Onions, cut into pieces
Celery, cut into pieces
Green pepper, cut in strips
Garlic, chopped
2 tbsp corn starch
1/2 cup water
Salt and pepper

Metric
2 kg beef, cut in strips
500 ml chicken stock
or
1 can beef consommé
3/4 can water
75 ml Japanese soy sauce
Onions, cut into pieces
Celery, cut into pieces
Green pepper, cut in strips
Garlic, chopped
30 ml corn starch
125 ml water
Salt and pepper

Brown the beef. Add the chicken stock or the beef consommé with additional water. Add the soy sauce and simmer over low heat for 2 hours to tenderize the meat.

Thirty minutes before serving, add the onions, celery and green pepper. Salt and pepper. Add the garlic.

Simmer for another 10 minutes. Mix corn starch with water and add to the mixture. Continue cooking for 10 minutes.

NAMEKO MIZORE-AE

Standard
2 cans mushrooms
5 radishes, peeled and finely grated
2 tsp lemon juice
1/4 tsp salt
1 tsp zest of grated lime

Metric
2 cans mushrooms
5 radishes, peeled and finely grated
10 ml lemon juice
1 ml salt
5 ml zest of grated lime

Bring 2 cups (500 ml) water to a boil in a small pan. Add the mushrooms and boil again. Drain. Run the mushrooms under cold water. Drain.

In a small bowl, combine the radish, lemon juice and salt. Mix in the mushrooms.

Divide into 4 portions, sprinkle with zest of lime and serve at room temperature.

CRAB AND CUCUMBER SALAD

Standard	Metric
3 large cucumbers	3 large cucumbers
2 tsp salt	10 ml salt
1 lb crab, fresh or canned	500 g crab, fresh or canned
3 tbsp grated ginger	45 ml grated ginger

Sauce

Standard	Metric
1/4 cup lemon juice	50 ml cup lemon juice
1/4 cup beef broth	50 ml beef broth
2 tbsp sugar	30 ml sugar
3 tsp soy sauce	15 ml soy sauce
1/2 tsp salt	2 ml salt
Monosodium glutamate	Monosodium glutamate

Peel cucumbers leaving a touch of skin for color. Cut in two lengthwise, and remove seeds. Slice into small pieces.

In a small bowl, combine 1/2 cup (125 ml) cold water and 1 tsp (5 ml) salt. Add the cucumber slices. Let soak for 30 minutes at room temperature. Drain and dry.

Flake or chop the crab. Combine with the cucumber. Separate into individual portions. Wrap the ginger in cheese cloth and squeeze over each bowl.

Mix the sauce ingredients together in a pan. Bring to a boil, stirring constantly. Remove from heat and let cool.

The sauce serves as a dip for the crab and cucumber.

MANDARIN CUP

6 fresh or tinned mandarin
oranges
Strawberry ice cream
6 candied green cherries,
chopped

Peel the mandarins and separate into sections. Place scoops of strawberry ice cream in 6 bowls. Top with mandarin sections. Sprinkle with chopped cherries.

Mandarin Cup

Mexican Cuisine

Serve with a dry white wine, and rosé.

Menu

Serves 6

Mexican Cream of Vegetables
Mexican Cucumber Mousse
Montezuma Pie
Mexican Spicy Peas
Veracruz Carrot Salad
New World Cake

Mexican Cream of Vegetables

Standard	Metric
4 cups chicken broth	1 liter chicken broth
1 can macedoine (mixed vegetables), drained	1 can macedoine (mixed vegetables), drained
2 tbsp tomato paste	30 ml tomato paste
2 tbsp celery leaves, finely chopped	30 ml celery leaves, finely chopped
2 tbsp butter	30 ml butter
Salt and pepper	Salt and pepper
Pinch of cayenne pepper	Pinch of cayenne pepper

Bring the chicken broth to a boil in a pot. Add the macedoine and cook uncovered. Put through the blender and pour into the pot. Add the tomato paste, celery leaves, salt, pepper and cayenne pepper.

Cook over medium heat, stirring from time to time. Mix in 2 tbsp (30 ml) butter and serve.

Mexican Cucumber Mousse

Standard	Metric
1 package lime jelly powder	1 package lime jelly powder
3/4 cup boiling water	150 ml boiling water
1 cup cottage cheese	250 ml cottage cheese
1 cup mayonnaise	250 ml mayonnaise
2 tbsp grated onion	30 ml grated onion
3/4 cup grated cucumber	150 ml grated cucumber
1 cup crushed almonds	250 ml crushed almonds

Dissolve the jelly powder in the boiling water. Mix in the cottage cheese, mayonnaise and onion. Fold in the cucumber and almonds.

Pour into a mold and refrigerate until the jelly is set.

Mexican Cream of Vegetables

Mexican Spicy Peas

MEXICAN SPICY PEAS

Standard

2 packages frozen, dainty green peas
2 tbsp butter or margarine
1/2 cup chopped onion
3 red peppers, cut into 1 inch strips
Salt and pepper

Metric

2 packages frozen, dainty green peas
30 ml butter or margarine
125 ml chopped onion
3 red peppers, cut into 2.5 cm strips
Salt and pepper

Cook peas until tender. Meanwhile, melt the butter in a small pan. Add the onion and cook for 5 minutes. Add the red peppers and stir.

Drain the peas. Mix the onions, peppers and peas. Salt and pepper.

MICROWAVE METHOD

To Cook Frozen Peas

Open the package and place frozen peas on a glass plate. Put in the oven and cook at HIGH for 5 to 7 minutes.

MONTEZUMA PIE

Standard

1 lb chopped lard
1 lb ground lean beef
1/2 green pepper, chopped
2 onions, chopped
1/2 cup catsup
1/2 cup relish
1/2 cup chili sauce
Pastry dough for 2-crust pie
1/2 cup mozzarella cheese
Butter

Metric

500 g chopped lard
500 g ground lean beef
1/2 green pepper, chopped
2 onions, chopped
125 ml catsup
125 ml relish
125 ml chili sauce
Pastry dough for 2-crust pie
125 ml mozzarella cheese
Butter

Preheat oven to 475°F (190°C).

Place the lard, beef, green pepper and onions in a pot and cook for 20 minutes. Add the catsup, relish and chili sauce.

Roll out pastry dough into two crusts. Place one in a buttered pie plate. Fill with meat mixture. Sprinkle with grated mozzarella cheese.

Cover with top crust and bake for 40 to 45 minutes.

VERACRUZ CARROT SALAD

Standard

6 large, fresh carrots, cut fine or grated
3/4 cup raisins
1-1/4 cups orange juice
1 tsp sugar
1/2 tsp salt

Metric

6 large, fresh carrots, cut fine or grated
150 ml raisins
300 ml orange juice
5 ml sugar
2 ml salt

Combine all ingredients. Refrigerate for at least 30 minutes before serving.

NEW WORLD CAKE

Standard

2 cups all-purpose flour
2 cups sugar
2 tsp baking soda
1 cup chopped nuts
1 can crushed pineapple with juice
1/2 cup Philadelphia cream cheese
1/4 cup butter or margarine
1 cup icing sugar
1/2 tsp vanilla

Metric

500 ml all-purpose flour
500 ml sugar
10 ml baking soda
250 ml chopped nuts
1 can crushed pineapple with juice
125 ml Philadelphia cream cheese
50 ml butter or margarine
250 ml icing sugar
2 ml vanilla

Combine the flour, sugar, baking soda, nuts and pineapple with juice. Bake at 350°F (180°C) for 45 minutes.

Combine the cheese, butter or margarine, icing sugar and vanilla. Mix thoroughly to make a smooth cream.

Remove cake from oven. Let cook for 10 minutes. Spread with the cream.

Montezuma Pie

328

Quebec Regional Cuisine

Serve with a semi-dry white wine and a rosé.

Menu

Serves 6 to 8

Gourgane Soup
Eggs au Gratin
North Shore Fish Dish
Cabbage and Celery Casserole
Townships Salad
Raspberry Upside-Down Cake

North Shore Fish DIsh

Gourgane Soup

Standard	Metric
4 pints water	1 liter water
1 soup bone (beef)	1 soup bone (beef)
or	or
1/4 lb salt pork	125 g salt pork
1 large onion	1 large onion
Bouquet garni (herb bouquet)	Bouquet garni (herb bouquet)
2 cups gourganes (navy beans)	500 ml gourganes (navy beans)
1/4 cup barley	50 ml barley
Salt and pepper	Salt and pepper

To the water in a pot, add the bone or salt pork, the onion and seasonings. Let boil for 1-1/2 hours. Add the gourganes and the barley. Cook for another 2-1/2 hours.

Eggs au Gratin

Standard	Metric
12 eggs	12 eggs
Salt	Salt
1 tbsp butter	15 ml butter
3/4 cup grated Gruyère cheese	150 ml grated Gruyère cheese
3 pinches finely chopped parsley	3 pinches finely chopped parsley

Preheat oven to 400°F (200°C). Put the butter and 5 tbsp (75 ml) of the Gruyère cheese in a baking dish. Place in the center of the oven for 4 to 5 minutes.

Break the eggs into the dish. Season and sprinkle with the remaining cheese. Cook the eggs in the oven at 375°F (190°C) for 5 minutes.

North Shore Fish Dish

Standard	Metric
2 cups onions, chopped	500 ml onions, chopped
6 cups potatoes, cooked and sliced	1.6 liters potatoes, cooked and sliced
1-1/2 lb cod and/or trout	750 g cod and/or trout
1/2 cup crab and/or clams	125 ml crab and/or clams
3 tbsp butter	45 ml butter
1-1/2 cups béchamel sauce	375 ml béchamel sauce
1/4 cup Parmesan or cheddar cheese	50 ml Parmesan or cheddar cheese
Parsley	Parsley
Salt and pepper	Salt and pepper

Brown the onions in 3 tbsp (45 ml) butter.

Prepare a béchamel sauce (See chapter on sauces).

In a 4 inch (10 cm) deep oven dish, place successively 1 cup (250 ml) onion, 3 cups (750 ml) potatoes, the cod and/or trout, the crab and/or clams, the parsley, salt, pepper, béchamel sauce and the grated cheese.

Bake in the oven at 375°F (190°) for 30 to 40 minutes, depending on thickness of the fish.

CABBAGE AND CELERY CASSEROLE

Standard	Metric
3-1/2 cups chopped cabbage	875 ml chopped cabbage
1 cup chopped celery	250 ml chopped celery
6 tbsp butter	90 ml butter
2 tbsp all-purpose flour	30 ml all-purpose flour
1-1/2 cups milk	375 milk
1/2 tsp salt	2 ml salt
Pinch of pepper	Pinch of pepper
1/2 cup breadcrumbs	125 ml breadcrumbs
Walnuts, finely chopped	Walnuts, finely chopped
or	or
Grated Parmesan cheese	Grated Parmesan cheese

Preheat oven to 375ºF (190º).

Melt 4 tbsp (60 ml) butter and add the chopped cabbage and celery. Sauté for 10 to 15 minutes, stirring frequently. Place in a buttered baking dish.

Melt the remaining 2 tbsp (30 ml) butter and add the flour, milk and seasonings. Cook, stirring until thickening occurs. Pour over the cabbage mixture.

Mix the breadcrumbs, nuts and cheese. Sprinkle over the mixture. Bake in the oven for about 15 minutes.

TOWNSHIPS SALAD

Standard	Metric
3 cups fresh mushrooms, sliced	750 ml fresh mushrooms, sliced
2 cups curd cheese	500 ml curd cheese
1 small onion, finely chopped	1 small onion, finely chopped
1 tomato, finely diced	1 tomato, finely diced
1 grated carrot	1 grated carrot
1 stalk celery, diced	1 stalk celery, diced
2 tbsp chopped celery	30 ml chopped celery
2 tbsp lemon juice	30 ml lemon juice
1 tbsp vinegar	15 ml vinegar
2 tbsp vegetable oil	30 ml vegetable oil
1/4 tsp garlic powder	1 ml garlic powder
1/4 tsp marjoram	1 ml marjoram
1/4 tsp salt	1 ml salt
Pinch of pepper	Pinch of pepper
Lettuce leaves	Lettuce leaves

In a mixing bowl, carefully combine all the vegetables and the cheese. In another bowl, combine the liquid ingredients and season to create a vinaigrette.

Just before serving, pour the vinaigrette over the vegetables. Mix carefully. Serve on lettuce leaves.

RASPBERRY UPSIDE-DOWN CAKE

Standard	Metric
1-3/4 cups sugar	400 ml sugar
1/2 cup melted butter	125 ml melted butter
3/4 cup milk	150 ml cup milk
1 tbsp lemon juice	15 ml lemon juice
1-3/4 cups all-purpose flour	400 ml all-purpose flour
2 tsp baking powder	10 ml baking powder
2 cups frozen raspberries	500 ml frozen raspberries
1/4 tsp salt	1 ml salt
6 eggs	6 eggs

Preheat oven to 375ºF (175ºC).

In a bowl, beat the eggs, sugar, salt and melted butter. Sift the flour and baking powder. Add the lemon juice and milk to the egg mixture, then fold in the dry ingredients.

Place the raspberries in a 10 x 6 x 2 inch (25 x 15 x 5 cm) pyrex mold and sprinkle generously with sugar. Butter the baking tins and fill with the mixture.

Bake for 40 minutes. Let cool and turn out upside-down on serving plates. Serve with Custard Sauce (see page 160).

Raspberry Upside-Down Cake

QUEBEC REGIONAL CUISINE

Serve with a white Bordeaux, or sparkling rosé.

MENU

Serves 6 to 8

Herb Soup
Mushroom Muffins
Miroton with Beer
Broccoli au Gratin
Grandma's Chicken Salad
Apple Turnovers

HERB SOUP

Standard	Metric
2 tsp "herbes salées"	10 ml "herbes salées"
5 tbsp chopped onions	75 ml chopped onions
3/4 cup grated carrots	150 ml grated carrots
1/4 cup butter or shortening	50 ml butter or shortening
6 cups water	1.5 liters water
1/4 cup rice	50 ml rice
2 tbsp vermicelli	30 ml vermicelli
3 leeks, chopped	3 leeks, chopped
6 carrots, chopped	6 carrots, chopped
5 pinches of finely chopped parsley	5 pinches of finely chopped parsley
1/2 cup shallots (green section), finely chopped	125 ml shallots (green section), finely chopped
1/2 cup celery leaves, finely chopped	125 ml celery leaves, finely chopped
1/2 cup chives, finely chopped	125 ml chives, finely chopped
1/2 cup cooking salt	125 ml cooking salt
Salt and pepper	Salt and pepper

Combine the vegetables and fine herbs with the cooking salt and set aside.

Put the butter in a pot and moisten the mixture of vegetables, fine herbs and "herbes salées". Add water. Pepper. Bring to a boil. Add the rice and the vermicelli. Boil for about 20 minutes. Salt. Serve.

MUSHROOM MUFFINS

Standard	Metric
2 tsp butter	10 ml butter
1-1/2 cups fresh mushrooms, finely chopped	375 ml fresh mushrooms, finely chopped
1 cup all-purpose flour	250 ml all-purpose flour
or	or
1 cup whole wheat flour	250 ml whole wheat flour
1/2 cup cheddar cheese	125 ml cheddar cheese
1 tbsp brown sugar	15 ml brown sugar
2 tsp baking powder	10 ml baking powder
1 beaten egg	1 beaten egg
1 tbsp melted butter	15 ml melted butter
1/2 cup milk	125 ml milk
Pinch of salt	Pinch of salt

Preheat oven to 375°F (190°). Butter a 6-cup muffin pan and sprinkle with flour.

Fry the mushrooms in the melted butter. Drain them.

Sift the dry ingredients. Mix with the cheddar cheese. In another bowl, mix the beaten egg with the melted butter, milk and mushrooms. Incorporate the dry ingredients. Spoon the mixture into the muffin pan. Cook for 20 to 25 minutes.

Mushroom Muffins

Miroton with Beer

MIROTON WITH BEER

Standard
2 lb beef cubes
1/4 cup all-purpose flour
1 tbsp paprika
1/2 tsp fines herbes
Pinch of ground cloves
5 medium carrots, sliced
1 tbsp corn starch
6 tbsp vegetable oil
1 onion
1 garlic clove, finely
chopped
1 cup beef broth
1 small bottle of beer
6 sprigs fresh parsley
1 can mushrooms
24 small onions
or
6 large onions, cut in
quarters
Salt and pepper

Metric
1 kg beef cubes
50 ml all-purpose flour
15 ml paprika
2 ml fines herbes
Pinch of ground cloves
5 medium carrots, sliced
15 ml corn starch
90 ml vegetable oil
1 onion
1 garlic clove, finely
chopped
250 ml beef broth
1 small bottle of beer
6 sprigs fresh parsley
1 can mushrooms
24 small onions
or
6 large onions, cut in
quarters
Salt and pepper

Combine the flour, salt, pepper and paprika. Coat the meat with this mixture. Heat the oil. Sauté the onion and garlic. Add the meat and the rest of the seasoned flour. Brown for a few minutes at high. Add the beef broth. Stir. Add the beer, parsley, cloves and fines herbes. Simmer over low heat for 1-1/2 hours.

Meanwhile, drain the mushrooms and reserve the juice. Add the vegetables and adjust seasoning. Cook for about 45 minutes. Thicken with the corn starch mixed with the mushroom juice. Check seasoning. Serve with mashed potatoes.

BROCCOLI AU GRATIN

Standard
2 cups broccoli
1 tbsp butter
1/2 cup grated cheese
1/4 cup bread chunks
Seasonings

Metric
500 ml broccoli
15 ml butter
125 ml grated cheese
50 ml bread chunks
Seasonings

Béchamel Sauce

Standard
2 tbsp butter
2 tbsp all-purpose flour
1 cup milk
1/4 tsp salt

Metric
30 ml butter
30 ml all-purpose flour
250 ml milk
1 ml salt

Cook the broccoli in boiling water for 10 to 15 minutes. Drain. Separate into flowerlets and cut into large pieces.

Meanwhile, melt the butter and stir in flour. Gradually add milk, stirring constantly with a wooden spoon. Season well. Cook for 20 minutes.

Butter a deep baking dish. Alternate the broccoli, the cheese and the sauce. Season each layer.

Cover with the buttered bread chunks and bake in the oven at 350°F (175°C).

GRANDMA'S CHICKEN SALAD

Standard	Metric
2 cups chicken, in small pieces	500 ml chicken, in small pieces
2 cups celery, finely chopped	500 ml celery, finely chopped
1/2 cup dainty peas	125 ml dainty peas
1/2 cup chopped olives	125 ml chopped olives
1/2 cup sweet pickles	125 ml sweet pickles
Mayonnaise	Mayonnaise

Combine all the ingredients. Add enough mayonnaise to hold the salad together. Refrigerate. Serve cool.

APPLE TURNOVERS

Standard	Metric
2 cups all-purpose flour	500 ml all-purpose flour
1 tbsp baking powder	15 ml baking powder
1 tsp salt	5 ml salt
1/2 cup vegetable shortening	125 ml vegetable shortening
1-1/2 cups milk	375 ml cup milk
6 apples	6 apples
6 tbsp sugar	90 ml sugar
1/2 tsp cinnamon	2 ml cinnamon
1/2 tsp nutmeg	2 ml nutmeg

Preheat oven to 325ºF (150ºC).

Combine the flour, baking powder, salt and vegetable shortening. Add the milk and mix well. Roll out the pastry and cut out 6 circles.

Pare the apples and cut in quarters. Remove cores. Cook them with the sugar, cinnamon and nutmeg for about 20 minutes. Allow to cool. Place a small amount of apple compote in the center of each pastry sphere. Baste with milk. Fold over and seal edges well. Bake for 30 minutes. Pour caramel sauce over baked turnovers.

Caramel Sauce

Standard	Metric
1/2 cup brown sugar	125 ml brown sugar
1/4 cup corn syrup	50 ml corn syrup
1 cup light cream (15%)	250 ml light cream (15%)
2 tbsp butter	30 ml butter
Pinch of salt	Pinch of salt

Heat all the ingredients in a pot over low heat. Pour over apples. Serve hot or cold.

Makes 6 turnovers.

Apple Turnovers

QUEBEC REGIONAL CUISINE

Serve with a dry white wine, white Bordeaux, or rosé.

MENU

Serve 6 to 8

Beauce County Punch
Grapefruit with Crab
Country-Style Roast Moose
Potatoes as Baked in the Beauce
Cucumber and Smoked Salmon Salad
Maple Mousse

BEAUCE COUNTY PUNCH

Standard	Metric
1/2 cup maple syrup	125 ml maple syrup
2 cups orange juice	500 ml orange juice
1/2 cup cherry juice	125 ml cherry juice
1 cup lemon juice	250 ml lemon juice
1/2 cup pineapple juice	125 ml pineapple juice
2 bottles non-sparkling cider	2 bottles non-sparkling cider
2 bottles sparkling cider, cold	2 bottles sparkling cider, cold

Place ice cubes in a punch bowl. Add the first 6 ingredients and leave for several hours. Add the chilled sparkling cider. Garnish with washed, fresh strawberries, and slices of orange and banana.

Variation: Add Calvados or brandy.

GRAPEFRUIT WITH CRAB

1/2 grapefruit per person
2 cans crab meat
Mayonnaise
Lemon juice
Cayenne pepper
Paprika

Cut the grapefruit in half. Scoop out the fruit and mix with the crab. Bind with the mayonnaise. Add lemon juice and a pinch of cayenne pepper. Garnish the grapefruit. Sprinkle with a bit of paprika. Serve chilled.

COUNTRY-STYLE ROAST MOOSE

Standard	Metric
2 lb lean moose meat, cut in cubes	1 kg lean moose meat, cut in cubes
2 cups chopped onions	500 ml chopped onions
3 tbsp fat	45 ml fat
2 tsp fines herbes	10 ml fines herbes
1 bay leaf	1 bay leaf
1 bottle of beer	1 bottle of beer
Salt and pepper	Salt and pepper

Place the flour, fines herbes, salt, pepper and meat cubes in a plastic bag. Shake well.

Heat the fat in a skillet and brown the onions. Add the floured meat and brown it. Pour in the beer and cover the meat with water. Add the bay leaf. Simmer over low heat for 2 hours. If there is too much liquid at the end of the cooking, add 1 tsp (5 ml) of flour dispersed in a little water and allow to boil for several seconds. Serve very hot.

Beauce County Punch

Potatoes as Baked in the Beauce

POTATOES AS BAKED IN THE BEAUCE

Standard	Metric
6 potatoes	6 potatoes
1 onion, finely chopped	1 onion, finely chopped
2 tbsp butter	30 ml butter
1 tbsp vegetable oil	15 ml vegetable oil
3 large tomatoes, chopped	3 large tomatoes, chopped
6 garlic cloves, finely chopped	6 garlic cloves, finely chopped
3 tbsp chopped parsley	45 ml chopped parsley
Salt and pepper	Salt and pepper

Bake the potatoes in the oven at 425°F (220°C) for 50 minutes. Melt the butter in a pot. Add the oil and fry the onion for 5 minutes. Add the tomatoes, garlic and parsley. Set aside.

When the potatoes are cooked, cut them in two and scoop out centers. Mash the potato and combine with the first mixture. Fill the potatoes and return to the oven at 400°F (200°C) for 15 to 20 minutes.

MICROWAVE METHOD

To Bake Potatoes

Scrub the potatoes. Prick them with a fork and arrange them in the form of a star on a plate covered with absorbent paper. Cook at HIGH for 14 minutes. Let stand for 4 minutes before serving.

CUCUMBER AND SMOKED SALMON SALAD

Standard	Metric
6 small carrots	6 small carrots
2 small cucumbers	2 small cucumbers
3 small onions	3 small onions
1/2 lb smoked salmon, cut in strips	250 g smoked salmon, cut in strips

Vinaigrette

Standard	Metric
2 tbsp corn oil	30 ml corn oil
Salt, pepper and curry powder	Salt, pepper and curry powder

Cut the carrots, cucumbers and onion in thin slices. Add the smoked salmon. Prepare the vinaigrette and pour over the vegetables. Mix well. Refrigerate for several hours.

MAPLE MOUSSE

Standard	Metric
3 cups sugar	750 ml sugar
1 cup cold water	250 ml cold water
1 cup maple syrup	250 ml maple syrup
3 egg whites	3 egg whites
Salt	Salt

Cook together the sugar, maple syrup and water until slightly thickened. Whip the egg whites into peaks. Gradually pour the syrup into the egg whites, stirring constantly. Spoon into sherbet glasses. Garnish with nuts.

QUEBEC REGIONAL CUISINE

Serve with a dry white wine, or rosé.

MENU

Serves 6 to 8

Cabbage and Partridge Soup
Strong Cheddar Cheese Soufflé
Sole Filets Stuffed with Mushrooms
Baked Noodles and Celery
Exquisite Chicken Salad
Beauce County Maple Cake

CABBAGE AND PARTRIDGE SOUP

Standard	Metric
1 partridge	1 partridge
8 cups water	2 liters water
1 medium cabbage	1 medium cabbage
2 small carrots	2 small carrots
2 shallots	2 shallots
1 tsp thyme	5 ml thyme
1/2 cup rice	125 ml rice
Salt and pepper	Salt and pepper

Boil the partridge with the shallots, salt, pepper and thyme. Add the cabbage, grated carrots and the rice. Boil until the vegetables are well cooked.

STRONG CHEDDAR CHEESE SOUFFLÉ

Standard	Metric
3/4 cup beer	150 ml beer
1/2 cup butter or margarine	125 ml butter or margarine
1 tsp salt	5 ml salt
1 cup all-purpose flour	250 ml all-purpose flour
4 eggs	4 eggs
7 tbsp strong cheddar cheese, grated	105 ml strong cheddar cheese, grated

In a pot over high heat, heat the beer, butter, and salt until the butter melts and the mixture boils. Reduce the heat to low, add the flour and mix with a wooden spoon until the mixture forms a ball and pulls away from the sides of the pot. Add the eggs, one at a time, and beat vigorously for 1 minute after each addition.

Grease a soufflé baking dish and fill with the egg mixture. Sprinkle the grated cheddar on top.

Bake at 350ºF (175ºC) for about 40 minutes or until the soufflé is golden. Let cool on a rack Serve.

Strong Cheddar Cheese Soufflé

SOLE FILETS STUFFED WITH MUSHROOMS

Standard
2 lb sole filets,
or pike (doré)

Metric
1 kg sole filets,
or pike (doré)

Mushroom Stuffing

Standard
3 tbsp butter
4 tbsp chopped onion
1-1/2 cans chopped
mushrooms
1 tsp tarragon
1 tsp salt

Metric
45 ml butter
60 ml chopped onion
1-1/2 cans chopped
mushrooms
5 ml tarragon
5 ml salt

Slice filets into 6 x 2 inch (15 x 5 cm) strips. Season both sides. Roll into well-greased muffin cups.

Melt butter in a pan over low heat. Add the other ingredients and cook until the vegetables are tender. Drain. Place 2 tbsp (30 ml) of this filling into each rolled sole filet. Place in the oven at 450°F (230°C) for 15 minutes.

BAKED NOODLES AND CELERY

Standard
3 cups celery, cut in
1/4 inch pieces
1/2 cup boiling, salted water
1/4 cup butter
1 can water chestnuts, sliced
1 can cream of chicken,
undiluted
1 package (5 oz) fried
noodles
Salt and pepper

Metric
750 ml celery, cut in
0.65 cm pieces
125 ml boiling, salted water
50 ml butter
1 can water chestnuts, sliced
1 can cream of chicken,
undiluted
1 package (145 g) fried
noodles
Salt and pepper

Preheat oven to 400°F (200°C). Butter a baking dish.

Bring salted water to a boil in a pot. Cook the celery for about 10 minutes. Remove from heat. Add the water chestnuts and the cream of chicken. Mix together gently. Salt and pepper.

In the baking dish, spread alternating layers of noodles and the mixture. Cover. Cook in the oven for 10 minutes. Remove the cover and continue cooking for another 5 minutes.

Sole Filets Stuffed with Mushrooms

Exquisite Chicken Salad

EXQUISITE CHICKEN SALAD

Standard	Metric
2 lb chicken, cooked and diced	1 kg chicken, cooked and diced
2 cups pared apples, diced	500 ml pared apples, diced
1 cup celery, diced	250 ml celery, diced
1/2 cup heavy cream (35%)	125 ml heavy cream (35%)
1/4 cup nuts	50 ml nuts
2 tbsp mayonnaise	30 ml mayonnaise
2 tbsp vinegar	30 ml vinegar
Salt and pepper	Salt and pepper
Lemon Juice	Lemon Juice
Lettuce leaves	Lettuce leaves
Hard-boiled eggs	Hard-boiled eggs

Sprinkle apples with lemon juice. Combine the mayonnaise, vinegar, salt and pepper to yield a salad sauce. Whip the cream and add to the sauce. Mix in the chicken, celery, apples and nuts, stirring carefully.

Serve on lettuce leaves. Garnish with hard-boiled egg slices.

BEAUCE COUNTY MAPLE CAKE

Standard	Metric
1 cup whole wheat flour	250 ml whole wheat flour
1 tsp cinnamon	5 ml cinnamon
1 tsp baking soda	5 ml baking soda
1/4 tsp salt	1 ml salt
1/2 cup vegetable oil	125 ml vegetable oil
2 medium eggs	2 medium eggs
1 cup maple syrup	250 ml maple syrup
1 cup grated carrots	250 ml grated carrots
1 cup grated apples	250 ml grated apples
1/2 cup chopped nuts	125 ml chopped nuts
1/3 cup grated coconut	75 ml grated coconut

Custard Topping

Standard	Metric
1/4 cup milk	50 ml milk
1/2 cup maple sugar	125 ml maple sugar
1/4 tsp baking soda	1 ml baking soda
4 tsp butter	20 ml butter

Preheat oven to 350ºF (180ºC).

Sift the dry ingredients together. Mix together the oil, eggs, syrup, carrots, nuts and coconut. Gradually fold in the dry ingredients. Pour into a buttered 9 inch (23 cm) cake pan.

Bake for about 40 minutes. Turn out the cake and prick in several places.

Place the milk, sugar, baking soda and butter in a pot. Bring to the boil. Cook for 5 minutes. Pour hot over the cake.

Scandinavian Cuisine

Serve with a dry white wine, and champagne.

MENU

Serves 6 to 8

Norrlandsk Laxsoppa
(Norwegian Salmon Soup)
Fyllda Skinkrulader
(Swedish Ham Rolls)
Kålpudding
(Cabbage Pudding)
Finnish Cream Carrots
Krabbsallad
(Swedish Crab Salad)
Risgrynsgröt
(Norwegian Rice Pudding)

NORRLANDSK LAXSOPPA

Standard	Metric
4 cups liquid (juice from a can of salmon plus additional water)	1 liter liquid (juice from a can of salmon plus additional water)
3 tbsp barley	45 ml barley
2 medium carrots, diced	2 medium carrots, diced
1 medium size turnip, diced	1 medium size turnip, diced
1 medium onion, chopped	1 medium onion, chopped
1 can red salmon	1 can red salmon
1 tsp salt	5 ml salt
2 tbsp chopped parsley	30 ml chopped parsley
Pepper	Pepper

In a pot, bring to a boil the salmon juice plus additional water. Add the barley and boil for 30 minutes. Add the vegetables and continue cooking for 10 to 15 minutes or until the vegetables are tender.

Mix in the salmon. Salt and pepper. Heat. Garnish with chopped parsley. Serve hot.

FYLLDA SKINKRULADER

Standard	Metric
1 cup cooked dainty peas	250 ml cooked dainty peas
1 apple, diced	1 apple, diced
1 tsp lemon juice	5 ml lemon juice
2 tbsp capers	30 ml capers
2 hard-boiled eggs, chopped	2 hard-boiled eggs, chopped
1/2 cup heavy cream (35%), whipped	125 ml heavy cream (35%), whipped
1/2 cup mayonnaise	125 ml mayonnaise
1 tbsp grated horse radish	15 ml grated horse radish
1 package (10 oz) frozen asparagus tips, cooked and chilled	1 package (280 g) frozen asparagus tips, cooked and chilled
12 slices boiled ham (about 3/4 lb)	12 slices boiled ham (about 275 g)

Combine the peas, the apple, lemon juice, eggs and capers. Refrigerate.

Mix the cream, mayonnaise and horse radish together in a bowl. Refrigerate.

Combine 1/2 cup (125 ml) of the cream mixture with the first mixture. Place about 1/4 cup (50 ml) of this on half of the ham slices. Roll up the slices. Place the asparagus on the other ham slices. Roll up. Serve with the remaining cream mixture.

Fyllda Skinkrulader

Kålpudding

KÅLPUDDING

Standard	Metric
1 cabbage (1-1/2 lb)	1 cabbage (750 g)
1 lb ground beef	500 g ground beef
1 lb ground pork	500 g ground pork
3 tbsp butter	45 ml butter
1 tsp salt	5 ml salt
1/2 tsp pepper	2 ml pepper
2 cups mashed potato	500 ml mashed potato

Remove the heart of the cabbage. Cut the cabbage into large pieces. Cook in boiling, salted water to tenderize it. Let drain.

Melt the butter in a pot. Brown the ground beef and pork.

Mix the cooked meat with the mashed potato. Salt and pepper.

In a baking dish, alternate layers of cabbage and the meat mixture. Cover. Cook in the oven at 350ºF (180ºC) for 45 to 50 minutes.

KRABBSALLAD

Standard	Metric
2 cans (6-1/2 oz) crab meat	2 cans (175 g) crab meat
4 stalks celery, chopped	4 stalks celery, chopped
1 tbsp grated onion	15 ml grated onion
2 to 3 tbsp lemon juice	30 to 45 ml lemon juice
1/2 tsp fresh fennel, chopped	2 ml fresh fennel, chopped
3/4 cup sour cream	150 ml sour cream
Lettuce leaves	Lettuce leaves
Pepper	Pepper

Drain the crab meat and flake. Combine the crab, onion, lemon juice, fennel and sour cream. Pepper. Stir carefully. Place on lettuce leaves.

FINNISH CREAM CARROTS

Standard	Metric
2 tbsp butter	30 ml butter
3 tbsp all-purpose flour	45 ml all-purpose flour
1 tbsp sugar	15 ml sugar
Pinch of white pepper	Pinch of white pepper
1 cup milk	250 ml milk
1/2 cup equal parts milk and cream	125 ml equal parts milk and cream
1 lb carrots, sliced and cooked	500 g carrots, sliced and cooked
Chopped parsley	Chopped parsley

Melt the butter in a pot. Add the flour, sugar and pepper. Stir to obtain a well-blended mixture. Remove from heat. Gradually add the milk and milk-cream mixture. Return to the stove. Simmer, stirring constantly, until mixture thickens.

Add the carrots. Heat. Sprinkle chopped parsley on top.

RISGRYNSGRÖT

Standard	Metric
3 cups cooked rice	750 ml cooked rice
4 cups milk	1 liter milk
1 tbsp butter	15 ml butter
1/8 tsp salt	0.5 ml salt
2 to 3 tbsp sugar	30 to 45 ml sugar
1/4 cup raisins	50 ml raisins

Combine the rice and milk in a heavy pot. Cover. Cook over low heat until the milk is absorbed, stirring occasionally. Add the butter, salt and sugar. Refrigerate. Serve with cream or applesauce.

Risgrynsgröt

FREEZING

FREEZING METHODS

Freezing is a modern method of food preservation which makes it possible to serve fresh foods all year long. Foods kept at very cold temperatures (ideally -10°F or -25°C) retain their color, flavor, texture and vitamins.

BASIC RULES

* Select the freshest and best quality products available.

* Do all the preparation, cooking and wrapping of frozen foods in the most hygienic conditions possible.

* To maintain the quality of your frozen foods, keep them frozen at a temperature of -10°F (-25°C) or lower.

* Freeze foods as rapidly as possible. If foods freeze slowly, large ice crystals are formed which cause the cells in vegetables and fruit to burst, and which tear the tissues in meats. Rapid freezing forms smaller crystals.

* If possible, adjust the freezer temperature to below -10°F (-25°C) when putting in foods to freeze. After 24 hours, the temperature can be readjusted and maintained at 0°F (-18°C).

* Avoid freezing too much unfrozen food at once.

* Place foods to be frozen next to the freezer walls. Once they have frozen solidly, move them to the centre and put new stock to be frozen next to the walls.

* Label the contents of each package with a tag or water-proof marker.

*Be sure to consult the instruction manual for your freezer for advice about your particular model.

* Keep the freezer full. A full freezer retains its cold temperature better.

*In case of electricity failure, avoid opening the freezer. If you know in advance that the power will be cut temporarily, fill any empty spaces in the freezer with bags of ice or cans of water. If the power failure lasts more than 6 hours, keep the freezer closed and cover it with newspapers and blankets to prevent cold loss. If the power failure lasts more than 12 hours, cook or discard all the contents, and clean the interior of the freezer before using it again.

* Observe the recommended storage period for each type of food. Food kept frozen longer than the recommended time loses flavor and nutritive value.

PACKAGING

Foods that are not carefully wrapped to protect them from the cold and dry air of a freezer compartment will dry out and suffer from 'freezer burn'. As a result the food loses flavor, color, weight and nutritive content.

Proper wrapping or packaging will prolong the life-span of frozen foods by preventing dehydration, loss of nutritive value and the transfer of flavors and odors from other foods.

All packaging materials used should be especially designed for freezer use; they should be impervious to water, grease, odors or water vapor, and should be able to stand up to intense cold for several months without drying out.

It is useful to have freezer containers in various materials, shapes and sizes. Aluminum containers with covers are handy for storing foods that you want to cook, freeze, and reheat in the same container; rigid plastic containers with lids are ideal for storing liquids, soups and sauces; heavy-duty aluminum foil is useful for wrapping meat; plastic freezer bags can hold prepared fruits and vegetables; freezer paper with waxed surfaces allows you to store stacks of steaks or burgers and thaw one at a time; plastic wrap which adheres to the surfaces of foods prevents the formation of air pockets and ice crystals.

SEALING AND LABELLING

Freezer packaging should be as air-tight as possible. You should remove as much air as possible from flexible packages or freezer bags. On the other hand, liquids tend to expand when frozen, so do not fill rigid containers right to the rim before freezing.

Every package should be tightly sealed and labelled. It is advisable to note the contents, the amount by weight or number of servings, the freezing date and the 'best before' date right on the package.

To make this job easier, use self-sticking tags designed for freezer use, with different-colored stickers for each category of food. Mark the information with a grease pencil or indelible marker.

Keeping an inventory of all your frozen food will help you keep track of what you have on hand and what needs to be used before its expiry date.

ACCESSORIES AND UTENSILS FOR PREPARING FOODS FOR THE FREEZER

Stainless steel knives

Paring knife

Vegetable scraper

Boning knife

Saw-tooth knife

Cutting board

Measuring cups

Strainer

Skimmer

Hydrometer

Food processor

Timer

Scales

Pressure cooker

Steamer

Stainless steel saucepans

Thermometer

Meat thermometer

Rigid plastic containers with lids

Aluminum containers with lids

Plastic wrap

Aluminum foil

Freezer bags

Self-sticking freezer tags

Indelible marker or grease marker

Erasable wall-chart for freezer inventory

IMPORTANT

All utensils and containers must be perfectly clean. Freezer containers should have air-tight lids. Because aluminum is porous, it might cause some foods with high acid content to discolor.

PREPARATION OF FOODS FOR FREEZING

Vegetables

Select vegetables that are fresh, firm and completely ripe, and freeze them as soon as possible. Avoid bruised, damaged or over-ripe vegetables.

Vegetables should be thoroughly cleaned, peeled if necessary, and cut into pieces of the same size. Most vegetables must be blanched before freezing to halt natural enzyme action and preserve color and texture. (See the blanching chart on page 347.)

* Some vegetables do not require blanching, including: **tomatoes, zucchini, pumpkin, cucumbers and peppers**.

* **Raw potatoes** and **lettuces** do not freeze well.

* **Broccoli, Brussels sprouts** and **cauliflower** should be soaked in salted water for 15 minutes before blanching.

* Fresh **herbs** respond well to freezing. Just wash them, dry, and chop. Freeze them on a cookie sheet then pack in air-tight bags.

* Vegetables can be frozen immediately after simply washing them in cold water, but without blanching will last only about 2 months.

Fruit

Fruit for freezing should be of excellent quality and perfectly ripe. Fruit can be frozen whole, in pieces, in syrup, in sherbets, etc. Fruits do not need to be blanched. There are two basic methods for freezing fruit, **dry**, or in **syrup**.

Fruit that can be **dry frozen** (without sugar or syrup) include **blueberries, raspberries, gooseberries, rhubarb**, etc.

A second version of dry freezing involves layering the fruit with sugar and stirring so that each piece is coated.

With the **syrup** method, the fruit is packed into rigid containers, and then covered with a sugar syrup. The density of the syrup depends on the acidity of the specific fruit type (see the syrup density chart on page 347) and individual taste. Be sure to leave about 1 inch (2.5 cm) of air space at the top of each container to allow for expansion.

* Since most fruit is usually already very juicy, it is usually better to use dry sugar than syrup. Use about 1 cup of sugar for every 5 cups of fruit.

* Pit **cherries** before freezing.

* **Apricots** and **plums** should be cut in half and the pits removed. Sprinkle with sugar and freeze, or blanch and cover with syrup with a bit of lemon juice or citric acid added.

* **Peaches** should be halved, pitted and peeled. Freeze using the same method as for apricots.

* **Pears** should be firm and juicy. Peel, quarter and remove the core. Cover with sugar syrup to which a little lemon juice has been added.

* Peel **apples** and cut into segments, removing the core. Layer the apple slices in a rigid container, covering each layer with a sprinkling of sugar and lemon juice and a sheet of aluminum foil.

* **Melons** should be peeled and the seeds and fibers removed. Cut into slices, sprinkle with sugar and wrap each slice in aluminum foil until completely frozen. Repack in plastic bags.

* Fruit **juice** freezes conveniently in ice cube trays.

* **Strawberries** and **raspberries** freeze very well without any sugar. Just wash, dry, and store in plastic bags.

Meats

The best meats for freezing are lean cuts with fat trimmed. Animal fat turns rancid quickly, so fatty frozen meats will not keep as long. It is better to freeze multiple small packages than one large one. Once frozen meat has thawed, cook it immediately.

* **Steaks, chops, cutlets,** and **roasts** should be wrapped and frozen individually, then consolidated into larger packages if desired. Be sure to use two layers of aluminum foil over any bones to avoid puncturing the foil.

* **Sausages** and **blood sausage** should be blanched for 1 minute in boiling water before being wrapped individually in aluminum foil. Consolidate into larger packages after they are frozen hard.

* Variety or **organ meats** (liver, sweetbreads, kidneys, brains) should be soaked in cold water for 2 hours before being wrapped individually in aluminum foil. Consolidate into larger packages after they are frozen, if desired.

Poultry and Game Birds

Commercially raised poultry can be stored longer in the freezer than game birds. Game birds should not be hung to age before freezing. Use giblets to make stocks for eventual use in gravies, etc.

Fish and Seafood

Fish for the freezer must be very fresh and prepared as soon as possible. Scale and gut the fish, and remove heads and fins. Cut large fish into pieces or filets. Wrap pieces individually in aluminum foil, freeze, and consolidate in plastic bags.

* **Shellfish** should be shucked, rinsed in fresh water, and frozen in containers topped up with salted water.

* **Shrimp** can be frozen raw or cooked.

Dairy Products

* Pasteurized and homogenized **milk** can be easily frozen in its carton or other container.

* Fresh heavy **cream** freezes well. We recommend that you beat it lightly first. Store in an air-tight container.

* Sweet or **unsalted butter** can be stored longer in the freezer than salted butter.

* **Cheese** is best frozen in small portions, since it tends to dry out quickly once it has been frozen. Grated cheese will keep longer than solid pieces.

Eggs

Eggs should be lightly beaten, with salt and/or pepper added, before freezing.

Breads, Cakes and Pastries

Pastry dough of various types freezes well, although you should not add sugar to the dough. Freeze pastry shells (baked or uncooked) and cream or custard-type fillings separately. If you are freezing dough containing yeast or a leavening agent that is meant to rise after being defrosted, double the amount of the leavening agent. Baked fruit pies freeze well.

Breads, brioches-type breads, and **cookies** freeze well as long as they are put in the freezer while still slightly warm.

Plain cakes freeze very well, but cakes covered with frosting or whipped cream should be covered with aluminum foil before being frozen. Butter icings freeze better than frostings made with eggs, and a plain cake will keep better than a frosted cake.

Cooked Dishes

Almost any cooked dish can be frozen as long as you observe a few basic rules:

* Use only fresh and high quality ingredients.

* Cut down the fat content and use butter, olive oil or peanut oil. Do not add cream or extra butter until reheating.

* Cut down the amount of flour, salt and spices or herbs when preparing the dish, since the flavors can change when frozen. Adjust seasonings when reheating.

* Reduce the cooking time by 1/3 to adjust for cooking that will take place during reheating.

*Thicken and bind sauces only after reheating.

* Remember that liquids expand when frozen. Do not fill freezer containers to the brim.

* Cool dishes as soon as they are cooked and before freezing, in the refrigerator if possible. This cuts down on the possibility of bacterial growth.

Sandwiches

Sandwiches containing fillings of poultry, meat, cheese or fish can be stored in the freezer for up to 2 weeks. Put frozen sandwiches straight into lunch boxes in the morning — they will be thawed and fresh at lunchtime. Do not freeze sandwiches containing mayonnaise (replace with commercial salad dressing), tomatoes, cucumbers or lettuce.

Defrosting

Almost any food in small quantities can be cooked or heated without defrosting. Large quantities, such as roasts or legs of lamb, can be defrosted and roasted in the oven in one operation. If this is not possible, put frozen foods in their freezer wrappers into the refrigerator to thaw. Vegetables are best defrosted in boiling water. Only plain cakes, fruit cakes, breads, or baked fruit pies should be thawed at room temperature.

Density Chart for Sugar Syrups (for 1 liter or 4 cups water)

Light syrup (20%)	1 cup sugar	250 ml sugar
Medium Syrup (30%)	2 cups sugar	500 ml sugar
Heavy syrup (40%)	3 cups sugar	750 ml sugar
Extra-heavy syrup (50%)	4-1/2 cups sugar	1.125 ml sugar

Mix together the sugar and water and bring to a boil. Let simmer for 3 minutes.
Let cool before using.

Light syrup: apples, apricots, grapes, raspberries, pears

Medium syrup: blueberries

Heavy syrup: cherries, peaches, pineapples, plums

Extra-heavy syrup: cranberries, rhubarb

Blanching Times for Vegetables (in boiling water)

Artichokes (chokes removed)	3 minutes
Asparagus	3 minutes
Beans, green or yellow	2 minutes
Broccoli (split stalks)	3 minutes
Brussels sprouts	4 minutes
Cabbage (chopped)	4 minutes
Carrots (sliced or diced)	2 minutes
Cauliflower	3 minutes
Celery	3 minutes
Eggplant	3 minutes
Mushrooms	2 minutes
Leeks	4 minutes
Onions (small)	2 minutes
Peas	1 minute
Snow Peas	3 minutes
Spinach	1 minute
Turnips	5 minutes

Storage Limits for Frozen Foods

Raw Food	at 0°F (-18C°)	at -10°F (-25°C)
Vegetables (blanched)		
Artichokes	10 months	18 months
Asparagus	10 months	18 months
Brussels sprouts	12 months	18 months
Cabbage	12 months	18 months
Carrots	10 months	18 months
Cauliflower	10 months	18 months
Celery	10 months	18 months
Eggplant	10 months	18 months
Green vegetables	8 months	16 months
Herbs	8 months	16 months
Peppers	5 months	10 months
Tomatoes	5 months	10 months
Turnips	10 months	18 months
Zucchini	5 months	10 months
Fruit		
Apricots	6 to 8 months	12 months
Cherries	6 to 8 months	12 months
Fruit in syrup	6 to 8 months	10 months
Other fruit	8 to 10 months	15 months
Peaches	6 to 8 months	12 months
Plums	6 to 8 months	12 months
Stewed fruit	6 to 8 months	10 months
Meat		
Lean meat	8 to 10 months	16 to 18 months
Fatty meat	4 to 5 months	8 months
Organ meat (liver, heart, kidneys, sweetbreads, brain)	3 months	3 months
Blood sausage	1 month	1 month
Sausages	1 month	3 months
Poultry, lean (chicken, guinea fowl, etc.)	10 months	15 months
Poultry, fatty (duck, goose, etc.)	4 months	6 months

Storage Limits for Frozen Foods

Raw Foods	at 0°F (-18C°)	at -10°F (-25°C)
Turkey	6 months	10 months
Chicken	6 months	10 months
Rabbit	3 to 4 months	5 to 6 months
Wild game	3 to 4 months	5 to 6 months
Fish		
Fatty fish	1 to 2 months	3 months
Lean fish	3 months	5 months
Shrimp	4 months	6 months
Shell fish	4 months	6 months
Dairy Products		
Pasteurized, homogenized milk	3 months	5 months
Sweet butter	8 months	12 to 15 months
Heavy cream	3 months	5 months
Cheddar cheese	6 to 8 months	10 months
Cream cheese	4 to 5 months	6 to 8 months
Custards	2 months	3 to 4 months
Eggs lightly beaten	4 to 6 months	18 months
Pastry and Doughs		
Dough with leavening agent	1 month	18 months
Other dough	2 months	18 months

Storage Limits for Frozen Foods

Cooked Dishes	at 0°F (-18C°)	at -10°F (-25°C)
Vegetables		
Vegetables without fat	3 months	6 months
Vegetables with fat	1 to 2 months	3 to 4 months
Soup without fat	3 months	6 months
Soup with fat	1 to 2 months	3 to 4 months
Meat		
Blanquettes of veal	3 months	5 months
Beef bourguignon	3 months	5 months
Stews	1 month	2 months
Sautéed meals	1 month	2 months
Meat sauce	1 month	2 months
Roasts	3 months	5 months
Meat stock	1 month	1-1/2 months
Poultry stock	1 month	1-1/2 months
Poultry	3 months	5 months
Fish		
Cooked fish	1 month	2 months
Breaded fish	1 month	2 months
Croquettes	1 month	2 months
Dairy Products		
Butter crèmes	3 weeks	1 month
Egg crèmes	3 weeks	1 month
Ice cream	1 month	2 months
Fruit sherbets	3 months	5 months
Pastries		
Plain cookies	6 months	10 to12 months
Génoises	6 months	10 to 12 months
Brioches	6 months	10 to 12 months
Plain cakes	1 month	1-1/2 months
Cake rolls	1 month	1-1/2 months

Storage Limits for Frozen Foods

Cooked Dishes	at 0°F (-18C°)	at -10°F (-25°C)
Frosted cakes	1 month	2 months
Pastas and Pastries		
Stuffed crêpes	1 month	2 months
Pasta	1 month	2 months
Pizza	1 month	2 months
Pies	1-1/2 months	2 months
Breads	1-1/2 months	3 months
Croissants	1-1/2 months	3 months
Brioches	1-1/2 months	3 months
Puff pastries	1-1/2 months	3 months

Freezer Meals

African Beef Stew

Standard	Metric
2 lb cubed beef	1 kg cubed beef
2 onions, diced	2 onions, diced
1 green pepper, diced	1 green pepper, diced
5 celery stalks, diced	5 celery stalks, diced
1 can cream of tomato soup	1 can cream of tomato soup
1 cup cold water	250 ml cold water
1 can tomatoes	1 can tomatoes
1 tsp pepper	5 ml pepper
2 cloves garlic	2 cloves garlic
10 to 12 carrots, sliced in rounds	10 to 12 carrots, sliced in rounds
1/3 cup brown sugar	75 ml brown sugar
1/4 cup vinegar	50 ml vinegar
2 tbsp Worcestershire sauce	30 ml Worcestershire sauce
1 can mushrooms (reserve the juice)	1 can mushrooms (reserve the juice)
2 tbsp butter	30 ml butter
3 tbsp vegetable oil	45 ml vegetable oil

Sauté the vegetables in the butter. In another pot brown the beef cubes in oil and degrease. Place the beef, sautéed vegetables and remaining ingredients (including mushroom liquid) in a baking dish. Bake at 350°F (180°C) for 1 hour. Serve with boiled potatoes.

This dish freezes well in large quantities.

Boiled Beef

Standard	Metric
3 lb beef brisket	1.5 kg beef brisket
1 cabbage, in wedges	1 cabbage, in wedges
3 potatoes, cut in half	3 potatoes, cut in half
2 carrots	2 carrots
4 onions, cut in half	4 onions, cut in half
1 leek cut in half	1 leek cut in half
Salt and pepper	Salt and pepper
1 bouquet garni: parsley, basil and thyme	1 bouquet garni: parsley, basil and thyme
2 onions, chopped	2 onions, chopped
Parsley, chopped	Parsley, chopped

Place the beef into a pot. Cover with cold water and bring to a boil. Remove the scum from the surface and set the beef aside.

Rinse the pot and put back the beef. Cover with cold water and add the bouquet garni, salt and pepper. Bring to a boil. Reduce the heat and simmer for 2 hours and 15 minutes.

Thirty minutes before the end of the cooking period, add all the vegetables except the chopped onions. Season to taste and remove the various vegetables when done. Place the vegetables in a serving dish. Cover with a bit of stock to keep them warm.

When all vegetables are done, discard the bouquet garni and place the beef and stock in the serving dish. Garnish with parsley and the chopped onions.

Beef Bourguignon

Standard	Metric
2 to 4 lb cubed beef	1 to 2 kg cubed beef
3 tbsp butter	45 ml butter
12 small onions or	12 small onions or
3 large onions	3 large onions
2 carrots, cut in pieces	2 carrots, cut in pieces
1 clove garlic	1 clove garlic
2 stalks celery	2 stalks celery
1 bay leaf	1 bay leaf
1/2 tsp thyme	2 ml thyme
Dry red wine	Dry red wine
1 cup stock or water	250 ml stock or water
2 tbsp beef concentrate stock	30 ml concentrated beef stock
2 tbsp tomato paste	30 ml tomato paste
1/2 lb mushrooms	250 g mushrooms
4 tbsp all-purpose flour	60 ml all-purpose flour
Parsley	Parsley

Sauté all the vegetables, except mushrooms, in butter. Dredge the beef in flour and brown on all sides. Add the water or stock and enough red wine to cover the meat. Cover and simmer for about 3 hours.

Add the mushrooms and chopped parsley 30 minutes before the end of the cooking time.

Cool and freeze.

MEATBALLS IN TOMATO SAUCE

Standard	Metric
1 lb lean ground beef	500 g lean ground beef
1 tsp salt	5 ml salt
1 tsp breadcrumbs	5 ml breadcrumbs
Pepper to taste	Pepper to taste
1/4 tsp thyme or savory	1 ml thyme or savory
1/3 cup tomato juice	75 ml tomato juice
1 can tomato sauce	1 can tomato sauce
1/2 tsp sugar	2 ml sugar
1 tbsp vegetable oil or butter	15 ml vegetable oil or butter

Combine the first five ingredients and shape into small meatballs. Sprinkle with flour and brown on all sides in oil or butter. Add the tomato sauce, tomato juice and sugar. Simmer for 15 minutes. Cool before freezing.

Makes approximately 20 meatballs.

STEWED CARROTS

Standard	Metric
2 tbsp olive oil	30 ml olive oil
1 Spanish onion, sliced	1 Spanish onion, sliced
4 large carrots, sliced	4 large carrots, sliced
2 tbsp all-purpose flour	30 ml all-purpose flour
2 cups water	500 ml water
Salt and pepper	Salt and pepper

Heat the oil in a large skillet over medium heat. Add the onion and sauté for 4 minutes. Add the carrots and flour. Stir and continue cooking until the flour begins to brown. Add the water, salt and pepper and bring to a boil. Simmer for 16 to 18 minutes.

Cool and freeze. Reheat and garnish with chopped parsley.

DATE SQUARES

Standard	Metric
1-1/2 cups flour	375 ml flour
1/4 cup sugar	50 ml sugar
1 tsp baking powder	5 ml baking powder
1 tsp salt	5 ml salt
3 eggs	3 eggs
1 cup corn syrup	250 ml corn syrup
1 tsp vanilla extract	5 ml vanilla extract
1/4 cup vegetable oil	50 ml vegetable oil
1 cup chopped nuts	250 ml chopped nuts
1 package dates, pitted and chopped	1 package dates, pitted and chopped

Sift the first four ingredients together. In another bowl, beat the eggs while adding the corn syrup, vanilla extract and oil. Add the chopped nuts and dates. Incorporate the dry ingredients. Mix gently. Pour this mixture into a greased pan and bake at 350°F (180°C) for approximately 40 minutes.

Cool and cut into squares. Freeze in the pan or in a plastic container. Sprinkle with icing sugar when ready to serve.

BEEF AND MACARONI CASSEROLE

Standard	Metric
3/4 cup light cream (15%)	150 ml light cream (15%)
1 cup breadcrumbs	250 ml breadcrumbs
1 tsp monosodium glutamate	5 ml monosodium glutamate
1 egg	1 egg
1 tsp salt	5 ml salt
1 tsp dry mustard	5 ml dry mustard
1/4 tsp thyme	1 ml thyme
1 onion, minced	1 onion, minced
1 lb ground beef	500 g ground beef
1 lb uncooked macaroni	500 g uncooked macaroni
1 tbsp butter	15 ml butter
1 tbsp chopped parsley	15 ml chopped parsley
1 cup grated cheddar	250 ml grated cheddar
Salt and pepper	Salt and pepper

Combine the milk, breadcrumbs, egg, seasoning and onions. Add the beef and mix with a fork. Pour this mixture into a greased 12 x 8 x 2 inch (30 x 20 x 5 cm) pan. Bake at 350°F (180°C) for about 30 minutes.

In the meantime, cook the macaroni and drain well. Add salt, pepper and butter and mix well. Remove the pan of meat from the oven and sprinkle with half the cheese. Cover with the macaroni and the rest of the cheese.
Place the pan under the broiler until the cheese begins to brown.

This dish freezes well in large quantities.

COQ AU VIN

Standard	Metric
1 whole chicken, about 4 to 5 lb	1 whole chicken, about 2 to 2.5 kg
2 tbsp butter	30 ml butter
24 small onions	24 small onions
1/8 lb salt pork, cubed	65 g salt pork, cubed
1 tbsp all-purpose flour	15 ml all-purpose flour
1/4 cup warmed Cognac	50 ml warmed Cognac
1 cup chicken stock	250 ml chicken stock
1 cup red wine	250 ml red wine
1 tsp each thyme and marjoram	5 ml each thyme and marjoram
1 bay leaf	1 bay leaf
12 mushrooms	12 mushrooms
1 carrot, whole	1 carrot, whole
Salt and pepper	Salt and pepper

Prepare the chicken and cut into individual serving pieces. In a large heavy saucepan, sauté the onions in butter and add the salt pork, cut up. Sauté until the salt pork has rendered its fat. Remove and drain the onions and pork bits. Set aside.

Dredge the chicken pieces in seasoned flour. Brown in the pork fat on all sides. Pour in the Cognac and flambé. Add the onion, pork bits, wine and stock. Add the bay leaf and herbs, correct the seasoning and add the carrot.

Cover and simmer for 1-1/2 hours until the chicken is done. Sauté the mushrooms and add to the Coq au Vin at the last minute.

Cool and freeze. Serve garnished with garlic croutons and fresh parsley sprigs.

COQUILLES SAINT-JACQUES

Standard	Metric
2 cups béchamel sauce	500 ml béchamel sauce
1/2 lb cooked shrimp	250 g cooked shrimp
1/2 lb cooked scallops	250 g cooked scallops
1/2 lb cooked fish, any kind	250 g cooked fish, any kind
1 cup mashed potatoes	250 ml mashed potatoes
1-1/4 cups grated cheese	300 ml grated cheese

Prepare the béchamel sauce (see chapter on sauces). Add the shrimp, scallops and fish. Pour this mixture into scallop shells or individual baking dishes. Using a pastry bag with a fluted tip, pipe the mashed potatoes around the edges of the shells. Top the seafood with grated cheese. Bake at 425°F (220°C) until the surface becomes golden brown. Cool.

Wrap individually in plastic and freeze.

Makes 6 to 8 portions.

BAVARIAN CREAM WITH GRAND MARNIER

Standard	Metric
8 egg yolks	8 egg yolks
4 egg whites	4 egg whites
1 lb sugar	500 g sugar
4-1/2 cups milk	1 liter milk
4 tsp unflavored gelatin	20 ml unflavored gelatin
2 cups whipped cream	500 ml whipped cream
1/4 cup candied fruit	50 ml candied fruit
Grand Marnier extract	Grand Marnier extract

Heat the milk, sugar, beaten egg yolks and gelatin. Stir frequently and cool until mixture becomes quite thick. Beat the egg whites and fold into the gelatin mixture. Fold in the whipped cream gently. Add candied fruit and Grand Marnier extract to taste. Pour into individual custard cups. Allow to set.

Cover each ramekin with plastic wrap and freeze.

BAKED PORK CHOPS

Standard	Metric
4 thick pork chops	4 thick pork chops
1 can cream of onion soup	1 can cream of onion soup
1 soup can water	1 soup can water
1/4 tsp pepper	1 ml pepper
1/8 tsp ground cloves	0.5 ml ground cloves
1/8 tsp cinnamon	0.5 ml cinnamon

Heat a skillet and brown the pork chops on both sides. Mix the soup and water and pour over the chops. Simmer for 20 minutes. Season to taste. Transfer the contents of the skillet into a baking dish. Cover and bake at 350°F (180°C) for about 1 hour, until pork chops are tender.

Cool before freezing.

ANISEED COOKIES

Standard	Metric
1/2 cup shortening	125 ml shortening
1/2 cup margarine	125 ml margarine
1-1/2 cups sugar	375 ml sugar
2 eggs	2 eggs
2 tsp baking powder	10 ml baking powder
3 cups all-purpose flour	750 ml all-purpose flour
1 cup milk	250 ml milk
1 tsp baking soda	5 ml baking soda
1 tsp vanilla extract	5 ml vanilla extract
1 to 2 tbsp aniseed	15 to 30 ml aniseed

Combine all the ingredients and mix thoroughly. Use a rolling pin to roll out the dough to 1/4 inch (5 mm) thickness. Add a bit of flour if dough begins to stick. Use an upside down glass or a cookie cutter to cut out cookies. Place on a cookie sheet and bake at 400°F (200°C) for 10 to 15 minutes.

Makes about 2 dozen cookies. Cool before freezing.

MOLASSES CAKE

Standard	Metric
1 egg	1 egg
1/2 cup sugar	125 ml sugar
1/2 cup molasses	125 ml molasses
3/4 cup milk	150 ml milk
1/4 tsp salt	1 ml salt
1 tsp baking soda	5 ml baking soda
1 tsp baking powder	5 ml baking powder
2 cups all-purpose flour	500 ml all-purpose flour

Beat the egg. Add the sugar and molasses. Mix thoroughly. Gradually add the dry ingredients, mixing well after each addition. Pour the batter into a cake pan and bake at 350°F (180°C) for 30 minutes.

Cool before freezing.

TOMATO SOUP CAKE

Standard	Metric
2 cups all-purpose flour	500 ml all-purpose flour
2 tsp baking powder	10 ml baking powder
1 tsp baking soda	5 ml baking soda
1/2 tsp ground cloves	2 ml ground cloves
1 tsp cinnamon	5 ml cinnamon
1 tsp ground nutmeg	5 ml ground nutmeg
1/2 cup shortening	125 ml shortening
1 cup sugar	250 ml sugar
1 cup cream of tomato soup	250 ml cream of tomato soup
1/2 cup chopped nuts	125 ml chopped nuts
1 cup raisins	250 ml raisins

Sift together the flour, baking powder, baking soda, cloves, nutmeg and cinnamon. Set aside. Melt the shortening and beat in the sugar until the mixture becomes frothy. Add the dry ingredients alternating with the cream of tomato soup. Mix thoroughly. Fold in the nuts and raisins. Pour the batter into a greased cake pan. Bake at 350°F (180°C) for 50 to 60 minutes.

Cool before freezing.

VEGETABLES AU GRATIN

Standard	Metric
1 lb carrots, broccoli, zucchini or cauliflower	500 g carrots, broccoli, zucchini or cauliflower
2 cups water	500 ml water
1 tsp thyme	5 ml thyme
1 cup béchamel sauce	250 ml béchamel sauce
1/3 cup breadcrumbs	75 ml breadcrumbs
1/4 cup butter	50 ml butter

Slice the vegetables or break them into flowerets. Add salt and thyme to the water and cook until barely tender. Drain the vegetables and save the water. Place the vegetables into greased individual baking dishes. Set aside.

Prepare the béchamel sauce (see chapter on sauces) using equal quantities of vegetable water and milk. Cover vegetables with the béchamel. Sprinkle with breadcrumbs and dot with butter. Bake at 350°F (180°C) for 30 minutes. Cool before freezing.

MUSHROOM AND MACARONI CASSEROLE

Standard	Metric
2 lb macaroni	1 kg macaroni
1 onion, chopped	1 onion, chopped
2 cups mushrooms, sliced	500 ml mushrooms, sliced
1 cup cooked ham, chopped	250 ml cooked ham, chopped
1 can cream of mushroom soup	1 can cream of mushroom soup
1 cup grated cheese	250 ml grated cheese
Salt, pepper, paprika	Salt, pepper, paprika

Sauté the onion and mushrooms in a heavy casserole. Add the ham and cook until lightly browned. Add the cooked macaroni and cream of mushroom diluted with a bit of milk. Stir. Add salt and pepper to taste and a pinch of paprika. Cover with grated cheese. Bake at 350°F (180°C) for about 20 minutes then broil for 5 minutes.

Cool before freezing.

MACARONI WITH MEAT SAUCE

Standard	Metric
2 tbsp vegetable oil	30 ml vegetable oil
1 large onion, thinly sliced	1 large onion, thinly sliced
1 green pepper, finely chopped	1 green pepper, finely chopped
1 lb ground beef	500 g ground beef
1 clove garlic, finely chopped	1 clove garlic, finely chopped
2 celery stalks, thinly sliced	2 celery stalks, thinly sliced
2 medium cans tomato juice	2 medium cans tomato juice
1 can tomatoes	1 can tomatoes
2 cans tomato paste	2 cans tomato paste
1/2 tsp rosemary	2 ml rosemary
1/2 tsp marjoram	2 ml marjoram
1/4 tsp crushed chili peppers	1 ml crushed chili peppers
4 bay leaves	4 bay leaves
1 tsp parsley	5 ml parsley
2 lb macaroni	1 kg macaroni

Sauté the first six ingredients in a heavy saucepan for 10 minutes. Add the remaining ingredients, except macaroni, and simmer for 3 hours over low heat.

In the meantime, cook the macaroni in salted boiling water. Drain and add to the sauce. Mix well. Cool before freezing.

BRAN MUFFINS

Standard	Metric
1 cup all-purpose flour	250 ml all-purpose flour
1 tsp baking powder	5 ml baking powder
1/2 tsp baking soda	2 ml baking soda
1/2 tsp salt	2 ml salt
1 cup bran	250 ml bran
1/3 cup chopped nuts	75 ml chopped nuts
1 egg	1 egg
3 tbsp honey	45 ml honey
3/4 cup sour milk	150 ml sour milk
3 tbsp melted butter	45 ml melted butter

Sift the flour, baking powder, baking soda and salt into a bowl. Add the nuts and the bran. Mix well. In a separate bowl, mix the egg, honey and sour milk. Add the dry ingredients all at once. Add the butter. Stir gently to combine without over-stirring.

Pour the batter into greased muffin tins and bake at 425°F (220°C) for about 15 minutes.

Cool before freezing. Makes approximately 2 dozen.

CREATIVE
LEFTOVERS

CREATIVE LEFTOVERS

FISH COQUILLES AU GRATIN

Standard	Metric
1-1/2 lb leftover cooked fish	750 g leftover cooked fish
1-1/2 cups thick béchamel sauce	375 ml thick béchamel sauce
1-1/2 cups grated Cheddar or Gruyère cheese	375 ml grated Cheddar or Gruyère cheese
Paprika	Paprika

Prepare the béchamel sauce and bring to a boil. Remove from heat and cool. Fill buttered scallop shells or individual baking dishes with fish. Cover with the sauce and sprinkle generously with grated cheese and paprika. Bake at 325°F-350°F (160°C-180°C) for about 30 minutes. Serve.

Makes 6 to 8 servings.

STUFFED SUMMER SQUASH

Standard	Metric
3 medium zucchini (or marrow)	3 medium zucchini (or marrow)
2-1/2 cups breadcrumbs	625 ml breadcrumbs
1 cup leftover cooked meat	250 ml leftover cooked meat
1 onion, finely chopped	1 onion, finely chopped
2 tbsp melted butter	30 ml melted butter
2 tbsp tomato ketchup	30 ml tomato ketchup
2 tsp Worcestershire sauce	10 ml Worcestershire sauce
Beef stock to moisten	Beef stock to moisten
Salt and pepper	Salt and pepper

Wash and dry the zucchini. Cut in two lengthwise and remove seeds and filaments. Pour a bit of melted butter into each cavity. Sprinkle with salt and pepper. Place in a glass baking dish and bake for 30 to 40 minutes at 400°F (200°C), until tender.

In the meantime, combine the breadcrumbs, meat, onion and ketchup. Add Worcestershire sauce and beef stock to moisten. Mix well. Fill the zucchini halves with this mixture and bake for an additional 15 minutes. Serves 6.

CHICKEN DIVAN

Standard	Metric
1 cauliflower, in flowerets	1 cauliflower, in flowerets
1 to 2 cups cooked chicken	250 to 500 ml cooked chicken
1 can cream of celery soup	1 can cream of celery soup
1 tbsp milk	15 ml milk
1/2 cup grated cheese	125 ml grated cheese

Cook the cauliflower in salted boiling water for 8 minutes. Drain and place in a baking dish. Add a layer of chicken. Cover with mixture of milk and cream of celery and sprinkle with grated cheese. Bake at 350°F (180°C) for 35 minutes, until cheese is golden brown.

Variation: Replace the cauliflower with green beans or broccoli or any combination of these vegetables. Substitute cream of asparagus or mushroom soup.

Makes 6 servings.

TURKEY AU GRATIN

Standard	Metric
2 cups rice	500 ml rice
2 cups chicken stock	500 ml chicken stock
2 to 3 cups cooked turkey	500 to 750 ml cooked turkey
1 can cream of mushroom soup	1 can cream of mushroom soup
1/2 cup mayonnaise	125 ml mayonnaise
1/2 cup milk	125 ml milk
Grated cheese	Grated cheese

Bring the chicken stock to a boil and cook the rice in it. Arrange the rice in an ovenproof dish. Arrange chopped or sliced cooked turkey on top and set aside.

Combine the cream of mushroom, mayonnaise and milk. Mix well and pour over the turkey. Sprinkle with grated cheese. Bake at 375°F (190°C) for 35 minutes, until cheese is golden brown.

Makes 6 to 8 servings.

Chicken and Asparagus Fricassee

Standard	Metric
3 cups cooked chicken, cubed	750 ml cooked chicken, cubed
1 cup frozen green peas	250 ml frozen green peas
1 cup carrots, chopped	250 ml carrots, chopped
1/2 cup parsley, finely chopped	125 ml parsley, finely chopped
1/2 cup celery, chopped	125 ml celery, chopped
1/2 cup green pepper, chopped	125 ml green pepper, chopped
1 lb cooked asparagus	500 g cooked asparagus
2 cups skim milk	500 ml skim milk

Combine the chicken, peas, carrots, celery and green pepper in a bowl. Put the milk and the asparagus through the blender at high speed for 3 minutes.

Pour the milk and asparagus into a saucepan and bring to a boil. Add the chicken and vegetables. Simmer over medium heat for 4 minutes. Garnish with parsley and serve.

Makes 6 to 8 servings.

Meat and Potato Galette

Standard	Metric
2 cups mashed potatoes	500 ml mashed potatoes
2 beaten eggs	2 beaten eggs
1/2 lb ground meat	250 g ground meat
Pinch thyme	Pinch thyme
1/2 onion, chopped	1/2 onion, chopped
2 cloves garlic, chopped	2 cloves garlic, chopped
3 tbsp butter	45 ml butter
Grated cheese	Grated cheese
5 tbsp vegetable oil	75 ml vegetable oil

Melt the butter in a skillet. Sauté the onion, garlic, thyme and ground meat. Cook over low heat for 10 minutes. Remove from heat and add the mashed potatoes and eggs. Mix thoroughly. Heat the oil in a cast iron skillet or any ovenproof frying pan. Place the meat and potato mixture in the skillet and press down with a spatula to make one large patty. Bake at 350°F (180°C) for about 30 minutes. Sprinkle with grated cheese and serve.

Makes 4 servings.

Ham n' Rice

Standard	Metric
3 cups tomatoes	750 ml tomatoes
1/2 cup uncooked rice	125 ml uncooked rice
2 cups water	500 ml water
3 cups leftover ham	750 ml leftover ham
1 finely chopped onion	1 finely chopped onion
Grated cheese	Grated cheese

Place the tomatoes and water in a saucepan and bring to a boil. Add the rice, cover and simmer for 15-20 minutes. Add the ham and onion. Pour the mixture into a baking dish and sprinkle with grated cheese. Bake at 350°F (180°C) for 20 minutes.

Makes 6 servings.

Rum Roll

Standard	Metric
3-1/2 cups dry cake	875 ml dry cake
1-1/4 cups icing sugar	300 ml icing sugar
4 tbsp cocoa	60 ml cocoa
2 tbsp sugar	30 ml sugar
4 tbsp chopped nuts	60 ml chopped nuts
1/2 cup rum	125 ml rum
3/4 cup butter	150 ml butter

Crumble the cake into crumbs. Add the icing sugar, cocoa, sugar and chopped nuts. Pour in the rum and work in the butter. Shape the mixture into a sausage shape.

Tightly wrap the cake in aluminum foil and place in the freezer for 3 hours. Serve frozen and cut into thin slices.

Turkey and Broccoli au Gratin

Standard	Metric
2 to 3 cups leftover turkey or 2 turkey breasts, cooked	500 to 750 ml leftover turkey or 2 turkey breasts, cooked
1 can cream of chicken soup	1 can cream of chicken soup
1 can condensed milk	1 can condensed milk
1 cup grated Gruyère	250 ml grated Gruyère
1 broccoli cut into flowerets	1 broccoli cut into flowerets
Butter	Butter
Salt and pepper	Salt and pepper

Line the bottom of a baking dish with the turkey. Combine the condensed milk and cream of chicken soup and pour over the turkey. Add salt and pepper to taste. Dot with butter and sprinkle with grated cheese. Broil for several minutes then bake at 350°F (180°C) for 15 minutes.

Makes 6 servings.

Cottage Pie

Standard	Metric
2 cups boiled beef, chopped	500 ml boiled beef, chopped
1 onion, coarsely chopped	1 onion, coarsely chopped
All-purpose flour	All-purpose flour
1/2 cup white wine	125 ml white wine
1/2 cup beef stock	125 ml beef stock
3 tbsp tomato paste	45 ml tomato paste
2 cups mashed potatoes	500 ml mashed potatoes
Salt and pepper	Salt and pepper

Chop the boiled beef into bite-size pieces. Sauté the onion in a large skillet. Sprinkle with flour and stir. Pour in the white wine and half the stock. Add the meat, tomato paste, salt and pepper and simmer for 45 minutes.

In the meantime, thin the mashed potatoes with the remaining stock. Place a layer of beef and onion mixture at the bottom of a baking dish and cover with a layer of mashed potatoes. Alternate these layers and finish off with potatoes. Place under the broiler until golden brown.

Pour a bit of melted butter on the surface when it begins to form a light crust.

Note: A beaten egg yolk may also be used to brush onto this crust.

FISH AU GRATIN

Standard	Metric
2 to 3 cups leftover fish	500 to 750 ml leftover fish
2 onions, finely chopped	2 onions, finely chopped
3/4 cup fresh mushrooms, sliced	150 ml fresh mushrooms, sliced
2 cloves garlic, chopped	2 cloves garlic, chopped
Parsley, finely chopped	Parsley, finely chopped
Flour	Flour
1/2 cup milk	125 ml milk
1/2 cup heavy cream (35%)	125 ml heavy cream (35%)
Breadcrumbs	Breadcrumbs
2 tbsp butter	30 ml butter
Salt and pepper	Salt and pepper

Lightly sauté the onions in butter. Remove from the pan and set aside. Sauté the mushrooms until all liquid has evaporated. Add small pieces of fish, garlic and parsley. Blend well. Add the onion and sprinkle with flour. Stir with a wooden spoon over high heat. Pour in the milk to make a thick béchamel sauce. Add salt and pepper to taste and the cream, stirring gently.

Pour this mixture into a buttered baking dish. Sprinkle with breadcrumbs and dot with butter. Bake at 400°F (200°C) for 10 to 15 minutes. Serve.

HAM OR PORK WITH PASTA

Standard	Metric
2-1/2 cups leftover ham or pork, cubed	625 ml leftover ham or pork, cubed
6 cups cooked pasta	1.5 liters cooked pasta
1 onion, finely chopped	1 onion, finely chopped
1 green pepper, finely chopped	1 green pepper, finely chopped
1 cup fresh mushrooms	250 ml fresh mushrooms
1 can ground tomatoes	1 can ground tomatoes
1 can cream of tomato soup	1 can cream of tomato soup
1 tsp brown sugar	5 ml brown sugar
1/2 cup grated cheddar	125 ml grated cheddar
Salt and pepper	Salt and pepper

Sauté the onions, pepper and mushrooms in butter. Add salt and pepper. Add the meat and all remaining ingredients

except grated cheese and cooked pasta. Stir and simmer for 20 minutes. Incorporate the pasta and cheese, stir and serve as soon as the cheese has melted.

Makes 6 to 8 servings.

NOODLES AND ONIONS

Standard	Metric
4 cups cooked noodles	1 liter cooked noodles
3 tbsp butter	45 ml butter
2 onions, finely chopped	2 onions, finely chopped
Salt and pepper	Salt and pepper
1/3 cup grated Parmesan cheese	75 ml grated Parmesan cheese

Brown the onions in the butter. Add the cooked noodles and reheat, stirring constantly. Season to taste. Add the Parmesan once the pasta is hot. Serve as soon as the cheese has melted.

Makes 4 servings.

EGGS IN TOMATO SAUCE

Standard	Metric
4 hard-boiled eggs, cut in half	4 hard-boiled eggs, cut in half
1-1/2 cups tomato coulis (see page 370)	375 ml tomato coulis (see page 370)
1 tbsp sugar	15 ml sugar
1 tbsp chopped parsley	15 ml chopped parsley
1 tbsp sweet basil	15 ml sweet basil
Pinch thyme	Pinch thyme
1/4 cup grated mozzarella cheese	50 ml grated mozzarella cheese
Salt and pepper	Salt and pepper

Pour the tomato coulis into a skillet and bring to a boil. Add parsley, basil thyme, salt and pepper. Place the eggs in the sauce and cook until the sauce becomes quite thick. Transfer the contents of the skillet to a baking dish and sprinkle with mozzarella. Place under the broiler until golden. Serve.

Makes 2 servings.

OMELET WITH CRETONS

Standard	Metric
10 eggs	10 eggs
3/4 cup cretons	150 ml cretons
4 tsp chopped parsley	20 ml chopped parsley
2 cooked tomatoes, coarsely chopped	2 cooked tomatoes, coarsely chopped
Salt and pepper	Salt and pepper

Cook the cretons in a skillet for several minutes to render most of the fat. Drain and set aside.

Beat the eggs and season to taste. Incorporate the cretons and the drained tomatoes. Correct the seasoning. Pour the mixture into a hot frying pan and cook as you would any omelet.

Note: It is much easier to prepare 2 separate omelets of 5 eggs apiece than a single 10-egg omelet.

Serves 6 to 8.

APPLE OMELET

4 old apples, sliced, with peel
Icing sugar
4 eggs

Sprinkle icing sugar into a casserole (with a cover) arrange apple slices on top. Shake the pan to coat the apples. Cook over low heat and turn frequently to caramelize the apples.

Oil individual custard dishes and place an apple slice in each. Beat the eggs and pour into each custard dish. Bake at 400°F (200°C) until the eggs are light and fluffy. Turn out each dish onto a warm plate, apple side up. Serve immediately.

HAM AND TURKEY PIE

Standard	Metric
1 can cream of chicken soup	1 can cream of chicken soup
1 cup cooked turkey, cubed	250 ml cooked turkey, cubed
1 cup cooked ham, cubed	250 ml cooked ham, cubed
2 tsp dried parsley	10 ml dried parsley
1/4 cup milk	50 ml milk
1 tsp pepper	5 ml pepper
1/8 tsp crushed cloves	0.5 ml crushed cloves
1 cup canned peas	250 ml canned peas
1 cup all-purpose flour	250 ml all-purpose flour
1 tsp baking powder	5 ml baking powder
1/2 tsp salt	2 ml salt
1 cup mashed potatoes	250 ml mashed potatoes
1/3 cup vegetable oil	75 ml vegetable oil
1 egg, beaten	1 egg, beaten

Combine the cream of chicken soup and the milk and pour into a saucepan. Add the ham, turkey, parsley, pepper and cloves. Place half the mixture in a 8 inch (20 cm) baking dish. Cover with the peas and add the other half of the ham and turkey mixture. Set aside.

Sift together the flour, baking powder and the salt. Incorporate cold mashed potatoes, vegetable oil and the egg. Blend well and refrigerate for 1 hour until firm.

Shape the dough into a ball and roll out to 1/4 inch (5 mm) thick. Place over the the ham and turkey filling. Coat fingers with flour and crimp the edges of the dough to seal the pie. Make a few cuts in the pastry and bake at 425°F (220°C) for about 30 minutes.

Serves 6 to 8.

CHICKEN PIE

Standard	Metric
3 cups cooked chicken, cubed	750 ml cooked chicken, cubed
1 cup mushrooms	250 ml mushrooms
1/4 cup green pepper, diced	50 ml green pepper, diced
1 cup peas	250 ml peas
1 cup cooked carrots, diced	250 ml cooked carrots, diced
1/2 cup Chinese cabbage, diced	125 ml Chinese cabbage, diced
1/2 cup cooked celery, diced	125 ml cooked celery, diced
2 cups chicken stock	500 ml chicken stock
1 cup light cream (15%)	250 ml light cream (15%)
1/4 cup all-purpose flour	50 ml all-purpose flour
1/4 cup butter	50 ml butter
2 tsp salt	10 ml salt
1/2 tsp pepper	2 ml pepper
1/4 tsp paprika	1 ml paprika
Double crust pastry recipe	Double crust pastry recipe

Sauté the mushrooms in a bit of butter. Add the chicken stock, chicken, cream, salt, pepper, paprika and vegetables. Simmer for 5 minutes, stirring occasionally. Knead together the flour and butter until smooth and add to the other ingredients. Stir and cook until sauce thickens.

Line a baking dish with pastry and fill with the chicken sauce. Cover with another sheet of pastry and seal well. Prick with a fork and brush with milk.

Bake at 425°F (220°C) for 10 minutes; reduce heat to 375°F (190°C) and bake for another 20 minutes.

Serves 6 to 8.

FLAN À LA RATATOUILLE

Standard	Metric
2-1/2 cups cold ratatouille	650 ml cold ratatouille
5 eggs	5 eggs
3 tbsp chopped parsley	45 ml chopped parsley
Salt and pepper	Salt and pepper

Heat the ratatouille in a small saucepan. Stir constantly with a wooden spatula and continue cooking until the ratatouille is quite dry. Cool and refrigerate for at least 1 hour.

Beat the eggs with the parsley and seasonings. Combine with the chilled ratatouille.

Butter 6 little custard molds (or muffin tins) and fill with the egg and ratatouille mixture. Place the molds in a pan filled with water to about halfway up the sides of the molds. Bake at 325°F (160°C) for about 40 minutes.

Serve hot or cold with a tomato sauce.

Makes 6 servings.

HAM AND LEEKS

Standard	Metric
2 cooked leeks, cut in half lengthwise	2 cooked leeks, cut in half lengthwise
4 ham slices	4 ham slices
4 cheese slices	4 cheese slices
1 cup béchamel sauce	250 ml béchamel sauce
Salt and pepper	Salt and pepper

Place one slice of cheese and 1/2 a leek on each slice of ham. Roll and place in a buttered baking dish. Cover with the béchamel (see chapter on sauces) and bake at 350°F (180°C) for 20 minutes.

Makes 4 servings.

BREAD PUDDING

Standard	Metric
4 to 5 slices bread, lightly buttered and cut into large cubes	4 to 5 slices bread, lightly buttered and cut into large cubes
1-1/2 cups milk	375 ml milk
2 eggs	2 eggs
1/4 cup sugar	50 ml sugar
1 tsp vanilla extract	5 ml vanilla extract
1 cup raisins	250 ml raisins

Combine the last five ingredients and mix well. Add to the bread. Place in a baking dish and bake at 350°F (180°C) for about 1-1/2 hours. Place a bowl of water in the oven to prevent the top of the pudding from drying out. Serve with maple syrup.

Serves 6.

SECOND CHANCE CAKE

Standard	Metric
4 cups white or chocolate cake, in pieces	1 liter white or chocolate cake, in pieces
2-1/2 cups milk	625 ml milk
4 eggs	4 eggs
1/4 cup sugar	50 ml sugar
1 tsp vanilla extract	5 ml vanilla extract
1/2 cup raisins	125 ml raisins
1/2 cup candied fruit	125 ml candied fruit

Combine the cake, raisins and candied fruit. Place in a lightly buttered mold.

Pour the milk and vanilla extract into a saucepan and bring to a boil. In the meantime, beat the eggs and sugar until quite thick. Pour the boiled milk into the egg mixture, beating vigorously all the while.

Pour this mixture over the cake, raisins and fruit. Place the cake mold in a pan of water and bake at 300-325°F (150-160°C) for about 40 minutes.

ROAST BEEF SALAD

Standard	Metric
2 lb cold roast beef	1 kg cold roast beef
3/4 cup sour pickles, coarsely chopped	150 ml sour pickles, coarsely chopped
1 sweet red pepper, finely chopped	1 sweet red pepper, finely chopped
1 sweet green pepper, finely chopped	1 sweet green pepper, finely chopped
1 onion, chopped	1 onion, chopped
2 cloves garlic, chopped	2 cloves garlic, chopped
1/3 cup fresh parsley, chopped	75 ml fresh parsley, chopped
1 cup cooked or canned corn kernels	250 ml cooked or canned corn kernels
1/2 cup of mustard vinaigrette	125 ml of mustard vinaigrette

Cut the roast into thin slices, then into strips. Place in a salad bowl with the remaining ingredients. Mix thoroughly. Correct the seasoning and serve.

TUNA AND MUSHROOM SALAD

Standard	Metric
2-1/2 cups cooked elbow macaroni	300 g cooked elbow macaroni
14 oz can tuna	400 g can tuna
1 can mushrooms	1 can mushrooms
1 lemon	1 lemon
1/2 cup Gruyère, cubed	125 ml Gruyère, cubed
Black olives	Black olives
1 cup oil and vinegar dressing	250 ml oil and vinegar dressing

Drain the tuna and the mushrooms. Rinse the mushrooms. Cut the tuna into small pieces. Combine all the ingredients, except olives, and mix thoroughly. Decorate with the black olives.

Serves 6.

SHRIMP AND CHICKEN SOUP

Standard	Metric
2 cups cooked chicken, cubed	500 ml cooked chicken, cubed
3 tbsp butter	45 ml butter
1 cup shrimp	250 ml shrimp
5 cups chicken stock	1.25 liters chicken stock
1/2 onion, minced	1/2 onion, minced
2 cloves garlic, chopped	2 cloves garlic, chopped
4 tbsp chopped parsley	60 ml chopped parsley
1 tsp thyme	5 ml thyme
1/2 tsp cayenne	2 ml cayenne

Melt the butter in a skillet and lightly sauté the onions. Add the shrimp and cook for about 5 minutes. Add the garlic, parsley, thyme and cayenne. Set aside. Pour the chicken stock into a pot and bring to a boil. Add the shrimp and chicken cubes and cook for 3 minutes. Serve.

Add rice and curry powder, if desired.

Serves 6.

POTATO SOUFFLÉ

Standard	Metric
2 cups mashed potatoes	500 ml mashed potatoes
1/2 cup light cream (15%)	125 ml light cream (15%)
5 egg yolks	5 egg yolks
5 egg whites	5 egg whites
Salt and pepper	Salt and pepper

Bring the cream to a boil and add to the mashed potatoes. Add the egg yolks and stir vigorously for about 1 minute over high heat. Remove from heat. Beat the egg whites until stiff and gently fold into the potato and cream mixture. Add salt and pepper to taste. Butter six individual soufflé dishes and fill to 2/3. Bake at 325°F (160°C) for 30 minutes.

CHEESE TARTS MAISON

Standard	Metric
1 cup leftover cheeses	250 ml leftover cheeses
2 cups milk	500 ml milk
4 tbsp butter	60 ml butter
4 tbsp all-purpose flour	60 ml all-purpose flour
1/2 onion with one clove	1/2 onion with one clove
1/2 tsp cayenne	2 ml cayenne
1/4 tsp nutmeg	1 ml nutmeg
Salt and pepper	Salt and pepper
Shortcrust pastry	Shortcrust pastry

Melt the butter in a saucepan without letting it bubble. Add the flour and cook over low heat for 3 minutes, stirring constantly with a wooden spoon. Remove from heat. Pour the milk into a separate saucepan and bring to a boil. Stir the milk into the flour and butter using a whisk. Add the onion and spices. Continue cooking over low heat for 10 minutes. Remove from heat. Take out the onion. Add the cheeses and stir until melted.

Line tart pans with shortcrust pastry and fill to 3/4 with cheese mixture. Bake at 350°F (180°C) for 30 minutes. Serve hot or cold.

Makes 6 to 8 tarts.

BAKED HOT CHICKEN SANDWICHES

Standard	Metric
6 slices bread	6 slices bread
2 tbsp butter	30 ml butter
2 cups béchamel sauce	500 ml béchamel sauce
1 cup sliced mushrooms	250 ml sliced mushrooms
1 cup cooked chicken, chopped	250 ml cooked chicken, chopped
2 eggs, beaten	2 eggs, beaten
Salt and pepper	Salt and pepper

Butter a large ovenproof pan. Place the bread slices in the pan with a slight space between each. Prepare the béchamel (see chapter on sauces) and incorporate the eggs, using a wooden spatula. Cook over high heat for 1 minute, stirring constantly. Set aside.

Brown the butter in a skillet and sauté the mushrooms. Drain and add to the sauce. Add the chicken and stir. Season to taste. Spread a layer of sauce and chicken mixture over the bread slices. Bake at 350°F (180°C) for 15 minutes and serve.

MEAT PIE

Standard	Metric
2 cups leftover beef and vegetables	500 ml leftover beef and vegetables
3 tbsp butter	45 ml butter
1 large onion, chopped	1 large onion, chopped
2 canned tomatoes, chopped	2 canned tomatoes, chopped
Pinch thyme	Pinch thyme
1 unbaked pastry shell	1 unbaked pastry shell
3/4 cup grated cheese	150 ml grated cheese

Melt the butter in a saucepan and sauté the onion and tomatoes. Coarsely chop the beef and vegetables and add to the onion and tomatoes. Cook for about 5 minutes. Pour this mixture into the pie shell, cover with grated cheese and bake at 350°F (180°C) for 30 minutes.

BREADED PORK SLICES

Standard	Metric
1-1/2 lb leftover roast pork	750 g leftover roast pork
5 tbsp butter	75 ml butter
2 eggs, beaten	2 eggs, beaten
1/2 cup milk	125 ml milk
Seasoned flour	Seasoned flour
Breadcrumbs	Breadcrumbs

Cut the leftover pork into thin slices. Mix the eggs and milk together. Dredge each pork slice in seasoned flour, dip in milk and egg mixture and coat with breadcrumbs. Melt the butter in a skillet and sauté the pork slices until crisp.

Serve with a mushroom sauce (see chapter on sauces).

Serves 6.

SAUCES

BASIC STOCKS AND SAUCES

CONSOMMÉ

Standard	Metric
2 lb veal bones, quite meaty (preferably shin or knuckle)	1 kg veal bones, quite meaty (preferably shin or knuckle)
10 cups cold water	2-1/2 liters cold water
2 unpeeled onions, cut in four	2 unpeeled onions, cut in four
2 carrots	2 carrots
3 stalks of celery	3 stalks of celery
2 tomatoes	2 tomatoes
3 garlic cloves, crushed (unskinned)	3 garlic cloves, crushed (unskinned)
1 tsp thyme	5 ml thyme
1 bay leaf	1 bay leaf
5 sprigs of parsley	5 sprigs of parsley
2 tbsp vegetable oil	30 ml vegetable oil

Blanch the bones in boiling water for 5 minutes, then rinse under cold water. Place on a baking sheet and baste with the oil. Brown them slightly in the oven at 400°F (200°C) for 5 minutes.

Wipe the oil from the bones and place them along with the rest of the ingredients in a large pot. Cook for about 4 hours. Add some water from time to time. Do not stir the consommé. Strain carefully through moistened cheesecloth.

CLARIFIED CONSOMMÉ

To provide a sparkling clear consommé, the stock must be clarified.

Allow 1 egg per 4 cups (1 liter) of consommé. Beat 1 egg white with 1 tbsp (15 ml) of cold water. Add the egg shell, crumbled. Pour the white and shell into the cold broth and bring to a boil, stirring constantly. Boil gently for 2 to 3 minutes. Reduce the heat and continue cooking for another 20 minutes. Strain.

Note: if the consommé is too light, adjust the color with a little beef concentrate. A perfect consommé allows you to see the bottom of the bowl. If some tiny droplets of oil remain on the consommé, touch a sheet of paper towel to the surface while it is still warm, to absorb the oil. Serve with added port or pasta, as a base for Chinese soups, and as a bouillon for Chinese fondues.

WHITE POULTRY STOCK

Standard	Metric
2-1/2 lb chicken bones	1.25 kg chicken bones
1 carrot	1 carrot
2 onions	2 onions
3 stalks of celery	3 stalks of celery
1 white turnip, pared	1 white turnip, pared
1 leek (white part)	1 leek (white part)
2 tomatoes	2 tomatoes
3 cloves garlic, crushed	3 cloves garlic, crushed
1 tsp thyme	5 ml thyme
1 bay leaf	1 bay leaf
6 sprigs parsley	6 sprigs parsley
20 peppercorns	20 peppercorns
1 tsp coarse salt	5 ml coarse salt
1 clove	1 clove
1 tsp ginger (optional)	5 ml ginger (optional)
1/2 cup mushroom stems	125 ml mushroom stems

NOTE: It is always preferable to blanch the bones or carcasses a few minutes in boiling water, then rinse them under cold water. This cleans the bones to provide a very clear stock.

Bring the water to a boil in a large pot, add the cut-up chicken bones, and let boil for 3 minutes. Rinse the bones in cold water and place them in a large pot. Add the whole tomatoes, the white turnip, 1 crushed clove, the thyme, salt, bay leaf, parsley, peppercorns and mushroom stems. Cut the onions in quarters and stick the clove in one of the quarters. Cut the leek in four crosswise along with the carrot and celery stalks. Add to the other vegetables. Pour in the cold water. Bring to a boil. Continue cooking for 2 hours over very low heat.

After cooking, pass the stock through the finest possible sieve or through cheesecloth.

Let stand for 2 hours at room temperature, then refrigerate. When about to serve, absorb the thin film of grease that may form on the surface of the stock using an absorbent paper towel.

Add this stock to soups, basic sauces and various baked dishes.

Brown Poultry Stock

Standard	Metric
2-1/2 lb chicken bones, broken up	1.25 kg chicken bones, broken up
2 carrots	2 carrots
2 onions	2 onions
3 stalks of celery	3 stalks of celery
2 tomatoes	2 tomatoes
6 cloves garlic, unskinned and crushed	6 cloves garlic, unskinned and crushed
1 tsp thyme	5 ml thyme
7 tbsp tomato paste	105 ml tomato paste
1 bay leaf	1 bay leaf
7 sprigs of parsley	7 sprigs of parsley
16 cups water	4 liters water

The bones may be blanched when making a brown stock, but this is less important than for a white stock.

In a large, sufficiently deep baking dish, combine the broken up chicken bones, the carrots, the onions, the tomatoes and garlic. Place in the oven at 400°F (200°C) until well browned, stirring occasionally. Add the tomato paste. Mix well and return to the oven for about 20 minutes.

Remove from the oven and add a little water to loosen the bones. Place everything in a pot, cover with water and bring to a boil. Allow to bubble. Add the thyme, bay leaf and parsley. Skim the surface frequently with a skimmer or ladle, and simmer for about 3 hours. Add water from time to time.

Let stand, then pour through a very fine sieve. Before using, remove any fat which may have set on the surface of the brown stock.

Use to deglaze pans and as a basic stock for brown sauces, stews and brown sauce dishes.

White Stock

Standard	Metric
2-1/2 lb veal bones, broken up	1.25 kg veal bones, broken up
2 carrots	2 carrots
2 onions	2 onions
3 stalks of celery	3 stalks of celery
2 tomatoes	2 tomatoes
5 cloves garlic, crushed	5 cloves garlic, crushed
1 tsp thyme	5 ml thyme
1 bay leaf	1 bay leaf
20 peppercorns	20 peppercorns
5 sprigs of parsley	5 sprigs of parsley
16 cups cold water	4 liters cold water

Blanch the bones in salted water for 3 minutes, then rinse under cold water. Place in a large pot with all the rest of the ingredients. Proceed as for "White Poultry Stock", but cook for about 3-1/2 hours. Add some liquid from time to time. Refrigerate once it has cooled.

Makes about 8 to 12 cups (2 to 3 liters) of light stock.

Brown Stock

Standard	Metric
2-1/2 lb veal bones, broken up	1.25 kg veal bones, broken up
2 carrots	2 carrots
2 onions	2 onions
2 tomatoes	2 tomatoes
6 cloves garlic, crushed	6 cloves garlic, crushed
1 tsp thyme	5 ml thyme
1 bay leaf	1 bay leaf
20 peppercorns	20 peppercorns
7 parsley sprigs	7 parsley sprigs
16 cups cold water	4 liters cold water

Blanch the veal bones in the boiling water for about 3 minutes. Proceed as for "Brown Poultry Stock", but let cook for 4 to 5 hours, adding some water from time to time.

Use to deglaze pans and as a basic stock for various combination sauces, brown sauce dishes, stews and baked dishes (braised meats or vegetables).

Fish Stock

Standard	Metric
2 lb fish trimmings and bones	1 kg fish trimmings and bones
2 onions, chopped	2 onions, chopped
3 stalks of celery, chopped	3 stalks of celery, chopped
1 leek (white part), chopped	1 leek (white part), chopped
1/2 carrot, chopped	1/2 carrot, chopped
1 tomato	1 tomato
1 cup mushroom stems	250 ml mushroom stems
1 tsp thyme	5 ml thyme
1 bay leaf	1 bay leaf
6 sprigs celery	6 sprigs celery
4 to 6 tbsp dry white wine	60 to 90 ml dry white wine
1/2 lemon, peeled	1/2 lemon, peeled
10 peppercorns	10 peppercorns
2 tbsp butter	30 ml butter
6 cups water	1-1/2 liters water

Melt the butter in a large pot, without browning it. Add the fish bones and trimmings, and the rest of the ingredients, except the white wine and the water. Cover and sauté until the water has been drawn out of the vegetables. Be careful not to brown the fish trimmings and bones.

Add the white wine and the water. Simmer for about 40 minutes over very low heat. Do not stir during cooking. Pass through a fine sieve or through two layers of moistened cheesecloth. Let stand, then place in the refrigerator. Remove any droplets of grease before using.

Use as liquid for poaching fish, in creamy fish sauces, as a base for fish sauces, Chinese soup or seafood chowders.

Lobster Bisque

Standard	Metric
2 lb lobster shells, broken up	1 kg lobster shells, broken up
1 carrot, finely chopped	1 carrot, finely chopped
2 onions, finely chopped	2 onions, finely chopped
3 stalks celery, finely chopped	3 stalks celery, finely chopped
6 cloves garlic, skinned	6 cloves garlic, skinned
3 tomatoes, cut into pieces	3 tomatoes, cut into pieces
5 tbsp butter	75 ml butter
3 tbsp tomato paste	45 ml tomato paste
3 tbsp flour	45 ml flour
7 sprigs parsley	7 sprigs parsley
1 tsp thyme	5 ml thyme
1 bay leaf	1 bay leaf
2 tbsp ground peppercorns	30 ml ground peppercorns
1/4 cup dry white wine	50 ml dry white wine
1 tsp cayenne pepper	5 ml cayenne pepper
1 tsp paprika	5 ml paprika
2 tbsp cognac	30 ml cognac
1 cup heavy cream (35%)	250 ml heavy cream (35%)
12 cups fish fumet or water	3 liters fish fumet or water

Melt the butter in a large pot and sauté the lobster shells with all the vegetables. Add pepper. When everything has been browned, add the tomato paste and mix well. Add the flour and cook for 2 minutes, stirring constantly. Add the white wine and the cognac, stir and flambé.

Then add the fish fumet or water, the paprika, cayenne pepper, bay leaf and thyme. Season. Simmer for 2 to 3 hours, frequently skimming the surface of the stock. Add some water from time to time. At the end of the cooking period, strain through a sieve and reserve.

If the stock is too thin, return to the heat and cook to the desired consistency. Just before using, add the cream and boil for 2 to 3 minutes. Correct seasoning and serve.

Note: should be amply seasoned.

Serve in fish sauces, shrimp soups, creamy dishes to accompany fish. Freezes well.

Vegetable Stock

Standard	Metric
2 onions, chopped	2 onions, chopped
2 stalks of celery, finely chopped	2 stalks of celery, finely chopped
2 carrots, finely chopped	2 carrots, finely chopped
1 bay leaf	1 bay leaf
7 sprigs of parsley	7 sprigs of parsley
1 tsp thyme	5 ml thyme
10 peppercorns	10 peppercorns
2 tbsp butter	30 ml butter
1 tsp salt	5 ml salt
10 cups water	2-1/2 liters water

Melt the butter in a pot and add all remaining ingredients except salt and water. Cover and cook for 10 to 15 minutes, over low heat. Stir from time to time. Add water and salt and continue cooking for 45 minutes to 1 hour. Pass through a fine sieve or through 2 layers of moistened cheesecloth.

Use as a base for creamed vegetables and vegetable soups.

Tomato Coulis

Standard	Metric
6 large, very ripe tomatoes	6 large, very ripe tomatoes
1 onion, finely chopped	1 onion, finely chopped
3 cloves garlic, chopped	3 cloves garlic, chopped
4 tbsp parsley, chopped	60 ml parsley, chopped
3 tbsp tomato paste	45 ml tomato paste
1 cup tomato juice	250 ml tomato juice
1 tsp oregano	5 ml oregano
1 tsp thyme	5 ml thyme
1 tbsp basil	15 ml basil
2 tbsp sugar	30 ml sugar
1 tsp Tabasco	5 ml Tabasco
2 to 3 tbsp olive oil	30 to 45 ml olive oil
Salt and pepper	Salt and pepper

Place the tomatoes in boiling water for 2 minutes. Run under cold water and peel. Cut in half and remove seeds. Cut tomatoes into small pieces.

Gently heat the olive oil in a pot and add the onions and tomatoes. Cook slowly until the water has been drawn out of the vegetables. Do not brown. Add garlic and mix well for 30 seconds. Then add the tomato paste, tomato juice and all remaining ingredients. Cook over very low heat for 30 minutes. Cool and put through the food processor.

If the coulis is too thin, simmer until you obtain the desired consistency.

Use with pastas. Also use in vinaigrettes, as a light sauce for poached fish, and in various sauces and soups. Helps enliven the taste and color of many dishes. Keeps for several days, refrigerated.

Roux and Binders

Beurre Manié

Standard
5 tbsp butter
5 tbsp all-purpose flour

Metric
75 ml butter
75 ml all-purpose flour

In a small bowl, cream the butter until soft. Add the flour and knead it in with your hands. The resulting paste is used in small quantities to thicken cooked sauces or dishes.

For example, if a sauce is too thin, bring it to a boil and add a large pinch of beurre manié. Use a whisk to combine. If the sauce still seems too thin, wait at least 1 minute before adding more beurre manié.

Toasted Flour

Standard
1 cup all-purpose flour

Metric
250 ml all-purpose flour

Spread the flour on a baking pan or cookie sheet and bake in a 350°F (180°C) oven, stirring from time to time, until flour is browned.

To thicken a liquid, put the flour in a fine sieve and shake some on top of the boiling liquid. Blend in with a whisk.

You can also combine the toasted flour with cold water or stock, then stir it into the boiling liquid.

White Roux

Standard
5 tbsp all-purpose flour
6 tbsp butter

Metric
75 ml all-purpose flour
90 ml butter

Melt the butter gently in a small heavy saucepan without allowing it to foam. Add the flour gradually, stirring it in with a wooden spoon.

The texture should be completely smooth.

Cook for about 5 minutes over medium heat, stirring frequently and gently so the flour does not brown. Let cool and reserve.

This makes enough roux to thicken 4 cups (1 liter) of liquid. Add it to consommé, poultry stock, fish stock, vegetable stock etc.

Brown Roux

Standard
5 tbsp all-purpose flour
7 tbsp vegetable oil

Metric
75 ml all-purpose flour
105 ml vegetable oil

Brown roux is used to thicken brown sauces. Follow the same procedure as for white roux, but continue cooking, stirring from time to time, until the roux is brown. Be careful not to let the roux stick to the pan or it will develop a burned flavor.

Brown roux can also be prepared in a 325°F (160°C) oven, but must be watched carefully and stirred as often as on the stovetop.

Brown roux should be uniform in color with a smooth, fairly thick consistency.

Using Roux

Both brown and white roux should be used cold.

Pour the boiling liquid over the cold roux and stir with a whisk until smooth and thickened. If the sauce is still too thin, stir in a little beurre manié.

WHITE SAUCES

CLARIFIED BUTTER

Standard	Metric
1/2 lb butter	250 g butter

To make successful Hollandaise or Béarnaise sauces, it is best to use clarified butter.

Melt the butter over very gentle heat in a small saucepan. Let stand, and spoon off the white foam on the surface.

Pour the melted butter through a double layer of cheesecloth, being careful not to include the sediment at the bottom of the pot. The filtered butter should be completely clear.

Clarified butter is less likely to burn than regular butter, and can be used for sautéing, frying and other cooking purposes.

BÉCHAMEL SAUCE

Standard	Metric
4 cups milk	1 liter milk
3/4 cup white roux	150 ml white roux
1/2 onion, stuck with 1 clove	1/2 onion, stuck with 1 clove
2 tsp salt	10 ml salt
1 tsp white pepper	5 ml white pepper
1/2 tsp grated nutmeg	2 ml grated nutmeg

In a saucepan, prepare the roux, cooking it for the normal 5 minutes. Let cool. Bring the milk to a boil and pour it gradually over the roux, stirring with a whisk. Add the onion, salt and spices. Let simmer for 15 to 20 minutes. Remove from heat and discard the onion.

Spread a bit of butter over the top of the béchamel to prevent the formation of a crust.

The sauce can be thinned to the necessary consistency for whatever dish you are preparing with the addition of a little more milk.

For a richer version, stir in heavy cream.

VELOUTÉ OF CONSOMMÉ

Standard	Metric
4 cups clarified veal consommé	1 liter clarified veal consommé
1/2 cup white roux	125 ml white roux
3/4 cup heavy cream (35%)	150 ml heavy cream (35%)

Follow the same procedure as for béchamel sauce, but add a little more cream. Veal velouté should be a little lighter than other veloutés.

If sufficiently reduced, this recipe can also be used as a sauce base.

Variation: Add sautéed mushrooms and cooked asparagus tips to make a delicious soup.

VELOUTÉ OF CHICKEN

Standard	Metric
4 cups chicken stock	1 liter chicken stock
3/4 cup white roux	150 ml white roux
1/2 cup heavy cream (35%)	125 ml heavy cream (35%)

Make the roux in a large saucepan and let cool. Bring the 4 cups (1 liter) of chicken stock to a boil, and pour gradually over the roux, stirring in with a whisk. Simmer gently for about 10 minutes, stirring from time to time. Add the cream and mix with a whisk.

Let boil for 1 minute, then remove from heat. Pour the sauce through a fine sieve. Season to taste.

This serves as a basic sauce in many sauces to be served with poultry.

VELOUTÉ OF FISH

Standard	Metric
4 cups fish fumet (stock)	1 liter fish fumet (stock)
3/4 cup white sauce	150 ml white sauce
1/2 cup heavy cream (35%)	125 ml heavy cream (35%)

Follow the same procedure as for Chicken Velouté. This is an excellent basic sauce for all poached or steamed fish.

Note: If the sauce is not to be used immediately, wait until serving time to stir in the cream.

Egg Yolk and Butter Sauces

Hollandaise Sauce

Standard	Metric
4 egg yolks	4 egg yolks
1 cup clarified butter	250 ml clarified butter
1 tsp salt	5 ml salt
1 tsp cayenne pepper	5 ml cayenne pepper
Juice of 1/4 lemon	Juice of 1/4 lemon
2 to 3 tbsp water	30 to 45 ml water

Put the egg yolks in a metal bowl. Sit the bowl over a saucepan filled with cold water. Heat the water, beating the eggs constantly with a wire whisk. The water in the pan should not boil, and the bowl should stay cool enough to hold with your hand.

Continue beating the yolks constantly until they thicken. The yolks have thickened enough when you begin to see the bottom of the bowl between strokes and the mixture forms a light cream on the wires of the whisk.

Immediately remove the bowl from over the water and gradually incorporate the cool, clarified butter with the whisk. The resulting mixture should be very smooth and light.

Pass the sauce through a fine sieve and stir in the seasonings and lemon juice. Thin if desired with cold water. Keep in a warm place. If the finished sauce starts to separate, beat in 1 tbsp (15ml) or so of cold water.

This sauce can be served with poached salmon or other poached fish, as well as with steamed vegetables including asparagus and broccoli. It can also be used as a glaze; brush it over cooked fish and put under the broiler for a minute or two, watching carefully to avoid burning.

Note: This sauce should never be boiled.

Makes approximately 1-1/4 cups (300 ml).

Béarnaise Sauce

Standard	Metric
5 egg yolks	5 egg yolks
1-1/2 cups clarified butter	375 ml clarified butter
5 tbsp wine vinegar	75 ml wine vinegar
4 chopped shallots	4 chopped shallots
1 tsp crushed peppercorns	5 ml crushed peppercorns
2 tsp chopped parsley	10 ml chopped parsley
1 tsp chopped tarragon	5 ml chopped tarragon
1 tsp chopped chives	5 ml chopped chives
1 tsp salt	5 ml salt
1/2 tsp cayenne pepper	2 ml cayenne pepper
Juice of 1/4 lemon	Juice of 1/4 lemon

Prepare the clarified butter and keep it in a relatively cool place. In a saucepan, combine the wine vinegar, chopped shallots, pepper, tarragon, parsley and chives. Cook over high heat until liquid is reduced by half. Let cook before adding the egg yolks.

Cook the yolks following the same procedure as for Hollandaise sauce, and add the clarified butter, stirring with a whisk to combine. Pour through a fine sieve and stir in the salt, cayenne pepper and lemon juice.

Keep this sauce covered and chilled.

Serve with grilled meats or fish.

Makes approximately 1 cup (250 ml).

Variation: Stir in warmed tomato sauce to make a tomato-flavored Béarnaise (Sauce Choron).

Mousseline Sauce

Standard	Metric
1 cup Hollandaise	250 ml Hollandaise
1/4 cup heavy cream (35%)	50 ml heavy cream (35%)
1/4 tsp salt	1 ml salt

Prepare the Hollandaise. Whip the heavy cream with the salt in a small cold bowl. Just before serving, gently stir the whipped cream into the Hollandaise with a rubber spatula.

Serve with poached fish or fresh cooked asparagus tips.

Makes approximately 1-1/4 cups (300 ml).

Maltaise Sauce

Standard	Metric
1 cup Hollandaise	250 ml Hollandaise
Juice of 1 orange	Juice of 1 orange
Zest of 1 orange, blanched	Zest of 1 orange, blanched
1 tsp sugar	5 ml sugar
Juice of 1/6 lemon	Juice of 1/6 lemon

Blanch the grated orange zest in boiling water for 2 minutes. Let cool.

Make the Hollandaise sauce and at the end, stir in the lemon and orange juice, sugar and orange zest.

Serve with poached or boiled fish. This is particularly good with salmon and boiled green or white asparagus.

Makes approximately 1-1/4 cups (300 ml).

SAUCES

CURRY SAUCE

Standard	Metric
4 cups chicken stock	1 liter chicken stock
3 tbsp butter	45 ml butter
3 tbsp all-purpose flour	45 ml all-purpose flour
1 chopped onion	1 chopped onion
1 stalk celery, chopped	1 stalk celery, chopped
1 small carrot, chopped	1 small carrot, chopped
1 peeled apple, chopped	1 peeled apple, chopped
1/2 cup diced pineapple	125 ml diced pineapple
1 peeled pear, chopped	1 peeled pear, chopped
1/2 cup coconut	125 ml coconut
1 tbsp curry powder	15 ml curry powder
1 tbsp paprika	15 ml paprika
1 tsp cayenne pepper	5 ml cayenne pepper
1 tsp ground ginger	5 ml ground ginger
1/2 tsp ground nutmeg	2 ml ground nutmeg
Salt and pepper	Salt and pepper

Melt the butter in a large saucepan and sauté the onion, celery, carrot, apple, pear, and pineapple until slightly browned. Sprinkle on the flour and stir for 1 minute.

Add the stock and stir with a wooden spoon until the mixture starts to boil. Add the curry, paprika, cayenne, ginger, nutmeg, salt and pepper. Continue to cook over low heat for about 30 minutes, scraping the bottom of the pan from time to time to prevent the sauce from sticking.

Pass the sauce through a sieve, if a smooth sauce is desired. Add a bit of cream to make a richer sauce.

Serve with fish, seafood, chicken or eggs.

ESCARGOT SAUCE

Standard	Metric
1 cup velouté of chicken or fish	250 ml velouté of chicken or fish
12 chopped escargots	12 chopped escargots
2 tbsp butter	30 ml butter
1/4 cup tomato coulis	50 ml tomato coulis
3 tbsp Port	45 ml Port
1/4 cup heavy cream (35%)	50 ml heavy cream (35%)
1 tbsp chopped dried shallots	15 ml chopped dried shallots
1 chopped clove garlic	1 chopped clove garlic
1 tbsp chopped parsley	15 ml chopped parsley
1 tsp cayenne pepper (or to taste)	5 ml cayenne pepper (or to taste)
Salt and pepper	Salt and pepper

Melt the butter in a saucepan and stir the chopped escargots in it for a few minutes over medium heat. Add the shallots and continue cooking about 30 seconds. Stir in the chopped garlic. Pour on the Port and flambé.

Add the velouté, tomato coulis, cayenne, salt and pepper. Let simmer until thickened to the desired consistency. Add the cream and cook for another few minutes. Season.

Serve with salmon or chicken.

MUSHROOM SAUCE

Standard	Metric
2 cups basic brown sauce (veal)	500 ml basic brown sauce (veal)
2 cups mushrooms, finely sliced	500 ml mushrooms, finely sliced
2 tbsp butter	30 ml butter
4 tsp all-purpose flour	20 ml all-purpose flour
1/2 cup dry white wine	125 ml dry white wine
1 cup heavy cream (35%)	250 ml heavy cream (35%)
Salt and pepper	Salt and pepper

Melt the butter in a saucepan and add the sliced mushrooms. Cook until the mushrooms have given up all their liquid and are lightly browned. Add the flour and stir for 1 minute.

Pour in the white wine and continue cooking for 2 minutes. Stir in the brown sauce and cook until thickened to the desired consistency. Add the cream and cook for a few more minutes. Season to taste.

This sauce can be served with many types of dishes.

ORANGE AND PORT SAUCE

Standard	Metric
1 cup thickened brown sauce	250 ml thickened brown sauce
1/2 cup Port	125 ml Port
Juice of 2 oranges	Juice of 2 oranges
Juice of 1/2 lemon	Juice of 1/2 lemon
2 tbsp sugar	30 ml sugar

In a small, heavy saucepan, combine the Port, lemon and orange juices and sugar. Bring to a boil and cook until the mixture resembles light syrup. Add the brown sauce and boil until the desired consistency.

Serve with white meats such as chicken, pork, veal or turkey. Garnish with orange slices just before serving.

HAM SAUCE

Standard	Metric
2 cups velouté of consommé	500 ml velouté of consommé
1/4 lb diced cooked ham	125 g diced cooked ham
1/4 lb smoked pork shoulder, cut in strips	125 g smoked pork shoulder, cut in strips
2 tbsp chopped shallots	30 ml chopped shallots
3 tbsp chopped parsley	45 ml chopped parsley
1 tbsp butter	15 ml butter
Salt and pepper	Salt and pepper

Melt the butter in a saucepan and sauté the ham and pork until golden brown. Degrease and add the chopped shallots. Stir for 30 seconds. Add the velouté of consommé. Simmer for a few minutes.

Add the parsley, salt and pepper.

Serve as a sauce with roast veal, breast of chicken, or ham steak.

PEPPER COULIS SAUCE

Standard	Metric
2 cups velouté of chicken or fish	500 ml velouté of chicken or fish
2 red or green bell peppers	2 red or green bell peppers
Pinch thyme	Pinch thyme
1 chopped garlic clove	1 chopped garlic clove
2 tbsp olive oil or butter	30 ml olive oil or butter
1 tsp Tabasco sauce	5 ml Tabasco sauce
Salt and pepper	Salt and pepper

Cut the peppers in half and remove the seeds. Chop them coarsely and place in the food processor with the thyme, garlic and olive oil. Process until very smooth.

Put the pepper mixture in a saucepan and cook gently until the water from the peppers has evaporated.

Meanwhile, bring the velouté of chicken or fish to a boil. Stir in the puréed pepper with a wire whisk.

Serve with chicken, seafood or fish.

PISTOU SAUCE

Standard	Metric
1 cup tomato coulis	250 ml tomato coulis
5 tbsp fresh chopped basil	75 ml fresh chopped basil
3 tbsp chopped garlic	45 ml chopped garlic
3 to 5 tbsp olive oil	45 to 75 ml olive oil
Salt and pepper	Salt and pepper

Chop the basil and garlic in the food processor and add in the olive oil. Put the mixture in a saucepan and cook for 1 minute. Remove from heat.

Meanwhile, bring the tomato coulis to a boil. Gently whisk it into the basil mixture.

Serve with pasta, fish or seafood.

Variation: Stir a little pistou sauce into vinaigrette or blend it into a vegetable soup for a fresh Mediterranean flavor.

SHALLOT SAUCE

Standard	Metric
2 cups thick brown sauce	500 ml thick brown sauce
1 cup chopped dried shallots	250 ml chopped dried shallots
2 tbsp butter	30 ml butter
Pinch thyme	Pinch thyme
1 cup dry white wine	250 ml dry white wine
2 tbsp chopped parsley	30 ml chopped parsley
Salt and pepper	Salt and pepper

Melt the butter in a saucepan and add the shallots and thyme. Cook over gentle heat until the shallots are slightly browned.

Pour in the white wine and continue cooking until the wine has nearly evaporated. Stir in the brown sauce and cook for another 2 minutes. Add the parsley, salt and pepper.

Serve with grilled beef or fish.

CREAMY SHALLOT SAUCE

Follow the same procedure as for shallot sauce, but double the quantity of shallots and process the cooked sauce in the food processor until smooth.

Baby Onion and Tomato Sauce

Standard	Metric
2 cups velouté of fish	500 ml velouté of fish
20 baby onions	20 baby onions
2 tbsp butter	30 ml butter
1 large firm tomato	1 large firm tomato
2 tbsp chopped parsley	30 ml chopped parsley
Salt and pepper	Salt and pepper

Cut the skin off the tomato about 1/8 inch (3 mm) thick. Cut the skin into small dice and set aside. Reserve the rest of the tomato for other uses.

Melt the butter in a saucepan and sauté the onions and tomato dice for about 5 minutes, without letting them brown. Add the velouté and boil about 2 minutes. Add the parsley, salt and pepper.

Serve with poached or steamed white fish.

Bacon and Tomato Sauce

Standard	Metric
1/2 lb bacon, cooked crisp and crumbled	250 g bacon, cooked crisp and crumbled
1 large onion, chopped	1 large onion, chopped
1-1/2 cups tomato coulis (page 370)	375 ml tomato coulis (page 370)
1 tsp sugar	5 ml sugar
2 tsp vinegar	10 ml vinegar
1/2 tsp basil	2 ml basil
1/4 tsp ground cloves	1 ml ground cloves
1/4 tsp monosodium glutamate	1 ml monosodium glutamate
Salt and pepper	Salt and pepper

Sauté the onion in a skillet with a bit of bacon fat. Add the rest of the ingredients and simmer for about 5 minutes.

Serve with veal or sausages.

Barbecue Sauce

Standard	Metric
1 onion, sliced thin	1 onion, sliced thin
2 tbsp butter or vegetable oil	30 ml butter or vegetable oil
2 tbsp vinegar	30 ml vinegar
2 tbsp brown sugar	30 ml brown sugar
1/4 cup lemon juice	50 ml lemon juice
1 cup catsup	250 ml catsup
3 tbsp Worcestershire sauce	45 ml Worcestershire sauce
1 tbsp prepared mustard	15 ml prepared mustard
1 cup water	250 ml water
1/2 cup fresh parsley, chopped	125 ml fresh parsley, chopped
1 tsp salt	5 ml salt
1 tsp paprika	5 ml paprika

Sauté the onion in the butter until tender. Add the rest of the ingredients and simmer for about 30 minutes.

Serve with spare ribs or chicken wings, or use as a basting sauce for grilled or barbecued meats.

Danish Sauce

Standard	Metric
2 cups velouté of fish (page 372)	500 ml velouté of fish (page 372)
1/2 cup chopped smoked salmon	125 ml chopped smoked salmon

Boil the velouté very gently. Put the salmon in the food processor and process until it forms a light mousse-like consistency. Pour a little of the hot velouté in with the salmon and process briefly. Use a wire whisk to stir the thinned salmon mousse into the velouté.

This is delicious with poached salmon or salmon trout.

Duxelles Sauce

Standard	Metric
2 cups velouté of chicken or fish, or consommé	500 ml velouté of chicken or fish, or consommé
3/4 lb chopped mushrooms	350 g chopped mushrooms
2 tbsp butter	30 ml butter
1 tbsp chopped shallots	15 ml chopped shallots
2 tbsp dry white wine	30 ml dry white wine
2 tbsp chopped parsley	30 ml chopped parsley
Pinch thyme	Pinch thyme
1/2 cup heavy cream (35%)	125 ml heavy cream (35%)
Salt and pepper	Salt and pepper

Bring the stock of your choice to a boil. Meanwhile, prepare the mushroom duxelles.

Melt the butter in a heavy saucepan and sauté the shallots and mushrooms until their liquid has evaporated. Add the thyme and white wine. Cook, stirring, until the wine has evaporated (the mushrooms should not brown). Add the parsley and cream and boil until the mixture is thick. Stir mushroom mixture into the velouté.

Can be served with almost any meat or fish dish.

Gazpacho Sauce

Standard	Metric
1 cup gazpacho (see Spanish Cuisine)	250 ml gazpacho (see Spanish Cuisine)
2 cups velouté of chicken or fish	500 ml velouté of chicken or fish

Follow the procedure for RatatouilleSauce.

This is delicious with baked chicken breast and with hot fish, lobster, or scallops.

Béarnaise Sauce

Standard	Metric
5 egg yolks	5 egg yolks
1-1/2 cups clarified butter	375 ml clarified butter
5 tbsp wine vinegar	75 ml wine vinegar
4 chopped shallots	4 chopped shallots
1 tsp crushed peppercorns	5 ml crushed peppercorns
2 tsp chopped parsley	10 ml chopped parsley
1 tsp chopped tarragon	5 ml chopped tarragon
1 tsp chopped chives	5 ml chopped chives
1 tsp salt	5 ml salt
1/2 tsp cayenne pepper	2 ml cayenne pepper
Juice of 1/4 lemon	Juice of 1/4 lemon

Prepare the clarified butter and keep it in a relatively cool place. In a saucepan, combine the wine vinegar, chopped shallots, peppercorns, tarragon, parsley and chives. Cook over high heat until liquid is reduced by half. Let cook before adding the egg yolks.

Cook the yolks following the same procedure as for Hollandaise sauce, and add the clarified butter, stirring with a whisk to combine. Pour through a fine sieve and stir in the salt, cayenne pepper and lemon juice.

Keep this sauce covered and chilled.

Serve with grilled meats or fish.

Makes approximately 1 cup (250 ml).

Variation: Stir in warmed tomato sauce to make a tomato-flavored Béarnaise (Sauce Choron).

Lobster Sauce

Standard	Metric
1-1/2 cups lobster bisque	375 ml lobster bisque
1/2 cup diced lobster meat	125 ml diced lobster meat
2 tbsp butter	30 ml butter
1 tbsp chopped shallots	15 ml chopped shallots
1 garlic clove, chopped	1 garlic clove, chopped
2 tbsp cognac	30 ml cognac
1/4 cup heavy cream (35%)	50 ml heavy cream (35%)
Salt and pepper	Salt and pepper

Melt the butter in a small saucepan and sauté the lobster pieces. Add the shallots and chopped garlic, and stir. Pour on the cognac and flambé. Add the lobster bisque and the cream. Heat until the desired consistency.

Serve with various fish, shellfish, chicken and veal.

Mornay Sauce

Standard	Metric
2 cups béchamel sauce	500 ml béchamel sauce
3 egg yolks	3 egg yolks cheese
1/2 cup grated Gruyère cheese	125 ml grated Gruyère cheese

Make the béchamel sauce. Add the egg yolks and stir briskly with a wooden spoon over medium heat for about 1 minute. Remove from heat and stir in the grated cheese.

Mustard Sauce

Standard	Metric
1 cup velouté of chicken	250 ml velouté of chicken
2 tbsp Dijon mustard	30 ml Dijon mustard
3 tbsp chopped shallots	45 ml chopped shallots
2 tbsp butter	30 ml butter
1/3 cup dry white wine	75 ml dry white wine
1/2 cup heavy cream (35%)	125 ml heavy cream (35%)
Pinch thyme	Pinch thyme
Salt and pepper	Salt and pepper

Melt the butter in a saucepan and add the shallots. Sauté until the liquid has evaporated. Add the mustard, mix well, and stir in the wine. Cook, stirring, over high heat until the liquid has reduced by two thirds.

Add the thyme and the velouté of chicken and the cream and cook until the sauce is the desired consistency. Season and serve with pork, veal, steaks, kidneys or chicken.

Note: It is important to stir the mustard into the white wine before adding the cream, or the final sauce will not be smooth.

Ratatouille Sauce

Standard	Metric
1/4 lb cold ratatouille (see page 96)	125 g cold ratatouille (see page 96)
2 tbsp olive oil or butter	30 ml olive oil or butter
2 cups velouté of chicken or fish	500 ml velouté of chicken or fish
Salt and pepper	Salt and pepper

Put the ratatouille into the food processor and process until it becomes a smooth mousse. Put the mixture into a saucepan with the olive oil or butter and cook until combined.

Bring the velouté to a boil and stir it into the ratatouille mousse.

Serve with chicken or white fish.

FLAVORED BUTTERS

GARLIC BUTTER

Standard	Metric
1/2 lb butter	250 g butter
6 to 8 cloves garlic, chopped	6 to 8 cloves garlic, chopped
2 tbsp parsley	30 ml parsley
Juice of 1/4 lemon	Juice of 1/4 lemon
Pinch of salt	Pinch of salt
Pinch of ground pepper	Pinch of ground pepper

Cream the butter and place in food processor. Add the rest of the ingredients. Roll in a sheet of foil wrap and refrigerate.

Cut into small round slices and place on broiled meats, especially beef.

Use to butter canapés topped with snails and placed in the oven for a few moments. Use to butter small croutons or to enliven sauces for shrimp, lobster or broiled trout.

MUSTARD BUTTER

Standard	Metric
1/2 lb butter	250 g butter
2 tbsp Dijon mustard	30 ml Dijon mustard
2 tbsp chopped shallots	30 ml chopped shallots
Pinch of thyme	Pinch of thyme
1 clove garlic, chopped	1 clove garlic, chopped
2 tbsp parsley, chopped	30 ml parsley, chopped
1 tsp curry powder	5 ml curry powder

Cream the butter and place in the food processor. Add the rest of the ingredients. Roll in a sheet of foil wrap and refrigerate.

Melt on broiled steaks and sausages cooked on the barbecue.

ALMOND BUTTER

Standard	Metric
1/2 lb butter	250 g butter
1/4 lb almonds, ground	125 g almonds, ground
2 pinches of salt	2 pinches of salt

Place softened butter in the food processor with the ground almonds and salt. Goes well with "papillote" or fried trout.

FINE HERBES BUTTER

Standard	Metric
1/2 lb butter	250 g butter
1 tbsp parsley, chopped	15 ml parsley, chopped
1 tsp thyme	5 ml thyme
1 tsp tarragon	5 ml tarragon
1 tsp basil	5 ml basil
1 tsp beef concentrate	5 ml beef concentrate
Juice of 1/2 lemon	Juice of 1/2 lemon
2 pinches of salt	2 pinches of salt
Pinch of pepper	Pinch of pepper
1 tsp Tabasco (to taste)	5 ml Tabasco (to taste)

Cream the butter and place in a food processor. Add the rest of the ingredients. Roll the butter in a sheet of foil wrap. Refrigerate. May be kept frozen for 2 to 3 months.

Cut into small rounds and serve with fish or kidneys or add to sauces served with fish.

ANCHOVY BUTTER

Standard	Metric
1/2 lb unsalted butter	250 g unsalted butter
1/4 lb anchovy fillets	125 g anchovy fillets
Juice of 1/4 lemon	Juice of 1/4 lemon
A few drops of Tabasco	A few drops of Tabasco
3 to 4 black olives, pitted	3 to 4 black olives, pitted
1 tbsp parsley	15 ml parsley
Salt and pepper	Salt and pepper

Cream the butter and place in the food processor. Add the rest of the ingredients.

Blend to obtain a smooth paste. Roll the butter in a sheet of foil wrap and refrigerate.

Use to butter canapés and broiled, poached or fried fish.

SHALLOT BUTTER

Standard	Metric
1/2 lb butter	250 g butter
5 tbsp dried shallots, chopped	75 ml dried shallots, chopped
1 tbsp Dijon mustard	15 ml Dijon mustard
Juice of 1/4 lemon	Juice of 1/4 lemon
1 tbsp chopped parsley	15 ml chopped parsley
Pinch of thyme	Pinch of thyme
Salt and pepper	Salt and pepper

Cream the butter and place in the food processor. Add the rest of the ingredients. Roll the butter in foil wrap and refrigerate.

Slice into rounds and place on a half broiled lobster, or on very hot broiled steak.

SHRIMP BUTTER

Standard	Metric
1/2 lb butter	250 g butter
1/2 lb shelled and deveined shrimp	250 g shelled and deveined shrimp
1 tsp tomato paste	5 ml tomato paste
1 clove garlic, chopped	1 clove garlic, chopped
1 tsp salt	5 ml salt
2 tbsp shallots, chopped	30 ml shallots, chopped
1 tsp pepper	5 ml pepper
1 tsp cayenne pepper	5 ml cayenne pepper
Juice of 1/4 lemon	Juice of 1/4 lemon

Cream the butter and place in the food processor. Place the shrimp in a clean towel and squeeze to remove water. Add the shrimp and the remaining ingredients to the butter. Blend well and roll in foil wrap. Refrigerate.

Use to butter shrimp canapés, to enliven sauces, and pep up fried, boiled or poached fish.

LOBSTER BUTTER

Standard	Metric
3/4 lb lobster shells	350 g lobster shells
1/2 lb butter	250 g butter
4 cups water	1 liter water

Grind the lobster shells as fine as possible. Place in a heavy pot. Add butter and water. Bring to a boil and cook for 10 minutes over medium heat. Continue cooking in the oven at 350 °F (180°C) for 15 to 20 minutes until the water is almost completely evaporated. Remove from the oven and strain the liquid through a double layer of cheesecloth. Collect the water in a plastic container and place in the freezer for several hours. (The freezing process separates the butter from the water.) Drain and refrigerate.

Use to enliven a smooth fish sauce or lobster bisque. May be kept frozen for 2 to 3 months.

NUT BUTTER

Standard	Metric
1/2 lb butter	250 g butter
4 tbsp nuts, finely chopped	60 ml nuts, finely chopped
Salt and pepper	Salt and pepper

Cream the butter. Place in a food processor and add the rest of the ingredients.

Serve on broiled beef or chicken.

SMOKED SALMON BUTTER

Standard	Metric
1/2 lb butter	250 g butter
1/4 lb smoked salmon	125 g smoked salmon
1 tsp tomato paste	5 ml tomato paste
Juice of 1/4 lemon	Juice of 1/4 lemon
Salt and pepper	Salt and pepper

Cream the butter. Place in the food processor and add the rest of the ingredients. Blend well. Roll the butter in a sheet of foil wrap and refrigerate.

Use to butter canapés or to enliven sauces accompanying salmon or trout.

TOMATO BUTTER

Standard	Metric
1/2 lb butter	250 g butter
2 tbsp tomato paste	30 ml tomato paste
1 tbsp chopped parsley	15 ml chopped parsley
2 tbsp dried shallots, chopped	30 ml dried shallots, chopped
2 to 3 cloves garlic	2 to 3 cloves garlic
1/2 tsp thyme	2 ml thyme
1 tsp fresh or dried basil, chopped	5 ml fresh or dried basil, chopped
1 tsp sugar	5 ml sugar
Salt and pepper	Salt and pepper

Cream the butter. Place in a food processor and add the rest of the ingredients. Blend until you obtain a smooth butter, uniform in color.

To keep the butter, spread in a straight line on a sheet of foil wrap. Roll up and pinch both ends of the wrap to tightly pack the butter. Refrigerate.

May be cut in round slices and placed on broiled, poached or boiled fish. Use to butter canapés.

CANAPÉS AND DECORATIONS

CANAPÉS AND DECORATIONS

ANCHOVY CANAPÉS

Standard
24 small crackers or rusks
1/2 cup anchovy butter (see page 378)
2 hard-boiled eggs
24 anchovy filets cut in half lengthwise

Metric
24 small crackers or rusks
125 ml anchovy butter (see page 378)
2 hard-boiled eggs
24 anchovy filets cut in half lengthwise

Spread each cracker with a thin layer of anchovy butter and cover with chopped hard-boiled egg. Cross 2 anchovy pieces on top and decorate with a tiny parsley sprig.

ASPARAGUS CANAPÉS

Standard
12 small rusks or crackers
24 asparagus points
1/2 cup mayonnaise
1 red bell pepper
Salt and pepper

Metric
12 small rusks or crackers
24 asparagus points
125 ml mayonnaise
1 red bell pepper
Salt and pepper

Spread each cracker with mayonnaise and garnish each with 2 asparagus points. Top with 2 strips of red pepper, crossed. Sprinkle with salt and pepper.

AVOCADO AND EGG SANDWICHES

Standard
6 hard-boiled eggs, chopped
2 chopped avocados
2 pinches cayenne pepper
1 onion, minced fine
3 tbsp chopped fresh parsley
2 tbsp vinegar
1 tsp salt

Metric
6 hard-boiled eggs, chopped
2 chopped avocados
2 pinches cayenne pepper
1 onion, minced fine
45 ml chopped fresh parsley
30 ml vinegar
5 ml salt

Combine all ingredients until the consistency is fairly smooth. Refrigerate.

Meanwhile, cut fancy bread shapes with cookie cutters. Toast. Spread the avocado mixture on top. Decorate each with a piece of black olive and a parsley sprig

MUSHROOM PATÉ CANAPÉS

Standard
2 cups mushrooms, sliced thin
1 small onion, finely chopped
4 tbsp butter
2 slices bacon, chopped
1 cup chopped tomatoes
2 eggs, beaten
1 tsp salt
1 tsp cayenne pepper

Metric
500 ml mushrooms, sliced thin
1 small onion, finely chopped
60 ml butter
2 slices bacon, chopped
250 ml chopped tomatoes
2 eggs, beaten
5 ml salt
5 ml cayenne pepper

Melt the butter in a skillet and sauté the onion. Add the bacon, tomatoes and mushrooms. Simmer for about 15 minutes. Pass the mixture through the food processor until smooth, then return to the skillet and stir in the beaten eggs. Stir constantly until thickened. Chill in the refrigerator. Serve on toast points, and garnish with slices of fresh mushrooms and parsley.

ONION AND PARMESAN CANAPÉS

Standard
1/2 cup onions, sliced thin
1/2 cup mayonnaise
2 tbsp grated Parmesan cheese
24 crackers or small rusks

Metric
125 ml onions, sliced thin
125 ml mayonnaise
30 ml grated Parmesan cheese
24 crackers or small rusks

Combine the mayonnaise and grated Parmesan. Lay a slice of onion on each cracker, and cover generously with the mayonnaise mixture. Bake at 375°F (190°C) for about 10 minutes, or until the topping is golden and puffy. Be careful not to burn the canapés. Serve hot.

ONION MARMALADE CANAPÉS

Standard
1 lb sliced onions
1 cup sugar
1/4 cup vinegar
1/2 bottle red wine

Metric
500 g sliced onions
250 ml sugar
50 ml vinegar
1/2 bottle red wine

Slice the onions as thinly as possible, and cook them in a

saucepan with the other ingredients over very low heat. Cook until the onions are a deep red color and have the consistency of marmalade.

Serve with toast points.

ROQUEFORT CANAPÉS

Standard	Metric
24 small crackers or biscuits	24 small crackers or biscuits
1/2 cup Roquefort cheese	125 ml Roquefort cheese
1/2 cup butter	125 ml butter
Fresh parsley	Fresh parsley

Cream together the roquefort and butter in the food processor. Spread on the crackers and decorate with a fresh parsley sprig.

SALMON ROE CANAPÉS

Salmon roe
Crackers
Butter

Spread a thin layer of butter on each cracker. Top with salmon roe.

SHALLOT CANAPÉS

Standard	Metric
24 small crackers	24 small crackers
1/2 cup shallot butter	125 ml shallot butter
(see page 378)	(see page 378)
8 dry shallots, chopped	8 dry shallots, chopped
2 tbsp butter	30 ml butter
2 tbsp chopped fresh parsley	30 ml chopped fresh parsley

Cream the shallot butter and spread it on the crackers. Chop the shallots. Brown them in butter, then drain. Let cool and sprinkle on the crackers with chopped parsley.

SHRIMP CANAPÉS

Standard	Metric
2-1/2 cups shrimp, shelled and chopped fine (reserve the shells and heads)	750 ml shrimp, shelled and chopped fine (reserve the shells and heads)
3 tbsp butter	45 ml butter
1/2 tsp all-purpose flour	2 ml all-purpose flour
2 beaten egg yolks	2 beaten egg yolks
Lemon juice	Lemon juice
Cayenne pepper	Cayenne pepper
3 tbsp water	45 ml water

Cook the shrimp shells and heads in the water for 30 minutes, covered. Filter the cooking liquid through a double layer of cheesecloth and reserve.

Melt the butter in a saucepan and stir in the flour and cayenne. Add the reserved shrimp liquid to make a roux.

Bring the roux to a boil, stir in the chopped shrimp, and heat again to boiling point. Stir in lemon juice to taste. Remove from heat and stir in the beaten egg yolks to bind the sauce. Spread on toast points. Garnish with small whole shrimp and serve hot.

SMOKED SALMON CANAPÉS

Standard	Metric
36 small rusks or crackers	36 small rusks or crackers
1 cup smoked salmon	250 ml smoked salmon
1/4 cup plain yogurt	50 ml plain yogurt
2 dry shallots, minced	2 dry shallots, minced
2 tbsp chives, chopped fine	30 ml chives, chopped fine
2 tbsp lemon juice	30 ml lemon juice
Salt and pepper	Salt and pepper

In the food processor, mix the salmon, lemon juice, salt, pepper, yogurt and shallots until smooth. Transfer to a small bowl and stir in the chopped chives. Put the mixture in a pastry bag with a fluted tip and pipe onto the crackers.

Decorate with small pickles cut fan-shaped (see page 387) or 3 sprigs of chive.

WATERCRESS CANAPÉS

Standard	Metric
1/2 cup butter	125 ml butter
1 bunch watercress	1 bunch watercress
2 tbsp lemon juice	30 ml lemon juice
2 hard-boiled eggs, sliced into thin rounds	2 hard-boiled eggs, sliced into thin rounds
Salt and pepper	Salt and pepper

Blanch the watercress in boiling salted water for 1 minute. Chill under cold running water and drain well. Place in the food processor with the softened butter, salt, pepper and lemon juice. Work just until smooth.

Butter small crackers or bread pieces with the watercress spread and garnish with an egg slice. Decorate with chopped fresh watercress, if desired.

LEMON FLOWERS

1 Lay the lemon on its side.

2 Insert a paring knife on an angle in the lemon.

3 Insert the knife in the opposite direction next to the first cut.

4 Continue cutting until lemon can be separated in 2 halves.

FLUTED ORANGES AND LEMONS

1 Cut off both ends of the fruit.

2 Score the peel from top to bottom at equal distances.

3 Slice the fruit thin.

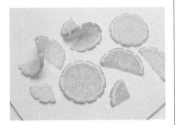

4 Trim and arrange as desired.

STUFFED KIWI

1 Peel the kiwi fruit.

2 Cut in half crosswise.

3 Use a melon scoop to gently scoop out the insides.

4 Fill the cavity with raspberry coulis and use to decorate a cheese cake, for example.

ORANGE BASKETS

1 With orange upright, make 2 vertical cuts 1/2 inch (1.25 cm) apart to about halfway down.

2 Make sawtooth cuts horizontally, leaving the handle intact.

3 Remove the cut pieces.

4 Trim out the center flesh and decorate with a cherry.

ORANGE BUTTERFLY

1 Cut the orange in half lengthwise.

2 Cut each half in thin segments.

3 Arrange 2 slices back to back.

4 Cut strips of peel for antennae and decorate with a cherry half.

OVEN-GLAZED APPLES

1 Cut apples in half lengthwise. Peel and core.

2 Slice into thin wedges, leaving them attached at one end.

3 Butter and sugar a baking dish. Bake the apples at 450°F (220°C) for 10 minutes.

4 Spread the apple segments.

ORANGE SUPREMES

1 Cut the ends off the orange.

2 Peel completely, removing all white pith.

3 Slide a knife blade down both sides of each membrane.

4 Gently pull out the orange segments.

CARAMELIZED GRAPES

1 Caramelize some sugar with water.

2 Cut grapes into small bunches.

3 Dip the grapes into the caramel to cover well.

4 Cool the bunches on a greased plate (do not refrigerate).

CHOCOLATE CURLS

1 Melt chocolate in a double boiler.

2 Spread on a cookie sheet and refrigerate until hard.

3 Scrape gently with a spatula to make large curls.

4 Scrape with a spoon to make small curls.

PAPER CUFFS

1 Fold a paper rectangle in half.

2 Cut through the folded side in thin strips, leaving other sides attached.

3 Roll and fasten with stapler or tape.

4 Spread the leaves for volume.

CREAM STAR

1 Pour cream in a thin stream in a large circle.

2 Make 2 smaller circles.

3 Cut through the circles towards the center.

4 Cut through the circles towards the edge.

ALMOND PASTE

1 Shape almond paste into small ball.

2 Roll into cigar shape.

3 Flatten and trim with knife into leaf shape.

4 Trace leaf pattern gently with a knife.

PASTRY GRAPES

1 Make 9 shortcrust pastry balls the same size.

2 Make leaves and trace vein pattern with knife.

3 Roll a stem.

4 Arrange in grape bunch pattern on top of pie or pastry.

SUGARED RIM

1 Cut lemon into wedges.

2 Slice across segment.

3 Rub lemon wedge over lip of glass.

4 Dip in sugar.

PÂTÉ DE FOIE PORCUPINES

1 Shape 4 tbsp (60 ml) pâté de foie into egg shape.

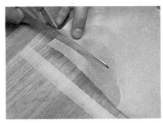

2 Use spatula dipped in hot water to smooth surface.

3 Toast sliced almonds in the oven.

4 Stick almonds in pâté to resemble porcupine. Use black olive pieces for eyes and nose.

ICING SUGAR CROSS

1 Cut 2 paper strips.

2 Arrange in cross shape on surface to be decorated.

3 Sift icing sugar on top.

4 Gently remove paper strips.

393

CANDIES AND COOKIES

Candies and Cookies

Festive Shortbread

Standard	Metric
1 cup butter	250 ml butter
1/4 cup sugar	50 ml sugar
2 cups all-purpose flour	500 ml all-purpose flour
1-1/2 cups coconut	375 ml coconut
2/3 cup red or green maraschino cherries, chopped	150 ml red or green maraschino cherries, chopped
1/4 cup raisins or currents	50 ml raisins or currents
1/3 cup walnuts, chopped	75 ml walnuts, chopped
1 can sweetened condensed milk	1 can sweetened condensed milk

Preheat oven to 350ºF (180ºC).

Cream the butter and sugar together. Add the flour and work until you have a dough that is still somewhat lumpy. Press the dough into a buttered 9 inch (22 cm) square baking pan. Bake for 20 minutes.

Combine the rest of the ingredients. Spread the mixture evenly over the cooked base. Place in the oven for 35 minutes or until the topping is golden in color. Cool completely and cut into 1/2 x 3 inch (1.25 x 7.5 cm) rectangles.

Sprinkle with sifted icing sugar.

Chocolate Balls

Standard	Metric
1 cup dates, finely chopped	250 ml dates, finely chopped
1 cup coconut	250 ml coconut
1 cup nuts, finely chopped	250 ml nuts, finely chopped
1 cup icing sugar	250 ml icing sugar
3/4 cup peanut butter	150 ml peanut butter
1 egg	1 egg
1/4 tsp vanilla	1 ml vanilla
1 package semi-sweet chocolate chips	1 package semi-sweet chocolate chips

Combine the dates, coconut and nuts with the icing sugar. Add the remaining ingredients. Mix well, using a mixer, if necessary.

Shape into small balls, or marble-sized balls. Melt the chocolate over low heat. Coat the balls in chocolate and place on wax paper.

Refrigerate for 3 hours.

Chocolate Cream Cookies, Chocolate Shortbread Cookies, Marshmallow Puffed Rice, Golden Cream Buttons, Sugar à la Crème Nicole, Chocolate Balls and Fudge.

Chocolate Cream Cookies

Standard	Metric
1 cup grated, semi-sweet chocolate	250 ml grated, semi-sweet chocolate
1/2 cup heavy cream (35%)	125 ml heavy cream (35%)
Cat's tongue pastry (see page 400)	Cat's tongue pastry (see page 400)

Grease a cookie sheet and arrange small disks of cat's tongue pastry, about 1-1/2 inch (3 cm) in diameter. Cook and set aside.

Bring the cream to a boil in a pot, then remove immediately from heat. Slowly mix in the grated chocolate, using a wooden spatula. Cool in the refrigerator. Shape into small balls. Place each one between two cat's tongue disks and press together with your thumb and index finger. Return to the refrigerator.

Chocolate Shortbread Cookies

Standard	Metric
2 cups pastry flour	500 ml pastry flour
1 cup sugar	250 ml sugar
1-1/4 cups unsalted, softened butter	350 ml unsalted, softened butter
3 eggs	3 eggs
3 egg yolks	3 egg yolks
1 tsp salt	5 ml salt
1 package semi-sweet chocolate	1 package semi-sweet chocolate

Preheat oven to 350ºF (180ºC).

Combine together in a bowl the eggs, egg yolks, sugar and butter to give a well-blended mixture. Mix the salt and flour and add gradually to the first mixture. Work the dough as little as possible. It should be sticky but not elastic.

Place the dough in a pastry bag and form small rosettes or petit fours about 2 inches (5 cm) long on a greased cookie sheet. Decorate with maraschino cherry quarters and bake for 10 to 15 minutes. Remove from the oven and cool at room temperature.

Melt the chocolate in a bowl over a pan of boiling water. Remove from heat. Work with a wooden spatula until the chocolate is lukewarm. Dip the biscuit ends into it, wait for the excess chocolate to drip off, then place on wax paper. (*Continued on next page*)

Variation: Arrange biscuits on a cookie sheet, dip a wooden spoon into the chocolate and coat the ends of the shortbread.

FRUIT BALLS

Standard	Metric
3 cups icing sugar	750 ml icing sugar
1 cup dates, finely chopped	250 ml dates, finely chopped
2 cups coconut	500 ml coconut
1 cup peanut butter	250 ml peanut butter
2 eggs	2 eggs
1 cup chopped nuts	250 ml chopped nuts
1/3 paraffin wax tablet	1/3 paraffin wax tablet
8 oz chocolate chips	227 ml chocolate chips

Mix all the ingredients well and shape into small balls. In the top of a double boiler, melt the 8 oz (227 ml) chocolate chips in the 1/3 paraffin tablet. Roll the balls in this wax-chocolate mixture and place on waxed paper. Let cool and serve.

SURPRISE BALLS

Standard	Metric
1 package cream cheese	1 package cream cheese
2 tbsp milk	30 ml milk
2 cups sifted icing sugar	500 ml sifted icing sugar
2 squares unsweetened chocolate	2 squares unsweetened chocolate
1/4 tsp vanilla	1 ml vanilla
Pinch of salt	Pinch of salt
3 cups miniature marshmallows	750 ml miniature marshmallows
1 cup grated coconut	250 ml grated coconut

Combine the cream cheese with the milk. Set aside. Melt the chocolate in the top of a double boiler. Add the vanilla and salt. Gradually mix the icing sugar and melted chocolate into the cheese-milk mixture. Add the marshmallows.

Drop the mixture by heaping teaspoonfuls into the coconut and coat the balls. Place on a cookie sheet and let cool in the refrigerator.

GOLDEN CREAM BUTTONS

Standard	Metric
1/2 cup butter	125 ml butter
1 cup water	250 ml water
3 eggs	3 eggs
2 cups heavy cream (35%)	500 ml heavy cream (35%)
1/4 tsp salt	1 ml salt
1 cup all-purpose flour	250 ml all-purpose flour
1 cup sugar	250 ml sugar
1/4 cup water	50 ml water

Preheat the oven to 425°F (220°C).

Bring the water and butter to a boil. Remove from the heat. Mix in the flour and salt and stir for 1 to 2 minutes. Let cool.

Break in the eggs one by one. Mix well after each addition. Grease a cookie sheet and shape the mixture into balls about 2 inches (5 cm) in diameter. Bake for 15 minutes at 425°F (220°C), then reduce the heat to 375°F (190°C) and continue baking for another 5 minutes.

Remove the balls and let cool. Press a hole in each one and garnish with whipped cream.

Caramelize the sugar and water. Set aside for 2 minutes, then dip tops of the balls into the caramel. Place on a lightly oiled plate. Wait several minutes before re-turning.

PINEAPPLE SQUARES

Standard	Metric
1 cup all purpose flour	250 ml all purpose flour
1 tsp baking powder	5 ml baking powder
1/4 tsp salt	1 ml salt
1/2 cup butter	125 ml butter
2 eggs	2 eggs
1 tbsp milk	15 ml milk
1 can crushed pineapple	1 can crushed pineapple
1/4 cup melted butter	50 ml melted butter
1 cup sugar	250 ml sugar
1 cup grated coconut	250 ml grated coconut
1 tsp vanilla	5 ml vanilla

Preheat the oven to 350°F (180°C).

Sift the flour. Add the baking powder and salt. Cut in the 1/4 cup (50 ml) butter. Add 1 beaten egg mixed with the milk. Pour the combined mixture into a buttered 8 x 8 inch (20 x 20 cm) baking pan. Drain the pineapple and spread over the mixture. Beat the other egg and combine with the melted butter, sugar, coconut and vanilla. Pour over the pineapple. Bake for 40 to 45 minutes.

Cool and cut into squares.

PEANUT BUTTER SQUARES

Standard	Metric
1 cup sugar	250 ml sugar
1 cup corn syrup	250 ml corn syrup
6 cups "Special K" cereal	1.5 liters "Special K" cereal
1-1/2 cups peanut butter	375 ml peanut butter
1 package semi-sweet chocolate chips	1 package semi-sweet chocolate chips
1 package caramel chips	1 package caramel chips

Place the sugar and the syrup in a pot. Bring to a boil and continue boiling for several minutes. Remove from the heat.

Combine cereal and peanut butter in a bowl. Add to the first mixture. Mix well. Pour into a 9 x 13 inch (22 x 34 cm) pan. Refrigerate.

Meanwhile, melt the chocolate and caramel chips in the top of a double boiler. Pour over the first mixture. Refrigerate. Cut into squares.

Maple Syrup Squares (I)

Standard	Metric
1/2 cup butter	125 ml butter
1/4 cup maple syrup	50 ml maple syrup
1 cup all-purpose flour	250 ml all-purpose flour
1/4 tsp allspice or nutmeg	1 ml allspice or nutmeg

Topping

Standard	Metric
2/3 cup maple sugar	150 ml maple sugar
1 cup maple syrup	250 ml maple syrup
2 beaten eggs	2 beaten eggs
1/4 cup butter	50 ml butter
1/4 tsp salt	1 ml tsp salt
1/2 cup chopped nuts	125 ml chopped nuts
1/2 tsp maple flavoring	2 ml maple flavoring
2 tbsp all-purpose flour	30 ml all-purpose flour

Preheat oven to 325ºF (160ºC).

Using a fork, combine the butter, maple sugar, flour and spices. Place this mixture in a 7 x 7 inch (17 x 17 cm) square pan. Bake for 10 minutes.

Meanwhile, place sugar and syrup for the topping in a pot and bring to a boil. Allow to simmer for 5 minutes. Remove from the heat and cool to lukewarm. Mix well and add the rest of the ingredients. Pour over the still warm pastry base. Return to the oven at 350ºF (180ºC) for 30 minutes.

Cool and cut into squares in the pan.

Maple Syrup Squares (II)

Standard	Metric
1/2 cup softened butter	125 ml softened butter
1/4 cup brown sugar	50 ml brown sugar
1 cup flour	250 ml flour

Preheat oven to 350ºF (180ºC).

Combine all the ingredients and spread in the bottom of an 8 x 8 inch (20 x 20 cm) pan. Bake for 8 minutes.

Topping

Standard	Metric
3/4 cup brown sugar	150 ml brown sugar
1 cup maple syrup	250 ml maple syrup
1/4 cup butter	50 ml butter
2 eggs	2 eggs
Pinch of salt	Pinch of salt
1/2 cup nuts	125 ml nuts
1/2 tsp maple flavoring	2 ml maple flavoring
2 tbsp all-purpose flour	30 ml all-purpose flour

Boil the syrup and the brown sugar together for 5 minutes. Remove from the heat and let cool.

Add the beaten eggs and the rest of the ingredients. Pour over the cooked base and bake for a further 30 minutes at 350ºF (180ºC).

Cool and cut into squares.

Lemon Squares

Standard	Metric
1 pkg. lemon pie filling	1 pkg. lemon pie filling
1-3/4 cups crushed biscuits	400 ml crushed biscuits
3/4 cup all-purpose flour	150 ml all-purpose flour
3/4 cup butter	150 ml butter
1/2 cup grated coconut	125 ml grated coconut
1 tbsp baking powder	15 ml baking powder
1/2 cup granulated sugar	125 ml granulated sugar
1 tbsp milk	15 ml milk

Preheat oven to 350ºF (180ºC).

Prepare lemon pie filling according to package directions. Cool.

Cream the butter. Add the sugar and milk, followed by the rest of the ingredients. Spread slightly more than half of the mixture on a well-buttered baking sheet, pressing down lightly.

Cover with lemon cream. Spread the remaining portion of the mixture on top. Cook for 30 minutes. Cut into squares.

Sugar Squares

Standard	Metric
1/2 cup butter	125 ml butter
1 cup Graham wafer crumbs	250 ml Graham wafer crumbs
1 cup semi-sweet chocolate chips	250 ml semi-sweet chocolate chips
1 cup grated coconut	250 ml grated coconut
1 cup chopped nuts	250 ml chopped nuts
1 can sweetened condensed milk	1 can sweetened condensed milk

Melt the butter and pour into a square baking pan, coating all the sides. Add the other ingredients, in sequence. Bake at 350ºF (180ºC) for 25 minutes.

Cool and cut into squares.

Health Squares

Standard	Metric
2 large eggs	2 large eggs
1 cup brown sugar	250 ml brown sugar
1/4 cup vegetable oil	50 ml vegetable oil
1 cup whole wheat flour	250 ml whole wheat flour
3/4 tsp baking powder	3 ml baking powder
1-1/2 cups grated carrots	375 ml grated carrots
1/4 tsp salt	1 ml salt
3 tbsp butter	45 ml butter
1/4 cup whipped cream	50 ml whipped cream
1/8 tsp salt	0.5 ml salt
1/2 cup brown sugar	125 ml brown sugar
1/2 tsp vanilla	2 ml vanilla
1/2 cup sifted icing sugar	125 ml sifted icing sugar

Preheat over to 350ºF (180ºC).

Combine the first 7 ingredients, forming the consistency of a cake batter. Bake for 30 minutes.

Place the remaining ingredients in a pot, except for the
(*Continued on the next page*)

icing sugar. Bring to a boil and continue boiling for 1 minute. Add the icing sugar and spread over the cake. Cut into small squares.

CHOCOLATE NUT CANDY

Standard
1 package semi-sweet chocolate
1 can sweetened condensed milk
2 tbsp butter or margarine
2 cups nuts
1 bag of miniature marshmallows

Metric
1 package semi-sweet chocolate
1 can sweetened condensed milk
30 ml butter or margarine
500 ml nuts
1 bag of miniature marshmallows

In a heavy pot, melt the chocolate with the condensed milk and butter. Remove from heat.

Combine the nuts and marshmallows in a large bowl. Add the chocolate mixture. Spread this on a 9 x 13 inch (22 x 34 cm) cookie sheet covered with wax paper. Refrigerate for 2 hours or until the mixture is firm. Remove from the wax paper and cut into squares.

Cover and keep at room temperature.

FUDGE

Standard
2 cups brown sugar
2 cups white sugar
1/4 cup corn syrup
3/4 cup condensed milk
3 tbsp unsalted butter
3 tbsp cocoa

Metric
500 ml brown sugar
500 ml white sugar
50 ml corn syrup
150 ml condensed milk
45 ml unsalted butter
45 ml cocoa

Place all the ingredients in a heavy pot. Bring to a boil and continue boiling for 4 minutes. Remove from the heat and beat with a wooden spatula for 10 minutes until the fudge thickens. Pour into an 8 x 8 inch (20 x 20 cm) buttered pan. Refrigerate. Cut into rounds or squares or shape into balls.

5-MINUTE FUDGE

Standard
2 tbsp butter
1-1/3 cups sugar
2/3 cup condensed milk
2 cups miniature marshmallows
1-1/2 cups chocolate chips
1 cup walnuts, chopped
1 tsp vanilla

Metric
30 ml butter
325 ml sugar
150 ml condensed milk
500 ml miniature marshmallows
375 ml chocolate chips
250 ml walnuts, chopped
5 ml vanilla

In a pot, bring the butter, sugar and condensed milk to a boil. Continue boiling for 5 minutes, over medium heat. Stirring constantly, add the marshmallows, chocolate chips and vanilla. Add the chopped walnuts. Pour into a buttered pan, let cool and cut into small squares.

CAT'S TONGUES

Standard
1/4 lb unsalted butter, creamed
1/4 lb sugar
1/2 cup egg whites
1/4 lb all-purpose flour

Metric
125 g unsalted butter, creamed
125 g sugar
125 ml egg whites
125 g all-purpose flour

Preheat oven to 375ºF (190ºC).

Place butter, sugar and egg whites in a bowl and beat with an eggbeater to give a smooth mixture. Add the flour. Put the batter in a pastry bag with a small tip and make 2 inch long (5 cm) sticks on a greased cookie sheet. Do not place sticks too close together, since they expand in cooking. Bake until the cat's tongues are golden in color. Keep in a dry place.

COCONUT MACAROONS

Standard
2 egg whites
2-1/2 cups grated coconut
1 tsp vanilla
1/2 cup light cream (15%)

Metric
2 egg whites
625 ml grated coconut
5 ml vanilla
125 ml light cream (15%)

Preheat the oven to 375ºF (190ºC).

Beat the egg whites until stiff. Add the coconut, cream and vanilla. Mix well. Shape into small balls. Place on a lightly buttered cookie sheet. Cook in the oven for 15 minutes. Add cream, sugar or coconut to taste.

COCONUT MACAROONS OR BALLS

Standard
1 cup dates, chopped
1/2 cup sugar
1 tsp salt
1/2 cup butter
1 tbsp milk
1 beaten egg
3 cups "Rice Krispies"
1/2 tsp vanilla
Grated coconut

Metric
250 ml dates, chopped
125 ml sugar
5 ml salt
125 ml butter
15 ml milk
1 beaten egg
750 ml "Rice Krispies"
2 ml vanilla
Grated coconut

Cream the butter. Add the sugar, milk, salt and beaten egg. Mix well together and add the dates. Cook over low heat, stirring constantly, for 2 minutes.

Remove from the heat and add the vanilla and "Rice Krispies". Cool for 1/2 hour. Shape into small balls, then roll in grated coconut. Refrigerate.

MARSHMALLOW PUFFED RICE

Standard	Metric
3 cups puffed rice	750 ml puffed rice
2 cups marshmallows	500 ml marshmallows
1/4 cup unsalted butter	50 ml unsalted butter
1 tsp cinnamon	5 ml cinnamon

In a pot over medium heat, melt the butter and marshmallows with cinnamon, stirring constantly with a wooden spatula. When thoroughly blended, add the puffed rice and mix well. Pour into a buttered pan and place in the refrigerator. Cut into rounds or squares.

MAPLE CREAM SUGAR

Standard	Metric
1 cup maple syrup	250 ml maple syrup
3 cups brown sugar	750 ml brown sugar
1 cup white sugar	250 ml white sugar
3 tbsp all-purpose flour	45 ml all-purpose flour
2 tbsp baking powder	30 ml baking powder
1 cup milk	250 ml milk
1 cup heavy cream (35%)	250 ml heavy cream (35%)
1 tbsp butter	15 ml butter
2 tsp vanilla	10 ml vanilla
1/2 cup nuts and almonds, chopped in large pieces	125 ml nuts and almonds, chopped in large pieces

Combine the maple syrup, brown sugar, white sugar, flour, baking powder, milk and cream in a large pot. Cook over medium heat, stirring constantly, until the mixture boils. Continue cooking until it reaches 240°F (115°C) on a candy thermometer, or until a drop forms a soft ball in cold water. Cool for 15 minutes, then add the butter, vanilla and the nuts. Stir until the mixture is evenly mixed. Spread in a buttered pan, to about 1 inch (2.5 cm) deep.

Note: if the mixture is too hard, heat up again and add 2 tsp (10 ml) of cream, stirring until you obtain the desired consistency.

SUGAR À LA CRÈME NICOLE

Standard	Metric
2 cups brown sugar	500 ml brown sugar
2 cups white sugar	500 ml white sugar
1/4 cup corn syrup	50 ml corn syrup
3/4 cup condensed milk	150 ml condensed milk
3 tbsp unsalted butter	45 ml unsalted butter
1 tsp vanilla	5 ml vanilla

Combine all the ingredients in a heavy pot. Bring to a boil and continue boiling for 4 minutes. Remove from the heat and beat with a wooden spatula for about 10 minutes or until the sugar cream reaches a smooth consistency.

Pour into a buttered pan, about 8 inches (20 cm) square. Refrigerate. Cut into rounds or squares, or shape into small balls. Garnish with ground, roasted almonds.

WINE

TABLE WINES

Well-chosen wines are the perfect way to bring out the best in a beautifully prepared meal and to add a sense of festiveness to any occasion. Modern gastronomic meals usually include two good-quality wines to accompany the two main courses — a white wine to accompany the hors d'oeuvres and fish course, and a red wine to accompany the meat course and cheeses.

WINE SELECTION

Given the enormous range of wines available, it can sometimes seem a confusing task to match the appropriate wines with the dishes you are serving. However, you can easily be adventurous and expand your knowledge of wines by purchasing different wines and learn by experience which ones you prefer.

Keep a record of the wines you most enjoy, and their particular qualities, including which of your favorite dishes they work with best.

The rules regarding which wines can be drunk with which dishes are no longer observed as rigidly as they once were, but there are still a few basic rules you must observe.

You should not serve wine with courses which contain vinegar, such as salad or certain hors d'oeuvres, or with fruits which have a high acid content. Wine also does not go well with dishes containing chocolate or with cream cheeses. It is much better to serve water with such courses.

Red wine usually overwhelms the delicate flavor of certain foods such as shellfish, sauces which contain white sauce or Madeira, white cheese and sweet dishes.

MATCHING THE WINE WITH THE DISH

Not long ago, it was considered a hard and fast rule that red wines could only be served with red meats, and that white wines could only accompany white meats and fish.

Adventurous diners now feel free to break that rule on occasion. But still, white wines usually match up best with delicately flavored dishes, while heartier dishes with more pronounced flavors can stand up best to the full-bodied flavor of the reds. A dry wine tastes sour if drunk with a sweet dessert, and a red wine can take on a fishy taste if drunk with fish. A highly spiced dish will kill the flavor of a light wine.

The most important point to remember is that the wine should complement the food and the food should accentuate and blend with the qualities of the wine. Great combinations of wine and food are unforgettable.

As a general rule, coarser or heavier wines should be served with more highly seasoned foods; lighter wines should be reserved to accompany more delicate flavors. You will normally not want to match up red wines with fish or seafood. On the other hand, game will overpower the flavor of white wine, especially a sweet one.

Knowledge of wine is a lifetime hobby, and the only way you will be able to expand your knowledge is to experiment. When in doubt, ask for advice from your wine dealer to match a wine with a specific dish.

Give yourself the opportunity to experiment with a variety of wines from around the world, rather than only the French ones; you will find the Australian, Portuguese and Spanish wines, among others, can offer good flavor at reasonable prices.

Throughout this book, you will find basic wine suggestions to accompany various menus. Use these as a guide, but follow your own instincts and wine interests above all.

ORDER OF SERVICE

1. **Aperitif wines** (Pineau des Charentes, Muscadet, Rhine and Moselle wines, dry sparkling wines and champagnes)
2. **Table wines** (such as Bordeaux, Beaujolais, Chablis, Burgundies, champagne)
3. **Dessert wines** (Marsala, Port, Sauternes, sweet wines and sweet champagnes, as well as various liqueurs)

Champagnes and sparkling wines are very much appreciated as aperitifs. White wines go best with most hors d'oeuvres and entrées, but if you are serving a pâté or an entrée involving meat or meat sauce, you should probably select red wine.

If you are a great fan of champagne, there is no reason that it cannot be served throughout the whole meal.

Fish, seafood, shellfish and chicken are normally accompanied with a dry white wine; meats and games with a more full-bodied red selection. Cheeses are normally served with red wine; lighter varieties to accompany milder cheese, although strong cheeses such as cheddar and Stilton can hold up very nicely to a more emphatic red. Desserts, with the exception of those containing chocolate, match up successfully with sweet or dessert wines, sparkling wines or wine-based liqueurs.

Generally, white wines should be served before reds, younger wines before older ones, chilled wines before room temperature ones, dry wines before sweet ones, and light wines before more full-bodied wines.

On the other hand, better quality wines should be served before those of lesser quality. A high quality but light wine can bear up to a heavier dish. But as a general rule, you should start with the lighter wines and work through to the more full-bodied ones.

One old principle that you might consider observing - the grape and grain do not mix well, and can produce certain ill effects. If, for example, you serve a gin-based aperitif, do not serve a wine-based digestif, such as cognac, at the end of the meal.

SERVING

Temperature

Wines should be treated with respect before serving.

As a general rule, red wines should be served at room temperature rather than chilled (unless the wine is very young and light). Bear in mind that room temperature used to mean around 65°F (18°C), which is lower than standard room temperature today. Red wine that is served too warm loses some of its bouquet and flavor. If you keep your red wine in a wine cellar, never bring it to proper serving temperature artificially. Instead, take it out of the cellar at least 4 hours in advance to warm naturally. If necessary, it is better to pour the wine chilled and let it warm in the glass.

Rosé wines should be served reasonably cool, at somewhere between 38°F (6°C) and 50°F (12°C), depending on their age. Generally speaking, sweeter wines should be served colder than dry ones. (This holds for white wines as well.)

White wines should be chilled to a temperature of between 46°F (10°C) and 50°F (12°C). Never add ice or put them in the freezer. White wines should taste refreshingly fresh, but not icy cold, or their flavor will be affected.

Sparkling wines and champagnes should be chilled to between 36°F (5°C) and 46°F (10°C), but never icy cold. Sweet and young champagnes need to be chilled, but rare aged champagnes can be appreciated best at cellar temperature, or about 56°F (15°C).

Dessert wines such as Muscadet and Malaga should be served at between 38°F (6°C) and 42°F (8°C).

Port should be served at a temperature just below room temperature.

Chilling

The best way to chill any wine to the proper serving temperature is to put it in an ice bucket well-filled with ice or an ice-and-water mixture. If you put your wines in the refrigerator or outdoors in the winter, you have to make sure that they do not become too chilled. If you are in a hurry to chill the wine quickly, you can use the trick of adding some salt in with the ice in the bucket.

Chambrage

Chambrage is the term used for the process of bringing wine from cellar temperature to proper serving temperature. Ordinarily, wine kept in a cellar should be brought out up to 48 hours in advance of serving time, so that it can warm gradually to serving temperature but is able to rest after being moved, with the sediments settling to the bottom. Never put the wine in a warm area of the kitchen, near a radiator, or beside any other source of heat.

Unfortunately, given the high temperature at which most people keep their houses today, wine removed from the cellar 48 hours in advance will become too warm. It will probably require only about 4 hours in a normal room to bring it to proper serving temperature. If you do not have a cellar in which to store your wines, you can use an ice bucket for a few minutes to bring red wines down to slightly less then room temperature, but do not let them cool too much.

Uncorking

Most red wines should be uncorked for a certain period of time before serving, to allow the wine to breathe and permit the release of pent-up gases. There is not set rule, but generally a light red wine should be opened about 1/2 hour before serving, while a Bordeaux needs 3 to 4 hours. White wines, rosés and champagnes are uncorked just before serving. If you cannot uncork the wine ahead of time, decant it, which will aerate it.

Decanting

Decanting is an operation which separates the wine from any sediments which have formed at the bottom of the bottle. White and rosé wines do not have a sediment, so do not need to be decanted. Never decant a champagne or sparkling wine; it would destroy the bubbles.

To decant red wines, proceed as follows:
* Rinse you decanter with warm water and drain it well.
* Uncork the wine bottle.
* Place a funnel in the neck of the decanter.
* Pour the wine very slowly to allow it to be aerated at the same time.
* Stop pouring before the sediment leaves the bottle.

GLASSES

An enormous choice in wine glasses is available, but you want to make sure that you do not select such elaborate glasses that they defeat the purpose of a wine glass, which is to permit the full visual appreciation of the wine as well as serve as a drinking vessel.

The ideal wine glass should be made of crystal or fine glass. It should be clear rather than colored, so that you can appreciate the true color of the wine. It should have a stemmed based at least 2 inches (5 cm) high, and a stable base.

The glass should be as thin as possible, and the sides should be straight or angled inwards at the top or tulip-shaped rather than flared, so that the full bouquet of the wine is captured for your enjoyment. A standard wine glass should be able to hold 3 to 4 ounces (90 ml to 120 ml) when filled to the halfway mark, which is the best amount to serve at one time. The bigger (more important) the wine, the bigger the glass; a small glass gives no room for a magnificent bouquet to develop or for the drinker to swirl.

Red wine glasses are usually slightly larger that white wine glasses. Since white wine should be drunk chilled, it is better to pour smaller quantities at a time.

Champagnes and sparkling wines should be served in flute-shaped glasses rather than flat wide glasses, so that their effervescence and aroma can be fully appreciated.

Try to use a fresh glass for each different wine served, and rinse your mouth with water before tasting a new one.

KITCHEN EQUIPMENT AND SUPPLIES

Basic Ingredients

It is a good idea to keep a basic stock of ingredients on hand for emergencies. The list that follows includes basic ingredients you will need for the recipes in this book.

Alcohol:
cognac
Kirsch
rum
wine (dry white, dry red, etc.)

Canned Goods:
anchovy filets
artichoke bottoms
artichoke hearts
beef consommé
bouillon or stock (beef, chicken, vegetable)
condensed milk
crab
cream soups (mushroom, celery, asparagus, etc.)
fruit (mandarins, peaches, pears, pineapple, etc.)
salmon
shrimp
soups (bean, pea, tomato, etc.)
tomato paste
tuna
vegetables (beans, peas, tomatoes, etc.)

Dry Ingredients:
baking powder
baking soda
breadcrumbs
cocoa
cream of tartar
flour (all-purpose, pastry, etc.)
grated cheese (Parmesan)
monosodium glutamate
mustard, dry
sugar (brown, fruit, granulated, icing, etc.)

Miscellaneous:
bacon
butter
capers
catsup
cheese (cheddar, Gruyère, Parmesan)
chocolate chips
chocolate, unsweetened
coconut, grated
cocktail sausages
concentrates (beef, chicken, vegetable)
crackers
cream (heavy, light, sour)

Miscellaneous (continued)
extracts (almond, vanilla, etc.)
honey
jams
jelly powder (flavored and unflavored)
lard
lemons
margarine
marmalade
mayonnaise
molasses
mustard (Dijon, powder, regular)
nuts (almonds, hazelnuts, walnuts, etc.)
oatmeal
oil (corn, olive, vegetable, etc.)
olives (black, green, stuffed)
pasta (fettuccine, lasagna, spaghetti)
pickles
raisins
rice (long grain, wild, etc.)
salt pork
sauces (chili, soy, Tabasco, Worcestershire)
shortening
syrup (corn, maple, etc.)
tapioca
vinegar (tarragon, wine, white, etc.)

Spices and Herbs:
allspice
basil
bay leaves
cinnamon
cloves (powdered, whole)
coriander
cumin
curry
ginger (fresh, powdered)
mace
marjoram
nutmeg
paprika
parsley (fresh, dried)
pepper (black, cayenne, green, white, etc.)
poppy seeds
powders (celery, garlic, onion, etc.)
rosemary
salted herbs
savory
thyme

Basic Equipment and Accessories for the Kitchen

Most Useful Equipment

1. Double boiler
2. 4 quart saucepan
3. Rectangular grill
4. Mixing bowls, different sizes
5. Spring-form tube cake pan
6. Spring-form pie plate
7. Muffin tins
8. Loaf pan
9. Soufflé dish
10. Scale
11. Juicer
12. Measuring cup
13. Food processor
14. Colander
15. Strainer
16. Drainer
17. Wire whisk
18. Funnel
19. Grater
20. Tongs
21. Pastry cutter
22. Raclette
23. Knife set
    left to right:
    * paring knife
    * carving knife
    * fork
    * chef's knife
    * spatula
    * bread knife
    * sharpener
    * cleaver
    * spatula
24. Pastry bag and tips
25. Cookie cutters
26. Metal funnel
27. Icing tips
28. Basting brush
29. Rubber spatula
30. Candy thermometer
31. Measuring spoons
32. Meat thermometer

33. Cake knife
34. Cutting board
35. Pastry trimmer
36. Zester
37. Apple corer
38. Melon baller
39. Mushroom brush
40. Chocolate spoon and fork
41. Egg scissors
42. Garlic press
43. Egg poacher

411

UTENSILS AND ACCESSORIES FOR MICROWAVE COOKING

LIST OF MOST USEFUL UTENSILS

1. Ring mold

2. Muffin mold

3. Baking dish with cover

4 and 5. Divided baking dishes with and without covers

6 and 7. Glass baking dishes in varying sizes (2 to 4 liters), round and square

8. Plastic baking dishes

9. Covered ceramic-glass saucepan

10. Defrosting and roasting rack

11. Bacon grill (clayette)

12. Browning dish

13. Braising dish

14. Double-sided cooking dish, one side ridged to facilitate draining, the other side smooth

15. Glass cooking dish with plastic cover

16 and 17. All-purpose cooking dishes

18, 19, and 20. Various size cooking dishes for individual portions or cooking separate recipes

21. Dish for steam cooking (also useful for popping corn)

22. Microwave rack for space saving

23. Microwave-safe measuring cups

OTHER USEFUL ACCESSORIES

* Microwave-safe roasting bags
* Microwave-safe boiling bags
* Plastic wrap
* Paper towels
* Wax paper
* Microwave thermometer
* Pie plates
* Bread and soufflé molds
* Quiche mold

MICROWAVE TECHNIQUES

Microwave Cooking Techniques

Cooking with a Microwave

Before you try microwave cooking, you should understand what microwaves are and how a microwave oven works. Microwaves are a form of electromagnetic energy, similar to radio waves except that microwaves are shorter (micro) and have an extremely high frequency. Microwaves in a microwave oven operate in three ways: reflection, transmission and absorption.

Reflection

Microwaves reflect off of metal exactly as a ball bounces off a wall. This is why it is not recommended to use metal containers in a microwave oven, because metal does not allow the microwaves to pass through and can reflect the waves back to the oven, causing damage.

Transmission

Microwaves are able to pass through certain materials, such as glass, paper, and plastic, exactly as the sun passes through a window-pane. These materials neither absorb nor reflect microwaves.

Absorption

Microwaves are attracted to moisture, and are able to penetrate foods to a distance of about 1/2 inch (2 cm). The waves are absorbed by the water, fat or sugar molecules in the food, which start to vibrate as a result. Once the outer layers of molecules have begun to vibrate, it sets off a chain reaction as vibrating molecules rub against other molecules. The resulting molecular friction produces heat, much like the heat you are able to develop by rubbing your two hands together. As certain parts of the food start to heat up, the energy and heat are passed on to the adjacent areas of food, moving from the edges toward the center.

As soon as the microwave is turned off, the microwaves disappear from the inside of the oven and from the food.

Microwave Containers

As already explained, metal containers and containers containing metal such as lead are not recommended for use in the microwave oven. Instead, you should select cooking containers which allow the microwaves to pass through, so that the waves heat the food rather than the container. In fact, the cooking container should never become hotter than its contents. Covered containers will however become a little hotter, as a result of trapped steam from the food. Many containers and utensils suitable for use in conventional ovens can also be used in microwave ovens, especially containers made of glass, pyrex and various glass-ceramics. Paper products and plastic containers can also be used in the microwave for short periods and/or at low temperatures, and especially for warming foods; they may tend to melt or deform if they are left in contact with hot foods for any length of time.

There is a simple test for checking whether a specific container is safe to use in the microwave: put the container into the microwave oven, and put 1/2 to 1 cup (125 to 250 ml) of water into a glass. Put the glass beside or in the container being tested. Turn the oven on at HIGH for 1 to 2 minutes. If the container being tested becomes hotter than the glass of water, it is not safe to use in the microwave. Note: Do not use this test for plastic containers.

Types of Cooking

There are various types of microwave ovens available on the market. Some of them offer, in addition to microwave cooking, the option of convection cooking or a browning element.

Convection Cooking

A convection oven allows you to brown and roast meats by using an element which dries and heats the air in the oven. In addition, a fan circulates the air to provide even cooking.

Combination Cooking

Combination cooking is the ideal method for roasting meat and poultry. It can also be used for stewing, simmering, and other purposes.

This method automatically alternates between microwave cooking and convection cooking, so that the meat browns on the outside and the interior cooks faster than in a conventional oven.

Browning Element (broiler)

Broiling or grilling is only useful for high quality, well-marbled meats which have been coated or basted to prevent drying during the cooking process. This type of cooking involves very high heat, with the food placed close to the browning element.

MICROWAVE EQUIPMENT

Many microwave ovens are sold equipped with a number of accessories, which you should know how to use in order to get the best use out of your oven.

Drip Pan and Spatter Shield

Combination convection and microwave ovens usually are equipped with a drip pan and spatter shield which are used for broiling meat, poultry and fish, and make it possible to produce crisp surfaces on cooked foods since they do not stew in their own juices. You should spray both utensils with a vegetable oil coating to prevent food from sticking and make clean-up easier.

Grills and Roasting Pans

Regular grills and roasting pans can be used in the conventional oven or convection oven, but are not recommended for combination or microwave cooking. However, there are special grills and pans designed specifically for microwave use.

Temperature Probe

The temperature probe resembles a thermometer and performs the same function, measuring the interior temperature of foods cooked in the microwave.

COOKING UTENSILS

Although there are many microwave utensils on the market, it is still possible to use many household items to accomplish the same tasks.

Glassware, Ceramics and Porcelain

Practically all heat-resistant glassware without metal decorations can be used in a microwave. However, thin glassware may crack from the heat developed by the food in it.

Here are some brand names of heat-resistant glassware that can be used in a microwave oven: Pyrex without metal decorations, Fire King made by Anchor Hocking, Glassbake by Jeannette Glass, Glass Ovenware by Helle Designs and Federal Glass.

Certain glassware used in conventional ovens can also be used in microwave ovens, such as Temper-Ware made by Lenox.

Caution: Never put anything made of metal, or which has metal parts or decorations, in a microwave. Never use utensils that have cracks or chipped glazes. The handles on cups or other items must always be intact.

Jars and Bottles

Jars and bottles can be used to reheat food, but not to cook food in. Be sure to remove all metal tops of any containers you are using. When cooking with combination heat, including conventional ovens, you should avoid using jars and bottles altogether.

Browning Dishes

Browning dishes are used to grill meats. The bottom of these plates are covered with a special material that absorbs microwaves. As a result, the plates become hot enough to brown food. The plate must be preheated according to the manufacturer's instructions or according to the recipe. Cook the meat to your own preference and remember to use oven mitts when removing the dish from the oven. It is not recommended to use a probe thermometer with a browning dish.

Metal

Metal containers should never be used, as metal reflects microwaves and makes it impossible to cook the dish evenly. They should only be used in conventional ovens.

Aluminum

Aluminum also reflects microwaves (because it is a metal), but it can be used to slow down the cooking of certain parts of your dish, such as the tips of chicken wings, etc.

Containers Lined with Aluminum

No container, if it is lined with aluminum, should be used in your microwave oven.

Wrapping Pre-cooked and Frozen Foods

Specially wrapped pre-cooked and frozen foods can be reheated in a microwave oven as long as they are not thicker than 3/4 inch (2 cm). These foods can be reheated by microwave or conventionally, but not by the two methods combined. Reheat only one dish at a time, making sure that it does not touch the sides of the microwave oven.

Metal Skewers

Metal skewers can be used in microwave cooking and in combination or convection cooking. The volume of the food cooked on the skewers must be greater than that of the skewer itself. The skewers must not be allowed to touch one another nor the sides of the oven, as this could cause sparks. Ideally, wooden skewers should be used and can also be used for combined microwave and convection cooking.

Plastic Containers

Certain plastic containers that can be placed in the freezer can also be used in a microwave oven provided that they are labeled " safe for microwave use" or "safe for conventional or microwave oven use". Containers that say "only for use in microwaves" can also be used in combined microwave and convection cooking or convection cooking alone. You should avoid using plastic containers for long cooking periods for any foods that contain a lot of sugar or fat.

Cooking Bags

Cooking bags used for conventional cooking can also be used in microwave ovens. They are ideal for maintaining moisture in large pieces of meat.

First place the food in the bag and close it with plastic fasteners or string. Pierce a few holes in the bag to permit some evaporation and place the bag and its contents on a plate suitable for microwave cooking.

Caution: Do not use metal fasteners covered in paper or plastic. Never use plastic garbage bags to cook foods in.

Other

Napkins, paper plates, cups and napkins, wax paper, paper or freezer bags can all be used for microwave cooking, but not for combined microwave and convection cooking nor for convection cooking alone. The food must not be too greasy and must only be cooked for short periods of time.

Bamboo, Rattan and Wood

Baskets made from bamboo, rattan or wood can be used in the microwave oven to heat up bread, for instance, but cannot be used for combined microwave and convection cooking nor for convection cooking alone. Wooden containers such as salad bowls or chopping boards should not be used, as microwaves will dry them out over extended periods of use.

Thermometers

You cannot use conventional oven thermometers in the microwave, but you can use them for convection cooking. If you do need a thermometer for your microwave oven, these are available and can be purchased. Please note however, that neither kind of thermometer can be used in combined microwave and convection cooking.

SHAPE AND SIZE OF CONTAINERS

Round containers enable you to cook all of the food evenly because there is an even distribution of energy on all sides of the container.

Square or rectangularly shaped containers allow more microwaves on certain sides than on others and as a result the food is unevenly cooked.

Ring shaped containers are ideal for cooking food that cannot be stirred while being cooked. These containers permit microwaves to penetrate food from all over, and so the food is cooked very evenly and in the shortest time possible.

Containers with straight sides allow the food in the container to be spread evenly and thus cook evenly. Containers that have inclined sides must be avoided, as some parts of the

food will be cooked a lot and some won't be cooked enough.

The depth of the container is very important in microwave cooking. For example, food placed in a container that is very wide with a capacity of about 8 cups (2 liters), will take much less time to cook than food that is placed in a deeper container of equal volume. This is because a larger capacity of food is exposed in a wider container and the cooking time is reduced.

COVERS

Glass Covers

Glass covers help prevent moisture loss and accelerate cooking. They should certainly be used with foods that will lose a lot of moisture when being heated, such as vegetables.

Plastic Wrap

Plastic wrap permits you to cover your food evenly, it retains heat and permits food to cook rapidly. The plastic wrap can serve as the only cooking container if it is wrapped completely around a vegetable containing a lot of water, such as an ear of corn. It is also ideal for replacing a glass cover or to prevent splashing and it can be rolled back to release moisture and vapor from the container.

Never use plastic wrap for combined microwave and convection cooking or convection cooking alone.

Wax Paper

A piece of wax paper between your casserole and the glass cover of your container makes a wonderful seal against moisture loss by reducing evaporation from the container.

WATER, SALT, FAT AND SUGAR REACT TO MICROWAVES

Water, salt, fat and sugar absorb energy from the microwaves, changing the cooking time of foods that contain them. Certain points must be followed when cooking with these ingredients:

Water

Water retains energy from microwaves, permitting vegetables of high water content to cook well in microwave ovens. It is advisable to add a little bit of water when you are cooking vegetables that retain a lot of water, whether they are fresh or frozen. However, too much water will absorb too much energy and will slow down the cooking time of vegetables.

Salt

Salt can cause burn marks on your food if it is sprinkled

directly on it. To avoid this, it is recommended that you dissolve the salt first in a small amount of water and then place the salted water on the food or even better, salt your foods after they have been cooked in the microwave.

Fat

Fat can slow down the transmission of energy to meats and this will increase the cooking time. You should remove as much of the fat as possible before cooking such foods in the microwave oven.

Sugar

Sugar absorbs the energy from microwaves as well. As a result, the parts of the food that are coated with sugar will cook faster than the others. It is therefore recommended that you do not expose glazed foods for long in the microwave.

FOR BETTER COOKING IN MICROWAVE OVENS

Many factors should be considered to cook effectively and efficiently. Here are a few.

Small pieces of food cook faster than do large ones. For more evenly cooked food, cut pieces to equal size. Food of the same shape also cooks more uniformly.

When choosing mussels for cooking, choose the ones that have a more rounded or crowned shape, for more even cooking.

Heavy and compact food takes much more time to cook than does porous food.

Small quantities cook more rapidly than large quantities. When the quantity of food is increased, the cooking time must also be increased.

Foods that have a high water content cook better in microwaves if you add a small amount of water. On the other hand, if too much water is added the cooking time will be lengthened. Foods with low water content do not cook very well in a microwave oven.

Foods that are cooked in a microwave oven continue to cook even after they have been removed from the oven. Certain foods therefore may not appear to be cooked completely when they are first removed from the oven. Test to see that the food is cooked after the minimum cooking time and not later.

Foods that do not cook well in the microwave oven are foods that are not high in water content as well as foods that require dry heat to cook. Do not use a microwave oven to make preserves, fried foods or to cook unshelled eggs.

Bones and fats affect cooking in microwave ovens. Bones conduct heat irregularly and fat absorbs microwaves more quickly resulting in over-cooked meat.

Food that is already at room temperature will take less time to cook than will foods that have been frozen or refrigerated.

HOW TO ARRANGE FOOD IN A MICROWAVE OVEN

The way in which food is placed in a microwave will modify the rate at which it is cooked. Here are some useful pointers:

Place the thinnest parts of the food in the center of a rectangular or square shaped plate (for example, in the case of fish filets). The thicker parts will thus be exposed to more energy.

Place the most tender parts of your food towards the center of the plate so as to protect them from being exposed to too much energy and thus overcooked (broccoli, asparagus tips, for example).

Choose foods of the same thickness and place them at equal distances beside one another around the plate, making sure not to place any in the middle or on top of each other (for example, potatoes, mushrooms, etc.). This enables the food to cook evenly.

Place the smallest pieces of food in the center of the plate (for example, pieces of chicken). This enables the food to cook more evenly.

When using the oven shelf, arrange the containers so that the microwaves can penetrate each container.

HOW TO STIR FOODS

Besides knowing how to arrange food in the oven, other techniques can help to distribute the heat and result in more evenly cooked food.

Cover foods to retain the heat and moisture and to shorten the cooking time. However, always be careful when removing the cover so as not to get burned by steam.

Stir foods to distribute the heat evenly and to shorten the cooking time. This is usually recommended at the halfway point in the cooking process. Stir from the exterior of the dish to the center, in other words, stirring so that the most cooked parts are brought to the center.

Dishes that cannot be stirred should be rotated. This technique helps distribute the heat evenly.

Turn the food over when you are cooking pieces of food, like slices of salmon, or whole foods, like cauliflower.

Rearrange food from the outside of the plate to the center, since the outside receives more energy.

Protect the corners of a dish or the parts that will cook more rapidly by covering them with aluminum foil so that they are not overcooked. The foil should be placed so that it is at least 1 inch (2.5 cm) away from the edges of the oven.

The standing time after the food has been cooked permits the food to continue to cook by the conduction of heat throughout the food. More dense food, like roasts, poultry, etc. usually require a longer standing time. This standing time permits the center of the food to finish cooking without letting the exterior become overcooked.

Steam build-up often creates pressure under the skin, peel or membrane of certain foods. To release the vapor, it is recommended that you: pierce the membrane of the egg yolk and the egg white several times with a tooth pick; pierce clams and oysters several times with a tooth pick; prick all vegetables with a fork; cut a slice of peel about 1 inch (2.5 cm) wide off fresh apples and potatoes before cooking; pierce the skin of sausages with a fork before cooking them.

APPEARANCE OF FOOD COOKED IN MICROWAVE OVENS

Certain meats and poultry brown quite easily, especially those that require between 10 to 15 minutes cooking time. On the other hand, foods that cook faster do not have time to brown. It is, however, possible to improve the appearance of food by basting it with a sauce mixture before cooking (Worcestershire sauce, soya sauce, etc.), and by using a browning dish.

Cakes and breads cook too quickly to form a brown crust. You can replace white sugar with brown sugar or sprinkle the top with dark spices before baking.

CHECKING DONENESS

Use the same methods for checking degree of doneness as for foods cooked in a conventional oven.

Cakes are done when a toothpick inserted into the center comes out clean or when the cake shrinks back from the sides of the mold.

Chicken is done when the leg joint can be moved easily and the juices run clear.

Meat is cooked when the fibers can be separated easily with a fork.

Fish is cooked when the flesh is opaque and flakes easily.

DEFROSTING

Foods can be defrosted in the microwave very rapidly, which inhibits the natural growth of bacteria occurring when food is defrosted at room temperature. Meat thawed rapidly just before cooking does not lose as much moisture. Basic defrosting techniques are:

* Place the food on a plate or a rack and cover with wax paper. This encourages the heat to diffuse around the food so that it thaws more rapidly and uniformly.

* Cover small and thin parts of food with a layer of aluminum foil to prevent them from cooking prematurely. You can tell if the food is starting to cook before it is thawed if it starts to change color or becomes warm.

* Rearrange, rotate or stir foods to distribute heat uniformly. As soon as possible, break apart foods that are stuck together, and continue defrosting. Foods being cooked in a bag can be stirred by shaking or folding the bag.

* A standing time may be necessary to complete defrosting after the recommended microwave time. Standing time permits the heat to spread through parts of the food that are not completely thawed. Dense, compact or delicate dishes may require a longer standing time.

* Cakes, rolls, fruit and vegetables require only a few minutes of defrosting time.

* Danish pastries and rolls should be wrapped in paper towels before being defrosted.

HOW TO REHEAT MEALS AND LEFTOVERS

Microwave ovens offer several advantages when it comes to reheating meals. Dishes can be prepared in advance and cooked at the last minute; foods keep their flavor, and texture and leftovers taste better. In addition, microwaves make it easy to reheat a single meal for one person on a single plate. However, you have to observe a few basic rules:

* The foods should be properly arranged on the plate, that is, with smaller and thinner pieces placed in the center of the plate. Each food should be at the same temperature. Cover the plate and turn it once during the cooking process.

* Certain dishes cannot be stirred so rotating the plate several times during the cooking period will produce more even results.

* Brioches should be placed on a paper towel or napkin to absorb moisture. Arrange the paper towel in a dish or basket if you are reheating several brioches at once. Be careful not to overcook.

* Simmered dishes and stews should be covered and stirred from time to time to distribute the heat evenly.

* Breads and sandwiches should be wrapped in a paper towel or napkin before reheating. The paper absorbs excess moisture and keeps the bread from becoming soggy. If you heat bread too long, it will become hard.

* Sliced meats reheat more rapidly and uniformly than a single large piece. Arrange the slices flat on a plate and cover with wax paper. To prevent drying, top with sauce or lemon juice before reheating.

* Place the thickest parts of chops near the edge of the plate. Top with sauce and cover with wax paper before reheating.

* Dishes with a breadcrumb topping should be covered with a piece of wax paper to keep the breading crisp.

MELTING AND SOFTENING

To melt 1 to 3 squares of chocolate, place them in a small bowl and heat at MEDIUM HIGH for 3-1/2 to 4 minutes. Five squares of chocolate will take 4-1/2 to 5 minutes.

To melt 1 to 4 tbsp (15 to 60 ml) of butter, place it in a measuring cup or small bowl and heat at HIGH for 45 seconds to 1-1/4 minutes. Melting 1/4 to 1/2 cup (50 to 125 ml) of butter will take 1-1/4 to 1-3/4 minutes.

To melt jams or jellies heat the necessary quantity in a small bowl at HIGH for 30 to 60 seconds.

To soften cream cheese, unwrap it, place it in a bowl, and heat at HIGH until it is well-softened; about 30 seconds for 1/2 cup (125 ml) and 45 seconds for 1 cup (250 ml).

To soften ice cream slightly, remove any aluminum foil from the container and put it in the microwave for 15 to 30 seconds per pint.

ADAPTING TRADITIONAL RECIPES FOR THE MICROWAVE

It is very simple to adapt standard recipes for microwave use. You just have to make some simple modifications to adjust, for example, the amount of liquid, the cooking time, etc. Following are some rules and examples:

* Choose recipes that contain ingredients which cook well in the microwave.

* Foods with a high moisture content, such as vegetables, fruit, chicken and fish need less water added when cooked in the microwave.

* Simmered dishes such as stews usually adapt very well to microwave cooking.

* Foods such as candies, cakes, etc. cook well in the microwave due to their high sugar and fat content.

* Reduce the amount of liquid in each recipe by 1/4; add more liquid later if necessary.

* Cut down the amount of seasonings, especially of salt, spices and herbs with a very pronounced flavor such as cayenne pepper and garlic. Recipes in which only small amounts of seasonings are required, do not need to be adjusted, but it is always preferable to correct seasoning after cooking.

You can use small quantities of butter or oil for flavoring but you do not need them to prevent sticking.

Modify cooking times by referring to a microwave recipe for a similar dish.

PLANNING A MICROWAVE MEAL

First, prepare any dishes which do not need to be served hot, for example, cakes, puddings, chicken, etc. Next prepare dishes which can be easily reheated just before serving time, such as spaghetti sauce, soups, stews, etc.

Take advantage of the standing time for large pieces, such as roasts, to cook items that require minimal cooking, such as hors d'oeuvres and bread.

Certain foods, such as potatoes, can be wrapped in aluminum foil during the standing period to retain their heat.

At the last minute, heat rolls and vegetables which cook rapidly.

Microwave Defrosting Times for Meat and Fish

Food	Cut	Amount	Defrost Time Defrost Setting	Standing Time
Beef	Rolled Rib Roast	1-1/2 lb (750 g)	10 min	10 min
	Palette Roast	3 lb (1250 g)	15 min	10 min
	Cubed Beef	3 lb (1250 g)	15 min	10 min
	Stewing Beef	1 lb (500 g)	8 min	5 min
	Ground Beef	1-1/2 lb (750 g)	10 min	5 min
	Hamburger	1 lb (500 g)	5 min	5 min
Veal	Cutlets	4 oz (125 g)	2 min	3 min
	Ground Veal	1 lb (500 g)	10 min	5 min
Poultry	Whole	1 lb (500 g)	5 min	5 min
	Wings	2 lb (1 kg)	14 min	5 min
	Legs	1-1/2 lb (750 g)	8 min	5 min
	Thighs	1 lb (500 g)	10 min	5 min
	Breasts	1 lb (500 g)	10 min	5 min
Pork	Roast	3 lb (1250 g)	12 min	5 min
	Chops	3 lb (1250 g)	15 min	10 min
	Spareribs	2 lb (1 kg)	12 min	5 min
	Tenderloin	1-1/2 (750 g)	10 min	5 min
Fish	Whole	2 lb (1 kg)	10 min	5 min
	Filets	1-1/2 lb (750 g)	8 min	None
	Scallops	1 lb (500 g)	5 min	None
	Lobster	1 lb (500 g)	5 min	5 min
		1-1/2 lb (750 g)	6 min	5 min

Note: Freezer temperatures vary. If the food is not completely defrosted after the recommended standing time, return to the microwave for a few more minutes.

Microwave Cooking Fresh Vegetables

Vegetable	Quantity Weight Number	Cut	Cooking Time at HIGH		
			500 W	600 to 650 W	700 W
Artichokes	2 medium	Whole	15 min	12 min	10 min
Asparagus	1 lb (500 g)	Whole	12 min	10 min	9 min
Beans	1 lb (500 g)	2 inch (5 cm) pieces	16 min	14 min	13 min
Beets	1 lb (500 g)	Slices	25 min	20 min	15 min
Broccoli	1 lb (500 g)	Flowerets	10 min	8 min	7 min
Brussels Sprouts	1 lb (500 g)	Whole	7 min	6 min	5 min
Cabbage	1 medium	8, 10 pieces	12 min	10 min	9 min
		Whole	14 min	12 min	11 min
Carrots	1 lb (500 g)	Rings	12 min	10 min	8 min
		2 inch (5 cm) pieces	14 min	12 min	10 min
Cauliflower	1 medium	Flowerets	12 min	10 min	9 min
Celeriac	1 lb (500 g)	Sliced	10 min	8 min	7 min
Celery	6 stalks	3 inch (7.5 cm) pieces	10 min	8 min	7 min
Corn	4 ears	Whole	12 min	10 min	9 min
	2 cups (500 ml)	Kernels	10 min	9 min	8 min
Eggplant	1/2 lb (250 g)	Whole	7 min	6 min	5 min
Endives	1 lb (500 g)	Halved	10 min	8 min	6 min
Fennel	1 lb (500 g)	Sliced	10 min	8 min	6 min
Leeks	1 lb (500 g)	Sliced	10 min	9 min	7 min
Mushrooms	1 lb (500 g)	Sliced	6 min	4 min	3 min
Onions	4 medium	Whole	10 min	9 min	8 min
	1/2 lb (250 g)	Chopped	8 min	7-1/2 min	7 min
Peppers	1 lb (500 g)	Sliced	8 min	7-1/2 min	7 min
Potatoes	2 medium	Whole	8-1/2 min	8 min	7-1/2 min
	4 medium	Whole	15 min	14 min	13 min
	4 medium	2 inch (5 cm) slices	12 min	10 min	9 min
Spinach	1 lb (500 g)	Whole	6 min	4 min	3 min
Squash	2 pieces of 8 oz (250 g)		7 min	6 min	5 min
	4 pieces of 8 oz (250 g)		12 min	10 min	9 min
Turnip	1 lb (500 g)	3 inch (7.5 cm) slices	10 min	9 min	8 min
Zucchini	1 medium	Halved	10 min	8 min	6 min

Microwave Cooking Frozen Vegetables

Vegetable	Weight	Cooking Time at HIGH		
		500 W	600 to 650 W	700 W
Home-Frozen				
Brussels Sprouts	1/2 lb (250 g)	8 min	6 min	5 min
Carrots	1 lb (500 g)	15 min	12 min	10 min
Cauliflower	1/2 lb (250 g)	10 min	8 min	7 min
Green Beans	1/2 lb (250 g)	8 min	6 min	5 min
Peas	1 lb (500 g)	15 min	12 min	10 min
Spinach	1/2 lb (250 g)	8 min	6 min	5 min

Suggestion:

* Add 2 tbsp (30 ml) of water and cover. Halfway through cooking, stir and add desired seasonings.

Commercially Frozen

Package Type

Package Type	Weight	500 W	600 to 650 W	700 W
Box or Carton	7 to 12 oz (200 to 340 g)	10 min	8 min	7 min
Aluminum Plate or Container	10 oz (285 g)	10 min	8 min	7 min
Cooking Bag	9 to 12 oz (255 to 340 g)	8 min	6 min	5 min
Ordinary Plastic Bag	16 oz (500 g)	14 min	12 min	11 min

Recommendations:

* Cook directly in frozen state, remove outside wrap and cook in box.

* Remove original packaging and cook in covered glass container. Stir midway.

* Perforate plastic bags and redistribute contents midway through cooking.

* Cook in covered glass container. Stir at midway point.

Microwave Cooking Fish, Shellfish and Seafood

Food	Quantity Weight Number	Cut	Cooking Time at HIGH		
			500 W	600 to 650 W	700 W
Fish	1 lb (500 g)	**Thin Filets** 1/4 inch (7 mm)	5 min	4-1/2 min	4 min
		Medium Filets 1/2 inch (14 mm)	6-1/2 min	5-1/2 min	5 min
		Thick Filets 1 inch (28 mm)	9 min	8 min	7 min
		Medium Steaks 1/2 inch (14 mm)	7-1/2 min	6-1/2 min	6 min
		Thick Steaks 1 inch (28 mm)	10 min	9 min	8 min
	2 lb (1 kg)	**Whole**	15 min	13-1/2 min	12 min
Crab	2 lb (1 kg)	**Claws**	6 min	5-1/2 min	5 min
Shrimp	1 lb (500 g)	**Whole**	5 min	4-1/2 min	4 min
		Shelled	6 min	5-1/2 min	5 min
Lobster	2 lb (1 kg)	**Whole**	10 min	9 min	8 min
	1 lb (500 g)	**Tails**	6 min	5-1/2 min	5 min
Clams	6 large	**Shells**	5 min	4-1/2 min	4 min
Scampi	1 lb (500 g)	**Whole**	6 min	5-1/2 min	5 min
Scallops	1 lb (500 g)	**Whole**	5 min	4-1/2 min	4 min

Suggestions:

* Make sure fish are completely thawed. Cook uncovered.

* Arrange the fish in a single layer with thinner and smaller pieces towards the center.

425

Microwave Cooking Meat

Food	Quantity Weight Number	Cut Doneness	Cooking Time at HIGH		
			500 W	600 to 650 W	700 W
Beef	1/2 lb (250 g)	**Steak** - blue - rare - medium - well-done	2-1/2 min 3 min 3-1/2 min 4-1/2 min	2-1/4 min 2-3/4 min 3-1/4 min 4-1/4 min	2 min 2-1/2 min 3 min 4 min
	For 1 lb (500 g)	**Roast** - blue - rare - medium - well-done	13 min 16 min 18 min 20 min	11 min 13-1/2 min 15 min 17-1/2 min	10-1/2 min 12 min 13-1/2 min 15-1/2 min
	1 lb (500 g)	**Ground** - medium	6 min	5-1/2 min	5 min
Veal	4 medium	**Cutlets** - medium	6 min	5 min	4 min
	For 1 lb (500 g)	**Roast** - medium	20 min	17 min	15 min
Pork	1 lb (500 g)	**Chops** - medium - well-done	15 min 17 min	13-1/2 min 15-1/2 min	12 min 15 min
	For 1 lb (500 g)	**Roast** - medium - well-done	17 min 19 min	15 min 17 min	13 min 15 min
	For 1 lb (500 g)	**Ham** - medium	13 min	12 min	11 min
	1/2 lb (250 g)	**Bacon, sliced** - crisp	5-1/2 min	5 min	4-1/2 min
Lamb	4 medium	**Chops** - medium	6 min	5 min	4 min
	For 1 lb (500 g)	**Leg or Shoulder** - medium - well-done	17 min 21 min	15 min 18 min	13 min 15 min

Microwave Cooking Poultry

Food	Quantity Weight Number	Cut	Cooking Time at ROAST		
			500 W	600 to 650 W	700 W
Chicken	1 lb (500 g)	Pieces	10 min	9 min	8 min
	1/4 lb (150 g) x 2	Whole	29 min	27 min	25 min
	3 lb (1.5 kg)	Boneless breasts	6 min	5 min	4 min
Turkey	For 1 lb (500 g)	Quarters	10 min	9 min	8 min
	For 1 lb (500 g)	Whole	14 min	12 min	11 min
Quail	1 lb (500 g)	Whole	9 min	8 min	7 min
	2 lb (1 kg)	Whole	13 min	12 min	11 min
Duck	1 lb (500 g)	Breasts	8 min	7 min	6 min
	4 lb (2 kg)	Whole	20 min	18 min	17 min
Goose	For 1 lb (500 g)	Whole	11 min	9 min	8 min

Suggestions:

* Arrange in glass dish skin side down.
* Cook at MEDIUM-HIGH for chicken weighing more than 3 lb (1.5 kg) and extend cooking time if necessary.
* Cook boneless breasts on a plate or wrap in wax paper.
* Let turkey stand 5-10 minutes after cooking.
* Rotate the turkey 3 times at regular intervals during cooking. Cover with wax paper final 15 minutes.
* Stuff if desired.
* For rarer duck cut 2 minutes off cooking time.
* Spread with apricot jam at midway point.

PLANNING A RECEPTION

Planning a Reception

In a sense, every occasion on which you entertain family and friends is a party, a festive gathering which you want to have unroll without a hitch, in an atmosphere that will be remembered and appreciated whether or not you are entertaining for a truly grand occasion, or spontaneously for no reason at all.

That means that whether you are organizing a children's birthday party, a summer picnic, or an important occasion such as a wedding or holiday dinner, planning and organization are essential to the success of your event.

Details are important. You should take time to plan in advance the menu, table decoration, the choice of colors for tablecloths, candles and other accessories, even the garnishes and decorations for various dishes. Advance planning of every aspect of the meal will save you last minute panics and ensure that the occasion takes place in a pleasant and relaxed atmosphere.

If you take the time to consider every step of party planning in advance, you will eliminate unnecessary stress for yourself and be able to enjoy the occasion along with your guests.

1. Define the Event

Any time that you decide to entertain at home, you should try to have a clear idea of the occasion you are celebrating. This will help you in organizing your decor, determining your guest list to ensure that you have compatible people, and deciding the type of service that will be most appropriate; a sit-down dinner or a buffet, for example, involve different types of planning.

Brunch

Brunches are usually organized for Saturdays or Sundays to start between about 11:30 a.m. and 1:30 p.m. They are a great way to get together casually with friends after a morning of bicycling or other activity. Certain occasions, such as a wedding day, call for a reasonably formal brunch, but generally you will want this type of entertaining to be relaxed and casual, with decor and music to match.

Special Occasions

A major or minor holiday, a birthday or anniversary are all great excuses for getting together with friends and family to celebrate, whether on week nights or the weekend.

The specific time for which you invite your guests will depend on the day of the week and the kinds of activities that you plan for later in the evening. You should aim for a menu that offers plenty of variety but is not too complicated to prepare, so that you can complete most of the preparations before the guests even arrive.

Tea Time

A light meal planned for late afternoon around 4:00 p.m. is a delightful way to pass some pleasant hours with friends, to toast a marriage or to start off an evening at the theater. Most people serve light sweets, cakes and fancy breads at a tea, but you might also consider the charming English idea of "High Tea," in which the menu is made more substantial with the addition of cold meats and sandwiches.

You should be as careful about selecting your tea as you would be if serving wine or coffee; this is one time to avoid tea bags in favor of a special blend or exotic Indian, Ceylon or Chinese tea served from an attractive tea pot.

Children's Birthdays

Children love parties, and this is a wonderful occasion to let them participate in planning the menu and inviting the guests. An afternoon party is usually the simplest idea, especially for young children. Let them make their own invitations. Plan activities such as charades and contests to keep the children occupied, and serve a series of snacks between games rather than a single sit-down meal.

Cocktail Parties

A cocktail reception is a smart way to entertain a crowd without having to worry about having enough chairs for a seated meal. You will want to have cocktails and/or wine, of course, as well as nonalcoholic beverages for those who prefer them. Serve an assortment of hot and cold canapés, planning on at least 15 to 20 pieces per guest. Guests are usually invited to arrive between 6:00 and 10:00 p.m.

Buffets

A buffet reception is often the only sensible way to entertain a large group. Buffets are flexible in that they can be planned for lunch time or evening, and served outdoors or inside. Make sure that you have generous quantities of each dish.

2. Plan the Guest List

The guests you invite will play an important role in determining whether or not your party is a success. It is up to you to invite people who will get along with each other, but that does not mean they have to be the same kind of people; the most interesting parties have an assortment of different personalities.

The number of people you invite depends very much on your personal objective, although you should take the size of the party space into account. Outdoor parties obviously allow the greatest number of guests, but don't forget that the more people you invite, the more work is involved.

Only when you have established the basic plan for the event should you invite your guests. It is a good idea to try to give people 10 to 15 days notice.

A simple telephone call is the easiest way to invite people, but for special occasions you might want to send an invitation that reflects the theme of the event. Be sure to include all the necessary information:

* your name
* the guest's name (optional)
* the event
* the date
* the time
* the place
* the type of dress

Here are a few examples:

Mrs. _____

invites you to celebrate the birthday of
her husband George at dinner
Saturday, January 5
at 8:00 p.m. at their home

_____
(address)

Casual Dress   *RSVP 000-0000*

Mr. and Mrs. _____

request the pleasure of your company

_____
(guest name)

for a cocktail reception in honor of the
engagement of their son Michael
at their home

_____
(address)

Friday, October 10th between 7:00 and 10:30 p.m.

Semi-formal   *RSVP 000-0000*

---

3. Plan the Menu

Deciding on the menu is one of the most important elements for successful entertaining.

The menu plans outlined in this book have been designed to produce an appetizing and nutritious balance of foods.

Although you always want to have plenty to serve, it is important to select a menu which will not overburden your guests with rich foods, leaving them feeling overstuffed and sleepy. Also pay attention to the importance of including interesting vegetables and side dishes with your meal, rather than focusing all your energy on an elaborate main dish.

Always try to pay attention to the food habits and allergies of your guests; you don't want to serve pork to a vegetarian or salmon to someone allergic to fish. A range of interesting side dishes and desserts can help compensate for oversights in this regard.

Now that people have become more conscious of the health implications of food, you need to focus on food quality rather than quantity. A basic outline for a good meal includes:

Hors d'oeuvre: crudités, pâtés or mousses
Soup
Main course: fish, poultry or meat with vegetables
Salad: a refreshing note
Cheeses
Dessert

4. Plan the Decor

Imaginative, refined, or off-beat — you can give free reign to your powers of imagination when it comes to planning the decor.

There is no obligation to stick to the old standard clichés when planning your decor. Why not a yellow theme instead of red and green for Christmas, for example? Express your own personality by planning a theme that appeals to you.

You should, however, take into account the dominant color scheme of the room in which you are entertaining, and take it from there.

The important thing is to make sure that the entire event is harmonious, including the type of celebration, the menu, the theme, the decor and the dishes.

Make a list of the things you plan to use well in advance, so that you don't find yourself scrounging for the right color candles or napkins at the last minute.

And don't be afraid to take your inspiration from anywhere. Try ideas such as a Mexican Christmas or a party with a movie theme.

Lighting

Lighting makes the decor... the intensity of light can create a sense of intimacy or of excitement.

In most cases you will find diffused lighting and candlelight the most pleasant solution.

Table Linen

Before you decide on the table linen, make sure it fits

with the type of event you are planning. Coordinate your napkins with the cloth, in matching or contrasting colors.

Dishes

Stores now offer a vast selection of tableware to suit every taste and budget. It is no longer regarded as essential to have a matched set of dishes. You can select large plates and soup plates in different patterns, for example, as long as they harmonize.

Flatware

Not long ago, everyone thought it was necessary to get out the sterling silver flatware for entertaining guests. Today it is perfectly acceptable to use flatware made of different materials and in a range of colors.

Make sure the table is set with appropriate cutlery for all courses to be served. Knives and spoons are placed to the right of the table setting, and forks on the left, arranged in order of use: the cutlery to be used with the first course hold the outside positions, and the implements to be used with the last course are nearest the plate. Dessert spoons and forks should be brought out on the dessert plates. Bring out coffee or teaspoons with the coffee or tea.

Centerpiece

Since what you decide to put in the center of the table will be a focal point, you should select it with care. Make sure that whatever you use is not so large that it inhibits views and conversation.

You can choose a flower arrangement or a green plant, or take your inspiration from the occasion by using a pumpkin or a folklore doll, for example. Or take your inspiration from the season, using autumn leaves or branches with Christmas decorations.

Almost any attractive or interesting object can be used as a centerpiece, as long as it fits with the theme and basic color scheme of the event.

You might also consider opting for individual arrangements at each place setting, although these should be small.

It is not necessary to buy expensive flower arrangements from the florist. You can always find inexpensive flowers or wild flowers, or perhaps green branches decorated with ribbons.

Other Elements

Candlesticks or elaborate candelabras can make interesting table decorations, providing light as well.

If you plan to give small gifts to your guests, use them as part of the table decoration, making sure that they are wrapped in paper that harmonizes with the color scheme.

You might consider writing out the menu by hand and placing a copy at each setting.

Presentation

Make sure you have appropriate serving dishes for the menu being planned, and which harmonize with the dishes, tablecloth and cutlery.

Here is a list of the items you should have for table setting:

The Table

Tablecloth and napkins, assorted

Dishes:

Bread plate
Entrée plate
Main course plate
Soup bowl and plate
Dessert dishes

Flatware:

Entrée fork
Main course fork
Knife
If necessary: steak knife, fish fork and knife, lobster cracker, salad fork, butter knife

Glasses:

White wine
Red wine
Water
Beer
Champagne
Liqueur

Cups:

Regular coffee
Demi-tasse
Espresso
Tea

Serving Dishes

Soufflé dish
Individual ramekins
Serving platters for roasts, fish, crudités
Coquilles Saint-Jacques shells
Escargot dishes
Individual salad bowls and large salad bowl
Fruit salad bowl
Cheese tray
Carafe
Punch bowl and cups
Vegetable serving bowls (with covers)

Utensils

Ladle (soup and gravy)
Cake server

Salad servers (fork and spoon)
Fish fork
Bread knife
Bread basket
Butter dishes
Gravy boat

Additional

Salt and pepper shakers
Knife rest
Mustard dish
Oil and vinegar cruets
Heat protectors for table
Coasters
Ice bucket
Wine cooler
Chafing dish
Tea service
Coffee service
Finger bowls
Table brush for crumbs
Warming tray

Miscellaneous

It is desirable to have a few serving pieces representative of countries whose cuisine you want to serve. Here is a list of decorative elements handy for exciting table decoration.

Candlesticks and candles in different designs and styles
Chinese lanterns
Confetti
Masks
Ribbons
Wrapping paper
Party hats
Noisemakers
Lace
Flowers
Balloons
Small boxes and bags
Rattles
Mistletoe
Pine cones
Dried leaves
Chocolates
Wrapped gifts
Baskets and woven trays
Taffy
Candies
Sweets
Hearts
Cards
Shells
Coral
Feathers
Costume jewelry
Colored napkins
Flags

Folklore dolls
Artificial snow
Glass art

Attention to Detail

If you pay attention to all the tiny details, combining them with taste and imagination, you will be able to create a total effect which will add to the pleasure of your guests and the success of your entertaining.

5. Seating Arrangements

Take into account the personal areas of interest of each guest, and try to seat people beside someone with similar interests. Hosts can sit at the head of the table or among the guests.

6. Prepare a Schedule

Use a list to help you keep track of the various steps for organizing your party. Do as much as possible in advance, so that you are not too rushed at the last minute. As much as possible, do your purchasing and cooking in advance.

Make ahead of time all dishes that will keep their freshness, such as desserts, soups, etc.

Make sure you have the table decorations ready; napkins clean and folded, menus written out, etc.

Set the table well in advance.

Use this book as a guide for amusing and interesting decoration ideas.

Use your imagination to organize the party to reflect your own tastes and personality.

And then relax and enjoy yourself.

GLOSSARY

Al Dente: Food, usually pasta, that is cooked just enough to remain firm to the bite, rather than mushy.

Artichoke Heart: The tender inner leaves and trimmed base of the vegetable, with choke removed.

Aspic: Cooked meat or vegetables folded into transparent jelly and chilled in a mold to give the desired shape.

Au Gratin: A dish with a top layer of cheese or breadcumbs which is browned in the oven.

Bain-marie: A large container of water in which a smaller container of the food to be cooked is placed.

Baste: To spoon melted butter, fat or liquid over foods.

Bathe: To brush or spoon a liquid or sauce onto foods.

Beat: To mix liquids or foods thoroughly and vigorously with a spoon, whisk or electric beater.

Béchamel: A creamy white sauce made of milk bound with roux.

Beurre Manié: Mixture of equal parts butter and flour kneaded together. Used to thicken sauces.

Blanch: To plunge food into plenty of boiling water until it is wilted or partially cooked.

Bind: To thicken and smooth a sauce with the addition of egg yolks or flour and butter.

Boil: To cook food or liquids to a high enough temperature that it sends up bubbles. A rolling boil causes a liquid to climb the sides of the pot.

Bouquet Garni: Mixture of parsley, thyme and bay leaf used to flavor dishes.

Braise: To brown foods in fat, then cook, covered, with a small amount of liquid.

Bread: To encase a food in a coating of breadcrumbs.

Brochette: Food, usually meat, threaded and cooked on a skewer.

Caramelize: To heat sugar with a bit of water until it becomes golden brown and syrupy.

Choke: The fuzzy inedible center of an artichoke.

Clarified Butter: Butter than has been melted and the milk solids, water and salt removed.

Combine: To mix ingredients completely.

Crock Pot: An earthenware cooking pot with a cover.

Croutons: Small cubes of bread fried in butter or oil.

Deglaze: Once meat has been cooked in a pan, remove the meat and pour in liquid, stirring to loosen and combine the flavorful juices stuck to the bottom.

Degrease: To remove excess accumulated fat from a cooked dish. Can be done with a ladle or spoon, or you can chill a liquid until the fat congeals and remove the fat layer.

Dice: To cut food into square cubes, usually about 1/8 inch (3mm) in size.

Dissolve: To make a solid or powder completely disappear in the liquid.

Drain: To pour off all liquid.

Filter: To pass a liquid through a fine sieve, cheesecloth or paper towel to remove all solids.

Fines Herbes: A mixture of aromatic herbs: parsley, chives, tarragon, etc.

Flambé: To set fire to the liquid to evaporate the alcohol.

Flour: To sprinkle a cooking surface or container with a very thin coating of all-purpose flour.

Fold: To gently blend a fragile mixture, such as beaten egg whites, into a heavier mixture, usually with a rubber spatula. Also to stir in solids, such as artichoke hearts, without breaking or mashing.

Foam: A white foamy substance which often appears on the top of a boiled liquid.

Fricassee: A braised dish in which the sauce is bound with egg and cream mixture.

Galantine: A dish of cold boneless meat served in its jelly.

Glaze: To bathe the surface of meat or other food with liquid or sauce and put under high heat until golden and shiny.

Homogeneous: Uniform consistency.

Julienne: To cut food into small, even strips.

Liquefy: To reduce a mixture to a smooth liquid form, usually in the food processor or blender.

Marinade: A liquid mixture of oil, spices, herbs and acid ingredients (wine, vinegar, lemon juice) in which meat or fish is soaked before cooking.

Marinate: To place foods in a liquid so they will absorb flavor or become more tender.

Mash: To break solids down to a smooth consistency, as mashed potatoes.

Mince: To chop foods very fine.

Miroton: A kind of stew made with leftover meat and onions.

Mixed Spice: Mixture of, usually, cinnamon, nutmeg, cloves, allspice and coriander (sometimes ginger).

Monosodium Glutamate: Brand name "Accent".

Pare: To remove the skin or peel from a fruit or vegetable.

Poach: To submerge food in a liquid to cook.

Purée: To reduce solid foods to a mush with a food processor, blender or sieve.

Ramekin: A small baking dish; also used for bain-marie.

Reduce: To diminish the volume of a dish by evaporating the liquid.

Refresh: To plunge food into cold or ice water once it has been blanched.

Reserve: To set aside for later use.

Roux: A cooked mixture of flour and butter used to thicken sauces, soups, etc.

Sake: Japanese rice wine.

Sauté: To cook and/or brown food in a very small quantity of hot fat, usually in an open skillet or saucepan.

Shortcrust Pastry: Thinly rolled dough used for the crusts of pies and tarts.

Sift: To pass flour and other dry ingredients through a sifter or fine screen to remove lumps and aerate.

Simmer: To cook at a gentle boil so that the bubbles barely break the surface.

Snow Peas: Edible pod peas.

Sprinkle: To add a thin, even layer of cheese, crumbs, herbs, etc.

Stew: To cook foods slowly and gently in liquid.

Stock: A well-flavored liquid made from simmered bones or shells, with vegetables, used as a base for sauces or stews.

Strainer: An implement with small holes for separating solids from liquids.

Tomato Purée: Tomatoes with peel and seeds removed, and passed through a food processor or sieve.

Top: To cover foods with a sauce thick enough to adhere to the food.

Vanilla Sugar: Sugar flavored with vanilla beans.

Wok: A round-bottomed large pan used for stir-frying and Chinese dishes.

Zest: The outermost colored part of citrus fruit, cut in fine strips or grated.

INDEX

PARTY PLANNER

"The Great Moments in Cooking" Party Planner provided on the following pages has been designed to help you better organize your time and resources when you are entertaining. We want you to enjoy the event as much as your guests!

GREAT MOMENTS IN COOKING
Party Planner

EVENT

day _____ date _____ time _____

Type

☐ indoors   ☐ outdoors

☐ sit-down meal   ☐ buffet

Main activities

_____

_____

_____

INVITATION

sent by: ☐ telephone   ☐ written

☐ other

Date _____

GUESTS

Number _____

MENU   page _____

☐ Canapés   ☐ Main course and vegetables or side dishes

_____   _____

_____   _____

☐ Entrée   _____

_____   _____

☐ Soup   ☐ Salad

_____

☐ Cheeses   ☐ Dessert

_____   _____

BEVERAGES

☐ Spirits

☐ Wine

☐ Beer

☐ Liqueurs

☐ Coffee

☐ Tea

☐ Milk

☐ Juice

☐ Mineral water

☐ Soft drinks

PURCHASES	
Article	**Quantity**

☐ Flowers

BUDGET	
Total	

PREPARATIONS

Table

☐ Tablecloth
☐ Napkins
☐ Dishes
☐ Glasses
☐ Flatware and utensils
☐ Flowers
☐ Centerpiece
☐ Candles
☐ Serving dishes
☐ Warming tray
☐ Dessert table
☐ Corkscrew
☐ Finger bowls
☐ Menu cards
☐ Seating arrangements

House

☐ Cleaning
☐ Cloakroom
☐ Lighting
☐ Temperature
☐ Music
☐ Tables and chairs
☐ Decorations

Other

☐ Babysitter
☐ Gifts
☐ Room for children
(games, toys, books, video)

NOTES

GREAT MOMENTS IN COOKING
Party Planner

EVENT

day _____ date _____ time _____

Type

☐ indoors   ☐ outdoors

☐ sit-down meal   ☐ buffet

Main activities

_____
_____
_____

INVITATION

sent by: ☐ telephone   ☐ written

☐ other

Date _____

GUESTS

Number _____

MENU   page _____

☐ Canapés
_____
_____

☐ Entrée
_____

☐ Soup

☐ Cheeses
_____

☐ Main course and vegetables or side dishes
_____
_____
_____
_____

☐ Salad

☐ Dessert
_____

BEVERAGES

☐ Spirits

☐ Wine

☐ Beer

☐ Liqueurs

☐ Coffee

☐ Tea

☐ Milk

☐ Juice

☐ Mineral water

☐ Soft drinks

PURCHASES	
Article	**Quantity**

☐ Flowers

BUDGET	
Total	

PREPARATIONS

Table

☐ Tablecloth
☐ Napkins
☐ Dishes
☐ Glasses
☐ Flatware and utensils
☐ Flowers
☐ Centerpiece
☐ Candles
☐ Serving dishes
☐ Warming tray
☐ Dessert table
☐ Corkscrew
☐ Finger bowls
☐ Menu cards
☐ Seating arrangements

House

☐ Cleaning
☐ Cloakroom
☐ Lighting
☐ Temperature
☐ Music
☐ Tables and chairs
☐ Decorations

Other

☐ Babysitter
☐ Gifts
☐ Room for children
   (games, toys, books, video)

_____
_____
_____
_____

NOTES

GREAT MOMENTS IN COOKING
Party Planner

EVENT

day ———————————— date ———————————— time ————————

Type

☐ indoors   ☐ outdoors

☐ sit-down   ☐ buffet
   meal

Main activities

————————————————————————

————————————————————————

————————————————————————

INVITATION

sent by: ☐ telephone   ☐ written

☐ other

Date ————————————

GUESTS   Number ————————————

MENU   page ————————

☐ Canapés   ☐ Main course and
                       vegetables or side dishes
————————————   ————————————
————————————   ————————————
☐ Entrée   ————————————
————————————   ————————————
                       ————————————
☐ Soup   ☐ Salad
————————————   ————————————
☐ Cheeses   ☐ Dessert
————————————   ————————————

BEVERAGES

☐ Spirits

☐ Wine

☐ Beer

☐ Liqueurs

☐ Coffee

☐ Tea

☐ Milk

☐ Juice

☐ Mineral water

☐ Soft drinks

PURCHASES	
Article	**Quantity**
☐ Flowers	

BUDGET	
Total	

PREPARATIONS

Table

☐ Tablecloth
☐ Napkins
☐ Dishes
☐ Glasses
☐ Flatware and utensils
☐ Flowers
☐ Centerpiece
☐ Candles
☐ Serving dishes
☐ Warming tray
☐ Dessert table
☐ Corkscrew
☐ Finger bowls
☐ Menu cards
☐ Seating arrangements

House

☐ Cleaning
☐ Cloakroom
☐ Lighting
☐ Temperature
☐ Music
☐ Tables and chairs
☐ Decorations

Other

☐ Babysitter
☐ Gifts
☐ Room for children
  (games, toys, books, video)

NOTES

NOTES

GREAT MOMENTS IN COOKING
Party Planner

EVENT

day _____ date _____ time _____

Type   **Main activities**

☐ indoors   ☐ outdoors   _____

☐ sit-down   ☐ buffet   _____
   meal   _____

INVITATION

sent by: ☐ telephone   ☐ written   Date _____

                ☐ other

GUESTS   Number _____

MENU   page _____   ### BEVERAGES

☐ Canapés   ☐ Main course and   ☐ Spirits
                   vegetables or side dishes
_____   ☐ Wine
                 _____
_____   ☐ Beer
                 _____
☐ Entrée   _____   ☐ Liqueurs

_____   _____   ☐ Coffee

☐ Soup   ☐ Salad   ☐ Tea

_____   _____   ☐ Milk

☐ Cheeses   ☐ Dessert   ☐ Juice

_____   _____   ☐ Mineral water

                                              ☐ Soft drinks

PURCHASES

Article	Quantity

☐ Flowers

BUDGET

Total	

PREPARATIONS

Table

☐ Tablecloth
☐ Napkins
☐ Dishes
☐ Glasses
☐ Flatware and utensils
☐ Flowers
☐ Centerpiece
☐ Candles
☐ Serving dishes
☐ Warming tray
☐ Dessert table
☐ Corkscrew
☐ Finger bowls
☐ Menu cards
☐ Seating arrangements

House

☐ Cleaning
☐ Cloakroom
☐ Lighting
☐ Temperature
☐ Music
☐ Tables and chairs
☐ Decorations

Other

☐ Babysitter
☐ Gifts
☐ Room for children
   (games, toys, books, video)

NOTES

GREAT MOMENTS IN COOKING
Party Planner

EVENT

day ——————— date ——————— time ———————

Type

☐ indoors   ☐ outdoors

☐ sit-down meal   ☐ buffet

Main activities

———————————
———————————
———————————

INVITATION

sent by: ☐ telephone   ☐ written

☐ other

Date ———————

GUESTS

Number ———————

MENU

page ———————

☐ Canapés

———————
———————

☐ Entrée

———————

☐ Soup

☐ Cheeses

———————

☐ Main course and vegetables or side dishes

———————
———————
———————
———————

☐ Salad

———————

☐ Dessert

———————

BEVERAGES

☐ Spirits

☐ Wine

☐ Beer

☐ Liqueurs

☐ Coffee

☐ Tea

☐ Milk

☐ Juice

☐ Mineral water

☐ Soft drinks

PURCHASES	
Article	**Quantity**
☐ Flowers	

BUDGET	
Total	

PREPARATIONS

Table

☐ Tablecloth

☐ Napkins

☐ Dishes

☐ Glasses

☐ Flatware and utensils

☐ Flowers

☐ Centerpiece

☐ Candles

☐ Serving dishes

☐ Warming tray

☐ Dessert table

☐ Corkscrew

☐ Finger bowls

☐ Menu cards

☐ Seating arrangements

House

☐ Cleaning

☐ Cloakroom

☐ Lighting

☐ Temperature

☐ Music

☐ Tables and chairs

☐ Decorations

Other

☐ Babysitter

☐ Gifts

☐ Room for children
(games, toys, books, video)

NOTES

GREAT MOMENTS IN COOKING
Party Planner

EVENT

day ——————— date ——————— time ———————

Type

☐ indoors   ☐ outdoors

☐ sit-down meal   ☐ buffet

Main activities

———————————————
———————————————
———————————————

INVITATION

sent by: ☐ telephone   ☐ written

☐ other

Date ———————

GUESTS   Number ———————

MENU   page ———————

☐ Canapés
————————
————————

☐ Main course and vegetables or side dishes
————————
————————
————————

☐ Entrée
————————

☐ Soup
————————

☐ Salad

☐ Cheeses
————————

☐ Dessert
————————

BEVERAGES

☐ Spirits
☐ Wine
☐ Beer
☐ Liqueurs
☐ Coffee
☐ Tea
☐ Milk
☐ Juice
☐ Mineral water
☐ Soft drinks

PURCHASES

Article	Quantity

☐ Flowers

BUDGET

Total	

PREPARATIONS

Table

☐ Tablecloth
☐ Napkins
☐ Dishes
☐ Glasses
☐ Flatware and utensils
☐ Flowers
☐ Centerpiece
☐ Candles
☐ Serving dishes
☐ Warming tray
☐ Dessert table
☐ Corkscrew
☐ Finger bowls
☐ Menu cards
☐ Seating arrangements

House

☐ Cleaning
☐ Cloakroom
☐ Lighting
☐ Temperature
☐ Music
☐ Tables and chairs
☐ Decorations

Other

☐ Babysitter
☐ Gifts
☐ Room for children
(games, toys, books, video)

NOTES

GREAT MOMENTS IN COOKING
Party Planner

EVENT

day ———————— date ———————— time ————————

Type

☐ indoors   ☐ outdoors

☐ sit-down meal   ☐ buffet

Main activities

————————————————

————————————————

————————————————

INVITATION

sent by: ☐ telephone   ☐ written   Date ————————

☐ other

GUESTS   Number ————————

MENU   page ————————

☐ Canapés   ☐ Main course and vegetables or side dishes

————————   ————————

————————   ————————

☐ Entrée   ————————

————————   ————————

☐ Soup   ☐ Salad

————————   ————————

☐ Cheeses   ☐ Dessert

————————   ————————

BEVERAGES

☐ Spirits

☐ Wine

☐ Beer

☐ Liqueurs

☐ Coffee

☐ Tea

☐ Milk

☐ Juice

☐ Mineral water

☐ Soft drinks

PURCHASES	
Article	**Quantity**
☐ Flowers	

BUDGET	
Total	

PREPARATIONS

Table

☐ Tablecloth
☐ Napkins
☐ Dishes
☐ Glasses
☐ Flatware and utensils
☐ Flowers
☐ Centerpiece
☐ Candles
☐ Serving dishes
☐ Warming tray
☐ Dessert table
☐ Corkscrew
☐ Finger bowls
☐ Menu cards
☐ Seating arrangements

House

☐ Cleaning
☐ Cloakroom
☐ Lighting
☐ Temperature
☐ Music
☐ Tables and chairs
☐ Decorations

Other

☐ Babysitter
☐ Gifts
☐ Room for children
(games, toys, books, video)

NOTES

GREAT MOMENTS IN COOKING

Party Planner

EVENT

day _____ date _____ time _____

Type   **Main activities**

☐ indoors   ☐ outdoors   _____

☐ sit-down   ☐ buffet   _____
   meal
                                  _____

INVITATION

sent by: ☐ telephone   ☐ written   Date _____

            ☐ other

GUESTS   Number _____

MENU   page _____

☐ Canapés   ☐ Main course and
                      vegetables or side dishes
_____
                   _____
_____
                   _____
☐ Entrée
                   _____
_____

☐ Soup   ☐ Salad

_____   _____

☐ Cheeses   ☐ Dessert

_____   _____

BEVERAGES

☐ Spirits

☐ Wine

☐ Beer

☐ Liqueurs

☐ Coffee

☐ Tea

☐ Milk

☐ Juice

☐ Mineral water

☐ Soft drinks

PURCHASES	
Article	**Quantity**
☐ Flowers	

BUDGET	
Total	

PREPARATIONS

Table

☐ Tablecloth
☐ Napkins
☐ Dishes
☐ Glasses
☐ Flatware and utensils
☐ Flowers
☐ Centerpiece
☐ Candles
☐ Serving dishes
☐ Warming tray
☐ Dessert table
☐ Corkscrew
☐ Finger bowls
☐ Menu cards
☐ Seating arrangements

House

☐ Cleaning
☐ Cloakroom
☐ Lighting
☐ Temperature
☐ Music
☐ Tables and chairs
☐ Decorations

Other

☐ Babysitter
☐ Gifts
☐ Room for children
(games, toys, books, video)

NOTES

GREAT MOMENTS IN COOKING
Party Planner

EVENT

day _____ date _____ time _____

Type

☐ indoors   ☐ outdoors   **Main activities**

☐ sit-down   ☐ buffet   _____
   meal   _____
                                       _____

INVITATION

sent by: ☐ telephone   ☐ written   Date _____

                ☐ other

GUESTS   Number _____

MENU   page _____

☐ Canapés   ☐ Main course and
_____   vegetables or side dishes
_____   _____
                     _____
☐ Entrée   _____
_____   _____

☐ Soup   ☐ Salad
_____   _____

☐ Cheeses   ☐ Dessert
_____   _____

BEVERAGES

☐ Spirits

☐ Wine

☐ Beer

☐ Liqueurs

☐ Coffee

☐ Tea

☐ Milk

☐ Juice

☐ Mineral water

☐ Soft drinks

PURCHASES	
Article	**Quantity**
☐ Flowers	

BUDGET	
Total	

PREPARATIONS

Table

☐ Tablecloth
☐ Napkins
☐ Dishes
☐ Glasses
☐ Flatware and utensils
☐ Flowers
☐ Centerpiece
☐ Candles
☐ Serving dishes
☐ Warming tray
☐ Dessert table
☐ Corkscrew
☐ Finger bowls
☐ Menu cards
☐ Seating arrangements

House

☐ Cleaning
☐ Cloakroom
☐ Lighting
☐ Temperature
☐ Music
☐ Tables and chairs
☐ Decorations

Other

☐ Babysitter
☐ Gifts
☐ Room for children
   (games, toys, books, video)

NOTES

GREAT MOMENTS IN COOKING
Party Planner

EVENT

day ———————————— date ———————————— time ————————————

Type   **Main activities**

☐ indoors   ☐ outdoors   ————————————————

☐ sit-down   ☐ buffet   ————————————————
  meal   ————————————————

INVITATION

sent by: ☐ telephone   ☐ written   Date ————————

                ☐ other

GUESTS   Number ——————

MENU   page ——————

☐ Canapés   ☐ Main course and
                       vegetables or side dishes
————————   ————————————
————————   ————————————
————————   ————————————
☐ Entrée   ————————————
————————   ————————————
☐ Soup   ☐ Salad
————————   ————————————
☐ Cheeses   ☐ Dessert
————————   ————————————

BEVERAGES

☐ Spirits

☐ Wine

☐ Beer

☐ Liqueurs

☐ Coffee

☐ Tea

☐ Milk

☐ Juice

☐ Mineral water

☐ Soft drinks

PURCHASES	
Article	**Quantity**

☐ Flowers

BUDGET	
Total	

PREPARATIONS

Table

☐ Tablecloth

☐ Napkins

☐ Dishes

☐ Glasses

☐ Flatware and utensils

☐ Flowers

☐ Centerpiece

☐ Candles

☐ Serving dishes

☐ Warming tray

☐ Dessert table

☐ Corkscrew

☐ Finger bowls

☐ Menu cards

☐ Seating arrangements

House

☐ Cleaning

☐ Cloakroom

☐ Lighting

☐ Temperature

☐ Music

☐ Tables and chairs

☐ Decorations

Other

☐ Babysitter

☐ Gifts

☐ Room for children
(games, toys, books, video)

NOTES

NOTES

GREAT MOMENTS IN COOKING
Party Planner

EVENT

day _____ date _____ time _____

Type

☐ indoors   ☐ outdoors

☐ sit-down meal   ☐ buffet

Main activities

_____

_____

_____

INVITATION

sent by: ☐ telephone   ☐ written

☐ other

Date _____

GUESTS

Number _____

MENU

page _____

☐ Canapés

_____

_____

☐ Entrée

_____

☐ Soup   ☐ Salad

_____

☐ Cheeses   ☐ Dessert

_____

☐ Main course and vegetables or side dishes

_____

_____

_____

_____

BEVERAGES

☐ Spirits

☐ Wine

☐ Beer

☐ Liqueurs

☐ Coffee

☐ Tea

☐ Milk

☐ Juice

☐ Mineral water

☐ Soft drinks

PURCHASES	
Article	**Quantity**

☐ Flowers

BUDGET	
Total	

PREPARATIONS

Table

☐ Tablecloth
☐ Napkins
☐ Dishes
☐ Glasses
☐ Flatware and utensils
☐ Flowers
☐ Centerpiece
☐ Candles
☐ Serving dishes
☐ Warming tray
☐ Dessert table
☐ Corkscrew
☐ Finger bowls
☐ Menu cards
☐ Seating arrangements

House

☐ Cleaning
☐ Cloakroom
☐ Lighting
☐ Temperature
☐ Music
☐ Tables and chairs
☐ Decorations

Other

☐ Babysitter
☐ Gifts
☐ Room for children
(games, toys, books, video)

NOTES

GREAT MOMENTS IN COOKING
Party Planner

EVENT

day _____ date _____ time _____

Type

☐ indoors   ☐ outdoors

☐ sit-down meal   ☐ buffet

Main activities

_____

_____

_____

INVITATION

sent by: ☐ telephone   ☐ written

☐ other

Date _____

GUESTS   Number _____

MENU   page _____

☐ Canapés

_____

_____

☐ Entrée

_____

☐ Soup

_____

☐ Cheeses

_____

☐ Main course and vegetables or side dishes

_____

_____

_____

_____

☐ Salad

_____

☐ Dessert

_____

BEVERAGES

☐ Spirits

☐ Wine

☐ Beer

☐ Liqueurs

☐ Coffee

☐ Tea

☐ Milk

☐ Juice

☐ Mineral water

☐ Soft drinks

PURCHASES

Article	Quantity
	.

☐ Flowers

BUDGET

Total	

PREPARATIONS

Table

☐ Tablecloth

☐ Napkins

☐ Dishes

☐ Glasses

☐ Flatware and utensils

☐ Flowers

☐ Centerpiece

☐ Candles

☐ Serving dishes

☐ Warming tray

☐ Dessert table

☐ Corkscrew

☐ Finger bowls

☐ Menu cards

☐ Seating arrangements

House

☐ Cleaning

☐ Cloakroom

☐ Lighting

☐ Temperature

☐ Music

☐ Tables and chairs

☐ Decorations

Other

☐ Babysitter

☐ Gifts

☐ Room for children
(games, toys, books, video)

NOTES

GREAT MOMENTS IN COOKING
Party Planner

EVENT

day ——————————— date ——————————— time ———————————

Type   **Main activities**

☐ indoors   ☐ outdoors   ———————————————

☐ sit-down   ☐ buffet   ———————————————
   meal   ———————————————

INVITATION

sent by: ☐ telephone   ☐ written   Date ———————————

☐ other

GUESTS   Number ———————————

MENU   page ——————   **BEVERAGES**

☐ Canapés   ☐ Main course and   ☐ Spirits
                    vegetables or side dishes
———————   ☐ Wine
                    —————————————
———————   ☐ Beer
                    —————————————
☐ Entrée   ☐ Liqueurs
                    —————————————
———————   ☐ Coffee
                    —————————————
☐ Soup   ☐ Salad   ☐ Tea

                    —————————————   ☐ Milk

☐ Cheeses   ☐ Dessert   ☐ Juice

———————   —————————————   ☐ Mineral water

                                                 ☐ Soft drinks

PURCHASES

Article	Quantity

☐ Flowers

BUDGET

Total	

PREPARATIONS

Table

☐ Tablecloth

☐ Napkins

☐ Dishes

☐ Glasses

☐ Flatware and utensils

☐ Flowers

☐ Centerpiece

☐ Candles

☐ Serving dishes

☐ Warming tray

☐ Dessert table

☐ Corkscrew

☐ Finger bowls

☐ Menu cards

☐ Seating arrangements

House

☐ Cleaning

☐ Cloakroom

☐ Lighting

☐ Temperature

☐ Music

☐ Tables and chairs

☐ Decorations

Other

☐ Babysitter

☐ Gifts

☐ Room for children
(games, toys, books, video)

NOTES

GREAT MOMENTS IN COOKING
Party Planner

EVENT

day _____ date _____ time _____

Type   **Main activities**

☐ indoors   ☐ outdoors   _____

☐ sit-down   ☐ buffet   _____
   meal   _____

INVITATION

sent by: ☐ telephone   ☐ written   Date _____

            ☐ other

GUESTS   Number _____

MENU   page _____   **BEVERAGES**

☐ Canapés   ☐ Main course and   ☐ Spirits
                   vegetables or side dishes
_____   _____   ☐ Wine
_____   _____   ☐ Beer
☐ Entrée   _____   ☐ Liqueurs
                 _____
_____   ☐ Coffee
☐ Soup   ☐ Salad   ☐ Tea
_____   _____   ☐ Milk
☐ Cheeses   ☐ Dessert   ☐ Juice
_____   _____   ☐ Mineral water
                                                ☐ Soft drinks

PURCHASES	
Article	**Quantity**
☐ Flowers	

BUDGET	
Total	

PREPARATIONS

Table

☐ Tablecloth
☐ Napkins
☐ Dishes
☐ Glasses
☐ Flatware and utensils
☐ Flowers
☐ Centerpiece
☐ Candles
☐ Serving dishes
☐ Warming tray
☐ Dessert table
☐ Corkscrew
☐ Finger bowls
☐ Menu cards
☐ Seating arrangements

House

☐ Cleaning
☐ Cloakroom
☐ Lighting
☐ Temperature
☐ Music
☐ Tables and chairs
☐ Decorations

Other

☐ Babysitter
☐ Gifts
☐ Room for children
   (games, toys, books, video)

NOTES

GREAT MOMENTS IN COOKING
Party Planner

EVENT

day ——————— date ——————— time ———————

Type   **Main activities**

☐ indoors   ☐ outdoors   ———————————

☐ sit-down   ☐ buffet   ———————————
   meal   ———————————

INVITATION

sent by: ☐ telephone   ☐ written   Date ———————

                ☐ other

GUESTS   Number ———————

MENU   page ———————

☐ Canapés   ☐ Main course and
———————   vegetables or side dishes
———————   ———————
———————   ———————

☐ Entrée   ———————
———————   ———————

☐ Soup   ☐ Salad
———————   ———————

☐ Cheeses   ☐ Dessert
———————   ———————

BEVERAGES

☐ Spirits

☐ Wine

☐ Beer

☐ Liqueurs

☐ Coffee

☐ Tea

☐ Milk

☐ Juice

☐ Mineral water

☐ Soft drinks

PURCHASES	
Article	**Quantity**

☐ Flowers

BUDGET	
Total	

PREPARATIONS

Table

☐ Tablecloth
☐ Napkins
☐ Dishes
☐ Glasses
☐ Flatware and utensils
☐ Flowers
☐ Centerpiece
☐ Candles
☐ Serving dishes
☐ Warming tray
☐ Dessert table
☐ Corkscrew
☐ Finger bowls
☐ Menu cards
☐ Seating arrangements

House

☐ Cleaning
☐ Cloakroom
☐ Lighting
☐ Temperature
☐ Music
☐ Tables and chairs
☐ Decorations

Other

☐ Babysitter
☐ Gifts
☐ Room for children
   (games, toys, books, video)

NOTES

GREAT MOMENTS IN COOKING
Party Planner

EVENT

day —————————— date —————————— time ——————————

Type   **Main activities**

☐ indoors   ☐ outdoors   ——————————————

☐ sit-down   ☐ buffet   ——————————————
   meal   ——————————————

INVITATION

sent by: ☐ telephone   ☐ written   Date ——————————

                ☐ other

GUESTS   Number ——————————

MENU   page ——————

☐ Canapés   ☐ Main course and
                     vegetables or side dishes
——————————   ——————————————
——————————   ——————————————
☐ Entrée   ——————————————
                  ——————————————
——————————   ——————————————

☐ Soup   ☐ Salad
——————————

☐ Cheeses   ☐ Dessert
——————————   ——————————

BEVERAGES

☐ Spirits

☐ Wine

☐ Beer

☐ Liqueurs

☐ Coffee

☐ Tea

☐ Milk

☐ Juice

☐ Mineral water

☐ Soft drinks

PURCHASES	
Article	**Quantity**
☐ Flowers	

BUDGET	
Total	

PREPARATIONS

Table

☐ Tablecloth
☐ Napkins
☐ Dishes
☐ Glasses
☐ Flatware and utensils
☐ Flowers
☐ Centerpiece
☐ Candles
☐ Serving dishes
☐ Warming tray
☐ Dessert table
☐ Corkscrew
☐ Finger bowls
☐ Menu cards
☐ Seating arrangements

House

☐ Cleaning
☐ Cloakroom
☐ Lighting
☐ Temperature
☐ Music
☐ Tables and chairs
☐ Decorations

Other

☐ Babysitter
☐ Gifts
☐ Room for children
(games, toys, books, video)

NOTES